Rivalry and Revolution in South and East Asia

Rivalry and Revolution in South and East Asia

Edited with an introduction by

Partha S. Ghosh

LONDON AND NEW YORK

First published 1997 by Ashgate Publishing

Reissued 2018 by Routledge
2 Park Square, Milton Park, Abingdon, Oxon, OX14 4RN
52 Vanderbilt Avenue, New York, NY 10017

Routledge is an imprint of the Taylor & Francis Group, an informa business

Publisher's Note
The publisher has gone to great lengths to ensure the quality of this reprint but points out that some imperfections in the original copies may be apparent.

A Library of Congress record exists under LC control number: 96040481

ISBN 13: 978-1-138-35291-9 (hbk)
ISBN 13: 978-1-138-35295-7 (pbk)
ISBN 13: 978-0-429-43437-2 (ebk)

Contents

Introduction

I

All the eleven chapters in this volume are carefully selected *Conflict Studies* papers published during the period between 1988 and 1995, a momentous phase when the edifice of the Cold War collapsed and the post-Cold War era began to crystallize. As an era of uncertainty and hope it evoked a worldwide scholarly response in order to fathom the exact nature of this transformation so that national priorities could be adjusted accordingly.

Logically, this rather abrupt cessation of hostilities between the two superpowers should have heralded an era of peace and stability since much of the earlier tensions were viewed as Cold War-generated. But that did not happen. The outbreak of the Gulf War and the persistence of rivalries between and among states, particularly in the Third World, tended to suggest that it was 'business as usual'. Moreover, the break-up of the Soviet Union and the loosening of its grip over its erstwhile empire gave rise to fresh ethnic and communal animosities. Another realization was that the end of bipolarity did not actually result in unipolarity of the world. On the contrary there was an evolving multipolarity in which the United States figured significantly but not exclusively.

This multipolarity expressed itself in various ways. While, on the one hand, its unit of expression was national, as in the case of China and to some extent of Germany and Japan, on the other its articulation became essentially regional, as in the cases of the European Union, the ASEAN, the APEC and so on. The cacophony thereby created demanded new approaches to international security. Thus while a universal 'UNism' was expedited to tame a recalcitrant Saddam Hussain only a Eurocentric UN exercise of limited efficacy was employed to provide succour to the bleeding Bosnians. The so-called 'New World Order' which George Bush had so fondly pioneered came to mean different things to different people.

In the populous and volatile regions of South and East Asia on which this volume focuses the forces of both nationalism and internationalism worked side-by-side. On the one hand there was serious international concern over certain problems such as those of Cambodia and the nuclearization of India, Pakistan and North Korea; on the other, there were strong nationalistic thrusts on military power to settle unresolved regional issues. At yet another level all these developments were overtaken by an irresistible popular pressure for economic integration with the global system, often without any corresponding commitment to political freedom. The cumulative effect of these diverse processes was a curious mix of international rivalries and national revolutions.

II

A question that is raised these days is whether the world is fast heading towards an 'Asian century'. Unlike the eighteenth and nineteenth centuries when world events used to be dictated by what happened in Europe, about which Immanuel Wallerstein theorized so forcefully, the twenty first century is likely to be influenced by developments in Asia. It is argued that the process is nearing completion and the entire twentieth century has acted as midwife to this transition.

The arrival of the 'Asian century' found its first manifestation in the early years of the twentieth century. It all started with the Japanese victory over Russia in the Russo-Japanese war of 1904–5 in which, for the first time in modern history, a European power had to face a humiliating defeat at Asian hands. The psychological impact of the event on other Asian peoples was tremendous. A breeze of pan-Asianism blew over many of the contemporary national movements, the best example of which was India. Sir Henry Cotton's *New India* noted: 'What an inspiration has been afforded by the character of these Eastern islanders. The example is not lost on India.' Indian nationalists asked, 'May we not also be able to challenge Great Britain some time in the future?'.

But, of course, it took many years for the Asian resurgence to crystallize. The convening of the Asian Relations Conference in New Delhi in 1947, and later the articulation of Afro-Asian solidarity at the Bandung Conference of 1955 were its slow but steady steps. The subsequent Sino-Soviet rift, America's defeat in Vietnam, the rise of Japan as a super economic power with a huge trade surplus with the United States, and lastly, the unprecedented growth of East and South-East Asian NICs as economic powers cemented the concept. In military terms too, the emergence of China as a nuclear power and, in a limited sense, that of India as a regional heavyweight completed the picture.

Any change inevitably also brings its strains. The Asian experience has been no different. It is an analysis of these strains and their undercurrents that constitutes the subject matter of this volume. While underlining the continuing relevance of military power in international affairs the authors have emphasized that it alone does not guarantee national security, nor does it provide the desirable political stability which is an essential prerequisite of power projection. How to harmoniously blend the demands of defence and development is what the Asian concern for a new world order is all about.

III

The chapters of this volume may be classified in three rather broad categories – security-orientated, political economy-orientated, and territorial dispute-oriented. Yet another category is that related to the issue of unification of bifurcated nationalities in which the Korean question has been addressed. It must, however, be quickly added that the categorization here is merely functional and each case study spills into the domains of one or more of the other categories.

Three chapters by K. Subrahmanyam, Michael Leifer and Partha Ghosh are primarily security-focused. Subrahmanyam's essay (Chapter 1) concentrates on India's security in relation to the threat posed by Chinese ambitions which are expressed more by deeds than words. His principal concern is Chinese duplicity.

> They said atom bombs were paper tigers – and went on to build them. According to them the primary contradiction in the world was between capitalism and socialism and subsequently they moved over to a perspective of three worlds. They railed against non-alignment as fence-sitting and have now a different view. Those who were denounced as capitalist-roaders and China's Khrushchevs are today in power, building enclaves of capitalist enterprise. ... They shouted *Hindi Chini Bhai Bhai* (Indians and Chinese are brothers) and their relationship with Vietnam was ... as between 'the lips and the teeth'. The Communist combination of the USSR and China was seen by Mao Zedong in 1957 as the 'East wind prevailing over the West' but that did not prevent the Chinese from waging war at different times on all the three neighbours – India, the Soviet Union and Vietnam.

Subrahmanyam indeed has a strong case. Recently, only hours before the CTBT negotiations were resumed for the final round on 29 July 1996 at Geneva, China undertook its forty-fifth nuclear test. The Chinese government which announced the detonation also announced a moratorium on nuclear tests. It was the height of audacity to proclaim that the moratorium 'is not only a response to the appeal of the vast number of non-nuclear weapon states, but also a concrete action to promote nuclear disarmament'. Given the fact that India's security concerns extend beyond the South Asian region and that there is turbulence in Tibet and Myanmar, Subrahmanyam is convinced that 'there can be no reasonable expectation that India will be able to relax its vigil for at least the next two decades', (since the essay was written in 1988, it thus means until 2008).

Michael Leifer's essay on the Cambodian conflict (Chapter 2) hinges on two closely interconnected realities – first, its centrality in Vietnam's security and, second, the strategic ambitions of other regional and extra-regional powers at Cambodia's cost. It was the conviction of Vietnam's leading military theorist, General Vo Nguyen Giap, that:

> ... Indochina is a strategic unit; a single theatre of operations. Therefore, we have the task of helping to liberate all of Indochina – specially for reasons of strategic geography,

> we cannot conceive of Vietnam completely independent while Cambodia and Laos are ruled by imperialism.

According to Leifer's reckoning this doctrine has never been revoked. While the ASEAN, as a regional grouping, may be said to have a coordinated security doctrine, when it comes to individual national interests the policies diverge depending upon hard geostrategic considerations.

Leifer also argues that lack of political development in Cambodia, at the core of which is the conspicuously absent political culture of power-sharing, is the real reason why its leaders consider politics only as a zero-sum game – the winner takes all – and the developments which have taken place since the internationally sponsored general election of May 1993 tend to vindicate this assumption. The next election is due in 1998 and, as US Secretary of State Warren Christopher noted recently, in Cambodia's case 'it is not the first, but the second elections that really count'.

Partha Ghosh's essay (Chapter 10) deals with the mysterious theme – Indo-Pak nuclear rivalry. His central argument is that it is not merely a question of bilateral competition in search of security against one another but that the whole issue has some complex moral and strategic overtones which have not merely extra-regional but also global ramifications. The China factor figures prominently in the analysis and so does the role of the nuclear weapon community in general in putting pressure on both India and Pakistan to cap their nuclear programmes. The CTBT experience suggests that since neither side is willing to accommodate the other's point of view the controversy is likely to persist.

Those chapters which deal with the political and economic dimensions of security constitute the bulk of the volume. There are six such chapters written by Dennis Austin and Anirudha Gupta, Anthony Hyman, Marko Milivojević, Manoj Joshi, Brian Bridges, and David Goodman. Of these, the essay by Austin and Gupta (Chapter 4) analyses the complex theoretical issue of the relationship between violence and democracy. Drawing from the experience of South Asia, a region eminently suitable for this kind of analysis, they start with the premise that 'democracy and political violence are surely incompatible'. Traversing a vast ground through the region's myriad social complexities rooted in its religious, linguistic, ethnic and caste pluralities they ask the critical question whether the fault is inherent in democracy itself.

> The state in South Asia is ... *responsive.* One can call that democratic, but the strength of its virtues is also its danger. Governments, parties and politicians not only respond to local animosities, they have begun to turn them into the stuff of politics.

In their envoi the authors put across a point which is for the consideration of all those who believe that democracies do not fight: 'if governments were fully responsive to popular pressure, India and Pakistan would already be at war.'

Anthony Hyman's essay on Pakistan (Chapter 3) deals with all the three aspects of the Pakistani scenario – its politics, economy and foreign policy and, necessarily, their interlinkages. The role played by the army in the overall game has been woven succinctly in his analysis as has also the problem of governance which is most evident in the growing influence of the drug and arms mafia. 'Army remains one of Pakistan's "three As" - Allah, the Army and America - three powers which, according to many Pakistanis, determine whatever happens of any importance in their country.' These phenomena eat into the vital organs of this fledgling democracy.

Mongolia which is otherwise in the backwaters of international politics receives a scholarly treatment in Marko Milivojević's essay (Chapter 5). It starts with Mongolia's glorious medieval past, passes through its sleepy withdrawal from global affairs during the Soviet domination and ends with its recent nationalistic and democratic resurgence. A pan-Mongol upsurge to reunite the scattered Mongol communities spread across Mongolia (2 million), China (3.5 million in Inner Mongolian Autonomous Region and Sinkiang) and Russia (0.7 million in Buryat-Mongol, Tuva and Kalmyk provinces) could one day take on serious proportions. The role of China, Japan and Russia would then become very relevant in the politics of Inner Asia. At the moment, however, the nation's thrust is towards economic liberalization and its gradual integration into the regional economy.

Manoj Joshi's essay on terrorism and secessionism in Punjab (Chapter 9) focuses on two most important dimensions of the problem – first, its international connection (that of Pakistan in particular but also that of the Sikh ethnic diasporas in the West) and, second, the question whether in dealing with the problem it is advisable first to have a mere political approach with due respect for human rights or to follow an eye-for-an-eye security method with the intention to first wipe out all the vestiges of terrorism before a political solution is conceived. The Punjab experience suggests that it is the latter that eventually worked. In that context the role of the controversial police chief K.P.S. Gill has received much attention. The issue that Joshi finally raises is as follows:

> The enormous powers of arrest, detention and seizure assumed by the police and security forces have implications for the whole country. The free hand given to the Punjab Police may become a 'model' for application elsewhere, and, more dangerously, everywhere in the country. Unchecked by a political system which is itself in a state of profound crisis, it could mean the collapse of democracy such as witnessed in Sri Lanka in the 1980s.

Brian Bridges' essay on Japan, reproduced as Chapter 8, has been appropriately subtitled 'Hesitant Superpower'. The author tries to provide an explanation as to why the country which accounts for about 15 per cent of the world's GNP and a trade surplus of $50 billion with the United States is not confident enough to translate that economic power into political clout. At the core of this hesitancy is its lack of will stemming from an uncertainty as to where it really belongs – Asia or the West. Also central to the question is the post-war convention not to spend more than 1 per cent of its GNP for the country's defence. At the moment Japan is lobbying hard for a permanent seat on the UN Security Council, and the attainment of this goal would probably lead to Japan playing a political role commensurate to its economic strength. But have the Japanese overcome their real problem – the dichotomy between their first-rate economy and third-rate politics?

David Goodman's essay on China (Chapter 9) focuses on political and economic changes introduced in the country since the late 1970s and which aimed at transforming the economy into a capitalist one without any commitment to democratic liberalization. Drawing comparisons from Eastern Europe it has been argued that probably this 'Chinese style' capitalism can be rationalized by the fact that China has little experience of people's participation in governance and that its Confucian philosophy stresses duties, not rights. It is uncertain how the experiment will ultimately fare but if it survives for several more years with little accompanying social turmoil and if the nation – or, more accurately, parts of it – become economically integrated with the neighbouring economies of East Asia, it would certainly make us all reconsider our premises about the relationship between economics and politics. Much of course would depend upon the future of Sino-American relations which have become hostage to a 'fettered dragon and caged eagle' syndrome.

There is no dearth of territorial disputes in South and East Asia but the one which is potentially most destabilizing to the region is the one over Kashmir. Iftikhar Malik's essay (Chapter 6) presents the case from a Pakistani perspective which is diametrically opposite to that of India. The problem has its roots in the mechanics of partition of the Indian subcontinent which has subsequently been further complicated by the processes of political development. It is a pity that, while both the nations are near the bottom of the international development index, they spend so much of their precious time and money on an issue that can be solved only through negotiations. Any other mode of solution would be devastating for the region and also for international security particularly when both seem to possess nuclear weapons.

The problem of peace on the Korean peninsula has haunted the world right from the closing days of the Second World War when the nation was vertically divided into two sovereign units. The Korean war had practically led the world to another world war. Barry Gills's essay (Chapter 11) addresses the various dimensions of the problem and speculates upon the chances of a Korean unification which, since the German reunification, has entered into the realm of possibility. The problem is, however, that during the past 50 years so much vested interest has been placed in the retention of the status quo, not only in both the Koreas but also in neighbouring countries, that there seems to be no simple solution. A further complication is North Korea's nuclear ambitions coupled with its relative backwardness in terms of economic development. The real challenge for Kim Jong Il now is how to save the *juche* ideology and 'socialism of our style' without totally shedding the legacy of his father, Kim Il Sung, which would amount to an ultimate betrayal.

IV

Asia's future – and more particularly that of South and East Asia – will largely influence the future of the world in the next century. With a population of about 2.5 billion these regions are at their developmental crossroads. Bubbling with economic and political activities these mostly poor nations are witnessing millions of social mutinies, to use V.S. Naipaul's phrase. What is actually in store no one can know. But the countries to be really watched are China, India and Japan, for much of the future developments in the region will be dictated by what happens in these countries.

Contributors

Dennis Austin is Professor Emeritus and former Pro-Vice Chancellor of the University of Manchester. He is the author of many works on Asia and Africa, including three other Conflict Studies.

Brian Bridges is Senior Lecturer in Social Sciences at Lingnan College, Hong Kong. He was formerly Head of the East Asia Programme at the Royal Institute of International Affairs. He has acted as Secretary to the UK–Japan 2000 Group and has written a number of books on the international relations of East Asia, including Japan and Korea in the 1990s.

Partha Ghosh is a Director at the Indian Council of Social Science Research, New Delhi. He was formerly a Humboldt Fellow at Heidelberg University, a Ford Visiting Scholar at the Program in Arms Control, Disarmament and International Security (ACDIS) of the University of Illinois and a Visiting Fellow at the Centre for Policy Research, New Delhi. He is the author of several books on the region and another Conflict Study, 'Ethnic and Religious Conflicts in South Asia' (No. 178).

Barry Gills is a Lecturer in International Politics at the University of Newcastle-upon-Tyne and formerly held a Fulbright Award in South Korea. He is a founding editor of the *Review of International Political Economy*.

David Goodman is Professor of Asian Studies and Director of the Australian Research Council's Asia Research Centre on Social, Political and Economic Change at Murdoch University, Western Australia. He has written extensively on China's regional development, political economy and leadership, including Deng Xiaoping and the Chinese Revolution.

Anirudha Gupta is Professor in the School of International Studies, Jawaharlal Nehru University, New Delhi and Editor of *International Studies* (New Delhi). He is the author of a number of studies of Asian and African politics.

Anthony Hyman is a specialist on Central Asia and has written three other Conflict Studies on the region. He is a contributor to the post-Soviet programme of the Royal Institute of International Affairs and Associate Editor of the journal, *Central Asian Survey*. He is the author of *Afghanistan under Soviet Domination 1964–91*.

Manoj Joshi is a journalist based in Delhi writing for *The Hindu*, *Frontline* and other publications. He was formerly Visiting Fellow at the Strategic and Defence Studies Centre of the Research School of Pacific Studies, Australian National University, Canberra.

Michael Leifer is Professor in the Department of International Relations at the London School of Economics. He was formerly Visiting Professor of Political Science at the National University of Singapore and has published extensively on South East Asia, including ASEAN and the Security of South East Asia.

Iftikhar Malik is a Senior Fellow at St Antony's College, Oxford University. He was previously at Qaid-i-Azam University, Islamabad and the Universities of Columbia and California. He is the author of many publications on South Asian history and politics.

Marko Milivojević is a writer and consultant on European affairs and Honorary Visiting Fellow at the University of Bradford.

K. Subrahmanyam was formerly Jawaharlal Nehru Visiting Professor at Cambridge University and served in the Indian Administrative Service for over 30 years, in the Ministry of Defence, on the Indian Joint Intelligence Committee and as Director of the Institute for Defence Studies and Analysis. He was Home Secretary in the Tamil Nadu State Government and has also served on UN Study Groups on nuclear deterrence and disarmament. He is the author of many publications on India's security.

[1]

India's Security

The North and North-East Dimension

K. Subrahmanyam

It is conventional wisdom in most of the strategic literature published in the Western world to discuss the Indian security issue entirely within the subcontinental framework. Some Indian strategic writings also tend to reflect this view, many of them having been influenced by Western thought. For most Indian policy-makers and for the Indian armed forces which have to deploy a substantial proportion of their capabilities against China and in North-East India this analysis of the Indian security problem does not make much sense. It puzzles most Indians why the Indian security problem vis-à-vis China should be overlooked these days by those very people who trumpeted about the Chinese threat to South and South-East Asia in the 1960s and why the Chinese nuclear threat, which was used to justify the deployment of anti-ballistic missiles (ABMs) in the United States by Defence Secretary MacNamara in September 1967, is no longer mentioned in the Western strategic literature.[1]

Recently the Chinese very obligingly reminded the world of their capabilities by transferring CSS-2 missiles to Saudi Arabia.[2] US Secretary of State George Shultz, during his recent visit to Beijing in mid-July 1988, expressed concern about the rumoured possibility of transfer of M-9 Chinese missiles to Syria[3] but those who continually tell the world (irrespective of Gorbachev's pronouncements) that it is the Soviet capabilities and deployment patterns that should influence Western military preparedness,[4] willingly suspend the application of this maxim when it comes to China's capabilities, deployments, actions and even pronouncements when they relate to India. The Soviet Union has no unresolved direct disputes with the Western Alliance but the Chinese have one with India. The Soviets and Western Alliance have not fought a war for over 70 years (since the Western interventions during the Bolshevik Revolution) but the Chinese launched an attack on India in 1962, delivered an ultimatum to India in 1965 and were being egged on to intervene militarily during the Bangladesh Liberation War in 1971.[5] Deng Xiao Peng talked of teaching a lesson to Vietnam in 1979 as the Chinese did to India in 1962.[6] According to US intelligence sources the Chinese have transferred the design of their fourth nuclear bomb test to Pakistan.[7]

In the 1950s and 1960s when Western strategists were turning out literature on the Chinese threat to South and South-East Asia and when there were frequent references to the effect that the Americans were fighting in Vietnam to stop the nuclear-armed Chinese over-running South-East Asia,[8] and when the domino theory was treated as the eleventh commandment,[9] India took a sober view of China. When the Chinese, solely because of their anti-Sovietism of the 1960s and 1970s, found favour with the West, India again had taken a sober view of its neighbour. Now that there is talk of possible Sino-Soviet rapprochement and of China overtaking the Soviet Union in terms of power rating, still India adopts a balanced, non-alarmist but a realistic view about China, its capabilities and its implications for South and South-East Asia. India did not change its vote in favour of seating the People's Republic of China in the Security Council even in 1962, when it was under Chinese attack.

The main problem with the Western strategic literature (with some exceptions) is that its framework is solely anti-Sovietism, irrespective of any changes in ground realities. Otherwise it is difficult to explain how 13 leading US strategists constituting the Commission on Integrated Long-Term Strategy, could produce the document *Discriminate Deterrence* which purports to look forward to the next two decades, makes the assessment that Japan and China might overtake the Soviet Union as powers, omits mention of Western Europe (especially after 1992 when the trade barriers are to go), accepts that a direct military confrontation with the Soviet Union is the least likely threat and yet proceeds to deal with the Soviet Union as the only major potential adversary.[10] This view of the US-USSR adversarial relationship as the axis around which all world events have to turn has cost the Americans dearly both in lives and material over the last four decades.[11] It has, among other facts, led to the US losing its hegemonic status. Exploiting the US obsession vis-à-vis the USSR, the Saudis and the Chinese, possibly through the intermediary of Pakistan, could conclude a deal to transfer intermediate-range ballistic missiles (IRBMs). But IRBM missiles are surely not purchased at a cost of several tens of million dollars each to deliver 1–1½ tons of conventional high explosives with circular error probability of a few thousand yards. Yet the real significance of the transfer – as the carrier for Pakistan's nuclear warheads – is rarely discussed in the literature produced by the military-industrial-academic-media complex of the West. They are prepared to delude themselves that these missiles are merely intended to give Saudi Arabia (China is not mentioned) influence in the region.[13]

Given this kind of intellectual conditioning (which should be the envy of the Chinese Politburo and the anti-*perestroika* sections of the Soviet Communist Party) it is not surprising that India's security problems vis-à-vis its North, North-Eastern and Eastern neighbours have received scant attention since the days when Nixon and Kissinger undertook their journey to Canossa (Beijing), their sense of penitence having been inspired by the virulent anti-Sovietism of the Chinese leadership of that dav and Chinese nuclear and missile capabilities.[14]

Legacy of the British Raj

As mentioned earlier, in India too there are those who look at India's security problems from the perspective of the glories of the British Raj which (not always under the strict control of London) often made its own policies and was the dominant power in Asia and the Indian Ocean. British India dominated the area from Suez to the Straits of Malacca, played the "great game" in

Afghanistan to stop the expansion of Tsarist Russia (with occasional debacles caused by the Afghan mujahideen of the time), influenced events in Xinjiang, lent its imperial support to nominal Chinese suzerainty over Tibet, sent in the Younghusband military expedition to Lhasa and attempted to determine the frontiers between Tibet and China (in the Simla Agreement of 1914).

Britain was then the foremost power of the world and, with the most advanced and best trained military and naval forces at their disposal, the Raj radiated power outward into Central Asia, Tibet, the Gulf and South-East Asia. This era came to an end on 15 August 1947 and this was reconfirmed when, in the words of Mao Zedong, China stood up.

Today's superpowers – the USA and USSR – can no longer dominate Asia. The US was forced out of Vietnam and the Soviet Union is withdrawing from Afghanistan after nine years of bitter struggle. The USSR, the US, China, Israel, Pakistan and India are all nuclear weapon powers (though the last three still practise a strategy of ambivalence). The eight-year Iraq-Iran war proved that the permanent members of the UN Security Council could not stop the war and in fact each member for its own reasons, was contributing to its continuation by the overt and covert supply of arms, and was prepared to look the other way as the 1925 Geneva Protocol on the use of poisonous gases was violated on a massive scale.[15] Their mighty navies could not safeguard the safe passage of oil out of the Gulf. The sponsors of the so-called Nuclear Non-Proliferation Treaty were also prepared to look the other way as various Western European and North American companies supplied machinery and material to enable Israel and Pakistan to achieve their nuclear weapon capability.[16]

Yet because of the conditioning of 100 years of the British in India, for many Westerners and some Indians the security perimeters for modern India are the boundaries of the former Raj (including Pakistan, Nepal, Bhutan, Bangladesh, Sri Lanka and the Maldives). Hence it is asserted that the nuclear issue is one to be settled between India and Pakistan.[17] It is often argued that if only India and Pakistan would live amicably with each other there would be no major security problems for either and both should be able to reduce their defence expenditures and accelerate their development correspondingly. The US administration and US academics propagate this view with such fervour that one is tempted to believe, against all reason, they are perhaps genuinely convinced of it, just as they believed, against all evidence in the 1950s, that China was a stooge of the Soviet Union and in the 1960s that Vietnam was a stooge of China. Their perceptions of South Asia today are as realistic as they were of China and Vietnam then.

Another major problem one meets in dealing with the Western strategic literature on the South Asian situation (and this applies to the Soviet and Chinese literature as well) is that their conclusions are reached mostly through one Westerner quoting another Westerner. There are voluminous studies on security issues in South Asia in which most of the citations are from Americans and other members of the Western strategic community which is usually like-minded, with an occasional quotation from an Indian who echoes the Western view. The vast Indian Press (which is less consensual than the Western Press in respect of its world view) and the strategic literature produced in India are either wholly neglected or mentioned in passing for convenient citations only.

EXTERNAL RELATIONS AFTER INDEPENDENCE

In the four decades since its independence India has had to fight major wars in 1947–48 (Kashmir secession), 1962 (the Chinese attack), 1965 (the Pakistani infiltration into Kashmir escalating to full-scale war), and 1971 (Bangladesh liberation and the return of ten million Bangladeshi refugees to their homeland). In addition, minor operations had to be undertaken for integration of princely states and colonial territories (Junagadh in 1947, Hyderabad in 1948 and Goa in 1961). Indian armed forces helped out Nepal in 1951–52 (to put down Communist insurgency of Dr K. I. Singh), Sri Lanka in 1971 (to help the Sri Lankan government against insurgency launched by the Maoist *Janata Vimukti Peramuna* (JVP)) and at present an Indian Peace-Keeping Force is assisting Sri Lanka to implement the Indo-Sri Lankan Accord of 29 July 1987 (see Conflict Study No 211 *Lions and Tigers* by D. Austin and A. Gupta). Prolonged counter-insurgency operations were conducted by the Indian army in Nagaland and Mizoram which finally resulted in the insurgents accepting autonomous statehood within the Indian union. Other counter-insurgency operations had to be launched in Punjab (*Operation Blue Star* and *Operation Woodrose* in 1984), against the Tripura National Volunteers (an agreement is reported to have been reached) and the Gurkha National Liberation Front (fortunately now reaching an agreement). Minor border clashes involving the army occurred in 1965 (the Rann of Kutch dispute with Pakistan), in 1967 (the engagement with Chinese forces on the Sikkim border) and 1987 (in Siachen Glacier involving Pakistani forces). Unlike the industralised world which has been at peace for over four decades and where the arms race is only a reflection of power rivalry, the Indian security perspective arises out of a series of inter- and intra-state wars most of which were either on Indian territory or involved vital national interests (10 million refugees on Indian soil) or were undertaken in pursuance of the requests of immediate neighbours whose security was threatened.

Until 1962 India felt that a modest defence expenditure of less than two per cent of GNP would be sufficient to keep an adequate force equipped to face Pakistan which was unrelenting in its attempts to undo the legal accession of the state of Kashmir to India, to which end it had allied itself with the Western powers by joining CENTO and SEATO while simultaneously cultivating China.

After the 1962 Chinese attack India realised that it had to be ready to face two fronts and that the Himalayas were no longer an insuperable barrier for forces deployed to the north. Consequently the Indian forces were almost doubled and the Indian defence burden reached four per cent of GNP, subsequently being stabilised at around 3.3 per cent (until about four years ago).

In the 1965 war, as Pakistan was running out of ammunition, the Chinese delivered an ultimatum[18] to India thereby making India conscious of the significant possibility of having to face a two-front war. At about the same time Indonesia, under Sukarno's leadership, aligned itself with Pakistan and China, renamed the Indian Ocean the Indonesian Ocean, laid claims to Nicobar Islands and stepped up hostile naval activities around the archipelago of the Andamans and Nicobars.[19] This confronted India with the possibility of a third front. Fortunately, with Sukarno's fall in the autumn of 1965, his successors did not continue his policies and Indian-Indonesian relations are now very cordial and the maritime boundary between the two countries has been demarcated.

However the maritime threat was revived when the United States despatched its Taskforce 74 headed by the nuclear-propelled and normally nuclear armed aircraft-carrier "USS Enterprise" into the Bay of Bengal in an intimidatory mission during the Bangladesh war in December 1971. By the time it arrived the Pakistani forces had surrendered at Dhaka.[20] The US has today created a Central Command in the Indian Ocean with contingent operational jurisdiction over 19 nations (all of them non-aligned) from Pakistan to Kenya. The US also keeps a carrier task force (which must be presumed normally to be equipped with nuclear weapons) on permanent station in the Arabian Sea.

Soviet switch

Although under Stalin the Soviet leadership decried Indian independence, called Nehru a "running dog of imperialism" and Gandhi a religious reactionary and the Communists in India launched an insurgency (in Telengana in 1947–50), as China become unified under Maoist control and began to attack the Soviet Union on border issues, on the status of Mongolia and on Marxist ideology the Soviet leadership started to change its attitude towards India. In the 1950s Soviet support was mostly in terms of assistance to set up heavy industry and of countering the Western support for Pakistan in the Security Council on the Kashmir issue. But from 1959 onwards, following a border clash between Chinese and Indian patrols at Longju (in Arunachal Pradesh), the Soviet Union began signalling its support for India in the dispute with China.[21] As the Sino-Soviet ideological dispute intensified the Soviet Union signed agreements with India to supply transport aircraft and helicopters to support Indian troops at high altitudes and to license India to manufacture MIG-21 supersonic fighters.

The 1962 Chinese attack coincided with the Cuban missile crisis. Initially the Soviet Union took a neutral position but once the missile crisis was behind it, it came out with strong condemnation of China and support for India.[22] In the immediate wake of the Chinese attack there was a promise of "massive military assistance" from the US and the Commonwealth; the Commonwealth nations duly fulfilled their promises but it became clear in 1963–64 that the US was not prepared to alienate Pakistan by providing India with military equipment.[23] US assistance was restricted to non-lethal items such as snowclothing, factory machinery, road-building equipment, communications equipment etc, and with the provision, supervised by a monitoring team, that the equipment was not deployed against Pakistan.[24]

Under these conditions India was compelled to turn increasingly to the Soviet Union for military supplies. The Soviet Union extended to India long-term credit (10 years) with low rate of interest (2.5 per cent) and also agreed to accept repayment in rupees (through the import of Indian goods). This enabled India to equip its forces without the strain of a balance of payments problem. The Russians imposed no conditions in terms of supervisory teams and were prepared to sell India a whole range of sophisticated equipment, fighter aircraft, submarines, patrol vessels, tanks, artillery, infantry combat vehicles, missiles and missile craft and were also prepared, when necessary, to transfer relevant manufacturing technologies to India.

In 1971, in the aftermath of Dr Kissinger's visit to Beijing – via Delhi and Islamabad – and the possibility of having to face a Pakistan-China-US alliance, with the Pakistanis having driven ten million refugees into India, an Indo-Soviet Peace and Friendship treaty was concluded. This treaty, unlike treaties concluded by the USSR with other countries, contained no military clause. It stipulated that the USSR respect India's policy of non-alignment and that in the face of security threats each country would consult the other as to ways and means of dealing with the situation. The real purpose of the treaty was to create a certain sense of deterrence through uncertainty in the minds of Chinese and American leaderships. Kissinger's book *The White House Years*[25] bears ample testimony that the treaty achieved this purpose since, when encouraged by the US to intervene in the Indo-Pakistan war which at that time was going badly for the Pakistanis, the Chinese declined to do so.

Reciprocal relations

Since then the Indo-Soviet relationship has remained cordial and steady. Even when the Janata government took office in 1977 with the avowed purpose of pursuing "genuine" non-alignment, they soon found it sufficiently genuine to require no change in the relationship with the Soviet Union. It is not that the Indo-Soviet relationship has been without its periods of strain. In spite of refraining from publicly condemning the Soviet Union for its intervention in Afghanistan, the Indian government made no secret of its disapproval. While preferring a secular (even if it had to be Marxist) government in Afghanistan to an Islamic regime, India was unhappy about the mode of Soviet intervention and this was conveyed to the Soviet leadership at the highest level. Similarly, earlier in 1971 the Soviet Union had had its reservations about a possible war between India and Pakistan on the Bangladesh issue and it was only after considerable pressure that the Soviet Union supported India during the war, both materially and in the UN, and in creating a sense of deterrence vis-à-vis China and the United States.

The Indo-Soviet relationship is based on a mutuality of strategic interests – that China presents a security problem for them both, though this is not articulated. However India would not support Brezhnev's Asian security plan which had an overt anti-Chinese bias. Each side recognises its need for the other without having to proclaim it in overt strategic terms. The Russians are aware of China's efforts to extend its influence along the soft belly of the

Soviet Union (the Islamic republics of Asia) by developing intimate relations with Pakistan, supplying arms to Afghan mujahideen, transferring missiles (Silkworms) and tanks to Iran, and IRBM missiles to Saudi Arabia. Similarly China is cultivating a close relationship with Thailand, arms the genocidal Pol Pot-Khieu Sampan clique, keeps up its military pressure on Vietnam, including naval action in Spratly Islands and, until some years back cultivating the Burmese Communist Party, various insurgent groups of North Burma and Naga and Mizo insurgents in India. Within the subcontinent China cultivates and intimidates the King of Nepal, provides arms to Bangladesh and to Sri Lanka. Once the US and China had established a cordial relationship the US extended significant help to the Chinese armaments industry.[26] This has an adverse impact on Indian security.

The Soviet Union has no interest in converting India to Communism. That would only produce one more ideological rival. Its relationship with India has been a model (as Gorbachev mentions in his book *Perestroika*) and mutually beneficial. Apart from Vietnam and Cuba, India is the only country which has used Soviet arms successfully in wars (without the benefit of any Soviet advisers in India). The relationship with India helps to legitimise Soviet relationships with the developing world. India is a countervailing factor vis-à-vis China and demonstrates that nationalist bourgeois democracies can deal with the Soviet Union without fear of being subverted. The USSR, though a superpower, does not attempt to dominate India in regard to its own perceptions of national interest, for example in respect of the Non-Proliferation Treaty. The Indian and Soviet interests in South-East Asia, in supporting Vietnam and hence recognising the Heng Samrin government to stem the Chinese influence, coincide.

The Indians will not become Communists as a nation but are mildly Left of centre in their international approach. On the issues relating to the developing world it costs the Soviet Union very little to support the developing nations in the United Nations.[27] It is not, as the Americans see it through their distorted prism of bi-polar conflict, that the developing world votes with USSR. It is the other way round. The USSR, and very often China, vote with the developing world while the US by voting against the vast majority of developing nations alienates them.

There is a distinct possibility of Sino-Soviet relations improving. To some extent this is inevitable since both China and the Soviet Union desire to have greater manoeuvrability in international relations. Neither of them is the ideological fanatic it was in the 1950s and 1960s. Both want rapid modernisation and are prepared to shed many of the Stalinist-Maoist dogmas. They have achieved mutual nuclear deterrence and hence have no fear of each other. Their differences are about third nations – Vietnam's presence in Kampuchea and Soviet presence in Afghanistan and Mongolia (the latter no longer serious issues). At the same time they compete for power and influence in South-West, South and South-East Asia. Consequently while their relations are likely to improve, there is no real possibility of a Sino-Soviet *entente* of the type the Western world perceived in the 1950s. Therefore in India Gorbachev's Vladivostock speech calling for an Asian collective security system (inclusive of

China) was received with some reservations and scepticism.[28] The quadrilateral interaction of US, Japan, China and USSR is likely to prove highly complex. Consequently while India watches closely the developments in Sino-Soviet relationships, most Indians feel confident that the Soviet Union would not make a deal with China at India's expense for the simple reason it just cannot afford to do so. Should it ever happen India will have its cards to play vis-à-vis the US, Japan and Western Europe. After all, options for such manoeuvrability is the very essence of non-alignment.

INDIA AND CHINA

India shares its longest border with China. The policy of the British Raj was to ensure the security of the Indian empire by creating three buffer zones. Afghanistan was the buffer between India and Tsarist Russia. Tibet, whose autonomy under the nominal suzerainty of a weak Chinese empire was acknowledged by Britain to keep off the Russians, was a buffer vis-à-vis both Russia and China. By occupying the entire Indian Ocean littoral, with small shares to the French, the Dutch and the Portuguese, the water spread was converted into a third buffer. When the Chinese Communists seized power in China and occupied Tibet, India lost the first buffer. The Chinese today acknowledge that Stalin was attempting to pressurise the Chinese Communists to come to terms with Chiang Kai-shek, and even to partition China along the Yangtze River. It was the enormous quantities of US arms supplied to Chiang Kai-shek which fell into the hands of Chinese Communists that enabled them to overrun Xinjiang and Tibet. At the same time, India was facing the hostility of Western powers in the Security Council on the Kashmir issue and Indian attempts to procure surplus arms from the US were rebuffed.[29] Nehru recognised the potential dangers of the long border with Tibet and warned as early as 1950 that the Himalayan crest was India's security perimeter and that no one could cross it without facing India's opposition.[30] At the same time he expressed the hope that, just as India was permitting Nepal, Bhutan, and at that time Sikkim too, to remain independent and autonomous, the Chinese would give autonomy to Tibet.

Though in the early years the Chinese Communists were supporting sections of Indian Communists in their insurgency, Nehru tried to assuage the Chinese hostility by prompt recognition of the new Beijing government and by pleading for its recognition by the international community. He also accepted Chinese sovereignty over Tibet but urged the Chinese to respect Tibetan autonomy. India also helped in restoring to the Nepali monarch his full powers, thereby abolishing the Shogunate of the Rana family. It was also perhaps Nehru's hope that Nepal would move towards a parliamentary democracy which would be the surest way of protecting it from possible Maoist subversion. He also renewed the treaty which the British Raj had had with Bhutan with the underlying objective of piloting Bhutan towards UN membership. In Sikkim, though there was a popular uprising in favour of integration with India in 1948 for reasons which are not clear, Nehru refrained from merging Sikkim with the Indian union as was done in respect of the 500 or so Indian Princely states. However Sikkim became a protectorate with an Indian official acting as the *Dewan* of Sikkim. Nehru also appointed a Committee under General Himmat Singhji to review the defences of India's northern borders.[31] Though the Committee produced its report in 1954 there was no significant follow-up action on its recommendations, especially in regard to developing communications in the northern border areas.

Following the Chinese occupation of Tibet, India extended its effective administration into the tribal area (which was then known as North-East Frontier Agency – NEFA – and is now the Indian state of Arunachal Pradesh) and set up border posts and stationed units of Assam Rifles; with the permission of the Nepali government, Indian personnel also manned border posts on the Nepal-Tibet border. India constructed the Kathmandu airfield and also connected Kathmandu with the Raxaul railhead through an all-weather road.

At the same time India concluded an agreement with China on regulation of border trade across the Indo-Tibetan border. The preamble to this 1954 agreement spelt out the five principles of peaceful co-existence (*Panch Sheel*). While there are indications that Nehru had reservations about China,[32] by and large in India there was general optimism about the future of Indo-Chinese relations. During this period Nehru tried to promote an Asian consciousness and bring together the Afro-Asian nations. An Asian Relations Conference was convened in 1947 in Delhi and the Bandung Conference followed in 1955. There was close co-operation and consultation between India, Burma, Indonesia and Sri Lanka. Decolonisation in Asia made further progress with the Indochinese States and Malaya becoming independent.

China's "Great Power" Aspirations

Two inter-related factors shattered this Nehruvian dream of the Asian role in world affairs. The US decided to encircle the Communist landmass (China as well as the USSR) through a series of military pacts; and Maoist China developed a grandiose vision of its role as a world power and the central engine of world revolution after the death of Stalin. The US promoted the CENTO and SEATO alliances and incorporated a part of the subcontinent – Pakistan – within them. Encouraged by the achievements of their first five-year-plan carried out with massive Soviet aid, China embarked upon the "Great Leap Forward", and a nuclear weapons programme. It began flexing its muscles as a great power.

The full facts of what happened within China in that period are yet to be made public. After the failure of the "Great Leap Forward" and opposition of pragmatic leaders – such as Liu Shaoqi and Deng Xiaoping – to Maoist policies – Mao appears to have started allying himself with Marshal Lin Biao and the People's Liberation Army (PLA) and decided on a totally adventurous course both within the country and in external relations. The Sino-Soviet ideological conflict worsened. There were attacks on Nehru for his economic and foreign policies which were attributed to his being a recipient of external aid. Khrushchev was attacked for his revisionism and internally leaders like

Liu Shaoqi and Deng Xiaoping were branded as "capitalist roaders" and China's Khrushchevs. Communist Parties in developing countries were encouraged to intensify insurgencies in an attempt for "the countryside" to encircle "the cities" (*ie* the developed world).[33] Maoism was prescribed as the universal revolutionary doctrine.

The suppression of the Tibetan uprising in 1959 and the steady Chinese advance into the Aksai Chin area of Ladakh and pressure on NEFA region, the attacks on Nehru, China's concern about growing Indo-Soviet friendship and its ideological dispute with the Soviet Union and the internal power struggle within China (which led to the elimination of a number of veteran leaders, millions of people being killed by Red Guards, and the rise to power of the Gang of Four and Lin Biao as well as the break with the Soviet Union), the Ussuri clash and the rapprochement with the US will appear to be interrelated – though without access to Chinese archives it is difficult to form a coherent pattern. One factor, however, that emerges clearly and continues to influence Chinese policies under the sober and pragmatic Deng, is China's continuous drive for recognition as one of the great powers.

The debacle at Bomdila suffered in 1962 by the famed Indian 4th division was not due to want of equipment or manpower but was a failure on the part of a few senior army officers[34] and politicans (Nehru and Krishna Menon) to prepare the army psychologically for a limited war with China.[35] The Chinese themselves were not apparently prepared for such a quick collapse of the Indian division. Knowing that snow would soon block their lines of communication to Tibet, the Chinese offered a unilateral ceasefire and withdrew from NEFA. They had succeeded in humiliating India – a humiliation from which Nehru did not recover. The purpose of the Chinese attack on 20 October 1962 is still shrouded in mystery. It was not provoked by India's so-called "forward" policy since by that term the Indians only meant establishing a chain of posts to prevent *further* Chinese incursions and did not include the recovery of territory lost nor pose any threat to the Chinese roads across Aksai Chin which were some distance from where fighting took place. In NEFA the Chinese withdrew, no doubt for fear of being cut off by snow but it validated in a sense India's title to NEFA. There appear to be three rational explanations for the attack: that it was part of China's internal power struggle and an attempt to boost the PLA's prestige which Mao was to use to strike at the Chinese Communist Party; that it was intended to humiliate India, in the process unleashing forces of disintegration (during that period the thesis of India's dangerous decade after Nehru's death was quite popular); and, thirdly, to force India to ally itself with the West, thereby proving Khrushchev wrong in the ideological debate. If these were its purposes, China may have succeeded fully in the first objective, partially in the second but not at all in the third. India was taught a lesson, as Deng Xiaoping claimed in 1979, that a country, though non-aligned, needs to be defended against great powers. India is not likely to forget this lesson for many decades to come.

BUFFER STATES AND BORDERS

The 1960s were an extremely dangerous period for the Indian security in the North-East. Not only did the Chinese strike directly at India but India's relations with Pakistan (then including East Pakistan) were deteriorating towards the war in 1965, Nepal, with its new young king Mahendra, was unfriendly and a coup in Burma toppled the co-operative U Nu. The Nagas had been sustaining an insurgency since 1954 and the Mizos also launched an insurgency of their own in 1966, both deriving training, armaments and asylum from East Pakistan and from China via East Pakistan. The tribals in Khasi and Jaintia hills were restive. The Chogyal of Sikkim attempted to exploit what he considered as India's moment of weakness. The central government and the Marxist Communist Party – CPI(M) – the larger of the two wings into which the Communist Party of India split in 1964, were at loggerheads and the CPI(M) cadres were detained for a period only to emerge victorious in the Provincial elections of 1967. The country underwent two changes in leadership in quick succession and in 1967 the Congress Party lost the elections in most of the states in the Hindi heartland, as well as in Bengal and Tamil Nadu.

A Maoist splinter group from the Communist Party calling themselves Naxalites (named after Naxalbari, the village in West Bengal where their uprising against the Marxist-oriented administration in Calcutta began) initiated acts of terrorism in various parts of India, mostly in areas where tribals or landless peasantry were under oppression by local landlords. They hailed the Cultural Revolution in China and raised the slogan "China's Chairman is our Chairman". Terrorism spread to the city of Calcutta. During this period the Chinese published an article, "Spring Thunder over India", predicting that soon revolution would sweep over India like a prairie fire.[35A]

Though in 1970, following some pleasantries between Mao Zedong and the Indian Chargé d'Affaires at a diplomatic reception in Beijing, there was an expectation of improved relations with China this did not materialise. The following year saw the Pakistan-China-US line-up against India. Following the liberation of Bangladesh, the Chinese withheld recognition from the Bangladesh government until after the assassination of Sheikh Mujibur Rahman in 1975. Thereafter relations between the two countries improved rapidly as tension began to develop between India and the military regime in Bangladesh. China became an arms supplier to Bangladesh, whose army today is equipped with Chinese T-59 and T-62 tanks, Chinese naval vessels and Chinese J-6 and Q-5 aircraft.[36]

The Chinese attempts to equip the Naga insurgents with arms via Burma was foiled in 1969 by the entire force returning from China being captured by Indian forces. After the Bangladesh war the Chinese training camps for the insurgents in East Bengal were closed down. While one lot of arms sent to Mizo rebels arrived, subsequent supplies were successfully intercepted by the Indian forces.

The Naxalite movement splintered further and at one time there were 21 separate groups. Though there are still Naxalite groups in operation in Tamil

Nadu, Andhra, Bihar and West Bengal, by-and-large they have ceased to be a meaningful factor in the political scene; most of them have rejoined the main political stream, while some became Khalistani extremists.

By the early 1970s the Naga insurgents had signed the Shillong Accord and accepted the Nagaland state within the Indian Constitution, though the statehood had been granted as far back as the early 1960s. In 1985, after nearly ten years of negotiations, the Mizo insurgent leader, Laldenga, also accepted the Mizo state within the Indian Constitution. His party won the elections and he is today the Chief Minister of Mizoram. Statehood was conferred on Khasi-Jaintia area (Meghalaya), Tripura and Manipur in the 1970s and, finally, on Arunachal Pradesh in 1986.

India's counter-insurgency experience is unique. India did not seek to eliminate the insurgents and their leaderships but offered them political autonomy. Initially the Nagas and Mizos, being Christians, had some reservations about the genuineness of Indian secularism. When the Church leaders recognised the risks of insurgents dealing with Communist China the Church itself became an influential factor in bringing about a rapprochement between the tribal insurgents and the government of India. India has also attempted to spend a much higher *per capita* rate of development outlays in the North-East tribal states.

The Indian constitutional process has been able to accommodate Marxism and India is the only country where the Marxists get elected in a fair and free multiparty competitive electoral system, conduct the legislative proceedings on liberal parliamentary procedure and leave office when the population votes them out. Out of three states where Marxists have held power (Kerala, West Bengal and Tripuna) two are in the North-East. While in West Bengal the Marxists have been able to provide a stable state administration for well over 11 years (they have won three successive elections), recently they were voted out of office in Tripura, after ten years in power.

Very recently the Gurkhas in Darjeeling District, who have been agitating for a separate state and have indulged in extremist violence over the last 3–4 years, have finally agreed to accept autonomous district councils within the state of West Bengal and have called off their agitational activities.[37] There is still some residual violence in Tripura (where the native tribals have been outnumbered by Bengali immigrants who flooded in in the wake of the partition of India and creation of East Pakistan in 1947) where the tribals are agitating for their "rights" against the immigrant majority.[37A] In Manipur there is a grievance among the Meiteyi population (the native Manipuri) about the recognition of their language as a national language. Similarly, the vast numbers of Gurkhas spread out all over the North-East want to have Nepali recognised as one of India's national languages. The Assam problem (though eased to some extent with the *Assam Gana Tantra Parishad* winning the elections and forming the administration) still remains, as the state government is not satisfied with the progress made in identifying alien immigrants and preventing further immigration into the area.

Different roads to nation-statehood

While all these problems remain and others may arise, it is important to note the resilience displayed by the Indian political system to accommodate various opposing views and to reach accords within the framework of the Indian constitution which assures basic autonomy and representational government on the basis of adult franchise and linguistic and ethnic identities. This process in India has to be contrasted with what happens in Tibet, Yunnan, Burma, Bangladesh and Nepal and the mutual impacts the Indian constitutional evolution process has on the neighbouring countries and *vice versa*. What is often overlooked is that India's security problem in the North and North-East mostly arises out of this basic dissonance between Indian democratic evolution and other paths to national consolidation, identity formation and the nation-state development India's neighbours have chosen to adopt. Given the interactions among the populations across frontiers, this basic dissonance is bound to cause security problems on both sides. One need not pass any judgements on the different roads to nation-statehood and national identity formation adopted by the nations concerned to reach the conclusion that the divergences in the constitutional evolutions of these nations is at the root of the problem of security.

To illustrate the divergences, India is a secular, democratic, federal (though not to the extent many people would desire) and linguistically autonomous polity; Nepal is a Hindu Kingdom; Bangladesh has just formally declared itself an Islamic state – though it has been this in practice since 1975; Bhutan and Burma are Buddhist states; and China in Tibet practises a dogmatic faith, with a prophet (Marx), and a church and priesthood (the Communist party). None of the states surrounding India is a democracy. While Nepal and Bhutan are monarchies, Burma, Bangladesh and Tibet are all directly ruled either by the military or military-dominated regimes. None of these surrounding states permit linguistic or ethnic autonomy. Tibet is being increasingly Hanified and the First Secretary of the Tibetan Communist Part is not a Tibetan. The Chins, Shans, Kachins, Akyabi Muslims and Karens in Burma, the Chakmas in Bangladesh, the Terai population in Nepal and the Nepali population in Bhutan do not enjoy the autonomy which the states in North-East India have within the Indian union. Nor does the development process in different minority areas in these countries get the preference received by the North-Eastern states in India under the Finance Commission's devolution of finances and plan allocations from the Planning Commission.

After 47 years of occupation, the Chinese have been forced to concede the status of Tibetan as the local language. In Burma the military overthrew the U Nu government as he was considering some devolution of powers to ethnic minorities. The Chakmas in Bangladesh do not see why they should not have the status of Nagas and Mizos in India. Consequently the different states feel a certain compulsion to raise barriers against India so as to avoid a wide-ranging people-to-people interaction. Nepal has an open border with India but the King's proposal for a zone of peace is intended to ensure that the Nepali Congress cannot obtain support or shelter from India in its struggle to bring about parliamentary democracy in Nepal.

The Burmese army has preferred to have an army-run regime within the Burman areas without their writ running effectively in the peripheral Chin, Shan, Kachin, and Karen areas, thereby providing a certain leverage to the Burmese Communist Party (till recently supported by China) and presenting a vulnerability to Chinese pressure. The Chakma rebels take refuge in India just as the Tripura National Volunteers do in Bangladesh. The explosive growth of population in Bangladesh, where orthodox Islam impedes population control, exerts enormous demographic pressure on Assam and Meghalaya. Hence the Indian proposal for border fencing which is resented in Bangladesh. The Indo-Burman relationship is tension-free, mainly because there is not much interaction between the populations of the two countries. India's concern is not about any action on the part of Burma itself but the fact that the sparsely-populated Northern Burmese tribal areas, where the writ of the Burmese government does not run effectively, may be vulnerable to Chinese demographic pressure and China's subversive dealings with Northern Burman tribes (though at present these have significantly decreased).

Bangladesh

Bangladesh has four disputes with India. One is about the transfer of a tiny strip of land of Tin Bigha. India is committed to it but, since the matter is pending in the High Court, the transfer has not been effected; one is left with the feeling that the Indian government has not pursued the case energetically. The second dispute is about the maritime boundary demarcation, which is complicated by the formation of a small sand bank island at the mouth of Haribanga river to which there are rival claims by both India and Bangladesh. The title to the island will influence the alignment of the maritime boundary. The third and most emotional issue is about the waters of the Ganges. There is no dispute that during the lean season there is not enough water in the Ganges to enable India to flush the Calcutta port and to prevent the salinity caused by the tidal surge as well as provide water for cultivation in Bangladesh and to prevent the tidal surge bringing salinity inland. The problem is how to get the surplus water. India feels that the waters of the Brahmaputra are so enormous and vastly more than can be used by India and Bangladesh that the best solution is to divert the Brahmaputra waters through a canal into the Ganges which will adequately cover the needs of both India and Bangladesh. Incidentally the canal will be traversing the northernmost parts of Bangladesh which suffer from frequent droughts.

Bangladesh is in favour of the Nepalis building storage dams in the tributaries of the Ganges in Nepal and releasing the waters during lean season. India argues that its water requirements exceed what can be stored by the Nepali dams. Bangladeshis feel that a canal across Bangladesh takes away some land from the densely populated country (they overlook the benefit to be obtained by the seepage from the canal to drought-prone northern districts). To many Indians the Bangladeshi stand appears emotional and irrational and against their own interests. There is a feeling in India that the Bangladeshis are interested in perpetuating the dispute mainly to create a certain amount of tension with India.

The final problem is tighter control over transborder migration of Bangladeshis into Assam and Meghalaya. People in Assam and Meghalaya do not want to be swamped by a steady influx of Bangladeshis. While the proposals of fencing the border and intensifying border patrols have not made significant progress, Bangladeshis resent the idea of being fenced off. At the same time Islamic Bangladesh has no effective population control policy and denies that such an exodus is taking place. If it is not, they should have no grounds for complaint.

The real problem for Bangladesh is its national identity. Until 1947 its history was part of Indian history. It shares language, religion, ethnicity and culture with West Bengal. Originally the emphasis on Islamic identity made the people vote for Pakistan in the 1946 elections even when the provinces which today constitute Pakistan did not do so. As part of Pakistan, they found their loyalty to their language and culture superseded their religious ties with Pakistanis. They seceded from Pakistan because they were denied an adequate share in national policy-making and neglected in terms of development. Now they are ruled by a military-dominated structure. They are surrounded on 95 per cent of their land border by an India with whom they have shared history for millenia and which has adopted totally different paths to nation-state evolution and national identity formulation. Bangladesh needs the friendly hinterland of India for its development, but is afraid of having close friendly relations with India lest it should call in to question the very *raison d'etre* for its separate existence.

Nepal

Nepal has been attempting to distance itself from India since the days of King Mahendra. India, as Nehru declared as far back as 1950,[38] acts on the assumption that, situated on the southern crest of the Himalayas, Nepal and Bhutan are within the Indian security perimeter. India is Nepal's largest aid-giver and has contributed significantly to its infrastructural development (as also to Bhutan), especially in terms of road construction and power generation.

The 1962 debacle in the war with China marked a turning point in Indo-Nepalese relations, though one could perhaps fix that point earlier when Prime Minister Nehru denounced the King's dismissal of the parliamentary government in Nepal.[39] The King demanded and obtained the withdrawal of Indians from the border posts between Nepal and Tibet. He permitted the Chinese to construct the Arnico highway linking Kodari on the Tibetan border with Kathmandu. He accepted Chinese aid and also started developing closer relations with Pakistan. In 1971 Nepal voted with the majority of UN members in calling on India to withdraw its forces, then in the process of liberating Bangladesh. Nepal also insisted on, and obtained, liberalisation in terms of transit of goods through India though there were Indian charges that vested interests in Nepal and India were colluding to divert the bulk of those goods (not permitted for import into India) into the Indian market.

In 1975, King Birendra made his proposal for declaring Nepal a zone of peace.[40] Nepal has borders with only two countries – China and India. The China-Nepal border is closed and Chinese forces are deployed along it. With India, Nepal has an open border and a special treaty relationship enjoins the two countries to consult each other in face of a security threat to either. Hundreds of thousands of Nepalis come into India to obtain employment and a significant number settle there. India does not keep any forces on the borders of Nepal.

It is quite obvious that the King's aim is to make Nepal a neutral country, equidistant from China and India. Such a decision on the part of Nepal cannot be questioned by India. However, if Nepal treats China and India on a par then it cannot expect India to keep the border open and accept Nepalis coming into India without visas to seek employment. India will be compelled to treat the Indo-Nepali border on the same lines as China treats the China-Nepali border. It would necessitate the Nepali border being patrolled by the Indian Border Security Force and India developing cantonments in Eastern Uttar Pradesh and Northern Bihar adjoining Nepal. But the Nepalis argue that, while they would like India to accept the principle of a zone of peace (Nepal equating India and China), they would still like to maintain the special relationship with India in every other respect.[41] In other words, Nepal would like to have their cake and eat it too. So far India has declined to accept this proposition.

Secondly, Nepal seeks, as part of the peace zone declaration, reciprocal obligation that neither country should permit any activities on its soil that are hostile to the other state. This is obviously a way of seeking a guarantee from India that it would not morally or materially support elements such as the Nepali Congress party which has been agitating for the restoration of parliamentary democracy and a multi-party system in Nepal. In the last referendum, the King's proposal for a partyless political system was approved only by a very narrow majority. It is difficult to say whether the King's proposal to declare Nepal a zone of peace is a way of bargaining with India to extract more concessions or is a genuine proposal. There is a good case to argue that it is in India's interest to have a closed border with Nepal and to stop further Nepali immigration into India. If India were to agree to the zone of peace proposal on the basis that India-Nepal relations would be on an equal footing to Nepal-China relations, the King's bluff would be called because he cannot afford it and Nepal would be the loser.

Nepal has also been bargaining hard with India in regard to a number of hydroelectric projects since many of the tributaries of the Ganges rise in Nepal. While it is reasonable that Nepal should bargain hard to obtain the maximum possible return from India, one sometimes has the impression that the Nepalese have been carrying the bargaining process too far and that in the process they could lose revenues and also delay the generation of power which could be of immense value for their own development.

Nepal has come far from the days of 1947. Yet there are pressures within the country for further democratisation and parliamentary rule. While progress in this direction is inevitable, the crucial issue is at what pace this development should take place. It could be argued that Nepali Congress and the younger generation want to reach that goal at too rapid a pace while the King and the Court are going about it too slowly. There is potential for conflict to develop on this account.

The Terai population in Nepal (south of the mountains, in the Gangetic plain) feels discriminated against by the Nepali ruling élite, in terms of language, employment opportunities and participation in national decision-making. If India accepts – in response to Gurkha National Liberation Front's (GNLF) demand – Nepali as one of India's national languages, one may expect a corresponding demand to make Hindi one of Nepal's national languages.

If, for reasons to be discussed further, Tibet becomes restive as a result of China's accepting Hong Kong on the basis of the "one nation – two systems" formula and demands a similar degree of autonomy, provoking the Chinese to crack down on Tibet, the impact will be felt on Nepal.

On the whole, though the Nepal-India relationship is not what it should be, there is very little risk of its getting out of control, mainly because of Nepal's dependence on India in a number of ways and the soft spot the Indians in the north have for the only Hindu king in the world.

Bhutan

India's relations with Bhutan are cordial and India fulfilled its pledge to pilot that country towards membership in the United Nations. The Bhutanese royal family has a tradition of popular consultation through an Assembly (the *Tsongdu*). The young King is devoting considerable attention to development of the country's infrastructure and administrative apparatus, mainly with assistance from India. There is an Indian military training mission in Bhutan. India has renewed the treaty which the British Raj had with the Maharajah of Bhutan. (Unlike Sikkim, whose prince used to be a member of the Indian Chamber of Princes, thereby acknowledging himself as an Indian Prince and where the Indian State's Congress – an offshoot of the Indian National Congress – functioned, Bhutan was never treated as part of the British Indian Raj.) Bhutan has yet to settle its border with Tibet and is now conducting border demarcation negotiations with the Chinese. Bhutan's external relations are somewhat limited because of its resource constraints and India, until recently, was the sole provider of external assistance. Of late Bhutan has tried to diversify its external assistance inflow, which is understandable.

Bhutan has a divided population. The Bhotiayas reside north of the Manas mountains and form the political and administrative élites; they are Buddhists with close cultural links with Tibet. On the southern slopes, with its plantations, the population is to a large extent Nepali. Though at present there are no problems, with the rising consciousness of the Nepalis in Sikkim where they constitute the largest single group, and the formation of autonomous councils in North Bengal to accommodate the Gurkhas, there is a possibility of the Nepali population in Southern Bhutan demanding increased participation in administration and the national developmental cake. If the King follows the tradition set by his father and the Indian example, there should be no difficulty in accommodating such legitimate political aspirations.

INDIAN DEFENCE DEPLOYMENT

The integration of India and its successful functioning as a secular, democratic union of autonomous linguistic and ethnic states is a unique experiment and, as Johan Galtung has suggested, may provide an example for ultimate European integration. The foregoing account shows that in the Eastern part of India such an integration has not come about without violence. India had and continues to have other secessionist problems. At one time seccessionism in Tamil Nadu was spearheaded by the *Dravida Munnetra Kazhagam.* Once elected, they found they could wield power in the state within the Indian constitutional system and they gave up their secessionism. In Jammu and Kashmir, Sheikh Abdullah originally fought for integration with India, subsequently started favouring secessionism and in the end also accepted the Indian constitution.

The Khalistani issue is slightly more complicated. It is not so much a secessionist issue as one of internecine struggle within the Sikh community – whether it should separate politics and religion and advance as the most enterprising community in India on a secular basis or be dominated by the clergy and clergy-influenced mediocre politicians. An attempt has been made to terrorise the non-Sikhs in order to invoke indiscriminate state violence against the Sikhs, thereby uniting the fragmented Sikh community. In this instance it is more difficult to accommodate the extremists within the constitutional framework. Initially the majority of the Sikh community has to assert its will to resist domination by clergy-dominated politics. Once that comes about political solutions will not be difficult to evolve.

India has had a number of advantages in its nation-style evolution. There is a millenia-old memory of an Indian culture and civilisation, distinct from the Sinic civilisation to the north, the Indo-Buddhist civilisation in South-East Asia and the Iranian and Arab Islamic civilisations to the west. A century-old freedom struggle, using liberal democratic, secular values as the goals, led by an all-India movement with the charismatic leadership of Gandhi and Nehru had significantly helped to bring about a deep commitment to Indian unity and democracy. There is no doubt still a long way to go in regard to total national integration, in eliminating the Untouchability in rural areas, integrating tribal populations without forcible cultural assimilation and blurring and eliminating the caste as a factor of division in politics. Overshadowing all this is the problem of population control and the alleviation and elimination of poverty.

This gigantic experiment in integration, development, and national consolidation is under continuous threat from cold war power politics between the two superpowers, the pressure of Chinese expansionism and drive towards great power status, religious fundamentalism, small nation chauvinism, tribalism and inter-caste tensions. The entire eastern region of India, while itself not entirely tension free, is surrounded on all sides by greater turbulence.

Tibet is struggling for autonomy and is being suppressed. The disturbances in Burma are a sign of the continued failure of the Burmese to solve their problems of ethnic autonomy and representational government. Bangladesh, though linguistically highly homogenous, has not been able to settle down to a degree of political stability which could facilitate optimum development and representational government. While Bangladeshis have obtained linguistic autonomy, they are still ruled by a military which had its origins in Pakistani military political theology, with all the elements of freedom-fighting having been eliminated from politics. The demand for a multiparty democratic system in Nepal has not weakened in intensity.

The building of a nation-state in India involves its development process being shielded from these external threats (primarily from China and the major powers pursuing their cold war politics) and surrounding turbulences in nations far less stable than India – Burma, Bangladesh, Nepal. This is the reason why India, even while saving and investing around 21–22 per cent of its GNP on development, is also compelled to spend around four per cent on its defence. An analysis of Indian security assessments and defence effort would explain the rationale underlying the Indian thinking. The following figures are from the *Military Balance 1987–88*, published by the International Institute of Strategic Studies.

On the Western Front

Pakistan	*India*
7 Corps	5 Corps (Part of one faces China in Ladakh) and 4 Corps deployed in the North and East against China
2 Armoured divisions	2 Armoured divisions 1 Mechanical division
17 Infantry divisions (13 divisions face India directly. Out of other 4 divisions on Western side 2 are earmarked against India).	20 Infantry divisions (inclusive of 3–4 divisions earmarked for the East and South).
4 Indep. Armoured Brigades	7 Armoured Brigades
8 Indep. Infantry Brigades	10 Independent Infantry Brigades

(While Pakistani cantonments are very close to the border and therefore Pakistan can mobilise its forces on battle stations within 72 hours many of the Indian divisions earmarked for Western front are quartered in Central and South-Central Indian and Indian mobilisation time is 10–14 days).

On the North and North East

China	*India*
Lanzhou Military Region	4 Corps
3 Corps, 2 missile battalions, 1 Armoured division, 13 infantry divisions	9 mountain divisions and 1–2 infantry divisions
Chengdu Military Region	
3 corps, 1 missile battalion	
15 infantry divisions	

While all the Chinese forces are not exclusively earmarked for deployment in Tibet, Indian calculations are that China can logistically support up to 22 divisions in Tibet. Unlike in 1962, the Chinese have laid an oil pipe line up to Lhasa, improved their roads along the Indo-Tibetan border and towards the Indian border and have four operational airfields in Tibet, as well as airfields in Xinjiang, and Yunnan. The Chinese also have the logistic advantage of operating on a plateau while the Indian troops have to face them on a slope. The Chinese road communications in Tibet and towards points of ingress into Arunachal Pradesh are better developed than the Indian road system on the slopes of Arunachal Pradesh (though rapid improvements have been undertaken in the last 2–3 years).

China has a modernisation programme for its military sector. Today it is the fifth largest arms exporter and has no hesitation in selling intermediate-range ballistic missiles to Saudi Arabia and other missiles (Silk Worm and M-9) to other countries. The Chinese navy came into the Indian Ocean in 1986 and called on ports in Bangladesh, Pakistan and Sri Lanka and held an exercise with the US navy in South China Sea. If China were to deploy its nuclear missile submarines against the Soviet Union the Arabian Sea would be an ideal deployment area, with port facilities in Pakistan. A programme of modernisation of aircraft using Chinese airframes, US engines, US avionics and weaponry has been contracted out to Grumman Aircraft Company for a feasibility study.

The security planners in India, after their bitter experience of 1962, 1965 and 1971, tend to apply the maxim popular in the West that, rather than declaratory positions, the actual military capabilities and their deployment are more relevant for threat assessments. If those criteria are applied, it is obvious that the size of the Indian forces is not disproportionate to the military capabilities and deployments of Pakistan and China.

This does not necessarily mean that active hostilities with either are anticipated. With Pakistan a kind of stable stand-off based on ambivalent deterrence has developed, with each power convinced that the other has nuclear weapon capability but neither side admitting to it itself. With China, too, such a situation could develop in a few years when India has missiles of 2,500km range which are under development.[42] At the present time, while China has certain logistic advantages in force deployments in the North-East, India has an edge in regard to use of airpower. (One of the main reasons for the 1962 debacle was Indian reluctance to use air power, on the assumption China had greater air capability. Actually at that stage the Chinese air force was in no position to operate for lack of spares since the Soviet Union had cut off supplies and they had very few operational airfields in and around Tibet). Now that the Chinese have learnt a few lessons in conventional war while trying to teach Vietnam a lesson in 1979, it is unlikely that China would attempt a military confrontation with India.

CONCLUSION

However, the fact remains that the Chinese have not been willing to negotiate a border agreement with India based on natural geographic features on a frontier which is very sparsely populated. On the East the Chinese have accepted the so-called MacMahon Line principle – namely that the Himalayan highcrest should be their boundary with Burma. Premier Zhou Enlai agreed to accept the same principle during his visit to India in 1960 provided India would accept the *status quo* as it then existed, in the West.[43] The Chinese, by occupying parts of areas south of the Himalayan Crest in NEFA during 1962 war and then unilaterally withdrawing, in effect validated the Indian claim to NEFA. In Ladakh the Chinese occupied areas beyond the 1960 *status quo*, beyond their claim line of 1959 (which itself was an augmentation of their claim line of 1956) during the war of 1962 but did not withdraw one millimetre there. Today popular opinion in India is in favour of a boundary settlement with China and the Indian government would in all probability settle in the Western sector for a boundary based on natural geographic features (for example, the watershed between the Indus and Tarim basins which will leave Aksai Chin area and the roads to Xinjiang in Chinese possession) and in the Eastern sector for a boundary along the Himalayan Crest which is an extension of the principle on which China settled its boundary with Burma. But the Chinese as of now insist on imposing an unequal settlement on India based on their military conquests of 1962. To make matters worse they have been dropping hints that if India were to insist on adjustments on the line of control in Ladakh they might revive claims to Tawang based on the traditional monasterial linkages between Tawang and Lhasa – a strange argument indeed coming from people who claim to be Marxists and hence anti-religious.[44] It is this claim which led India to put its troops in forward positions in 1986–87 in Kameng division in Arunachal Pradesh to shield and effectively defend Tawang.

Since then two important developments have taken place. Developments in Tibet have highlighted the degree of dissatisfaction and unacceptability of the Chinese efforts at Hanification of Tibet.[45] The Dalai Lama, in a speech distributed to the European Parliamentarians in Strasbourg, in June 1988, stated that he would be prepared to accept the Chinese presence in Tibet and Chinese direction of Tibet's foreign and defence policies, provided China would give sufficient autonomy to Tibetans.[46] Evidently the Dalai Lama is asking for Tibetans, who are not Han people, the autonomy the Chinese have agreed to extend to Hong Kong people who are Han Chinese (one nation, two systems) and which the Chinese say they are willing to extend to Taiwan. The Dalai Lama's proposals constitute a test of the sincerity of the Chinese in respect of their future observance of their commitments to Hong Kong. Tibet has already experienced the Chinese scrapping their earlier commitments for autonomy, agreed to in 1954 but dropped in 1959.

Even as China's admirers (Henry Kissinger, Zbignew Brzezinski and others participating in the Commission on Integrated Long-Term Strategy) recognise that while the Chinese economy may well grow faster than those of the US,

Europe or the USSR and by 2010 could be the world's second or third largest, great uncertainties attach to China's future.[47] If one reviews China's policy zig-zags in retrospect one finds that the only consistent strand is the quest for power – global power. They said atom bombs were paper tigers – and went on to build them. According to them the primary contradiction in the world was between capitalism and socialism and subsequently they moved over to a perspective of three worlds. They railed against non-alignment as fence-sitting and have now a different view. Those who were denounced as capitalist-roaders and China's Khrushchevs are today in power, building enclaves of capitalist enterprise. The much hailed "great leap forward", "one hundred flowers blooming" and the "great cultural revolution" were all subsequently repudiated. They shouted *Hindi Chini Bhai Bhai* (Indians and Chinese are brothers) and their relationship with Vietnam was at the time very close, said by Zhou Enlai to be as between "the lips and the teeth". The Communist combination of the USSR and China was seen by Mao Zedong in 1957 as the "East wind prevailing over the West" but that did not prevent the Chinese from waging war at different times on all three neighbours – India, the Soviet Union and Vietnam. More recently, Hu Yaobang admitted that their policy towards Tibet was mistaken and needed to be liberalised. Soon after he was demoted.

The many uncertainties of Chinese policies, their continuing dispute on the border with India and their reneging on the acceptance of the principle on which they settled the Arunachal Pradesh border problems, the turbulence in Tibet and in Burma, the unsettled politics and population explosion in Bangladesh all critically affect the shaping India's defence posture in the North-East and the North. There can be no reasonable expectation that India will be able to relax its vigil for at least the next two decades.

NOTES

[1] For Secretary McNamara's San Francisco speech of 18 September 1967, see *Keesing's Contemporary Archives*, 1967, p. 22325.

[2] *Facts on File*, 1988, p. 233.

[3] *The Independent*, 16 July, 1988.

[4] In Brussels, the NATO communiqué issued after the summit of 2–3 March 1988 reported that President Reagan and Prime Minister Margaret Thatcher pressed for keeping nuclear forces "updated". *Facts on File*, 1988, p. 139. Also see Defence Secretary Carlucci's remarks during his Moscow visit, reported in *The Times*, August 2, 1988.

[5] Henry A. Kissinger, *The White House Years*, London: Weidenfeld and Nicolson, 1979, pp. 906–907.

[6] *BBC Summary of World Broadcasts*, FE/6054/A3/2, dated 28 February 1979.

[7] "A bomb ticks in Pakistan", Hedrick Smith in the *New York Times Magazine*, 6 March 1988.

[8] When the present author toured the American "think-tanks" in 1967–68, this opinion was expressed almost universally by members of the US strategic community.

[9] This view of the US strategic establishment is brought out forcefully in *The Pentagon Papers*, Bantam Books, various editions.

[10] *Discriminate Deterrence*, Report of the Commission on Integrated Long-term Strategy, Superintendent of documents, US Government Printing Office, Washington DC, January 1988.

[11] See the article by Henry Kissinger in *The Australian*, 28 March 1988, on the rise of Japan and the decline in US power and influence. There are increasing demands in the US Congress and Administration that Japan and Western Europe assume a greater share of the defence burden, *The Independent*, 16 June 1988.

This bipolar world view of the US was debated between Indian and US scholars in two seminars in 1982 and 1984, and the discussions have been published in a monograph entitled *India and the United States*, Council on Foreign Relations, New York, 1985.

[12] This transaction has been analysed in detail in K. Subrahmanyam's articles in *India Abroad*, New York, 15 April and 29 April 1988, as well as in the *Times of India*, 5 April 1988.

[13] Western views were reflected by the US State Department spokesperson, and in articles in *The Sunday Times*, 1 May 1988, and *The Independent*, 2 May 1988.

[14] President Nixon's Press Secretary, Herbert Kline, justified the visit to Peking with the statement that a nation of 800 million, armed with nuclear weapons, could not be ignored. This is in line with the view mentioned in Note 8 *supra*.

[15] The UN Secretary-General issued reports on the allegations of use of chemical weapons in the Iran-Iraq war in March 1984, April 1985, February/March 1986, April/May 1987, March/April 1988, 20 July 1988 (S–20060), and 25 July 1988 (S–20063). The Security Council passed only platitudinous resolutions. The arms flow from other nations to the combatants is discussed in the *SIPRI Year Book, 1984*, Chapter 7, and the *SIPRI Year Book 1987*, Chapter 7.

[16] In respect of Israel, see Christopher Raj, "Israel Nuclear Weapons: A case of clandestine proliferation", in K. Subrahmanyam, (ed.), *Nuclear Myths and Realities*, Delhi: ABC Publishing House, 1982, The case of Pakistan is dealt with by Hedrick Smith (cited in Note 7, *supra*), and in the Congressional Research Service Report, order code IB 86110, especially in the attached chronology. For details of earlier flows of equipment into Pakistan, to enable it to reach nuclear weapon capability, see P.K.S. Namboodiri, "Pakistan's Nuclear Posture", in Subrahmanyam, (ed.), *Nuclear Myths and Realities, op. cit.* Also see Congressional Record – Senate – S–17894 to S–17909, of 11 December 1987.

[17] This was the stand of the Congress and Administration in the original Appropriation Bill, and this was modified during the Senate proceedings of 11 December 1987, cited above. The removal of this equation between India and Pakistan evoked the following comment from Senator Daniel P. Moynihan, "I especially welcome the extinction of what seems to many of us as gratuitous, unnecessary and offensive language concerning the Republic of India".

[18] *Keesing's Contemporary Archives*, 1965, p. 21118.

[19] The Indonesian arms shipment to Pakistan during 1965 is referred to in Lawrence Ziring, *The Ayub Khan Era*, Syracuse University Press, 1970, p. 62. On India-Indonesia relations in this period, including the burning of the Indian embassy at Jakarta, see *Keesing's Contemporary Archives*, 1965, p. 21117.

The present author was the secretary of the Indian defence delegation which negotiated the Soviet submarine deal in August 1965. It was on account of hostile Indonesian naval activities around the Andaman Islands that India was compelled to acquire Soviet submarines.

[20] This has been dealt with in detail in Barry Blechman, Stephen Kaplan, *et al. Force Without War: US Armed Forces as a political instrument*, Brookings Institution, Washington DC, 1978.

[21] John Gittings, *Survey of the Sino-Soviet Dispute*, London: Oxford University Press, 1968, p. 110.

[22] *Ibid.*, p. 178.

[23] The present author was the deputy secretary in the Indian Ministry of Defence during the period 1962–65, dealing with equipment procurement. In a letter to Ambassador Chester Bowles dated 10 April 1964, James Grant of the US State Department wrote: "Unless the Indians have decided to scale down the magnitude of their defence plan by the time they come here, there is the great danger that the talks here will consist largely of negative comments by us rather than a constructive discussion on how the Indians can meet their priority defence needs within a smaller financial frame".

[24] The US demanded that the radio (DA–PRC–215) to be licensed for manufacture in India should not be issued to Indian troops deployed against Pakistan. Since one army cannot have two kinds of radio for troops on two different fronts (and since the US mission in India was constantly urging standardisation of equipment), India refused to accept such conditions. This author negotiated the contract.

[25] See Henry Kissinger, *The White House Years, op. cit.*, chapter entitled "The Indo-Pakistan Crisis of 1971".

[26] See Henry J. Keeney, "Underlying Patterns of American Arms Sales to China", in *World Military Expenditure and Arms Transfers*, 1986; Sujit Dutta, "Recent trends in China's Foreign Policy: Implications for Asia Pacific", *Strategic Analysis*, (New Delhi), Vol. XI, (September–October), nos. 6/7; Larry M. Wortzel, "US technological transfer policies and the modernisation of China's armed forces", *Asian Survey*, June 1987. As against this, US-approved sales of military-related items to India amounted in 1983 to $61.5 million, and this rose to $263 million by 1987; *cf.* K. Subrahmanyam, "How the Media missed key points of Carlucci talks", *India Abroad*, New York, 29 April 1988.

[27] Barnard Wood, *Middle Powers in the International System*, (Monograph of the North–South Institute), Ottawa, 1988, p. 27.

[28] For the Indian perspective, see K. Subrahmanyam and Jasjit Singh, (eds.), *Security Without Nuclear Weapons*, Delhi: Lancer's International, 1986. The book is the result of a seminar between the Institute for Defence Studies and Analyses, New Delhi, and the Institute for Oriental Studies, Moscow, held between 1–3 October 1986.

24 The Centre for Security and Conflict Studies

[29] B. M. Kaul, *The Untold Story*, Delhi: Allied Publishers, 1967, p. 98.

[30] *Jawaharlal Nehru's Speeches*, Vol. II, Publications Division, Government of India, Delhi, p. 257.

[31] See K. Subrahmanyam, "Nehru and the India–China Conflict of 1962", in B. R. Nanda, (ed.), *Indian Foreign Policy: The Nehru Years*, New Delhi: Vikas Publishing House, 1976.

[32] *Ibid.*

[33] *Keesing's Contemporary Archives*, 1965, p. 20973.

[34] Lt. Col. J. R. Saigal, *The Unfought War of 1962*, Bombay, Allied Publishers, 1979.

[35] See Subrahmanyam, "Nehru and the India–China Conflict", *op. cit.*

[35A] *People's Daily*, 5 July 1967.

[36] *Military Balance, 1987–88*, International Institute of Strategic Studies, London.

[37] *The Hindu*, International Edition, week ending 30 July 1988.

[37A] An agreement has been reached with the insurgents – the Tripura National Volunteers, *The Independent*, 13 August 1988.

[38] See Note 30.

[39] *India's Foreign Policy*, Selected Speeches of Jawaharlal Nehru, Publications Division, Government of India, pp. 441–43.

[40] S. D. Muni, "Nepal as a Zone of Peace", *Strategic Analysis*, New Delhi, January 1984.

[41] *Ibid.*, p. 782.

[42] *The Hindu*, International Edition, week ending 23 July 1988.

[43] Neville Maxwell, *India's China War*, pp. 160–69. Mr Maxwell makes much of the argument that the Chinese were proposing to accept *status quo* while India insisted on the *status quo ante*. Now the Chinese are questioning the *status quo* on the MacMahon Line, which has existed for nearly 40 years, as may be seen from Note 44. For a critique of Mr Maxwell's thesis, see K. Subrahmanyam, "Neville Maxwell's War", *The Hindustan Times*, 18/25 October 1970.

[44] Sujit Dutta, "Sino-Indian Relations: Some issues", *Strategic Analysis*, New Delhi, February 1988. Also see Manoj Joshi, "Debate in China on Border", *The Hindu*, International Edition, week ending 30 April 1988, in which the author cites an article in Chinese by Hu Xiachen and Peng Zhong Huai, (*Liberation Army Daily*, 22 January 1988), wherein the Chinese accuse India of having reoccupied 90,000 sq. km. south of the MacMahon Line, and of calling it Arunachal Pradesh.

[45] On the 'Hanification' of Tibet, see Dawa Norbu, "The Chinese Strategic Thinking on Tibet and the Himalayan Region", *Strategic Analysis*, New Delhi, July 1988. For riots in Tibet, and Tibetan resistance, see *The Observer*, London, 13 March and 8 May 1988; also *Facts on File*, 1988, p. 360, and *Keesing's Contemporary Archives*, 1988, pp. 35716–17.

[46] *The Independent*, London, 16 June 1988. For the cold Chinese response, *The Independent*, 23 June 1988.

[47] *Discriminate Deterrence*, cited in Note 10 *supra*.

FURTHER READING

1. K. Subrahmanyam, (ed.), *India and the Nuclear Challenge*, Delhi: Lancer's International, 1986.
2. K. Subrahmanyam and Jasjit Singh, (eds.), *Security without Nuclear Weapons*, Delhi: Lancer's International, 1986.
3. K. Subrahmanyam, (ed.), *Nuclear Proliferation and International Security*, Delhi: Lancer's International, 1985.
4. K. Subrahmanyam, *Indian Security Perspectives*, Delhi: ABC Publishing House, 1982.
5. U. S. Bajpai, (ed.), *India's Neighbourhood*, Delhi: Lancer's International, 1986.
6. U. S. Bajpai, (ed.), *Our Security*, Delhi: Lancer's International, 1984.
7. *IDSA Journal*, Vol. XVIII, (1), July–September 1985, (Fourth India–Indonesia Conference).
8. *IDSA Journal*, Vol. XIX, (1), July–September 1986, (Indo–FRG Seminar).
9. Sujit Dutta, "Sino–Indian Relations: Some issues", *Strategic Analysis*, February 1988.
10. Aabha Dixit, "Sino–Pak relations and their implications for India", *Strategic Analysis*, December 1987.
11. G. V. C. Naidu, "Domestic Developments in Burma", *Strategic Analysis*, November 1987.
12. Dawa Norbu, "Chinese Strategic Thinking on Tibet and the Himalayan Region", *Strategic Analysis*, July 1988.

13. Sujit Dutta, "China and the Security of India", *Strategic Analysis*, May 1988.
14. Chintamani Mahapatra, "Implications of increasing Sino–Bangladesh relations", *Strategic Analysis*, March 1988.
15. Jasjit Singh, "Southern Asia and the Nuclear threat", *Strategic Analysis*, April 1988.
16. John W. Garver, "Chinese–Indian rivalry in Indo-China", *Asian Survey*, November 1987.
17. Henry J. Keeney, "Underlying patterns of American arms sales to China", in *World Military Expenditure and Arms Transfers*, (US Arms Control and Disarmament Agency), 1986.
18. B. P. Singh, *The Problem of Change: A Study of North-East India*, Delhi: Oxford University Press, 1987.
19. Michael E. Van Welt Van Prang, "Population Transfer and the Survival of Tibetan Identity", paper for the Seventh International Human Rights Symposium and Research Conference, Columbia University, New York, June 1986.
20. M. Rafiqul Islam, "The Ganges Water Dispute", *Asian Survey*, August 1987.
21. Saral Patra, "Bangladesh: Needed Mutual Trust", *World Focus*, Delhi, November/December 1986.
22. Gowher Rizvi, "Bangladesh: Insurgency in the Hills", *The Round Table*, 39–44, 1988.
23. Nirmala Das, "The Nepalese of North-East India and their politics", *IDSA Journal*, January–March 1983.
24. S. D. Muni, "Nepal as a Zone of Peace", *Strategic Analysis*, January 1984.
25. T. S. Murty, *India–China Boundary: India's Options*, Delhi: ABC Publishing House, 1987.
26. T. S. Murty, *Assam, the Difficult Years*, Delhi: Himalaya Books, 1983.

INDIA'S NORTHERN NEIGHBOURS

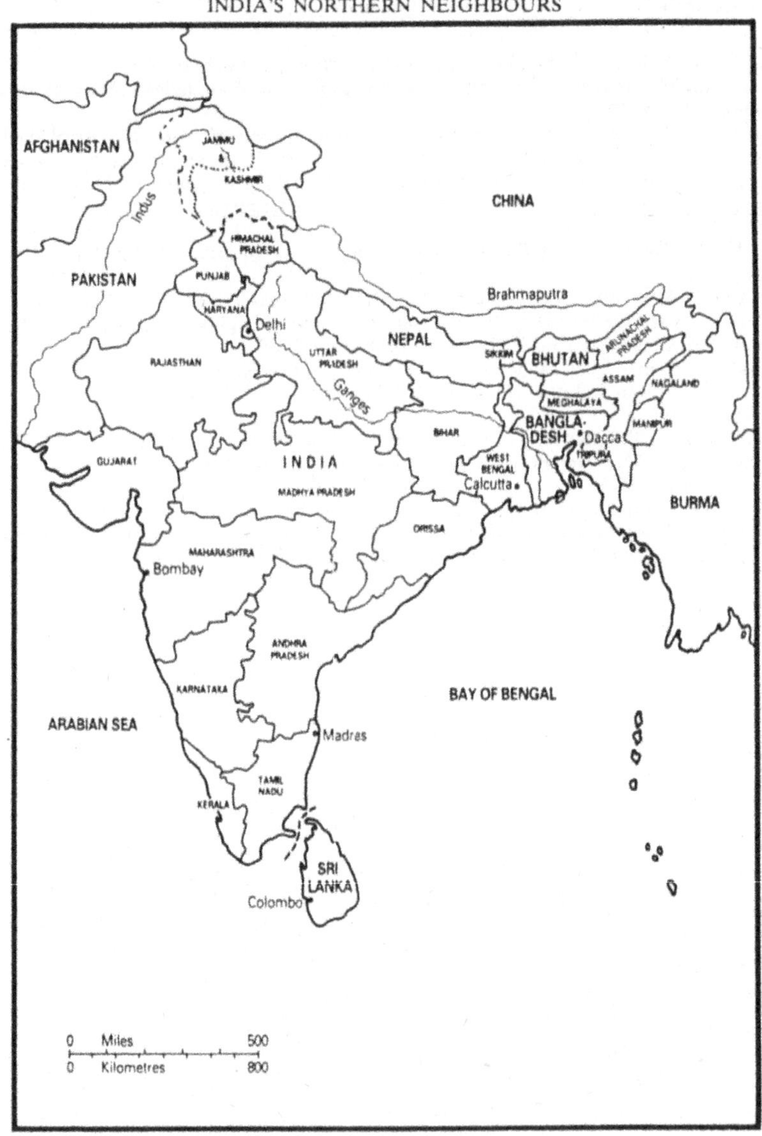

[2]

Cambodian Conflict – The Final Phase?

Michael Leifer

From the end of 1987, a succession of political initiatives generated strong expectations that a peaceful solution might be found to the protracted Cambodian (Kampuchean) conflict in South-East Asia. A number of significant diplomatic steps towards such a solution have been taken, by both global and regional States. An end to conflict is not quite at hand, however. Still unresolved is whether or not the government in Phnom Penh should remain subject to a subordinate political relationship to Vietnam which was imposed when its armed forces invaded and occupied Cambodia. A settlement endorsing that relationship – matching a longer established one with Laos – would confirm Vietnam's position of dominance throughout Indochina. An alternative settlement to the disadvantage of Vietnam would have less clearly foreseen political consequences. Tensions have long obtained among disparate Cambodian factions supported by external patrons who have collectively challenged the legitimacy of the People's Republic of Kampuchea since its establishment by Vietnam in January 1979.

The Cambodian conflict was precipitated by confrontation between governments in Phnom Penh and Hanoi. Its momentum was sustained by the intervention of parties to two rival international alignments which had materialised from the early 1970s. President Nixon's historic visit to China in February 1972 confirmed the revision of a pattern of international relationships forged at the height of the Cold War. That visit paved the way for the end of the Vietnam war but also served to draw new lines for conflict over Indochina at the end of the decade. The net effect was to expose and reinforce long-standing Sino-Vietnamese tensions in a context of Sino-Soviet hostility and Soviet–American alienation which encouraged a countervailing relationship between the Soviet Union and Vietnam. Cambodia was drawn into the vortex of that complex structure of competing relationships.

Over the past decade, Sino-Soviet hostility has given way to practical *rapprochement* concurrent with a substantial improvement in Soviet–American relations. It was in this changing context that convergent global and regional interests in a political settlement in Cambodia emerged. Such convergence has not been fully evident, however, in the respective positions of Vietnam and China whose differences have been at the heart of the Cambodian conflict. Correspondingly, their Cambodian clients have not been willing to translate a declared commitment to national reconciliation into a necessary accord on power-sharing. Despite the promising climate of international conciliation, the impasse over Cambodia has been sustained for the time being. This Study explores recent abortive attempts to overcome that impasse and the prospect for an eventual settlement.

ROOTS AND STRUCTURE OF CONFLICT

Cambodia had been a factor in regional conflict well before Vietnam's invasion in December 1978. It was incorporated within the geo-strategic perspective of Vietnam's Communist Party shortly after the end of the Pacific War. Nearly four decades ago, Vietnam's leading military theorist, General Vo Nguyen Giap, articulated a strategic doctrine which has never been revoked. He asserted:

> Indochina is a strategic unit; a single theatre of operations. Therefore, we have the task of helping to liberate all of Indochina – especially for reasons of strategic geography, we cannot conceive of Vietnam completely independent while Cambodia and Laos are ruled by imperialism.[1]

After the Geneva Conference on Indochina in 1954 and subsequent partition, Vietnam's Communist Party was obliged to limit its prerogative strategic outlook in the interest of unifying a divided country. That outlook, never subordinated in the case of neighbouring Laos, was revived after March 1970 when an ostensibly neutral Cambodia was subject to a Right-wing coup which deposed Prince Norodom Sihanouk as Head of State. To protect the western flank of its insurgent challenge to the government in Saigon, the Vietnamese Communist Party made a major military contribution to the revolutionary success of a Cambodian counterpart. That party seized power in April 1975 and, unlike its Laotian equivalent, refused to acknowledge direct lineal descent from a Vietnamese political core. The most recent phase of the conflict for Cambodia began when the armed forces of a united Vietnam invaded the country in order to overthrow a seemingly renegade party and government and replace them with compliant political alternatives.

From Hanoi's perspective, the imposition of a compliant administration in Phnom Penh was a matter of strategic necessity. The perspective was the same as that articulated by General Giap, even though the threatening "imperialism" had changed. Vietnam had been prompted to invade by months of marauding cross-border intrusions into its south-western provinces by the armed forces of Pol Pot's **Democratic Kampuchea**. Those intrusions had been an intolerable nuisance but not a major security threat in themselves. It was the perceived role of Cambodia in serving as "a bridgehead of aggression" on behalf of a menacing China which generated acute concern. After the invasion, it was alleged in justification that "they [the Chinese] used the reactionary and genocidal Pol Pot–Ieng Sary fascist gang to make war, nibbling at the south-western border of our homeland hoping to squeeze us in a vice".[2]

If Vietnam had reason to regard Pol Pot's Cambodia as an agency of a hostile China and acted accordingly, China had become correspondingly convinced of its southern neighbour's bad political faith and intent. From its unification in April 1975, Vietnam came to be viewed as the willing proxy of an aggressive Soviet Union which had replaced the United States as China's principal adversary. In the circumstances, Vietnam and the Soviet Union became natural geo-political partners. Vietnam's invasion of Cambodia was facilitated by a prior Treaty of Friendship with the Soviet Union in November

1978. It was intended to deter Chinese retaliation while Pol Pot's regime was being despatched. China's convictions were reinforced. On the day that Phnom Penh fell to Vietnamese troops, China's national news agency commented: "It is to serve the Soviet Union in its expansionist strategic plan that the Vietnamese authorities have invaded Kampuchea so recklessly".[3] A punitive Chinese military intervention into northern Vietnam in retaliation during February and March 1979 only confirmed Hanoi's geo-strategic perspective and its alliance with the Soviet Union.

ASEAN's role

The conflict over the political identity and external alignment of Cambodia was from the outset primarily a test of wills and resources between Vietnam and China. It extended regionally and globally beyond that antagonistic relationship, however. China's evident determination to bring Vietnam to heel politically gave heart to the government of Thailand, which viewed neighbouring Cambodia and Laos as a security zone. The invasion of Cambodia brought the country politically into line with Laos, whose special relationship with Vietnam had been registered by treaty in July 1977. A corresponding treaty between the newly-established People's Republic of Kampuchea and Vietnam was concluded in February 1979. In the process, Thailand's security environment had been violated. Of prime concern in Bangkok was the prospect of a novel concentration of power in Indochina being consolidated under Vietnamese auspices. The independence and identity of the Thai State were deemed to be at serious risk. In the way that the Soviet Union had become the natural geo-political partner of Vietnam, China came to assume a corresponding role for Thailand. The two States overcame historical and ideological differences in a division of labour to challenge Vietnam. China applied military pressure along Vietnam's northern border and also served as military quartermaster for Pol Pot's surviving Khmer Rouge army, which was restored as a fighting force by receiving territorial sanctuary in and material supply through Thailand.

Thailand's security priorities were central to the collective diplomatic stand against Vietnam adopted by its fellow-members of the Association of South-East Asian Nations (ASEAN). Employing regional credentials and high-lighting respect for national sovereignty, the ASEAN States played a notable role in denying international legitimacy to the government carried into Phnom Penh in the saddle-bags of Vietnam's army. They also played a major part in sustaining the international status of the ousted Democratic Kampuchean government which retained Cambodia's seat in the United Nations. To overcome political embarrassment because of the bestial record of that government, ASEAN was instrumental, in June 1982, in cobbling together a coalition of Cambodian resistance factions incorporating two non-Communist groups as well as the Khmer Rouge. The resulting **Coalition Government of Democratic Kampuchea** represented political form rather than political substance but attracted international support because it was presided over by former Head of State, Prince Norodom Sihanouk.

ASEAN's corporate position barely concealed mixed interests, in particular over the indirect association with China in challenging Vietnam. Solidarity with Thailand was required, however, to ensure the Association's cohesion and viability. Joined significantly to the alignment confronting Vietnam was the United States, which had responded to the invasion of Cambodia out of concern for the advantage reaped by the Soviet Union as well as from an interest in the security of Thailand. Japan and the European Community (EC) also joined in the diplomatic confrontation reflecting special ties with both ASEAN and the United States and also differences in their relationships with China and the Soviet Union. The United States and Japan, in particular, have played an important role in denying economic resources to both Vietnam and Cambodia in order to reinforce an overall strategy of attrition intended to weaken the political will of the government in Hanoi. Western relief aid supplied to the Thai border has served to succour refugees from Indochina and also to nourish and revitalise the fearsome soldiers of the Khmer Rouge.[4]

In meeting this mixed challenge to its forward policy in Indochina, Vietnam has been sustained materially and diplomatically almost entirely by the Soviet Union and its Eastern bloc allies. In return in March 1979 Vietnam granted the USSR military base facilities which extended the operational range of the Soviet Pacific fleet. Beyond the Soviet fraternal connection, but excluding North Korea and Romania, only India has lent significant diplomatic support to Vietnam. Its government has acted from a sense of shared antipathy towards China and from an attendant shared security relationship with the Soviet Union.

CHANGING INTERNATIONAL CONTEXT

The Cambodian conflict has been characterised by the engagement of extensive competing interests. In a regional expression of global competition, the policies of China and the Soviet Union have been of considerable significance. Their patron roles in sustaining respectively the Khmer Rouge and Vietnamese forces have prevented a conclusive resolution on the field of battle. They have also contributed to the political impasse. More recently, however, positive changes in Sino-Soviet relations have modified the overall context of the Cambodian conflict and it is these changes which have encouraged a number of political initiatives designed to promote a peaceful solution.

The Soviet government had indicated an early interest in repairing relations with China (further set back by the invasion of Afghanistan) in a speech by the late Leonid Brezhnev in Tashkent, in March 1982. A major undertaking to transform relations dates, however, from Mikhail Gorbachev's assumption of power in March 1985. He indicated a strong interest in *rapprochement* with China as part of a wider Asia–Pacific policy in a much-remarked speech in Vladivostock in July 1986. The opening to China should be seen as part of a global strategy. Acutely conscious of the economic weakness of the Soviet Union and the failings of military policy, Gorbachev has sought to revise the dominant structure of international alignments set during the 1970s through political initiatives. In an attempt to deal with both the United States and China on a different footing, he has sought to detach regional conflicts, and Soviet involvement in them, from global relationships. A demonstrated determination to disengage militarily from Afghanistan has been matched by a strong interest in promoting a political settlement in Cambodia.

The Soviet purpose has been to decouple the Cambodian conflict from the progressive transformation of Sino-Soviet relations. A withdrawal of support from Vietnam over Cambodia had been made the prime test of Moscow's political good faith by Beijing after July 1986, following the absence of any concession in Gorbachev's speech in Vladivostock. In response, the Soviet Union took steps to persuade Vietnam to expedite the withdrawal of its forces from Cambodia as the nexus for a viable relationship with China. In this exercise, the Soviet government has avoided being obliged to make a crude choice between sustained *rapprochement* with China and a conspicuous compromise of Vietnam's security interests. It has appeared to encourage rather than to dictate the pace of Vietnamese troop withdrawals from Cambodia; and it has apparently refrained from imposing economic sanctions on its ally despite wishing to ease the heavy burden of aid, estimated at more than $US3 million a day. Moreover, Vietnam has been supported diplomatically in upholding the legitimacy of the government in Phnom Penh and in refusing to compromise its political entitlement in negotiations for a settlement. At stake for the Soviet Union is a reputation as a reliable security partner as it reiterates its claim to be an Asia–Pacific power. Its military base facilities have assumed a lesser significance.

Beijing's priorities

China's positive responses to Soviet initiatives and indications of Vietnamese troop withdrawals have also not involved a conspicuous compromise of client interest. The Chinese government has been willing to countenance a progressive detachment of the Cambodian issue from its relationship with the Soviet Union and to welcome Mr Gorbachev in Beijing, but not at the expense of a long-standing determination to limit Vietnam's influence in Indochina. The Soviet factor has ceased to colour China's view of Vietnam in the way that it did over a decade ago, when it was represented as an oriental Cuba.

Nonetheless, China's own regional priorities have not wavered. An ostensible flexibility in opposing a return to exclusive power by the Khmer Rouge has been coupled with a consistency of purpose in supporting an equal role for them in a power-sharing political settlement among Cambodian factions. In addition, a declared willingness by Prime Minister Li Peng to phase out military aid to the Khmer Rouge "in step with Vietnam's pull-out" is not immediately relevant to the balance of forces within Cambodia. The awesome military reputation of the Khmer Rouge may not be matched by their military strength which has been the subject of conflicting reports.[5] Nonetheless, China has made provision for their material needs in any forthcoming civil war and in consequence, its government has been able to respond to Soviet initiatives and seeming Vietnamese concessions without necessarily abdicating a long-standing interest in the balance of power in Indochina.

Without doubt, China's interests have been well served by *rapprochement* with the Soviet Union. Of the two main external patrons in the Cambodian conflict, China would seem to be in the more advantageous position. Early on, its government was obliged to take serious account of Soviet military support for Vietnam, at close hand and in well-utilised base facilities. Nine years later, Moscow's muted response to China's deliberate military confrontation of Vietnam in the Spratly Islands in the South China Sea indicated concern not to jeopardise progress in Sino-Soviet relations.

Given sustained Soviet conciliation of China, the balance of diplomatic advantage would seem clear. Despite Mikhail Gorbachev's initiatives and China's progressive responses, the pattern of international alignments set by President Nixon's historic visit to China has not been transformed beyond recognition. For example, Foreign Minister Qian Qichen made clear shortly before President Bush visited Beijing in late February 1989 that, for the foreseeable future, China would maintain a special and closer relationship with the United States. Encouraged by President Bush's endorsement of Prince Sihanouk and his preferred solution to the Cambodian conflict, China has been able to persist in seeking to deny Vietnam undue political influence in Indochina. A surface flexibility has sustained *rapprochement* with the Soviet Union and has avoided international isolation over conspicuous identification with the cause of the murderous Khmer Rouge.

The wider context of conflict encompassing Cambodia has been changed significantly through the substantial improvement in Sino-Soviet relations. That improvement has encouraged, and has gone hand-in-hand with, political initiatives to find a peaceful solution for Cambodia. Sino-Vietnamese relations, which have remained at the heart of the Cambodian conflict, have continued to obstruct a settlement, however. China has not, so far, shown any willingness to concede Vietnam's special political relationship with Cambodia in return for a viable *rapprochement* with the Soviet Union. In turn, Vietnam has not been willing to concede that the government in Phnom Penh is less than legitimate as the necessary condition for protecting its security interests.

VIETNAM'S PREDICAMENT

In seeking to incorporate Cambodia within a structure of special political relations, Vietnam faced unexpected difficulty from the outset. Initial miscalculation was indicated in January 1979 when Ha Van Lau, its representative at the United Nations, informed his Singapore counterpart: "In two weeks, the world will have forgotten the Kampuchea problem."[6] In the event, Vietnam was confronted by international outrage. Instead of being applauded as an international benefactor for having rid Cambodia of political pestilence, it was denounced for having violated national sovereignty. Moreover, economic problems self-inflicted by socialist dogma were aggravated by denial of access to development aid, except from the Soviet Union and its partners.

In the circumstances, an overriding priority for Hanoi was to be able to demonstrate in good time that the government imposed in Phnom Penh, presided over by Heng Samrin, a Khmer Rouge defector, was both legitimate and viable. To uphold the claim that the situation in Cambodia was "irreversible", it was necessary to eliminate any insurgent challenge and to foster a local administration and army capable of assuming responsibility for government and security. An ability to hold general elections of a kind between March and May 1981 endorsed the leading role of the ruling People's Revolutionary Party. An announcement in February 1982 of annual withdrawals of Vietnamese troops served also to strengthen the claim of irreversibility, despite charges that they were disguised troop rotations.

Challenging that claim collectively from the middle of 1982 was a tripartite coalition of Cambodian resistance groups pressured into a united front under ASEAN's auspices. These three groups represented vestiges of the past political systems in Cambodia. Their fighting core was a revived Khmer Rouge under the less objectionable nominal leadership of Khieu Samphan. More significant in political terms were the republican-oriented **Khmer People's National Liberation Front** (KPNLF) headed by former Prime Minister, Son Sann, and loyalists to Prince Sihanouk known as the **United Front for an Independent, Neutral, Peaceful and Co-operative Cambodia** (FUNCINPEC in French acronym). This disparate and fragile coalition represented an attempt by the anti-Vietnamese alignment to refute the charge that it was supporting a return to power of the bestial Khmer Rouge. It was cobbled together in an attempt to provide a credible political alternative both to that prospect and to a Vietnamese-imposed government. The resistance groups drew support from Cambodian refugees and operated from base camps along the ill-demarcated border with Thailand. In order to shield the embryonic government in Phnom Penh, the Vietnamese set out to disrupt and destroy these camps which served as staging posts for armed penetration of the interior.

During the 1984–85 dry season, Vietnamese forces mounted a series of co-ordinated attacks. They overran the camps of all three resistance groups, driving the inhabitants into Thailand. Measures were then taken to seal the border. The operation was judged to be successful, particularly as China's threat of retaliation did not materialise. In consequence, at a meeting of Indochinese Foreign Ministers in Phnom Penh in August 1985, it was announced that all Vietnamese forces would be withdrawn from Cambodia by the end of 1990 whether or not a political settlement had been reached.

The public announcement of a terminal date was a calculated risk. It imposed a rigid deadline on Vietnam without necessarily ensuring a corresponding ability to determine the balance of forces bearing on Cambodia by the end of the decade. By 1986, the resistance forces, especially the Khmer Rouge, had begun to display an ability to regroup and to revise, to some effect, the nature of their military operations. Increasing numbers of small-scale forays were conducted into Cambodia. This changing pattern of military activity did not pose a major challenge to Vietnam's control of Cambodia as long as an effective blocking force was retained in the country. It did succeed, however, in restoring a stalemate on the ground with Vietnam committed publicly to military withdrawal and with serious doubts being expressed about the fighting quality of the local Cambodian army.

The renewed military stalemate coincided with a marked deterioration in Vietnam's economic circumstances expressed in failings in production and an accelerating inflation, against a background of uncontrolled population growth.[7] It also coincided with Mikhail Gorbachev's active search for *rapprochement* with China, with the prospect of Vietnam's interests in Indochina being compromised. A decisive factor in Vietnam's ability to impose its political will in Cambodia had been assured access to Soviet material and diplomatic support.

CONVERGENCE AND DIVERGENCE

Convergent interests in both Moscow and Hanoi encouraged a search for a political settlement, albeit not necessarily to the same end. Soviet foreign policy priorities had been revised as a consequence of fundamental economic weakness. For its part, the Soviet Union could pursue improved relations with both China and the United States – and to that end agree to withdraw from a military quagmire in Afghanistan – and serve national security ends at the same time. In this global exercise, the political identity of the government in Phnom Penh was a minor consideration. Vietnam, however, was confronted with a major problem in the light of an apparently unrelenting Chinese hostility, expressed in an adamant refusal to consider negotiations. The prospect of a Sino-Soviet *rapprochement* was a source of anxiety because of past experience, at the Geneva Conference on Indochina in 1954, of Vietnam's interests being subordinated.

For Vietnam, a political settlement in Cambodia without international endorsement of the Phnom Penh government installed in January 1979 would constitute a strategic defeat. The abiding prospect of the return to power of the Khmer Rouge as an agency of a hostile China has governed its priorities consistently over a long period. In December 1986, the sixth congress of Vietnam's Communist Party had approved important changes in the political leadership. The appointment of Nguyen Van Linh as General Secretary, following the death of Le Duan in the previous July, indicated a willingness to reconsider economic policy and, in principle, to follow the Soviet example of *perestroika*. If economic policy was made subject to debate, and revision, foreign policy was apparently not. The Political Report of the Congress affirmed that consolidating and developing Vietnam's special alliance relationship with Laos and Cambodia was "a sacred international duty and a task of strategic importance to the vital interests of independence, freedom and socialism in our own country and on the Indochinese peninsula as a whole".[8] But at that juncture, Vietnam had not demonstrated an ability to sustain that relationship other than through its military presence, which was dependent on Soviet material benefaction. That presence had been made the prime obstacle to an improvement in Sino-Soviet relations by the government in

Beijing. Vietnam's vulnerability to Soviet priorities was conspicuously evident.

In the circumstances, it became a matter of urgency to promote a political settlement that would safeguard Vietnamese geo-strategic interests. To this end, Vietnam sought to engage regional adversaries in a structure of negotiations that would divide an international coalition sustained by China's doggedness. Divisions had long existed within it over the role of China and also that of the Khmer Rouge, and Vietnam hoped to exploit those divisions to secure international endorsement of the political *status quo* within Cambodia. Its government, therefore, sought to represent the conflict in Cambodia in such a way that the terms of reference of any negotiations would serve to predetermine a favourable outcome.

Hanoi's preconditions

Vietnam had from the outset, represented the Cambodian conflict as being between internal parties. This position was in keeping with the initial claim that Pol Pot's government had been overthrown by a Cambodian "salvation" front, assisted only in its military task by Vietnamese volunteers. The presence of regular Vietnamese forces had been justified subsequently under the terms of the bilateral treaty concluded with the government in Phnom Penh in February 1979. Accordingly, Vietnam refused to acknowledge that it was directly party to the Cambodian conflict or to entertain direct negotiations with the "so-called" Coalition Government of Democratic Kampuchea. Vietnam's government had been willing to endorse the principle of national reconciliation among Cambodian parties but, as stated at the Party Congress in December 1986, without the participation of "the Pol Pot clique of genocidal criminals". A subsequent willingness to tolerate some form of Khmer Rouge participation in negotiations between Cambodian parties was made conditional on national reconciliation being discussed "on the basis of the elimination of Pol Pot". This formula was a euphemism for dismantling the military and political structure of the Khmer Rouge so that they could only be a nominal party to any formal power-sharing arrangement, thus safeguarding the political *status quo* in Phnom Penh.

In insisting on this precondition, Vietnam played skilfully on the gruesome reputation of the Khmer Rouge and on the stand of opposing non-Communist governments which also rejected a resumption of power by the Khmer Rouge. Publicly committed to a total withdrawal of its forces from Cambodia, the Vietnamese insisted in return on the elimination of the Khmer Rouge. Foreign Minister Nguyen Co Thach pointed out in December 1986 that "a fair compromise must be to link both positions". The exclusion of the Khmer Rouge from a primary role in a settlement would leave an acceptable balance of forces between the government in Phnom Penh and the two non-Communist resistance factions whose military capability was limited. If Prince Norodom Sihanouk could be persuaded to lend his personal authority to such an arrangement, so attracting internal and external support, the political ends sought initially through military invasion could be assured.

THE PATH TO NEGOTIATIONS

The extensive alignment confronting Vietnam had engaged in a strategy of attrition with the object of applying breaking strain on its government and society. The intention had been to coerce Vietnam to the negotiating table rather than to drive its forces physically from Cambodia. In this undertaking, ASEAN had played the leading diplomatic role, though with limited success. Vietnam had rejected any structure of negotiations in which it might be represented as the aggressor in Cambodia, with the solution to the conflict resting solely on the withdrawal of its forces. It had refused to participate in an international conference on Cambodia, held under United Nations auspices in July 1981, partly for this reason and also because the ousted government of Democratic Kampuchea had retained the Cambodian seat in the world body. A number of attempts to find an alternative format for negotiations proved abortive, partly because of ASEAN's strong reluctance to compromise its representation of the conflict as the product of external aggression. For example, in 1985 Malaysia's then Foreign Minister, Tengku Ahmad Rithaudeen, had suggested proximity talks, using the Afghanistan model, between the Heng Samrin government and that of the Democratic Kampuchean coalition. That deviant initiative was short-lived. ASEAN's Foreign Ministers closed ranks, amending the proposal so that proximity talks should take place between the Coalition Government of Democratic Kampuchea and Vietnam, with participation by the Phnom Penh government only as part of the Vietnamese delegation. Thai Foreign Minister, Sitthi Savetsila, explained: "The reason why ASEAN made the proposal is logical. As Vietnam is the aggressor and Kampuchea is the victim, the two sides should meet because they are directly involved in the conflict."[9]

ASEAN's public position, however, barely concealed a growing dissidence on Indonesia's part. President Suharto's government had indicated ambivalence over the Cambodian issue early on because of the way in which ASEAN had been drawn into an alignment with China against Vietnam. It had long regarded China as its prime source of external threat, while Vietnam, despite its Communist identity, was regarded as a potential security partner to be included in a structure of regional relations to counter Chinese influence. At the root of this perspective was a corresponding experience in challenging colonial domination from 1945 and an awareness of historical Sino-Vietnamese tensions. Vietnam's blatant violation of Cambodia's sovereignty had been politically offensive to Jakarta but as the conflict continued a sense of frustration appeared in Indonesia over the way it was distorting the country's regional priorities. At the formation of ASEAN in August 1967, President Suharto's government had advocated a system of regional order based on an exclusive managerial role for regional States.[10] In November 1971, at a meeting of ASEAN's Foreign Ministers in Kuala Lumpur, Indonesia had been instrumental in securing support for making South-East Asia "a Zone of Peace, Freedom and Neutrality". The prime purpose of the proposal was to exclude the competitive intervention of external powers. Although very much an ideal design which lacked operational utility, it came to serve as the symbol of the Association's declared regional purpose. The course of the conflict over Cambodia, however, moved ASEAN and South-East Asia in direct contradiction to this goal because of the way external quarrels had been drawn into the region.

Indonesia's abortive initiative

Indonesia's ambivalence over the Cambodian issue was expressed in its strong interest in promoting negotiations within an exclusively regional context. Its ASEAN partners tolerated that interest by according Indonesia the role of the Association's interlocutor with Vietnam. In fulfilment of that role, Indonesia's Foreign Minister, Professor Mochtar Kusumaatmadja, sought to arrange informal talks between the Cambodian parties to the conflict. He had been encouraged by Prince Norodom Sihanouk who had broken ranks with his coalition partners in May 1987, announcing that he would be taking at least one year's leave of absence from his post of President. In July, after consulting Prince Sihanouk, then living in Pyongyang, Professor Mochtar paid a long-postponed visit to Vietnam. In Ho Chi Minh City, he reached an agreement with his Vietnamese counterpart, Nguyen Co Thach, that an informal meeting of Cambodian parties should convene in Jakarta "on the basis of equal footing, without preconditions and with no political labels". Only later would Indonesia invite other concerned countries, including Vietnam, to participate. That bilateral accord did not constitute a compromise of contending diplomatic positions; it reflected clearly Vietnam's representation of the Cambodian conflict as one primarily between internal parties who had to settle matters among themselves. That representation, in separating the international and domestic dimensions of the conflict, was also linked to the prospect of a partial settlement in Vietnam's interest. An international settlement in which Vietnam's withdrawal of troops would be matched by withdrawing territorial sanctuary and military assistance from the resistance groups could leave the political *status quo* inside Cambodia undisturbed.

Any optimism in Hanoi and Jakarta at an apparent diplomatic breakthrough was short-lived as other ASEAN members – especially Thailand and Singapore – made it very plain that Professor Mochtar had conceded far too much in his eagerness to promote a political settlement. Stronger views were indicated by the Khmer Rouge whose spokesman described the accord as a trick. In August 1987, at a special conference of ASEAN's Foreign Ministers held in Bangkok, it was decided that an informal meeting on Cambodia could only be countenanced if Vietnam, as the invading and occupying power, took part immediately after the initial discussions between internal parties. A further limiting precondition was that a proposal put forward by the insurgent coalition in March 1986, calling for the establishment of a quadripartite government in Cambodia, including the Heng Samrin faction, to be headed by Prince Sihanouk, should serve as the basis for negotiations. These qualifications to the agreement reached in Ho Chi Minh City were immediately denounced by Vietnam, which reiterated its support for Phnom Penh's willingness "to discuss national reconciliation on the basis of the elimination of Pol Pot". A determination not to compromise over the status of that government had been indicated pointedly in late July on the very day that Professor Mochtar had journeyed to Vietnam. *Nhan Dan*, the Communist Party's daily newspaper, had affirmed that "the People's Republic of Kampuchea's international prestige has not ceased to grow. The fact is that nobody can reverse the situation in Kampuchea".[11] The diplomatic stalemate over Cambodia appeared to have become entrenched, with neither Vietnam nor ASEAN apparently prepared to compromise over how the conflict should be represented and, therefore, on the terms on which negotiations might begin to resolve it. At that juncture, compromise seemed impossible because of the stark alternative representations of the Cambodian conflict.

Sihanouk breaks ranks

Indonesia's abortive initiative had expressed a growing political frustration. Corresponding frustration had been registered by Prince Sihanouk in his role as President of the Coalition Government of Democratic Kampuchea. He served as its major political asset because of his standing as the personal embodiment of an independent and neutral Cambodia. Within that country he has attracted mixed views because of his political association with the Khmer Rouge. Nonetheless, he still personifies the monarchy, probably the only institution which still carries meaning for Cambodia's long-suffering people.[12] As the most credible symbol of political legitimacy and unity, he has long represented a major political asset to any party to the conflict able to attract his support. His lack of an adequate military organisation capable of revising the *status quo* in Cambodia on its own has made him less than a full subject of politics and in many respects its object. From June 1982, he became a political prize which ASEAN, China and the Khmer Rouge had won for their varied purposes. Prince Sihanouk had been the nominal head of a united front with the Khmer Rouge in 1970–75. He had returned to Cambodia from exile to suffer house arrest, and a number of his children and grandchildren had perished under Pol Pot's draconian regime. One reason that he had been persuaded to re-enter a coalition with such a loathsome partner was the rebuff he had received from the Vietnamese to whom he had made political overtures at an early stage in the conflict.[13] At the time, the Vietnamese felt sufficiently confident in their ability to entrench the position of the government set up under Heng Samrin in January 1979 but as its viability and Soviet support became suspect, the Vietnamese were attracted to the idea of detaching Prince Sihanouk from the coalition and drawing him into a power-sharing arrangement in Phnom Penh under their effective auspices.

Prince Sihanouk has long demonstrated a mastery of the political *coup de theâtre*, the most famous being his abdication as King of Cambodia in 1955 in favour of his father. He divested himself then of monarchy but not of a royal disposition. The prospect of resuming political leadership in Cambodia in keeping with that disposition depended on an ability to employ his personal assets as a bargaining counter. To do so, he had to free himself from the constraints imposed by membership of the coalition. In May 1987, he announced that he would be taking at least one year's leave of absence as head of the coalition, justifying his decision on the ground that resistance forces loyal to his person had been attacked by the Khmer Rouge. A strong factor in his decision was Vietnam's persistence in trying to draw him into direct negotiations with the Phnom Penh government.

After an abortive approach in 1984, further attempts were made during 1986, continuing into the following year when Prince Sihanouk visited Romania in January. In February 1987, Prince Sihanouk indicated a willingness to engage in informal talks but claimed that he had been thwarted by China's opposition. His act of temporary resignation in May expressed resentment at Chinese and also Khmer Rouge restrictions on his freedom of political manoeuvre. He made his views known in a cable to the UN Secretary-General in June 1987, claiming that within the framework of the coalition government he had been "completely neutralised by his partners and their sponsors in his quest for peace".[14]

Prince Sihanouk sought to break the diplomatic deadlock in the conflict, displayed subsequently by the abortive outcome of the meeting in July between the Indonesian and Vietnamese Foreign Ministers. He was engaged also in trying to broker a political settlement which would pivot on his personal role, seemingly acceptable to all sides. In breaking ranks, Prince Sihanouk's initiative was disturbing to most ASEAN members as well as to China and the Khmer Rouge but was well received by Vietnam and the Soviet Union. Both were keen to encourage a political settlement, if for mixed reasons. In September, Prince Sihanouk indicated a willingness to meet leaders of Phnom Penh's government in the company of his coalition partners, if a formal request for such a meeting were received from its Prime Minister, Hun Sen. That request was forthcoming in November, paving the way for bilateral meetings in France in December 1987 and again in January 1988. Prince Sihanouk's coalition partners refused to attend in the absence of Vietnamese representation. The Chinese government, in contrast with its American and even ASEAN counterparts, was conspicuously unenthusiastic at this turn of events but refrained from criticising Prince Sihanouk.

Coalition strains

The meetings between Prince Sihanouk and Hun Sen were cordial but significant only for the precedent which they established; they did not produce any agreement of political substance. A nominal accord was reached on an ideal common goal of a political settlement establishing an independent and neutral Cambodia, to be confirmed by an international conference. The issues of withdrawing Vietnamese forces and provision for power-sharing were not addressed in the joint statement after the talks but in private discussion deadlock arose over Hun Sen's insistence on a timetable linking Vietnam's withdrawal of troops before 1990 to the elimination of the Khmer Rouge.

A corresponding lack of progress was made over Prince Sihanouk's demand that the Phnom Penh government as well as his tripartite coalition be dismantled concurrently, to be replaced by a provisional four-party coalition administration which would assume responsibility for conducting elections under effective international supervision. Hun Sen refused to countenance either his government's dissolution or provision for international peace-keeping as preconditions for a political settlement; or to accept more than a nominal role for the Khmer Rouge. Prince Sihanouk was not prepared to endorse a government which had been established by Vietnamese force of arms nor to abdicate the political claims of his coalition partners. Both parties employed the idiom of national reconciliation but for irreconcilable purposes.

The effect was to expose strains within the coalition and among its supporters and to confer a measure of recognition on the government in Phnom Penh. In exasperation, and to mend fences with his Chinese patron, Prince Sihanouk denounced Hun Sen publicly as being completely manipulated by his masters in Hanoi. He refused to meet him again, as had been agreed, and called on Vietnam to deal directly. The Vietnamese government responded by insisting that the Cambodian parties must reach a solution among themselves before any of its representatives would meet Prince Sihanouk. For his part, Prince Sihanouk sustained the demand for a four-party provisional government and for an international peace-keeping force to hold the ring between the contending factions during the implementation of a political settlement. At the end of January 1988 he announced his formal resignation as President of the coalition government, described as "an abominable monster". This decision was reversed at the end of February, albeit not his intention of remaining on leave of absence. Clearly, Prince Sihanouk's attempt to trade the asset of his personal legitimacy in the interest of a political settlement had failed. The Vietnamese, through the government in Phnom Penh, had made it clear that Prince Sihanouk would be an acceptable partner only if he helped to consolidate the political *status quo* in Cambodia.

THE JAKARTA INFORMAL MEETING

Despite the measure of recognition secured by the meetings between Prince Sihanouk and Hun Sen, conclusive political authority remained beyond the grasp of the government in Phnom Penh. Vietnam's continuing occupation was still internationally contentious, and it faced economic distress and external pressure, including armed attacks by China in the South China Sea in March 1988. Moreover, by this juncture, the Soviet Union had been willing to have the subject of Cambodia addressed in preliminary discussions to the June summit meeting in Moscow between Mikhail Gorbachev and Ronald Reagan by Soviet Deputy Foreign Minister, Igor Rogachev, and America's Assistant Secretary of State, Gaston Sigur. Significantly, and not coincidentally, in May, Vietnam announced its intention of withdrawing an additional 50,000 troops from Cambodia by the end of 1988 and of transferring command of the remainder to local military authority. The object was both to help the Soviet Union in its relationships with the United States and China and to reduce Soviet pressure on Vietnam. There was no interest, however, in a political settlement being imposed through a deal between the major powers, foreshadowed by the new tone of Soviet–American and Sino-Soviet relations.

Moved by this concern and the failure of the bilateral talks in France, Vietnam sought to revive the diplomatic option of an informal regional meeting first raised by Indonesia. To this end, Vice Foreign Minister Tran Quang Co visited Jakarta in April 1988 shortly after President Suharto had been re-elected for a further five-year term of office and Ali Alatas had been appointed Foreign Minister in succession to Mochtar Kusumaatmadja. Ali Alatas had been a professional diplomat and previously Indonesia's ambassador to the United Nations. He was less sympathetic than his predecessor to the security concerns of Thailand and reflected the dominant view in Indonesia's military establishment that Vietnam's paramount influence in Indochina was in Jakarta's best interests. He was particularly keen to revive the idea of informal discussions and was encouraged and assisted by a novel flexibility in the position of Thailand. That flexibility had been encouraged during the course of a visit to Moscow in May 1988 by Prime Minister Prem Tinsulanond and Foreign Minister Sitthi Savetsila. They were offered convincing assurances that the Soviet Union would try hard to resolve Vietnam's occupation of Cambodia.

A meeting soon after between Foreign Minister Sitthi and Nguyen Co Thach and the announcement by Vietnam of substantial troop withdrawals also contributed to Thai flexibility. Thailand's position as ASEAN's front line State had given its government a virtual veto on the Association's diplomatic initiatives, invariably with strong support from Singapore. Objection to Vietnam's insistence that any informal meeting be convened in two distinct stages was now withdrawn: first, Cambodian parties alone would discuss internal issues; and secondly, both Cambodian parties and representatives of regional governments would together consider the international dimension of the conflict.

In the event, the so-called Jakarta Informal Meeting (JIM) convened in late July 1988 in the resort town of Bogor, close to Indonesia's capital. Two weeks earlier, Prince Sihanouk had again announced his resignation as head of the coalition and pointedly referred to the injustice of certain of its "godfathers" who favoured the Khmer Rouge in distributing arms. He acted to elevate himself in monarchical manner above factional rivalry by withholding the political prize of his legitimising person from either side in the conflict. Prince Sihanouk announced that he would not personally attend the talks but that his faction in the coalition would be represented by his son, Prince Ranaridh. Indonesia went along with Prince Sihanouk's political stage management by inviting him to Jakarta as the personal guest of President Suharto. He stayed in the capital while the Bogor meeting took place and subsequently had the satisfaction of receiving the Cambodian participants at the equivalent of an audience, reminiscent of court life in Phnom Penh before March 1970.

Political solution elusive

The Jakarta Informal Meeting was represented as a psychological breakthrough.[15] It was the first occasion on which all internal Cambodian and regional parties to the conflict had been willing to join in discussions to resolve it. It was significant that Khieu Samphan – the senior Khmer Rouge representative and Vice-President in the resistance coalition – was prepared to take part in negotiations with Hun Sen, Prime Minister of the Phnom Penh government. Correspondingly, the Vietnamese and their Cambodian affiliates were prepared to tolerate an acceptable representative of the Khmer Rouge, albeit within a structure of negotiations on their terms.

Any expectations of an early political settlement raised by the uniqueness of the diplomatic occasion were dashed, however. The outcome of these talks was no different from the bilateral ones held in France. No concessions of substance were made. Hun Sen was prepared to concede Prince Sihanouk's leadership of a four-party national reconciliation council charged with conducting elections but was adamant that his government should not be dismantled in advance of them. He insisted also that the withdrawal of Vietnamese forces before 1990 be tied to the termination of aid and denial of territorial sanctuary to the Khmer Rouge. He had argued before the meeting that a provisional government along the lines proposed by Prince Sihanouk would only pave the way for the return of the genocidal Pol Pot regime. A separate meeting of Indochinese Foreign Ministers earlier in July had reaffirmed the legitimacy of the People's Republic of Kampuchea whose status was put beyond negotiations.[16]

In Bogor, the terms of reference were changed. Hun Sen and Nguyen Co Thach demanded that the Khmer Rouge be eliminated as a military organisation and denuded of its objectionable political leadership as "the only correct way" to resolve the conflict. The onus for removing the main military challenge to the Phnom Penh government in the event of a complete withdrawal of Vietnamese forces was placed on the non-Communist participants. This tactic had mixed success and the meeting ended inconclusively, as did the separate discussions between all the Cambodian parties and Prince Sihanouk in Jakarta. There was no joint communiqué; only an agreement to convene a working group of officials in October. Despite the lack of a practical response to Hun Sen's demand for the elimination of the Khmer Rouge, he was successful in registering a conditional link to the pace of Vietnamese troop withdrawals and accordingly in revising the long-standing representation of the conflict. Indonesia's Foreign Minister, Ali Alatas, who acted as host for the meeting, contributed to that revision. At the end of the proceedings, he took it upon himself to announce:

> All participants shared the view that the two key issues of the Kampuchean problem which are interlinked are the withdrawal of Vietnamese forces from Kampuchea to be carried out within the context of an overall political solution and the prevention of the recurrence of genocidal policies and practices of the Pol Pot regime and to ensure the cessation of all foreign interference and external arms supplies to the opposing Kampuchean forces.[17]

Although this statement caused consternation among some ASEAN partners, it could not be repudiated because convening the Jakarta Informal

Meeting in a context of global changes indicated the strong possibility of a political settlement. All ASEAN governments understood that the closer the prospect of a political settlement came, the greater was the requirement to deal with the gruesome fact of political life which the Khmer Rouge represented.

Some Chinese flexibility

The outcome of the informal meetings in Bogor and Jakarta indicated the extent of political impasse over Cambodia. One effect of the revision of the terms of reference, however, was to place the Khmer Rouge and their Chinese patron on the defensive. To avoid diplomatic isolation and to show flexibility, Communist Party General-Secretary Zhao Ziyang announced in August that China would not support a monopoly of power for the Khmer Rouge in Cambodia. He insisted, nonetheless, that they participate as an equal partner in any political settlement. To this end, China's support was forthcoming for a Khmer Rouge proposal that the armed forces of all four Cambodian factions be merged under international supervision in addition to the coalition stand that a four-party provisional government headed by Prince Sihanouk assume responsibility for conducting national elections. This attempt to demonstrate the willingness of the Khmer Rouge to be contained within a controlled structure of both military and political power-sharing was intended to meet Hun Sen's powerful claim that the Khmer Rouge constituted the source of the Cambodian problem. In this, they enjoyed the pragmatic support of Prince Sihanouk. For example, during a visit to Singapore in September 1988, he explained:

> If you exclude them, they will try to destabilise the new government. So, in order for the new government to have a chance of establishing itself through democratic stability and peace, we must include the Khmer Rouge in the government.[18]

He reiterated, also in concert with China, a demand for the complete withdrawal of Vietnamese forces and the dissolution of the Phnom Penh government. China had initially declared a commitment to continue arms supplies to Cambodian insurgent factions until an approved timetable for withdrawal had been established. By the end of 1988, however, flexibility had crept into this position also. Prime Minister Li Peng announced:

> To put the minds of the international community at rest, all sides may even gradually reduce such military support in step with the tempo of the troop withdrawal.[19]

The defensiveness of China and the Khmer Rouge in the wake of the Jakarta Informal Meeting and in the context of sustained Sino-Soviet *rapprochement* was matched by ASEAN. Indonesia's political activism had visibly weakened its common front on Cambodia. The members of the Association were obliged to come to terms with the revised representation of the conflict in order to retain their voting support in the United Nations. To this end, they modified their annual resolution before the General Assembly calling for the withdrawal of Vietnamese forces from Cambodia, by urging the international community to work toward "the non-return to the universally condemned policies and practices of a recent past". Although the statement was elliptical, it was widely understood to register opposition to the resumption of power in Cambodia by the Khmer Rouge. Despite objections by Khmer Rouge representatives in the Cambodian delegation and from China, the modified resolution received overwhelming support when it was put to the vote in November 1988: 122 votes were cast in favour, with only 19 against and 13 abstentions, in the largest demonstration of support against Vietnam's military presence in Cambodia since the issue first came before the General Assembly in 1979. Needless to say, Vietnam was not mollified by the modified terms of the resolution.

Limited agreement

By the end of 1988, the Cambodian conflict had been the subject of a number of separate negotiations, all without practical outcome. The bilateral meetings between Prince Sihanouk and Hun Sen had been fruitless. The Jakarta Informal Meeting had been a breakthrough in political form but had failed to produce any substantial agreement. The prearranged Working Group of officials convened in Jakarta in October but in the absence of a Khmer Rouge presence, probably out of concern that the Indonesian hosts were in collusion with the Vietnamese to reinforce their diplomatic isolation. Nonetheless, deadlock prevailed among the participants over linking the timetable for withdrawal of Vietnamese forces to the elimination of the Khmer Rouge and of ending external aid to all Cambodian resistance groups. No headway was made either over the key issue of political power-sharing and international peace-keeping.

Agreement was reached only for the Working Group to meet again and also for a second round of the Jakarta Informal Meeting early in 1989. This procedural accord could not conceal the extent to which the diplomatic enterprise appeared to have ground to a halt. A visit to Vietnam in November by Ali Alatas was prompted by the prospect that major power *rapprochement* might take responsibility for resolving the Cambodian conflict out of regional South-East Asian hands. Indonesia's strong preference for a regionally-forged political settlement was suggested by its Foreign Minister's willingness to meet Cambodia's Prime Minister Hun Sen while in Hanoi. It was the first occasion on which an ASEAN Foreign Minister had met a political representative of the Phnom Penh government directly.

The abortive talks between Prince Sihanouk and Hun Sen were resumed in November 1988. On this occasion Son Sann participated on behalf of the Khmer People's National Liberation Front but Khieu Samphan did not appear for the Khmer Rouge. (Their attempt to substitute Cambodia's representative to UNESCO was unacceptable to the other parties.) The Phnom Penh government drew some satisfaction from the unprecedented tripartite structure of the meeting, which suggested a form of power-sharing excluding the Khmer Rouge. This round of talks was equally inconclusive, however, and also generated personal acrimony between Prince Sihanouk and Hun Sen whose earlier cordiality had aroused speculation about the possible conclusion of a bilateral deal. At issue still was Hun Sen's adamant refusal to accept any change in the political *status quo* in Cambodia before elections to decide the country's future. He reiterated his position during a stop-over in Hanoi on his way back to Phnom Penh from Paris, pointing out that "it is [only] the People's Republic of Kampuchea which can prevent the return of the Pol Pot clique". The adamant insistence on its perpetuation was repeated the following month in rejecting Prince Sihanouk's associated proposal for an international peacekeeping force. Hun Sen explained:

> The solution to the Cambodian problem necessitates the establishment of an international control. However, since Cambodia is not a losing country like Germany and Japan in World War Two, it is not necessary to bring in a peace-keeping force to keep control over the Cambodian government. Therefore all international control organisations must respect Cambodia's independence and sovereignty and must be placed under the authority of the Cambodian government. It must not be a force for occupation or control of Cambodia. Its duty is to monitor the implementation or violation of agreements reached and to report it to the Cambodian government for remedial action.[20]

This statement, more than any other, revealed the limits of accommodation in the conflict and reflected Vietnam's insistence from the outset that the situation in Cambodia could not be reversed. The measure of impasse was demonstrated at a meeting of the Working Group of Cambodian parties in Paris in December 1988 which managed no more than two hours of discussion before being suspended *sine die*. The only development of any significance was an attempt by the Khmer Rouge to overcome a tactical blunder. They had recognised the folly of their self-exclusion from previous abortive rounds of negotiations. Their absence from meetings in Indonesia and France had enabled their claim to political entitlement to be questioned. Khieu Samphan had acknowledged this failing when he met Prince Sihanouk in Paris earlier in December, in an attempt to rebuild a semblance of coalition solidarity against Vietnam and its client government. Accordingly a Khmer Rouge representative took part in the brief and abortive Working Group later in the month.

The barren prospect for a political settlement was also indicated in an attempt to promote negotiations through the good offices of the Non-Aligned Movement. This initiative further reflected the Phnom Penh government's determination not to compromise its established position. Yasser Arafat, the leader of the Palestine Liberation Organisation, whose representative in Pyongyang had played a part in promoting the initial bilateral talks between Prince Sihanouk and Hun Sen, was asked to convene talks under Non-Aligned auspices. The plan was to involve former leaders of the movement, including Fidel Castro, Robert Mugabe and Rajiv Gandhi – all sympathetic to Vietnam's position – in a negotiating structure. An additional attraction was the absence of any Cambodian representation to the Non-Aligned Movement because the seat had been declared vacant at Havana in September 1979. In the event, this initiative was arrested at the meeting of Non-Aligned Foreign Ministers in Cyprus in September 1988 when ASEAN representatives successfully insisted on more balanced participation in any mediation group.

THE SINO-SOVIET DIMENSION

The failure of the two sets of talks involving both internal Cambodian and regional parties to the conflict reinforced the significance of the *rapprochement* between the Soviet Union and China. Their patron roles had been instrumental in sustaining its momentum through support for Vietnam and the government in Phnom Penh and for Thailand and the Cambodian resistance groups. After the success of the Moscow meeting between Ronald Reagan and Mikhail Gorbachev in June 1988, the Soviet leader renewed his efforts to improve Sino-Soviet relations. China had made Cambodia the sticking point in the relationship, insisting on Soviet withdrawal of support for Vietnam's policy as the prime precondition for full normalisation.

An earlier Soviet attempt to remove that obstacle had been indicated in October 1986 when Deputy Foreign Minister Igor Rogachev had announced his government's willingness to discuss Cambodia in the ninth round of talks on normalising relations. Up to then, the Soviet Union had insisted as a matter of principle that it was not prepared to discuss the interests of third countries in its continuing dialogue with China.

Consideration of Cambodia assumed a significant stage in August 1988. Four lengthy sessions were held at Deputy Foreign Minister level in Beijing, at which "common ground" was reported to have been found between the two sides. A Soviet willingness to encourage Vietnam's withdrawal of forces from Cambodia appeared to be matched by China's willingness to consider measures for containing the Khmer Rouge. In mid-September 1988, in the Siberian city of Krasnoyarsk, Gorbachev returned to the theme of improving relations with China. He offered joint economic zones along the Sino-Soviet border and reiterated his request for a meeting with Deng Xiaoping. The momentum of *rapprochement* ceased to be retarded by Chinese reservations over Cambodia. At the end of the month, Soviet Foreign Minister Eduard Shevardnadze met his Chinese counterpart, Qian Qichen, at the United Nations in New York. This encounter paved the way for a substantial negotiation between the two in Moscow, early in December – the first time in over 30 years that a Chinese Foreign Minister had visited Moscow. During the visit Qian Qichen met Mikhail Gorbachev after which it was announced a Sino-Soviet summit would take place during the first half of 1989.

Measure of accord

Cambodia figured prominently in the discussions, which ranged over a number of contentious issues. The timely announcement from Hanoi that the promised withdrawal of 50,000 troops from Cambodia would be completed before the end of December 1988 improved the climate for the talks and the two sides agreed on China's phasing out support for resistance groups within Cambodia concurrently with Vietnam's withdrawal of forces. (This accord was confirmed by China's Prime Minister Li Peng later in the month.)

It is probable that it was at the meeting in Moscow that the Chinese government was persuaded to embark on direct talks with Vietnam on Cambodia. These began in Beijing in January 1989 after Vietnam had announced a willingness to withdraw all its forces from Cambodia by September in the event of a political settlement. The momentum of Sino-Soviet *rapprochement* accelerated when Eduard Shevardnadze visited China early in February when it was agreed that Gorbachev would pay a much-sought visit in the middle of May. The two Foreign Ministers held further discussions on Cambodia and at the end of the visit issued a joint nine-point statement.

That statement constituted a significant if limited accord. It referred to Vietnam's commitment to withdraw all its forces from Cambodia by September 1989 (but without the precondition of a political settlement) and registered the understanding that military aid to all parties in Cambodia should cease with that withdrawal. It was also agreed that, in order to ensure strict supervision of troop withdrawals, cessation of foreign military aid, the maintenance of peace and the conduct of free elections, "an effective international control mechanism" be established.

The measure of accord, as well as joint support for an internal settlement through negotiations among Cambodian parties, was not matched by a common view on the terms of such a settlement. On that fundamental issue, the statement was an agreement to disagree, with both States supporting contending positions held by Cambodian adversaries. To that end, it was stated that "the Chinese side stands for the establishment of a provisional coalition government in Kampuchea headed by Prince Sihanouk and with quadripartite representation". It was further stated that

> the Soviet side will support an agreement among the four parties in Kampuchea on the establishment of a provisional organ under the charge of Sihanouk and with quadripartite representation. This organ should not be subordinate to any party in Kampuchea, and its task is to implement agreements reached by the parties in Kampuchea and to conduct free elections.[21]

At issue was the right of the government in Phnom Penh to remain in power during the process of political settlement. The differing positions adopted by China and the Soviet Union indicated that neither State had completely abdicated its role as a patron power. At the same time, the terms of the joint statement, taken together with the agreement on the date of a summit meeting, suggested that Cambodia had been removed as an obstacle to sustained improvement in relations. That had long been the case on the Soviet side. The Chinese no longer saw any security or other interest in withholding the ceremonial seal of a meeting between Mikhail Gorbachev and Deng Xiaoping from the undoubted transformation of the bilateral relationship.

REGIONAL INITIATIVES

Between the meetings of the Soviet and Chinese Foreign Ministers in Moscow and Beijing, a number of regional initiatives occurred which revived expectations that a final settlement of the Cambodian conflict might be close. In the context of accelerating Sino-Soviet *rapprochement*, the Phnom Penh government had announced on 6 January 1989 that all Vietnamese forces would be out of Cambodia by September if a political settlement were concluded. Within three days, Thailand's Foreign Minister, Sitthi Savetsila, visited Hanoi – the first time a Thai Foreign Minister had been to the Vietnamese capital since 1976. It indicated a softening of Bangkok's position following the Thai elections in July 1988, after which General Prem Tinsulanond had been succeeded by Chatichai Chunhavan, a retired General and leader of the Chart Thai Party. In his first statement to the Press after assuming office he announced that his predecessor's policies would continue, with one exception; Indochina would be turned from a battleground into a trading market. Sitthi Savetsila, the leader of the rival Social Action Party, was retained as Foreign Minister in a coalition government. His visit to Hanoi reflected the changing climate of regional and global relations and also an element of domestic political tension.

In the Vietnamese capital, a measure of accord over Cambodia with Foreign Minister Nguyen Co Thach was publicly indicated over the so-called international aspect of the conflict. Sitthi even went so far as to declare: "There is no disagreement between us". Apart from endorsing an "international control and supervisory mechanism" of an undefined kind, there was no tangible progress, but the occasion was of political significance.

Of even greater political significance was China's decision to receive a Deputy Foreign Minister from Vietnam. On 14 January 1989, Dinh Nho Liem arrived in Beijing for talks with his Chinese counterpart, Liu Shuqing. It was the first ministerial encounter for nearly 10 years. China had insisted initially that Vietnam withdraw all its forces from Cambodia before any dialogue could begin, and then had revised that condition to demand a firm timetable for withdrawal. The announcement that Vietnam would withdraw all its forces by September 1989 in the event of a prior political settlement was interpreted as an adequate concession in the context of improved Sino-Soviet relations.

The two Deputy Foreign Ministers discussed Cambodia, indicating a measure of agreement and a willingness for their Foreign Ministers to meet in the near future. The talks constituted a cautious exchange after a decade of bitterness and invective but they seemed momentous for the Cambodian conflict, in which Sino-Vietnamese contention had always been the central factor. From the outset, the two States had been entangled in a hostile Sino-Soviet relationship. The progressive transformation of that relationship to one of working *rapprochement* had muted China's suspicion of a Vietnam in a condition of evident economic distress. The beginning of a limited Sino-Vietnamese dialogue served in turn to reinforce the pace of Sino-Soviet *rapprochement* reflected in Shevardnadze's visit to Beijing in February 1989.

ASEAN in disarray

The visit of the Thai Foreign Minister to Hanoi followed by that of a Vietnamese Deputy Foreign Minister to Beijing indicated a symmetrical pattern of flexibility and accommodation among external parties to the Cambodian conflict. That pattern had been shaped by Gorbachev's drive to decouple regional conflicts from the primary international relationships of the Soviet Union and by Deng Xiaoping's positive, if gradual, response. The pace of diplomatic interchange had prompted Indonesia and its regional partners within ASEAN to press ahead with arrangements for a second round of the Jakarta Informal Meeting. A meeting of its Foreign Ministers in Brunei confirmed the occasion and also support for Prince Norodom Sihanouk as the head of a future government in Cambodia.

Two days later on 25 January, Hun Sen, Prime Minister of the People's Republic of Kampuchea, arrived in Bangkok on a Thai military aircraft from Vientiane as the personal guest of Prime Minister Chatichai Chunhavan. His visit, ostensibly on an informal basis and without conceding recognition, had been arranged apparently without the prior knowledge of the Thai Foreign Ministry. It was exceedingly controversial, flouting the long-standing Thai and ASEAN policy not to have any dealings with representatives of a government which owed its existence to a Vietnamese act of force. Direct dealing with Hun Sen and discussions on a range of bilateral issues including trade and the return of Cambodian refugees, gave the impression that the government in Phnom Penh had been accepted as a political fact. This implied transformation of Hun Sen from an alleged Vietnamese puppet to a practical ruler was in direct contradiction to Thailand's long-standing support for the Coalition Government of Democratic Kampuchea, reaffirmed by its Foreign Minister only days previously. Prince Sihanouk's meetings with Hun Sen in France and even that between him and Indonesia's Foreign Minister, Ali Alatas, in Vietnam the previous November, had not constituted equivalent acts of recognition. By appearing to confer recognition without the Phnom Penh government modifying its stance on power-sharing, Thailand had considerably weakened the position of the resistance coalition backed by ASEAN, as well as exposing its diplomatic disarray.

Revised priorities

Prime Minister Chatichai's invitation to Hun Sen reflected a perception of change in global and regional relationships with which Thailand wished to keep pace. It also indicated a revision of national priorities based partly on the remarkable economic success of Thailand concurrent with the course of the Cambodian conflict. Vietnam's engagement in that conflict had weakened it to the point of exhaustion and had eliminated the acute sense of threat experienced in Bangkok in January 1979. Prime Minister Chatichai enjoyed the support of the Armed Forces Commander, General Chaovalit Yongchaiyudh, in reassessing the security threat posed by Vietnam, especially if its troops were to withdraw from Cambodia. It merits recalling that in April

1980, shortly after he became Foreign Minister, Sitthi Savetsila had remarked that his government would even be willing to accept a government headed by Heng Samrin "if this is the result of a political settlement and if it is not necessary for foreign forces to keep it in power".[22] In the circumstances, a role for Thailand as the economic power-house of mainland South-East Asia was judged likely to counter any adverse consequences from a Vietnam politically influential in Cambodia.[23]

Prime Minister Chatichai was encouraged in his opening to the Phnom Penh government by business interests and by an informal group of academic advisers, including his son, whose members had been critical of Thailand's policy of confrontation towards Indochina virtually from the onset of the Cambodian conflict. They calculated, *inter alia*, that a Cambodia under Hun Sen could have greater potential for serving as a stable buffer between Vietnam and Thailand than one in which Prince Sihanouk exercised a dominant role. Thai ambivalence towards Prince Sihanouk has been of long duration. Further confirmation of implicit Thai endorsement of the Phnom Penh government was a concurrent visit to the Cambodian capital by a parliamentary delegation from Bangkok. The political opening to Phnom Penh had been preceded by a vigorous attempt to improve relations with Laos. Prime Minister Chatichai's visit to Vientiane in November 1988 was reciprocated by Laos's Prime Minister Kaysone Phomvihan in February 1989.

Thailand's regional policy, revised at the expense of its ASEAN partners and the resistance coalition, did not involve foreclosing on access to external countervailing power provided by China and the resistance coalition. China had managed to mix *rapprochement* with the Soviet Union and limited détente with Vietnam with continued support for the position of the resistance. Correspondingly, Thailand managed to open up a political option without foregoing pressure on Vietnam. China offered only the mildest, and then indirect, criticism of Hun Sen's visit. Moreover, at the same time, Prime Minister Chatichai also played host to China's Minister of Defence, General Qin Jiwei. Prince Sihanouk reacted in an affronted manner, however, and refused to take part in the forthcoming Jakarta talks. The three resistance factions agreed to attend the regional meeting after their representatives had been persuaded personally by Prime Minister Chatichai.

Despite the new tone in global and regional relationships, the limited measure of agreement among external parties still left practical parts of a settlement unattended. The meeting between Chinese and Vietnamese ministers failed to agree on the form of international supervision and on how elections should be held after a Vietnamese withdrawal. Correspondingly, the Soviet and Chinese Foreign Ministers meeting in Beijing were obliged to agree to disagree over the terms on which an internal political settlement might be based. Prime Minister Chatichai's reception of Hun Sen undoubtedly stiffened Phnom Penh's position but without inducing any concessions on the part of the resistance coalition or its external backers. Divisions of major political magnitude between the Cambodian parties obstructed a political settlement but those divisions were also sustained by external parties which managed to reconcile their support for contending factions with détente and *rapprochement* among themselves. This was the situation when the Cambodian factions and representatives of the regional States met in Jakarta in mid-February 1989.

FROM JAKARTA TO JAKARTA

In the weeks prior to the second round of the Jakarta Informal Meeting, the prospects for a political settlement to the Cambodian conflict appeared to improve. An apparent willingness by Vietnam, with Soviet encouragement, to withdraw its forces from Cambodia quickened the pace of Sino-Soviet *rapprochement*. The announcement in January 1989 – coinciding with the 10th anniversary of the investment of Phnom Penh – that all Vietnamese forces would be withdrawn from Cambodia by September in the event of a political settlement encouraged Thailand and China to begin direct talks with Vietnam. All parties appeared to be agreed that external military aid to Cambodian factions should cease concurrently with the withdrawal of Vietnamese forces. The Vietnamese, who had always insisted that the Cambodian conflict was essentially an internal matter, sought to establish the conventional wisdom that its international aspect had been virtually resolved. All that was required was an accord between the Cambodian parties. If not, a partial settlement of the international aspect could be formally concluded.

The apparent climate of conciliation among the external parties to the Cambodian conflict was not matched by the state of relations among the internal ones. The informal meeting between Prince Sihanouk and Hun Sen in November 1988 had ended without any substantive accord and in some acrimony, which continued afterwards. At issue was Prince Sihanouk's realisation that Hun Sen had no intention of assuming a subordinate political role in his favour and that he had become a formidable political rival. Hun Sen's proposal articulated at the first round of the Jakarta talks was a formula for maintaining the political *status quo* in Cambodia imposed by Vietnamese force of arms. Correspondingly, Sihanouk's counter-proposal, backed by his coalition partners, was a formula for revising it. The political impasse between the contending Cambodian parties was not in any way eased by the apparent climate of conciliation among the external ones. Indeed, a significant feature of that climate was the extent to which there had been an agreement to disagree over Cambodia, in particular between the Soviet Union and China, which left both States free to hold opposing positions with respect to the contending internal parties. Vietnam's declared intention to withdraw from Cambodia did not indicate any willingness to compromise support for the legitimacy of the government in Phnom Penh. The surprising decision of Thailand's Prime Minister to welcome Hun Sen to Bangkok had the additional effect of reinforcing it. Indeed, this indication of backsliding on the part of an ASEAN member which had long provided territorial sanctuary and material supply for the Khmer Rouge was almost certainly responsible for Prince Sihanouk resuming his leadership of the resistance coalition from which he had "irrevocably" resigned in July 1988.[24] His closing ranks with his Communist and non-Communist coalition partners in February restored a political polarisation among the Cambodian groupings which had been blurred by his resignation. He was once again seeking to exploit his prime political asset – his legitimacy. By resuming the leadership of the resistance coalition, he signalled to Vietnam that he was withholding the prospect of his endorsing a political settlement which would attract strong domestic and international support as a consequence. The net effect was to diminish expectations for the second round of the Jakarta Informal Meeting.

Those expectations had been based on a fallacy about the Cambodian conflict encouraged by the format and procedure of the Jakarta talks. At Vietnam's insistence, the initial round in Bogor had represented the conflict as comprising two distinct domestic and international dimensions. In effect, those two dimensions have never been separated in practical political terms. Vietnam invaded Cambodia in December 1978 to drive out the Pol Pot regime and to impose an alternative government of its own choosing. That alternative government serves to safeguard Vietnam's security interests and Hanoi's willingness to withdraw its occupying forces is not intended to be at the expense of that safeguard. In that respect, the essence of the Cambodian conflict has not changed.

From impasse to dialogue

In the event, the second round of the Jakarta Informal Meeting proved to be as inconclusive as the first. The contending Cambodian parties were not able to bridge the political divide over how to share power in the interim period before a final settlement or over the terms of international supervision and control. The resistance factions rallied around the figure of Prince Sihanouk who remained conspicuously in Beijing for the duration of the talks. They were still determined not to accord legitimacy to a government installed by Vietnamese force of arms nor to allow it to influence an electoral process to determine Cambodia's political future. That government, backed doggedly by Vietnam, stuck rigidly to its insistence that the role of the Khmer Rouge in the resistance coalition obliged it to retain administrative responsibility. It presented itself as the sole obstacle to the resumption of power by the notorious Khmer Rouge. Its stance, as well as Thailand's unilateral initiative, could have been factors in Indonesia's decision, in February 1989, to normalise relations with China after a break of more than 21 years.

The political impasse in Jakarta brought to the surface the incompatible positions of the contending Cambodian parties which were not completely autonomous. Behind the government in Phnom Penh stood that in Hanoi which, in April 1989, announced that it would unconditionally withdraw all of its forces from Cambodia by September. That announcement did not constitute an abdication of support for the Phnom Penh regime. It reflected a judgement about its chances of military survival and an interest in influencing both the Soviet Union and China in advance of their summit in May, as well as encouraging Prince Sihanouk to come to terms with Hun Sen. And, although the Soviet Union had persuaded China of the merits of *rapprochement*, it had also not wavered in its diplomatic support for the political position of the Phnom Penh government.

Correspondingly, although Thailand had welcomed Hun Sen and also began to tighten control over Khmer Rouge encampments along the border with Cambodia, its government had not foreclosed on its support for the resistance coalition. For example, during his visit to Beijing in March 1989, Prime Minister Chatichai pointed out that Thailand continued to support Prince Sihanouk and the three parties of the Cambodian resistance and that his country did not recognise the Phnom Penh regime.[25]

China's line has been more consistent and decisive, with Communist Party General Secretary Zhao Ziyang stating that there were two aspects to the Cambodian conflict which required attention; first, the complete withdrawal of Vietnamese forces and, secondly, the establishment of a four-party coalition under Prince Sihanouk. He added that "without a settlement to the Kampuchean issue, there will be no improvement in Sino-Vietnamese relations".[26] Confirmation of China's doggedness has been a refusal so far to receive Vietnam's Foreign Minister in Beijing.

The announcement that Vietnam would withdraw all its forces from Cambodia by the end of September 1989, irrespective of a political settlement, encouraged a fourth round of talks between Prince Sihanouk and Prime Minister Hun Sen at the beginning of May, in Jakarta. Hun Sen made concessions over the name and flag of Cambodia and also offered Prince Sihanouk the post of Head of State if he returned to Phnom Penh; but he refused, once again, to dismantle his government in advance of national elections. Prince Sihanouk said he would not speak any more of dismantling but insisted that the Phnom Penh government be "reshaped", which amounted to much the same demand. The talks were significant for their climate of conciliation but Hun Sen did not succeed in prising Prince Sihanouk away from the Khmer Rouge and his Chinese backers. Still at issue was the exercise of power. Prince Sihanouk has long sought an executive presidency and not the role of a constitutional figurehead who would endorse the government established by Vietnamese force of arms. Although the principal Cambodian parties indicated progress and agreed to meet again in July, in Paris, a conclusive accord still eluded them.

CONCLUSION

Political impasse over Cambodia may appear to be due to the inability of the contending internal parties to come to terms. But behind the stand of Hun Sen is the interest and backing of Vietnam. Behind that of Prince Sihanouk is the interest and backing of China, which he apparently believes it is necessary to retain to uphold the independence of Cambodia and also to contain the Khmer Rouge.

This Conflict Study suggested at the outset that the central issue in the case of Cambodia has been the balance of power in Indochina defined with reference to Vietnam's advantage or disadvantage. That issue has, so far, been beyond resolution through political means because it possesses a zero-sum quality. The internal parties to the conflict may employ the idiom of national reconciliation but they lack a tradition of power-sharing. Their experience and culture of politics disposes them to think only in terms of either winning or losing. Neither side has been able to impose a military solution or been obliged to concede a political one from exhaustion or pressure from an external patron. Prince Sihanouk and Hun Sen may yet come to terms, particularly if Prince Sihanouk, from his perspective as a man of 67 years, becomes convinced there is no viable alternative. But, if they fail to do so in a context of unrepaired Sino-Vietnamese relations, the final phase of the Cambodian conflict will remain incomplete.

NOTES

[1] Cited in Gareth Porter, "Vietnamese Policy and the Indochina Crisis"; in David W. P. Elliot (ed.), *The Third Indochina Conflict*, Westview Press, Boulder, Colorado, 1981, p. 88.

[2] Vietnam News Agency 4 March 1979, cited in BBC Summary of World Broadcasts, FE/6059/A3/3.

[3] SWB *op. cit.*, FE/6072/A3/9.

[4] See, Josephine Reynell, *Political Pawns. Refugees on the Thai-Kampuchean Border.* Refugee Studies Programme, Queen Elizabeth House, Oxford, 1989.

[5] See Michael Richardson in *International Herald Tribune*, 18 October 1988, Nicholas Cumming-Bruce in *The Guardian*, 30 November 1988, and James Pringle in *The Independent*, 23 February 1989.

[6] Quoted in Kishore Mahbubani "The Kampuchean Problem: A Southeast Asian Perception", *Foreign Affairs*. Winter 1983/84, p. 410.

[7] For a self-criticism of Vietnam's economic condition, see Nguyen Xuan Oanh, "A Vietnamese Assesses Hanoi's Attempt at *Perestroika*", *International Herald Tribune*, 13 December 1988. See also Michael Richardson, *Ibid.*, 19 December 1988.

[8] Cited in SWB *op. cit.*, FE/8447/C1/11.

[9] See *Documents on the Kampuchean Problem 1979–1985*, Ministry of Foreign Affairs, Bangkok, 1985, p. 117.

[10] See Michael Leifer, *Indonesia's Foreign Policy*, George Allen and Unwin, London, 1983. Chapter 6.

[11] Cited in SWB *op. cit.*, FE/8633/A3/4.

[12] See Serge Thion, "The Pattern of Cambodian Politics", in David B. Ablin and Marlowe Hood (eds), *The Cambodian Agony*, M. E. Sharpe Inc., Armonk, New York, 1987.

[13] See Peter Schier and Manola Schier-Oum, *Prince Sihanouk on Cambodia*, Institut for Asienkunde, Hamburg, 1980.

[14] *The Bangkok Post*, 21 June 1987.

[15] For example, see Chang Pao-min "Kampuchean Conflict: The Diplomatic Breakthrough", *The Pacific Review*, Vol. 1, No. 4, 1988.

[16] Reported in SWB FE/0202 A3/5.

[17] SWB FE/0217 A3/1.

[18] *The Straits Times*, 15 September 1988.

[19] SWB FE/0340/A3/2.

[20] *Ibid.*, FE/0338/A3/2.

[21] *Sino-Soviet Statement on Cambodia*, cited in SWB FE/0378 C2/1.

[22] *The Bangkok Post*, 3 April 1980.

[23] See the analysis in *Far Eastern Economic Review*, 23 February 1989.

[24] Note the explanation provided by Prince Sihanouk in *International Herald Tribune*, 20 February 1989.

[25] SWB FE/0411/A3/2.

[26] *Ibid.*

SELECTED READING

David B. Ablin and Marlowe Hood (eds), *The Cambodian Agony* (M. E. Sharpe Inc., Armonk, New York, 1987).

Elizabeth Becker, *When the War was Over* (Simon and Schuster, New York, 1986).

Leszek Buszynski, "International Linkages and Regional Interests in Soviet Asia–Pacific Policy", *Pacific Affairs*, Summer 1988.

Nayan Chanda, *Brother Enemy: The War After the War* (Harcourt Brace Jovanovich, San Diego, California, 1986).

Chang Pao-min, "Kampuchean Conflict: The Diplomatic Breakthrough", *The Pacific Review*, vol. 1, no. 4 (1988).

Grant Evans and Kelvin Rowley, *Red Brotherhood at War* (Verso Books, London, 1984).

Justus M. van der Kroef, *Dynamics of the Cambodian Conflict*, The Institute for the Study of Conflict (Conflict Studies no. 183, London, 1986).

Michael Leifer, *ASEAN and the Security of South-East Asia* (Routledge, London, 1989).

Charles McGregor, *The Sino-Vietnamese Relationship and the Soviet Union*, The International Institute for Strategic Studies; *Adelphi Papers*, No. 232 (London, Autumn 1988).

John Pedler, "Cambodia: dangers and opportunity for the West", *The World Today*, February 1989.

Gareth Porter, "Cambodia: Sihanouk's Initiative", *Foreign Affairs*, Spring 1988.

Josephine Reynell, *Political Pawns. Refugees on the Thai-Kampuchean Border*. Refugee Studies Programme (Queen Elizabeth House, Oxford, 1989).

Robert S. Ross, *The Indochina Tangle* (Columbia University Press, New York, 1988).

Indochina

CHINA
YUNNAN
GUANGXI
Red R.
Black R.
Dien Bien Phu
HANOI
Haiphong
Gulf of
Tonkin
Luang Prabang
NGHIA
BINH
Hainan
LAOS
VIENTIANE
Mekong R.
17th PARALLEL
Paracel Is
Hue
Danang
THAILAND
VIETNAM
SOUTH
CHINA
SEA
Pakse
CHAMPASSAK
Central
Kontum
Aranyaprathet
Sisophon
RATANAKIRI
Siem Reap
CAMBODIA
(Kampuchea)
Highlands
Battambang
MONDOLKIRI
Cardomom
Mountains
Nha Trang
Mekong R.
Dung R
PHNOM PENH
Cam Ranh
Tay Ninh
LAM DONG
Phan Rang
Kompong Som
GULF OF
THAILAND
Ream
Ho Chi Minh
City
Con Son
Spratly I
0 Miles 200
0 Kilometres 300

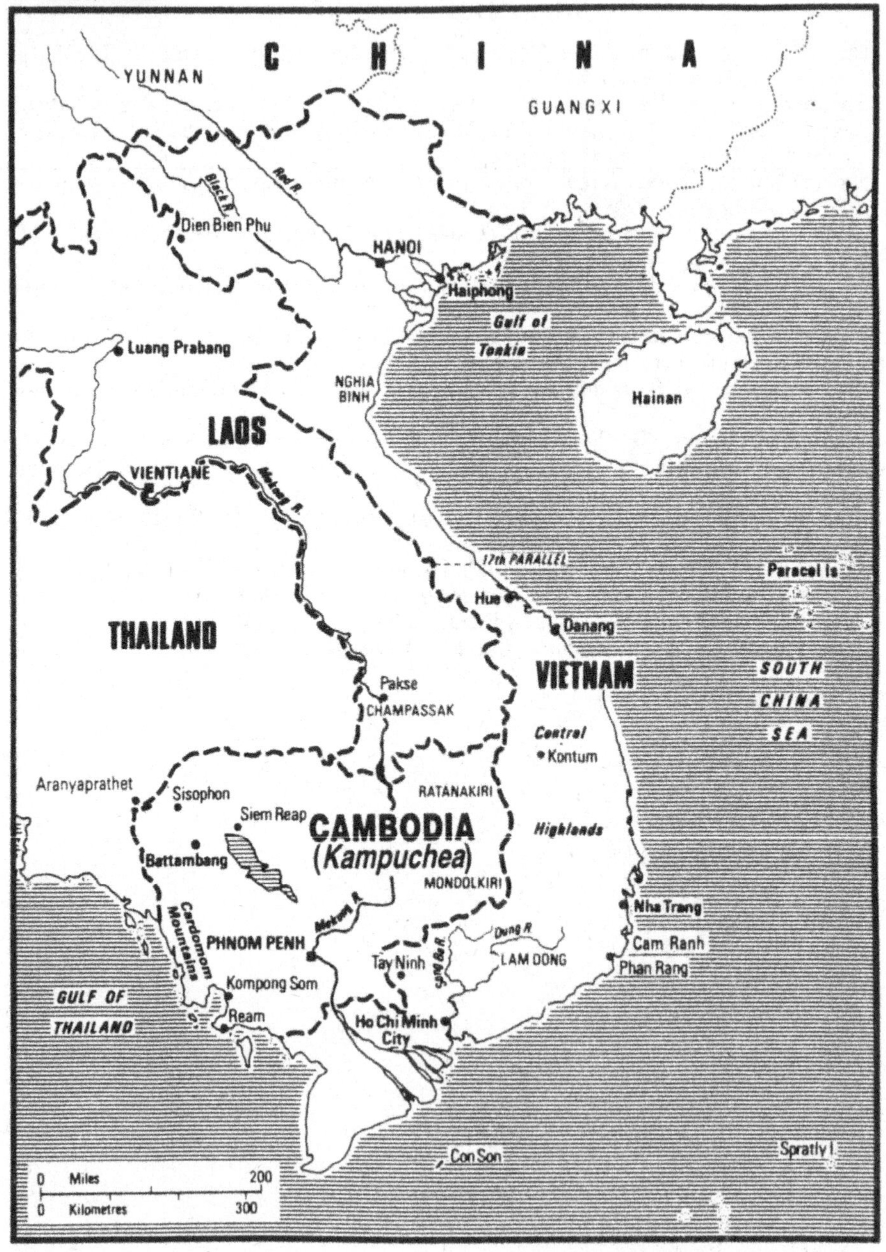

[3]

Pakistan: Towards a Modern Muslim State?

Anthony Hyman

Pakistan's experience as an independent state has oscillated between periods of civilian governments giving flawed democracy and military rule of varying degrees of harshness. Politicians, generals and senior bureaucrats all share the blame for the country's recurrent crises, and the failure to achieve a stable democratic system. Any serious analysis of Pakistan's problems has to take account of the unresolved issues which continue to dominate national and regional politics, and are discussed below under *Legacies from the Past*.

Pakistan's election campaign in the autumn of 1988 was followed with unusual attention in the international media. This was partly because the November elections were widely viewed in the West as an historic opportunity for the Pakistani people to choose a democratic government. It was also accounted for by Western media interest in what was obviously going to be a colourful election campaign, with a female politician in the starring role.

Benazir Bhutto's Pakistan People's Party (PPP) won millions of votes across the country, with sweeping gains in constituencies in rural Sind, but failing in the biggest province, the Punjab. The PPP secured 38 per cent of the popular vote and 45 per cent of the seats. This means the anti-PPP vote for the opposition alliance cannot realistically be dismissed as somehow insignificant. Though the PPP had failed to gain an overall majority, it won over independent MPs, gained 12 of the 20 Assembly seats reserved for women and offered alliances to regional parties in three provinces.

When, after a hiatus, in which the Sind-based Mohajir Qaumi Movement (MQM), holding the balance in the National Assembly, was hotly wooed by both sides, Benazir Bhutto was finally called upon to form a government the next month, huge international goodwill greeted the outcome. The young and glamorous Prime Minister, it was claimed, was the first woman leader of any modern Muslim nation, and deserved every chance to succeed in her stated mission of restoring democracy to Pakistan.

PROBLEMS OF THE BHUTTO GOVERNMENT

However, the problems of the Bhutto government became increasingly evident by the summer of 1989. Not one piece of legislation had gone through parliament. She had alienated many influential people by what was often described as an autocratic style, and unwillingness to take or follow advice. The powerful civil service was reliably said to be in a state of paralysis, with many new appointments and important decisions being delayed indefinitely.

The Prime Minister came into rivalry with the President, by challenging the latter's powers on appointments. She unilaterally ordered the retirement of the Joint Chief of Staff, Admiral Sirohey. Earlier, she had dismissed the director of the Inter Services Intelligence, (ISI), the Army's shadowy intelligence agency, successfully replacing General Hameed Gul with her own choice, the retired General Kullu.

A record number of appointments had been made to a cabinet which by September 1989 actually numbered 68, including senior advisers and ministers. It was not so much the size of the cabinet as the inexperience and generally low calibre of appointees which worried Pakistani observers. The increasing inaccessibility of Benazir was compounded by her frequent absences from the country. She made eight foreign trips in as many months in 1989, where she was received with warmth and enthusiasm by foreign dignitaries and the media alike. However, in Pakistan itself the new Prime Minister was criticised for running away from pressing problems at home.

The giving of the post of deputy prime minister to her own mother, Begum Nusrat Bhutto, in March 1989, was followed closely by the appointment of her father-in-law, rich businessman Hakim Zardari, to be chairman of the influential Public Accounts Committee of the Parliament. These moves alienated a considerable number of people who were initially well disposed to the Bhutto government. Widely credited rumours of nepotism, corruption, abuse of privileges and gross irregularities helping to enrich members of the Zardari family and other cronies badly dented the image of the struggling Prime Minister.

Problems with the government's key allies in the MQM emerged by the autumn of 1989. MQM leaders demanded four important cabinet posts as the price of continuing their alliance. After months of wrangling, the MQM abandoned its alliance, siding with the opposition Islamic Democratic Alliance (IDA) in the no-confidence vote sprung on the government in the National Assembly in October 1989. Only narrowly won by Benazir's government, it served as a salutary shock and warning to the Prime Minister. The resignation of the entire Cabinet was soon announced, and a reorganisation followed in November.

The opposition had gathered 107 votes in the 237-seat Assembly, just 12 short of the 119 needed to oust her as Prime Minister. As parliamentary leader of the IDA, the veteran Sindhi politician (himself a onetime senior leader of the PPP) Ghulam Mustafa Jatoi stated in November 1989 that the opposition would table further no-confidence motions until this "corrupt, inefficient and inept" government was brought down.

By the end of 1989 it was quite clear not only that democracy was not set on firmer foundations in Pakistan, but that there was also evidence of an absence of statesmanship and even of basic honesty on all sides of the political spectrum. The second half of 1989 had seen blatantly underhand tactics, together with offers (and acceptances) of huge sums of cash for defections by MPs. Their respective parties had to keep these "assets" under guard in remote hill resorts, so as to be sure of them.

It was a depressing spectacle – a travesty of democracy by the very people elected to help revive it in Pakistan. "The great mass of common people are sick of their performance to date", claimed the independent national newspaper, *The Muslim*, with good reason.

Pakistan: Towards a Modern Muslim State? 3

The "three As"

In the background there is always the Army. Benazir's personal relations are said to be very cordial with the present chief of army staff. The generals may be far from anxious to stage another coup, yet its potential for influencing events, in the case of a serious crisis, is obvious. The Army remains one of Pakistan's "three As" – Allah, the Army and America – the three powers which, according to many Pakistanis, determine whatever happens of any importance in their country.

There was much speculation about the "inevitability" of the Bhutto succession to power in Pakistan. Parallels were even claimed for Benazir between Corazon Aquino's sensational rise in the Philippines. What is certain is that leadership of political parties has often passed to dead politicians' widows or daughters in South Asia. But Benazir's inheritance of the PPP leadership does not necessarily mean she can hold onto power indefinitely. That will surely depend on her government's performance in office.

On behalf of the government, it could be argued that the PPP remains the only truly national party, with solid public backing in all four provinces of the country. In itself, though, this is hardly a guarantee of survival. Benazir represents a potent symbol, but certainly not a united or well organised political party. The prosperity and superficial stability brought to Pakistan since the 1977 military coup has made the middle classes all the more wary of the PPP. The party was identified with socialism and wholesale nationalisations of key sectors of the economy under Z. A. Bhutto.

Punjabi nationalism

It used to be stated as an axiom of Pakistani politics that no government in Islamabad could long survive without also controlling the Punjab, the country's biggest and wealthiest province, with close on 60 per cent of Pakistan's 107 million people and a larger proportion of its agricultural and industrial production, besides recruitment to the armed forces. Yet the PPP government coped with a bitterly hostile Punjab through 1989, even after the breakdown of its tactical alliances with other regionally-based parties in North West Frontier Province (NWFP) and Baluchistan.

Nawaz Sharif, chief minister of the Punjab and a major leader of the opposition, is of the same 1950s generation as Benazir, but of contrasting class origins, being a *parvenu* Punjabi industrialist, not a feudal Sindhi landlord. Far from inheriting a political party, as did Benazir from her charismatic father, Nawaz Sharif had joined the pro-Zia Muslim League, revived in 1985. On Zi ul-Haq's sudden death, Nawaz Sharif had to forge a larger coalition at great speed. from what looked like extremely unpromising material.

By keeping together scores of members of the National and Provincial Assemblies (of the IDA as well as independent deputies), Nawaz Sharif proved he had staying power as well as large financial resources – though hardly on a scale to compete with the central government. For all this, the

IDA had little obvious cohesion between its component parties. It remained a loose grouping of members united not by principles, but simply by a common appetite for achieving political power, and enjoying whatever fruits it offered.

Though the IDA lacks any coherent ideology, the Punjabi element is one of the keys to understanding it. Nawaz Sharif himself personifies Punjabi nationalism in a strident form. One of its strands is a fierce anti-Indian line, which claims that Benazir Bhutto is too "soft" on India, and altogether unreliable in maintaining Pakistan's national interests. Nawaz Sharif has also appealed, not without success, to popular Punjabi prejudices against a Sindhi prime minister, besides exploiting for all it is worth the conservative Muslim backlash against having a woman as a ruler.

Sindhi nationalism

A further worrying development for the government is growing opposition from Sindhi nationalists. There is sympathy for their demands – for full autonomy amounting to independence for Sind – among ordinary PPP members and even from its own MPs elected from Sind. Of all the four provinces of Pakistan, Sind is, after all, the party's heartland and crucial source of national support. Riots, arson and looting broke out in six towns of Sind province in October 1989, in protest at the arrest of G. M. Syed, the "grand old man" of Sindhi nationalism, and leader of the Sind National Alliance. This militant grouping had called for Sind's independence from Pakistan.

LEGACIES FROM THE PAST

The new state of Pakistan was carved out of Muslim-majority areas of British-ruled India in the 1947 Partition. Most of its people lived in West Punjab and East Bengal (now Bangladesh). With these two areas were combined three other provinces, Sind, NWFP and Baluchistan, soon joined also by the northern third of Kashmir. Millions of Muslim refugees from many areas of India crossed to Pakistan, while Hindu and Sikh refugees crossed in the opposite direction. Separated by one thousand miles of hostile Indian territory, the two wings of Pakistan contrasted strongly in most important aspects – language and culture, economy and climate. Islam was the most obvious link between them, but a shared religion gradually proved insufficient to compensate for major differences.

In 1947, Pakistan constituted the fifth largest state in the world, in terms of population. Even today, without Bangladesh, it is a major Asian country, with a rapidly growing population of 107 million. But the emergence of Pakistan as a separate state for Muslims of India failed to produce either a democratic, secular state or an Islamic order. Nor did it produce a united nation with a coherent ideology. Well might Mohammad Ali Jinnah have said, as the creator of a united Italy said of the Italians, "We have Pakistan, now it remains to make Pakistanis".

Pakistan: Towards a Modern Muslim State? 5

The ethnic factor

One of the basic facts about Pakistan is that it is made up of more than one nation. Yet the importance of ethnicity has often been blatantly ignored in the past. A fervently nationalistic version of history has been promoted by successive governments. On the right, Islamic idealism has been preached and, on the left, Marxist dogmatism. Between them, these various ideologies conspired to bury or obscure the awkward truth that Pakistan as a nation still barely existed.

In the 1980s, the ethnic factor behind contemporary Pakistani politics has even been claimed to be the artificial and deliberate creation of martial law rulers allied to sinister cliques. This is a gross simplification of a much more complex reality. Pakistan's ethnic rivalries and clashes, along with local issues, have come to dominate national politics in large part because of long-term failures by rulers and politicians alike.

In the early part of Pakistan's development, it became obvious that – apart from the inadequacies of the country's politicians – it was sharp tensions between politicians of the West and East wings which plagued the new state. From 1958, with Pakistan's first military coup, Bengali alienation grew. Army rule effectively meant Punjabi rule, because of the preponderance of Punjabis in military service.

Sentiments of Bengali nationalism, but not yet separatism, became widespread. Many Bengalis came to feel their Eastern wing of Pakistan was being unfairly exploited for the benefit of non-Bengali rulers, and that they were victims of a neo-colonial relationship to the Urdu-speaking elite which dominated the country. Certainly they had serious economic grievances. Bengali jute exports supplied most of the country's foreign exchange, yet this was devoted to industrial development almost entirely in West Pakistan. Language disputes, over the relative places of Urdu and Bengali with English, proved another fertile source for discontent.

On top of existing grievances, in 1970 political leaders of the Bengali majority felt cheated of the results of general elections. The Punjabi-dominated army and bureaucratic establishment refused to recognise the popular verdict of the 1970 elections, and yield power up to Sheikh Mujibur Rehman's Awami League, which had won a majority of seats. The political crisis soon resulted in mass killings, civil war, mass exodus of refugees and, finally, in decisive intervention by the Indian army, which brought about disintegration of the two wings of Pakistan in 1971–72.

The emergence of East Pakistan as the separate state of Bangladesh was a deeply traumatic event for Pakistanis, which even now some have not come to terms with. The crisis did, however, help to end a long period of military rule, with the armed forces discredited and demoralised. This crisis provided the opportunity for the remarkable politician Z. A. Bhutto to become Prime Minister.

The shadow of former leaders

A populist landowner and lawyer masquerading as a radical Socialist, this former Foreign Minister and young protege of General Ayub Khan had founded his own political party in 1967. Zulfikar Ali Bhutto, chairman of the PPP, had a major impact on the country as Prime Minister, tapping and mobilising popular backing from the poorest classes, and giving them for the first time a stake in politics. However, Bhutto's policies of harsh repression of political opposition, together with nationalisation and lamentable mismanagement of the economy, proved disastrous, and fuelled militant opposition.

General Zia ul-Haq took over on 5 July 1977 after months of turmoil and chaos in the major cities, in demonstrations by a united opposition against Z. A. Bhutto's rigging of the general elections. The soft-spoken general declared that calm would quickly be restored by the army, pledging that he himself had no political ambitions and that elections would be held within 90 days. The General went on to become Pakistan's President and dictator right up to his death in a sabotaged air flight in August 1988.

General Zia surprised everyone, perhaps even himself, by his unsuspected talent for politics. He learned quickly how to manipulate people, and ran rings around the opposition parties. He played on uncertainty and personal ambitions so as to divide his opponents, and marginalise the professional politicians. Pakistani journalist Ahmed Rashid aptly wrote that, Zia "had the humility to learn about politics and the arrogance to use his authority forcefully".

After the protracted trial of Z. A. Bhutto on a charge of conspiracy to murder, and the hanging of the fallen Prime Minister in February 1979, Zia's position looked increasingly shaky. The economy was in deep trouble, with few foreign loans or friends, while political parties were demanding the long overdue elections. Zia was saved, however, by an international event – the Soviet military invasion of Afghanistan.

General fears of Soviet aggression in the wider Gulf region gave Zia the respectability he could not otherwise have hoped for in the West. From 1980, Pakistan was seen widely as a "front line" state deserving strong support by the West, Japan, Saudi Arabia, China and other states. Zia ably exploited this new interest in Pakistan, attracting considerable aid and loans. Large scale relief aid came too, through the United Nations High Commissioner for Refugees, to cope with the flood of Afghan refugees into Pakistani camps.

Among the bitterest legacies of Zia's policies are the growth of ethnic and religious sectarianism – often violent – together with the extension of the Afghan war to Pakistani towns by a terrorist bombing campaign mounted from Kabul. In addition to ethnic rivalries, tensions between the Sunni majority and the Shi'a minority (placed at between 15 and 20 per cent) grew rapidly under Zia.

The Pakistani dictator's various "Islamic" reforms and initiatives, far from uniting Pakistanis as Muslims, added to existing enmities between rival Muslim sects. The influential fundamentalist Muslim party Jama'at Islami backed Zia uncritically almost until the end, though its activists had many reservations about his sincerity in claims to introduce an Islamic order in Pakistan.

The move to partial democratisation in 1985 proved a considerable success. The "partyless politics" notion introduced was a fraud, but many politicians took part, and the popular vote was high. The wider opposition Movement for Restoration of Democracy (MRD) failed in the attempted boycott of elections, and a revived pro-government Muslim League took shape from 1985. Zia's nominee as Prime Minister was the colourless, middle aged Sindhi politician Mohammad Khan Junejo. He was abruptly dismissed from office by Zia in 1988, and then failed to win enough backing to keep the Muslim League leadership when pressed by a younger, more ambitious contender, Punjabi businessman–politician Nawaz Sharif.

The shadow cast by two dead political leaders, Z. A. Bhutto and General Zia ul-Haq, still hangs heavy over Pakistan today. Both are claimed as "shaheeds" (or martyrs) by their respective followers; Bhutto as the victim of a deliberate plot by generals, bureaucrats and judges, and Zia as the victim of sabotage by agents of foreign powers. The legacy of Bhutto – albeit a flawed one, which is partially disavowed or discarded – is the thing which keeps together the PPP under his daughter. For many in the IDA, Zia ul-Haq is held to be the symbol of patriotism and Islamic rectitude.

Because the PPP is currently in power, official patronage is naturally at the disposal of the fans of Z. A. Bhutto. In the state-controlled press, on TV as on radio, the term "shaheed" is now used regularly for Bhutto – as it had been for Zia after his death, under another regime.

On the tenth anniversary of the death of the hanged Prime Minister in February 1989, the government issued special stamps bearing portraits of Z. A. Bhutto, with "shaheed" printed after his name. The cult of Bhutto is set to grow, especially in his home province of Sind, with various official initiatives. The Department of Culture, for example, ordered construction work to begin in February 1989 on a Z. A. Bhutto memorial in Thatta, an ancient town near Karachi. As the fulsome tribute of the adviser to the chief Minister on Culture and Tourism declared: "The sacrifices of the late Prime Minister Zulfikar Ali Bhutto for the cause of democracy will be written in golden words in the history of Pakistan. This library-cum-museum in Thatta will not only benefit the younger generation of the district in inculcating in them reading habits, but also keep alive the name of Z. A. Bhutto for all time to come."

ETHNIC TENSIONS

Renewed rioting and killings in Karachi in spring and autumn 1989 served as a reminder that just beneath the surface stability, dangerous ethnic tensions were still lurking. Benazir Bhutto denounced in no uncertain terms the ethnic riots in Karachi as a deliberate attempt to undermine her government. Many Pakistanis would agree with this explanation of the troubles. Some even trace the sudden rise of the new party, MQM, to theories of secret help from Zia's government.

But the violence in Karachi, Hyderabad and other cities of Sind has been seen by many shrewd observers as a recurrent symptom of ethnic strife and rivalry between members of the various groups living there – Pushtuns (Pathans), Punjabis, Sindhis and above all the Mohajirs (literally "refugee",

Muslim migrants from India since 1947). At first the violence was between Pushtuns and Mohajirs, then between Sindhis and Mohajirs. While the earlier killings in 1986, mainly by Pushtun gangs controlling the drugs trade in areas of Karachi, are plausibly explained as being caused largely by a drugs "Mafia", this does not hold for more recent violence between Sindhis and Mohajirs. The diversion of Kalashnikov assault rifles and other weaponry meant for the Afghan war has helped to increase the scale of the killings.

The plight of the Biharis

The sharp ethnic tensions may help to explain the emotional reactions at the prospect of a final settling of the vexed issue of the Biharis. Speculation mounted in Pakistan in the early months of 1989 about the imminent repatriation from Bangladesh of the Biharis, also known as "stranded Pakistanis". Most members of this tragic minority of some 250,000 Urdu-speakers – many originally from Bihar, but also from United Provinces and other areas of India and long left languishing in Bangladeshi camps – desire passionately to be repatriated to Pakistan. Many did reach Pakistan from there in the 1970s. The plight of the remaining Bihari community, stranded in Bangladesh ever since the 1970 war, mostly despised and treated as unwelcome aliens, is certainly a humanitarian issue. In Pakistan it represents also an acute political dilemma.

Baluchi and Pathan nationalists have reacted sharply against a Bihari "incoming". The very solidarity with Pakistan shown by many Biharis during the traumatic civil war of 1971, ending with the break-up of the two wings of Pakistan, seems suspect to many members of the smaller ethnic groups. There are already three million Afghan refugees living in Pakistan, with no likelihood of their voluntary mass-return from North West Frontier Province and Baluchistan at least until the end of the fighting inside Afghanistan. Many Pakistanis assume, rightly or wrongly, that the majority of these Afghans will continue to stay on. In addition, there are small numbers of Iranian refugees, and many illegal migrants from Bangladesh in Karachi and other cities.

Responsibility for accepting the remaining Biharis has been long avoided by Pakistan. A Saudi offer to bear the heavy expenses of an airlift to Pakistan has not been taken up. A unanimous resolution passed by Pakistan's senate in 1985 promised to speed their repatriation. Reports of the imminent arrival of the first contingent of the Biharis mass-repatriation sparked off riots in Karachi in the first months of 1989, with heated emotional debates in the Pakistani Senate and press.

One condition of the original pact between the MQM and the PPP, which formed the basis of Benazir's ability to form a government in November 1988, was actually the repatriation of the Biharis. Some of the leaders of the MQM are themselves Bihari in origin. Yet precisely because the refugees at issue are stranded in Bangladesh, not India, there seems to be no unanimity among the Mohajir community of Pakistan as a whole on the desirability or moral obligation of accepting and resettling them.

For Sindhis, members of a community already outnumbered in their province of Sind, the prospect of more Bihari settlement is unwelcome and vigorously opposed, even by those spokesmen usually judged moderate. The stated grounds for opposition are economic as well as political. Some Sindhi nationalist spokesmen have deliberately exaggerated the numbers of Biharis involved into millions, so as to further fan the flames. The factor in deciding responses on this issue seems to be ethnic loyalties, not party affiliations. Only members of the Fundamentalist party Jamaat-i-Islami are apparently united in backing the proposed early repatriation.

Though areas of the Punjab were proposed as possible places of resettlement Sindhi spokesmen maintained that wherever the Biharis are settled in Pakistan, they would inevitably gravitate to Karachi and Hyderabad in Sind for jobs, like so many other migrants before them. The nightmare of the Sindhi nationalists is that they will soon become a minority in their own province – "the Red Indians" of Pakistan, as one self-pitying Sindhi spokesman phrased it. The possibility of a new wave of Bihari outsiders into Karachi is viewed with frank alarm.

Sindhi nationalist spokesmen have demanded the "release of the demographic imbalance" of Sind, by which euphemism is meant the forced removal of Punjabis and Pushtuns from Karachi and other areas of Sind to their respective provinces of origin. Perhaps because there seems absolutely no likelihood of such state intervention, Sindhi nationalists resorted in 1989 to issuing warnings that the existing ethnic conflict was being aggravated by a "revolutionary upsurge" among Sindhis.

They maintain that Sind stands on the threshold of a social revolution. As proof, they point to the November 1988 elections, in which the rural electorate of Sind for the first time rejected prominent feudal landlords and traditional political figures (the "waderas" and "pirs"), notably Pir Pagara, G. M. Jatoi and M. Junejo. In fact, the older generation of politicians lost out in Pakistan as a whole, being to a large extent replaced or marginalised by younger men.

MQM's rise to power

The campaign for repatriation of the Biharis is certainly complicated by the strained relations between Sindhi nationalists, the PPP government and MQM, as champion of Mohajir interests. Mohajirs traditionally claimed to be simply Pakistanis, often voting for religious right-wing parties. Without separate political organisations, and making no territorial claims, they were distinct from the other four major nationalities of Pakistan, the Punjabis, Sindhis, Pushtuns (or Pathans) and Baluchis.

In place of the term "Mohajir", "New Sindhi" had come into vogue – though it was often resented as patronising by some Mohajir elements. The early slogan of MQM activists: "We have identity cards, but no identity" was rapidly made irrelevant after their sensational electoral gains in Karachi and other urban areas of Sind province at the end of 1987. With the rise of MQM to power in the main cities of Sind, the demand is growing fast among the younger generation of Mohajirs for full formal recognition of the Mohajirs as Pakistan's fifth nationality, with all that this implies in the way of state patronage and jobs, reserved places in educational institutions, and so on.

The rise of the MQM as the organised political force of Pakistan's fifth "nationality" marks the decline of the Pakistan ideal, and the frank recognition among a young generation of leaders sprung from the lower classes that aggressive demands for rights by community leaders pay off.

Baluch nationalism

Baluchistan used to be known as Pakistan's problem province, with internal tensions and grievances alienating the younger educated Baluchis to a dangerous degree. Baluch nationalism and the bitter legacy of the civil war in the 1970s are still to be reckoned with, but now it is Sind which presents the main challenge to the central government.

There was a crisis when the newly-elected Baluchistan Assembly was dissolved, early in 1989, but the PPP government wisely appointed the veteran Baluch politician Nawab Akbar Bugti to be chief minister of the province, in place of a fragile coalition of parties including the PPP. There are grounds for hoping that the dangerous power vacuum in Baluchistan may be over, and that Baluch political dissidence can be contained.

The dream of an independent Baluch state, taking in also the Iranian portion of Baluchistan, is steadily receding. Separatist sentiments lack grassroots appeal. Baluchis are in fact in a minority in both of the only true cities to be found in the entire Baluchi desert region, Quetta in Pakistan and Zahedan across the Iranian frontier.

The most vigorous centres of Baluch nationalism are actually outside Baluchistan, in Karachi and western areas of Sind province, besides the Gulf where many Baluch workers have prospered. Another small group of unreconciled Baluch tribesmen is still living in exile in Afghanistan's Qandahar province, where they fled 14 years ago, after joint Pakistani-Iranian forces put down the tribal uprising.

The Pakistani portion of Baluchistan is about equal in size to Italy. It is Pakistan's largest province but has by far the smallest population, mostly living in great poverty. The local economy has benefited in the 1980s, however, by large-scale US development aid. This is a valuable source of funding and work, but a controversial one, because the left-wing opposition is convinced that the operation is really meant to hide the building of US strategic bases on the Makran coast.

Besides the US-aid programmes, new business ventures have been started up there, mainly by entrepreneurial Punjabis and Pushtuns. Baluchis want a bigger share of the cake. They also want their distinct identity recognised, together with some form of autonomy. But the old goal of a separate, independent state for Baluchis of Pakistan, Iran and Afghanistan is seen by nearly all as unrealistic. More Baluchis now occupy posts of influence within the administration, making less valid the nationalist complaint that Baluchistan is nothing better than a colony of the Punjab, ruled by a Punjabi army.

Now, at least, the abundant natural gas of the area is available for heating homes in the province, instead of being piped eastwards from Sui and other gasfields to industrial centres of the Punjab and Karachi. This new availability of gas is a gesture, a token concession to Baluch nationalism. It does not go any way, though, towards satisfying the demand that the financial benefits of the gas should be devoted to development exclusively for the Baluchi's own backward province.

IMPACT OF HEROIN

The extraordinary spread and growth of drugs production and smuggling through the 1980s in Pakistan is beyond doubt. This has been the main factor behind the massive influx of money into the country. High-grade heroin is smuggled out to the world's markets via Karachi or Lahore, with connivance from officials of all grades, and goes to fuel corruption as well as inflation in Pakistan. The export of heroin and opium grown and processed inside Afghanistan and the Pushtun tribal belt of Pakistan's northern frontiers was stimulated by war and anarchy inside Afghanistan in the past decade, together with the decline of drug production in the "Golden Triangle" countries of southeast Asia.

Besides feeding an ever-expanding domestic market, Pakistani-smuggled heroin has had a big impact in Iran and Saudi Arabia, besides in its main markets of Western Europe and the USA. Estimates of Pakistan's share of the trade in heroin with Western countries placed it at around 60 per cent by 1989. With estimated drugs earnings reaching four billion dollars annually, they were worth more than Pakistan's legal exports, or even total remittances from overseas workers.

Drugs money has enriched many individuals, including prominent public figures, or their close relatives, and officials of the Pakistan government. However, it has brought few tangible benefits to Pakistan's economy. The bulk of Pakistan's "black money" is held in non-productive investments, mainly in the form of bank deposits, real estate and undeclared business assets.

A grim warning was given by a Pakistani committee which studied the drugs problem in 1986: unless checked by drastic measures – vigorous prosecution of offenders at all levels of the business, punishments by long prison terms and confiscation of assets – "the illegal transactions and black money will eventually equal, or perhaps surpass, the legitimate open economy". While penalties for drugs smuggling were sharply increased in 1988 by the Junejo government, they failed to bite. Official efforts since then to curb heroin production have proved, so far at least, by and large irrelevant.

Combating the drugs epidemic

Growing numbers of drugs addicts in Pakistan bear witness to the domestic impact of the flourishing drugs trade. The heroin culture has spread its insidious effects at all levels of society, especially among the young. Official estimates by the Pakistan Narcotics Board in 1988 stated there were 1.9 million drug users, mostly in the 20 to 30 age group, half of them heroin-users.

Even this alarming figure may be understating the problem.

Doctors and social workers in Karachi and Lahore believe there may be as many as two million addicts in the country as a whole. About 80 per cent of these heroin-users are believed to be in the 18 to 28 age group. A 1988 survey estimated that one in ten of Karachi's population was using drugs. This heroin epidemic is one of the most urgent problems facing the administration, and to some extent the government has recognised it. Despite the fact that Benazir Bhutto pledged at the time of the general elections to spend considerably more money to combat the drugs menace, the Pakistani drugs barons have powerful patrons. The formidable task of overcoming the heroin challenge will require enormous dedication, and consistent efforts as well as state money.

The impact of the official crusade against drugs, launched in April 1989, was being called into question within months. Of the scores of minor customs officials and police officers whose arrest had been ordered, many were freed on bail, while several others managed to abscond. Only one figure of real importance in the Pakistani drug smuggling business had been arrested by October 1989, Haji Iqbal Baig – proudly described by a senior official as "the kingpin of the world's heroin trade", operating from Lahore. But by a farcical sequence of events, Baig was soon released on bail because of what officials lamely described as lack of evidence.

The death in Karachi in October 1989 of a senior Pakistani anti-narcotics agent, (Altaf Ali Khan, regional director of Pakistan Narcotics Control Board), added to speculation that a Colombian-style drugs war was beginning in Pakistan. Though shoot-outs between well-armed gangs and customs or police units were common, there were in fact few other indications that Pakistan's drug barons were directly challenging state power.

In the Western Asia region there was growing recognition of the extent of drug smuggling from Pakistan and Afghanistan, and the need for drastic action. Iran initiated a national campaign against drug addiction from January 1989, with public executions of hundreds of smugglers, forced registration of addicts and setting up of labour camps to 'reclaim' victims of drugs in each province. Iran stated it was considering laying minefields across its long eastern border, so as to deter drug smugglers. Saudi Arabia, for its part, introduced the death penalty for drug trafficking in 1987.

POPULATION PRESSURES

Pakistan's population growth, at 2.9 per cent annually, is among Asia's highest. It deeply worries the country's planners, who see considerable economic progress swallowed up by the increasing numbers of extra mouths to feed. With 107 million people in 1989, Pakistan ranked as the ninth most populous country in the world. Its population will reach at least 150 million by the year 2000, if present trends continue.

It should be all the more surprising, then, that family planning in Pakistan lacks firm state backing and encouragement. Under Zia's rule, such neglect was generally explained by the government's sensitivity to the Islamic lobby, suspicious of any interference in what was generally regarded as a private matter. The idea of family planning and the availability of contraception have still barely penetrated the villages of Pakistan, and are by and large restricted to the middle classes.

Poverty varies greatly in rural areas of Pakistan. In the Punjab, for instance, many villagers have become better off over the past decade. Safe drinking water supplies are a major unresolved problem in rural Pakistan. "Only 9.7 per cent of the entire population of Pakistan enjoys proper sanitation and sewerage facilities; and only 26.8 per cent of the entire population has access to clean drinking water", according to Iqbal Khan (*Fresh Perspectives on India and Pakistan*, 1985).

The problems caused by rapid growth of population are particularly evident in Pakistan's cities. With their infrastructure already under heavy strain, the crowded urban areas are set to expand massively through the 1990s. Already accounting for 28 per cent of the population by 1986, the cities are likely to hold 44 per cent of an expanded population of some 150 million by the end of the century.

In standards of urban housing and sanitation, Pakistan is considerably ahead of India. However, severe shortages of houses for the lower income groups living in the cities have led to the proliferation of overcrowded slums and illegal *katchi abadis* (shanty towns). A conservative estimate at the beginning of the 1980s concluded that 116,000 new houses were needed annually to accommodate the additional number of households, while the actual total of housing units constructed was only 3,300 per year. The election campaign of the PPP in 1988 promised to provide houses and jobs for millions of the needy, but virtually nothing had been achieved towards this goal by the end of the Bhutto government's first year of power.

Rapid rural migration to the large cities has caused social and economic dislocation. In the 1980s, the spread of drugs and related activities of so-called "heroin mafias", together with the easy availability of automatic weapons filtered off from the Afghan war, combined to aggravate existing social tensions in the country's largest city, Karachi.

Karachi, with an estimated ten million people, has the greatest concentration of industry, and the country's sole large port. The breakdown of law and order and acute ethnic tensions among large sections of Karachi's slum-dwellers from 1986 became a focus of great concern and official enquiry. The Karachi disturbances, warned Pakistan's Institute of Policy Studies, were symptoms of a sense of deprivation and frustration which, "may cross the limit of tolerance if the situation is allowed to persist".

AFGHANISTAN ISSUES

The problem of Afghanistan has dominated Pakistan's foreign relations since 1980. Pakistan's role in the Afghan resistance to the Soviet-backed Kabul government remains crucial. As a safe haven for guerrillas, a base for exile parties and refuge for three million refugees, Pakistan has been vital to the Afghan opposition's long struggle against a communist regime backed by the Soviet Union's resources.

The image of the Afghan resistance has shifted gradually. In 1989, instead of conquering heroes, the Afghan *mujahidin* look more like pawns in a geopolitical chess game. Their inability to bring down the Najibullah regime within months of the completion of Soviet military withdrawal in February 1989 showed up their deficiencies. Their failure to capture Jalalabad, with heavy casualties inflicted, led to a crisis in morale. Either Jalalabad or Kandahar, the historic capital of the country and a major military base, would have made ideal centres for a provisional government to challenge that of the People's Democratic Party (PDPA) in Kabul. It would also have liberated parties from Pakistani and other outside influences.

The splits within the guerrilla resistance seem to be almost the greatest asset of the embattled PDPA regime. Repeated attempts to forge real unity between the rival parties, along with a credible alternative government have failed abjectly. Certainly there are cases of outstanding commanders who have created effective parallel administrations and genuine, cross-party unity in their respective areas. These achievements are rare, however, and there is no one guerrilla commander who has a serious prospect of gathering popular and cross-party backing throughout the country as a whole. The sole national figure commanding wide respect and support among the Afghan people is the 74 year old ex-king Zahir Shah, an exile in Rome since 1973. A compromise peace solution, with the ex-king as one element, is still conceivable, but unlikely.

The opposition "Islamic Alliance" simply papers the cracks between the seven rival party leaders based in Pakistan. These internal political divisions and continuing rivalries between the leaders in Peshawar were increasingly criticised by commanders in 1989, after the fiasco of a "Shura" or national Assembly which took place in Rawalpindi, Pakistan, during February 1989. Although the Shura declared an interim government formed from representatives of the seven parties, it was recognised by only four Muslim states, taking the vacant seat for Afghanistan in the Saudi-backed Islamic Conference Organisation.

The blatant manipulation and interference in the Shura by Pakistan's ISI alienated many Afghan nationalists, and many guerrilla commanders refused to attend, though nominated by the parties to which they were linked. Pakistan's most powerful military agency the ISI had long since taken responsiblity for allocating foreign weapons to the various parties and field commanders, but its crude interference in a supposedly independent Afghan initiative was bitterly resented. This, together with the Jalalabad offensive which followed, reportedly ordered by the ISI, proved definitely counter-productive.

The Kabul regime headed by President Najibullah, clearly expects to profit by the divisions within the resistance, believing that time is on its side, with the prospect of protracted fighting. It has repeatedly offered to acknowledge the power and authority of major guerrilla commanders in their respective regions, by recognising them as governors. To date, though, not one of the outstanding or really important commanders has defected to the PDPA side, although some are alienated from their leaders and the party system.

The PDPA itself is still plagued by factionalism, but it does have a core of solid support from activists who are organised, trained and well armed. The PDPA government, still enjoying firm backing from the USSR, represents itself as progressive, and the sole alternative to a wretched state of brutal anarchy. In Kabul, with over 1.5 million people, half of them internal war refugees, it has a natural constituency.

Support comes especially from the younger people of both sexes, attending schools, education courses and Kabul University. Youth is where propaganda for the regime is targeted. The regime is able to capitalise on people's worries for the future. Many Kabulis, though often hostile to the Soviet presence and communist rule, fear any takeover by Muslim extremists keen to enforce their own narrow, dogmatic views on how society should be organised.

There is a basic difference between the strict vision of a fundamentalist Islamic state, and the moderate, conservative ideal of many, probably most Afghans, of returning to the pre-communist past. Many yearn for the traditional society of the majority living in rural areas, co-existing with the modern, secular-minded society of Kabul, under the form of limited democracy introduced by King Zahir Shah in 1964.

The Alliance of Seven Parties

The tension between these irreconcilable visions is, of course, one reason (apart from personal rivalries and ambitions) why the Alliance of Seven Parties is only a very conditional one. Whether such an alliance can continue much longer, even in name, is a question being asked by many Afghans. Virtual civil war broke out in summer 1989 in northern areas between guerrillas of two major parties, Jamiat-i-Islami and Hizb-i-Islami of Gulbuddin Hekmatyar (the most controversial leader, favoured by the ISI and Pakistani fundamentalist circles). The trigger was an ambush by a commander of Gulbuddin Hekmatyar which killed a band of Jamiat guerrillas. This episode caused an open confrontation between the two leaders, and the resignation of Hekmatyar from his post as foreign minister for the interim government.

The opposition Alliance was clung to out of self-interest from 1985, because each of the seven parties benefited, even if unequally, by the existence of the "arms pipeline" through Pakistan. If US, Saudi and Chinese arms deliveries were ended, or possibly blocked by a Pakistan government at some stage, it would provide the impetus for the frank abandonment of the Alliance.

The removal of Zia from the political scene inevitably called into question Pakistan's policy of firm support for the Afghan opposition to the Kabul regime. Although it has been asserted since from Islamabad that there would be no change in the policy goal, no elected civilian government could ignore indefinitely the build-up of worries among Pakistanis about their country's deep involvement in the Afghan war.

This mood of disenchantment was aggravated by hundreds of bomb explosions in Pakistani cities and towns, attributed to the Afghan intelligence service KHAD. The Bhutto government is bound to try to end this war, sooner or later, rather than back indefinitely what looks like a stalemate, or a lost cause.

General Zia ul-Haq himself seemed quite impervious to deepening public worries and overt hostility over the Afghan war. Pakistani opinion has become polarised, with some keen supporters of the Afghan *jihad*, but many eager to see relations regularised with Kabul, and the refugees sent back across the border. Cynicism has become general about what is often called dismissively "an American war". Like so many refugees elsewhere, the Afghans have become scapegoats for the entire range of problems seen in Pakistan, from the many bomb explosions, flourishing heroin trade, violence and crime to overcrowding in the cities and unwelcome competition for scarce jobs.

An independent Pushtunistan?

One option for Kabul is the revival of the semi-dormant Pushtunistan issue. This is the demand for an independent state for the Pushtun and Baluch peoples of Pakistan – a demand by the Afghan government ever since Pakistan was created in 1947. The political pressures used by Kabul in the past included the symbolic trappings of a nation-state – a special flag, stamps and an annual ceremony for "Pushtunistan Day", meant to mark Afghan solidarity with the Pushtuns (Pathans) and Baluch of Pakistan. This campaign could be revived in the future.

The exodus of almost three million Afghan refugees into Pakistan has created many political consequences, besides the obvious economic burden on Pakistan. Its political impact is particularly clear in the two border provinces of Peshawar and Quetta. Some Pakistanis fear the creation of a second Lebanon, with the well-armed Afghans in their camps competing for power as the Palestinians did in Lebanon and Jordan.

One Doomsday scenario sees the Afghan refugees and guerrillas staying on in Pakistan permanently, but their leaders not giving up their political ambitions, nor their formidable armouries. It could have profound political consequences for Pakistan. Since most of the refugees are Pushtuns, their permanent settlement in Pakistan would effectively change the sensitive ethnic map along this tribal borderland region.

Ties with China

From the outset of the Afghan guerrilla war, China was a major supplier of weapons for the resistance based in Pakistan. There is no doubting the importance of Pakistan's ties with China. Most Pakistanis in fact look on China as a far more reliable ally and friend than the USA, based on experience over the past 25 years at times of crisis, especially during the war with India. When US military aid to Pakistan and India was cut off in the 1965 war between the two neighbours, China became the single most important supplier of weapons to Pakistan. After the war had ended, it was China again which stepped in to provide help with a new ordnance factory.

Though never the sole supplier of military technology, China has continued to give valuable military and economic assistance to Pakistan. Early doubts and hesitations at relying upon a communist state faded fast in Islamabad, and China began to be seen as a vital strategic counter-balance to India's goal of hegemony in the subcontinent. The building of the famous Karakoram Highway, linking Chinese and Pakistani territory across Central Asia, symbolised this mutual trust. This close relationship weathered successive changes of government in Pakistan without any repercussions. Predictably, the shooting in Tiananmen Square by the People's Liberation Army did not provoke critical comments from Islamabad, nor did it prevent the visit to Pakistan of Chinese Prime Minister Li Peng in November 1989.

Besides US tanks, F16s and French warships, Pakistan's armed forces have a large Chinese element in their weapons systems. In the building of short- and medium-range surface to surface missiles by Pakistan, Chinese technology played a big part, as it did in the semi-covert nuclear programme started under Z. A. Bhutto. The Air Force received a squadron of F7P fighter aircraft from China in November 1989, and Silkworm missiles are expected early in 1990.

IRAN AS A REGIONAL ALLY

Relations are rapidly improving between Iran and Pakistan. There are sound political and economic reasons why this process should continue, and become more important in economic and military areas. Pakistan is keen to develop the links which have grown considerably since the mid-1980s. Iran, for its part, is definitely looking to its non-Arab neighbours with more interest now than at any time since the Islamic Revolution. This comes from the strong sense in Tehran that the Arab world is irreconcilably hostile – with the exception of Syria. With President Rafsanjani in control, and the moderate Ali Akbar Velayati remaining Foreign Minister, a pragmatic rather than ideological foreign policy looks certain.

On the Afghanistan issue, the two governments have widely different views, though they both hope that a united grouping of Afghan guerrilla parties will eventually replace the Soviet-backed PDPA regime led by President Najibullah. Tehran was keenly disappointed over the failure of the Afghan "Shura" in Rawalpindi in February 1989 to agree terms for sharing power in a joint interim government with the Afghan Shi'a Muslim parties grouped in an eight-party council. In the event, the Shura proceedings were totally dominated by the seven exile parties, based in Pakistan. It is, of course, their Sunni leaders (dubbed the "seven dwarfs" by critical Afghans) who are favoured by Pakistan's ISI.

Holding out as patron of the Shi'a Muslim minority in Afghanistan, Iran is concerned to get this group's leaders represented in the interim government. Of the eight Shi'a "parties" in a Tehran-based Council, some do have well organised guerrilla groups active on many fronts, with backing from the Hazara minority of central Afghanistan and from Shi'a communities in Kabul, Herat and Kandahar. But the claims made for 30 per cent representation of Shi'as in an interim cabinet, appear exaggerated as well as potentially dangerous to many Afghans.

Iran and Pakistan have other significant differences over foreign policy. Pakistan maintains close relations with Saudi Arabia and the other Gulf states. The Pakistani military presence in the Gulf remains considerable, even after the return of army units from Saudi Arabia.

There is a marked contrast in official attitudes towards the USSR and Western countries, notably the USA. Pakistan may be a non-aligned state, but its government's closeness to the USA, and its dependence upon Western economic aid and loans are a fact of life. As far as the Pakistani establishment is concerned, its "Great Satan", if such there is, is surely India, not the USA. For Iran, on the other hand, India is a valued partner in trade and technological transfer, besides being a key member of the Non-Aligned Movement which Iran is keen to influence.

Economic co-operation

In the economic field, at least, co-operation is going forward. The ideal of a mini-Asian common market – something dear to the late Shah of Iran – has been revived between Iran, Pakistan and Turkey. If there is a change of regime in Kabul, Afghanistan would also be invited to join in a new Economic Co-operation Organisation.

The basis for a preferential trading system between Iran, Pakistan and Turkey was actually laid in March 1987. At that time, Iran's ambassador in Islamabad, Ali Musavi, claimed it would not be unrealistic to expect Iran–Pakistan annual trade to increase to 800 million dollars. During the war years, Iran found in Turkey a major supplier of goods, industrial as well as agricultural. Pakistan's trade has been only relatively modest in comparison. A barter agreement between Pakistan and Iran for a total value of 400 million dollars in 1988 exchanged 20,000 barrels per day of crude oil for 100,000 tonnes of Pakistani rice. Surplus sugar and wheat have also been exported.

There have been difficulties in expanding barter trade beyond a relatively modest level. Only limited quantities of Pakistani surplus agricultural products (mainly wheat, sugar and rice) have been available for barter trade against Iran's oil. There were disagreements over terms of trade in past years. Pakistan certainly wants Iranian oil at the right price, to make up its shortfall. Iran is keen to export non-oil items.

Military links

Currently, it is joint production ventures in the military field which are being actively explored. They follow on recent announcements of the development of Pakistani weapons systems, including two types of surface to surface missiles with ranges of 80 km and 300 km. Pakistan is building a jet trainer, with Chinese technical help, and also aims to manufacture tanks by 1991. Iran itself has made strides in military production from 1980, under the pressure of the long war against Iraq, but many factories were being turned over to civilian production in 1989.

An Iranian defence delegation which visited Pakistan in March 1989 was led, significantly enough, by Ali Shamkhani, Minister for the Revolutionary Guards Corps (Pasdaran), the parallel military force to the regular army of Iran. In Tehran, Shamkhani declared that Iran and Pakistan would form "an Islamic defence line in the region". Vague though this description was, it was taken to refer to the projected military alliance, or more likely a looser link-up, between the armed forces of Pakistan, Iran and Turkey, together with Afghanistan in future. Periodic diplomatic upsets between Tehran and Ankara do not augur well for a full-blown tripartite alliance.

PAKISTAN'S MILITARY ROLE IN THE GULF

As supplier of military manpower in the Third World, Pakistan was second by 1981, placed next to Cuba. It had military contingents or missions, large and small, in 22 countries, with most in seven states – Saudi Arabia, the United Arab Emirates (UAE), Oman, Kuwait, Jordan, Syria and Libya. This was, by any standards, a curious combination of states to be linked to Pakistan in the sensitive area of military aid. It reflected Pakistan's reputation for military competence, as well as earlier links with a variety of regimes in the Middle East, ranging from ultra-conservative Saudi Arabia to Libya and Syria.

In was in the Gulf region where Pakistan's military expertise was most in demand, not in carrying on wars but in training and internal defence. Military technicians of the army, air force and navy were being provided by Pakistan in many Gulf states, to help operate sophisticated equipment. Pakistani armour and artillery experts, engineers and pilots on contract were particularly numerous in the Gulf states. In 1983 Saudi Arabia and Pakistan signed two security co-operation agreements, with the emphasis on internal defence for the Kingdom.

The naval presence is striking in Saudi Arabia, Oman and the UAE. Besides the hundreds of Pakistani officers and technicians serving in warships and naval establishments in Gulf Co-operation Council (GCC) states Pakistani instructors were also prominent at the new Saudi naval school in Jubail, open to all six GCC states. A powerful Pakistani naval force visited GCC ports in 1985, and according to some reports a large part of Pakistani naval strength was stationed in Gulf waters from 1985. Karachi itself has the best naval and logistic facilities in the entire Gulf region.

Besides the loaning of Pakistani technicians and the deployment of units in the Gulf states, officers from Saudi Arabia and other Gulf states are regularly trained in military institutions in Pakistan itself.

This expanding military role of Pakistan became the target of fierce condemnation by domestic critics, who claimed that this development was proof that the 520,000 strong armed forces were simply mercenaries hired out to Arab potentates. Some published estimates, of a total of 40,000 or even 50,000 Pakistani military personnel serving abroad by 1985 were certainly exaggerated, but the numbers clearly were large before the phased withdrawal of a Pakistani division from Saudi Arabia from the end of 1987.

"Policeman of the Gulf"?

This formidable Pakistani military presence came about, so many critics claimed, because of US pressure on Pakistan to replace Iran as the "policeman of the Gulf", after the collapse of the Shah's regime. A number of factors came together. The emergence of the Khomeini regime in Iran along with the seizure of Makka's Great Mosque in 1979 and the outbreak of war between Iran and Iraq all combined to impress on the Arab Gulf rulers Iran's weakness in defence and security matters.

It was natural for them to turn to Pakistan, since they already enjoyed a close working relationship. And it was natural for the Pakistani military to agree to play a bigger role in return for enhanced financial rewards. Such a policy neatly combined the goals of Pakistan's military rulers with US security priorities in the wider region. On the other hand, this expanding Pakistani military role in the weaker conservative Arab states of the Gulf clearly had much to do with the strategic requirements of the US Central Command (Centcom). New port facilities were being developed at Gwadar and other places along Baluchistan's Makran coast. As American analysts were not slow to point out, by early 1982 the USA and Pakistan appeared ready to renew a defence relationship which had been in a state of suspension ever since 1965. It was built on the realisation in Washington that Pakistan represented high strategic–military value:

> "There has long been a propensity in Washington to regard the Pakistani military as first-rate, smart and professional, certainly on any comparative standard . . . Its military is among the few that can effectively assimilate high-technology weapon systems, if only in limited amounts."
>
> (Robert G. Wirsing and James M. Roberty, *The United States and Pakistan*, International Affairs, London, Autumn 1982)

The hiring out of military manpower paralleled Pakistan's export of manpower in the civil field. Individuals have benefited from it by enhanced pay, and at the same time Pakistan's armed forces also gain. As a provider of military personnel to Saudi Arabia, the Pakistan government and military personnel have gained alike financially. In addition to large payments for the supply of military units, the Saudis reportedly paid for large amounts of US weaponry supplied to Pakistan's armed forces in the early 1980s. Not only did this arrangement help generate income to buy weapons, it provided access for Pakistanis to the most sophisticated types of Western military hardware being bought by the GCC states.

Pakistan's military role in the Middle East had, of course, begun much earlier, in the era of the Baghdad Pact (1955), and its successor organisation the Central Treaty Organisation (CENTO), set up in 1959. Indeed, its antecedents can be traced back to the two World Wars, when the British Indian army played a major part in the fighting throughout the Middle East and North Africa.

RELATIONS WITH INDIA

The outlook for improved relations between Pakistan and India was looking considerably better by mid-1989, when it was frequently asserted in public that because both Rajiv Gandhi and Benazir Bhutto were markedly younger than previous holders of power, without the bitter personal memories of the tragic events of the Partition period, they would be able to bring about a rapprochement. But by the beginning of 1990, when Rajiv Gandhi had been replaced by V. P. Singh, the process of overcoming the longstanding and ingrained distrust between the two countries had been set back once more.

Cautious hopes for improving bilateral relations as well as promoting greater regional unity had come from membership of the South Asian Association for Regional Co-operation (SAARC). Pakistan's new Prime Minister met Rajiv Gandhi for the first time at SAARC's summit meeting in Islamabad in December 1988, where three agreements were signed – the first for 17 years. These were pledges not to attack each others' nuclear facilities, and agreements on cultural exchanges and avoiding double taxation. Admittedly, these agreements did not amount to much in themselves, but it was hoped they would be a foundation for future deals.

During her visits to the USA and Britain in summer 1989, Benazir Bhutto made plain Pakistan's apprehensions over India's rapidly growing military power, giving it regional Superpower status in the South Asia region. The test firing of India's Agni missile, capable of carrying a two-ton conventional or nuclear payload 1500 miles, made Pakistanis even more nervous than the massive expansion of India's ocean-going fleet.

Rajiv Gandhi's visit to Pakistan in July 1989 marked the first bilateral visit to Pakistan by an Indian Prime Minister in almost 30 years. In their speeches the two leaders talked of "an end to fear between their countries" and agreements on arms control and nuclear non-proliferation, but Rajiv Gandhi acknowledged "real problems" over the Siachen region.

An undeclared war

The disputed Siachen glacier has become since 1984 the world's highest battlefield, where soldiers fight in sub-zero conditions, breathing air with under half the standard oxygen content. The utterly barren Siachen region in the uppermost Himalayas is 19,000 feet high, with winter blizzards and temperatures of minus 60C making conditions highly dangerous. Estimated casualties were by 1989 in the thousands, with the costs also high: Pakistan was deploying 4000 troops and spending up to 60 million dollars annually, and India perhaps double that amount.

Siachen is, in fact, an undeclared war between the two neighbour states, the fourth fought since Partition and independence in 1947. The fighting in Siachen has no end in sight, despite the supposed improvement in relations between the two countries by mid-1989 and the personal warmth between Benazir Bhutto and the ex-Prime Minister of India. However, for reasons of prestige alone, neither government can afford to be seen as ceding an inch of disputed territory in the Kashmir region claimed by both states. Both governments have to face a chauvinistic element at home which would seize on any "softness" towards the traditional national enemy.

Far from warm before, Indo-Pakistani relations had deteriorated sharply from 1984. Two main factors were responsible: the Sikh terrorist movement in India's Punjab state and Pakistan's nuclear programme. After Mrs Gandhi's assassination in 1984, Rajiv Gandhi made much of Pakistan's role in arming and training Sikh terrorists. Some Kalashnikovs were traced to Pakistan – but was this government policy or the operation of market forces? Although the Indian population by and large believe in Indian claims about Pakistani help to Sikh terrorists, it is very difficult for an independent observer to check the validity of Indian evidence.

The nuclear rivalry of both states is three decades old, but became much more serious after 1974, when India exploded a nuclear device, and entered the nuclear club. The crash-programme ordered by Z. A. Bhutto was, of course, continued under General Zia ul-Haq, and fancifully named by many journalists "the Islamic Bomb". In denouncing Pakistan's alleged nuclear weapons programme, Rajiv Gandhi appeared to be exploiting Indian nationalist sentiments. Differences over the Afghanistan issue also contributed to the slide in bilateral relations.

There are many pointers indicating a strong current among ordinary Pakistanis and Indians alike to rebuild the frozen relations between the two states, and a conviction that the costly rivalry of the past should at last be discarded. Speaking for them in a speech made one week before Zia ul-Haq's death, Pakistani Senator Javed Jabbar declared:

> "The India–Pakistan situation is a unique example in the world whereby the people of both the countries desperately aspire for friendship and harmony, while powerful vested interests both inside and outside the two governments hold them back."

When Pakistan finally rejoined the Commonwealth in October 1989, the timing had much to do with India's veto, which had prevented a formal application by Pakistan to rejoin under Zia ul-Haq. It also seemed appropriate that its Prime Minister was the daughter of the very man who had taken the decision to quit the organisation in 1972.

Sri Lanka

Pakistan's policies towards its neighbours in the subcontinent have been largely determined by their relations with India. Sri Lanka is the prime example. Prior to the India–Sri Lanka accord of July 1987, it was India which had been aiding Tamil separatist groups, and Pakistan backing the small Sri Lankan army, to improve its training and equipment. When the Indian air force dropped food, medicine and other supplies over the Jaffna peninsula in June 1987, in an independent initiative to help Tamil civilians caught in the fighting, it was Pakistan which led criticism by other regional states for what was claimed to be violation of airspace and an infringement of international law.

The sending of Indian troops to Sri Lanka and their active involvement in fighting against Liberation Tiger guerrillas of Tamil Eelam was resented in Islamabad. To some Pakistani circles it was more evidence of India's ambitions to establish its predominance over the Indian Ocean region. This impression was reinforced by the rapidity with which Indian forces were sent to the Maldives in 1988 to quash a coup attempt.

Bangladesh

Though it took four years for Pakistan to recognise the independent existence of Bangladesh, relations gradually improved after 1974. There was limited trade and contacts remained correct rather than close. A somewhat closer relationship developed only after 1982, when General Ershad came to power in a military coup. Some observers see General Ershad's policies as closely modelled on those of his Pakistani counterpart. Certainly the disputes each state had with India helped to bring them together. The two generals were instrumental in the formation of SAARC, formally launched in Dhaka in December 1985. India was a somewhat reluctant member, fearing that the organisation would be exploited by its smaller neighbours whom Pakistan would lead on to criticise India.

PAKISTAN'S ECONOMIC PERFORMANCE

Pakistan's economy has had an impressive growth rate coupled with a significant rise in real wages over the past decade. Although the economy's general performance has been uneven, it produced some striking successes, with record crops of cotton, wheat and rice going to fuel an export drive. Annual economic growth has average almost seven per cent of GDP since 1979. However, most economists agree that this remarkable growth rate cannot be sustained over the long-term without much greater investment. Pakistan's domestic savings are a mere 4.5 per cent of its GDP, as contrasted with India's 20 per cent.

One of Pakistan's urgent needs is to mobilise existing domestic savings for productive purposes. One way this was attempted was by Islamisation of banking, and various other "Islamic" measures introduced, in part at least, to overcome past reluctance by pious Muslims to invest or lend their money through normal commercial banking channels. This strategy has, however, had little impact, to date, on the level of savings in Pakistan.

A fragile balance of payments position is something which Pakistani planners have long had to live with. But the scale of remittances from Pakistani workers in the Gulf during the 1980s – 3.2 billion dollars annually at their peak – served to relax the country's balance of payments problems, and reduce the trade deficit. The decision in 1982 to make the Pakistani rupee independent of the US dollar, and its gradual slide in value, helped to make Pakistani exports more price-competitive on world markets.

The Sixth Five-Year Plan (1983–88) set out to solve the basic problem that Pakistan regularly imported twice as much as it exported. The Plan envisaged a massive concentration of resources on agriculture together with energy development, along with much higher investment in neglected sectors such as health, rural water supply and basic education. However, economists had early on criticised the Sixth Plan – costed at Rs 490 billion (33 billion dollars) – as being totally unrealistic, and tailored more to IMF demands than to Pakistan's own priorities.

Their criticisms were largely justified. By the time the civilian government under Prime Minister Junejo came to power in February 1985, this Plan had effectively been scrapped. All of the Plan's targets for spending in these social areas, as in other fields, had fallen far behind, for lack of domestic resources. However, the government's determination to expand exports was further spelled out in June 1987 by the Commerce Ministry, which outlined details of a three-year trade policy, holding out as its goal the doubling of exports by 1990.

Foreign currency receipts

Estimates of Pakistan's total receipts of foreign currency placed these at 40 billion dollars in the period 1980–85. These were made up of: export earnings (15 billion dollars), remittances (15 billion dollars) and foreign aid (10 billion dollars). However, the potential benefits of these large sums to help fund the country's development were lost, for the most part, because they went largely to pay for imports of consumer goods and servicing foreign loans, which had grown by 1988 to 14 billion dollars. Pakistan's economy has been living "on borrowed time and borrowed money", according to one of the key architects of the country's financial planning, Dr Mahbubul Haq. Foreign aid and loans have regularly financed around one-fifth of the country's annual budget.

The decade 1978–88 saw non-development expenditure rise from Rs 25 billion (in 1977–78) to Rs 125 billion in 1987–88. Defence spending rose sixfold in this decade, accounting for between 32 and 38 per cent of total current expenditure. However, in the budget announced by the Bhutto government in 1989, half a year after taking office, defence spending rose just 1.3 per cent to Rs 51.76 billion. The scale of military spending by Pakistan has placed it among the highest in Asia. It is keenly resented by the majority of the public, which appears to believe the generals are pampering the military, rather than simply re-equipping the armed forces in dangerous times.

Although the World Bank and other institutions have repeatedly declared their concern over Pakistan's worsening budget deficits, yet the Pakistan Aid Consortium have committed aid over recent years at a higher level than anticipated. For 1987–88 the Consortium offered 2.4 billion dollars. Commitments of 2.5 billion dollars for 1988–89 were obtained in 1988 from the Consortium, made up of 12 governments and nine financial institutions. Total pledges for 1989–90 reached 3.1 billion dollars, split between projects, commodities and programme assistance.

The sheer size of Pakistan's budget deficit gives rise to fears that the country's long-term position will soon become untenable. There have been pressures on the government by the World Bank to implement long-requested measures to tackle macroeconomic issues. Many of the problems of Pakistan's economy are essentially structural. While the savings rate has stayed extremely low, Pakistan's taxation base has remained very narrow, and successive governments have failed to generate sufficient resources to meet spiralling expenditure, particularly in defence and debt-servicing.

The taxation system

Pakistan's taxation system contains many anomalies. Direct tax revenue has amounted to less than 25 per cent of revenues from excise, sales and customs duties. Direct taxes were being paid only by 11 000 companies, with almost three times as many firms left out of account. The failure to tackle the problem of missing revenues had come about through a lack of will on the part of successive governments, unable or simply unwilling to tackle the resistance of powerful vested interests.

Senior Pakistani officials made increasingly blunt complaints from 1987 as to the prevalence of tax evasion, corruption and smuggling. Stiffer penalties for tax evasion were finally introduced in 1988, together with a radically-restructured tax system. Dr Mahbubul Haq, as Minister for Finance, Planning and Commerce, presented a budget in June 1988 in which significant changes were outlined for Pakistan's taxation laws, with reforms on the lines long demanded by the World Bank and other financial institutions. The Minister bluntly declared that the country's sick economy, "needs surgery, not more debate".

The taxation system was both restructured and simplified in the budget, with national tax numbers allotted, while the wide discretionary powers of income tax officers were reduced. The explicit goal of this change was to provide an opportunity for businessmen to pay to the state money which they had been paying to corrupt officials. However, the new tax proposals provoked a vigorous campaign of protest by the business community in cities all over Pakistan.

Recent moves towards disinvestment in state enterprises and state-owned banks seem to owe their stimulus to privatisation in Mrs Thatcher's Britain and other Western experiments to tap domestic resources and private savings for productive investment. The long-awaited offering to the public of shares in the country's profitable Pakistan International Airlines (PIA) was still not finalised in 1989, after two years, and there was much less public interest in plans to sell off other parts of the ailing state sector.

Agriculture itself accounts for fully 25 per cent of GDP. The idea of introducing an income tax on agriculture is not new in Pakistan, and for decades, in fact, foreign aid donors have urged it. Under strong pressure from the World Bank, Pakistan agreed to introduce a selective water tax from mid-1989, over a period of four years. It will be levied on farmers benefiting from new irrigation schemes funded by the World Bank.

Taxation on land in Pakistan is a particularly sensitive issue because the landed lobby has remained very powerful throughout Pakistan's history, with members of rich landowning families tending to dominate national as well as local politics. This explains why, under the authoritarian populist government of Z. A. Bhutto, there was actually written into the Constitution of 1973 a special provision excluding agriculture from the income tax mandate of Pakistan's Parliament.

The omission of agricultural income from taxation has also hindered state efforts to obtain tax due from the wealthy business class, many of whom own farms as well as companies. Many rich assessees hide income from business sources, simply by ascribing it to their farms or orchards. Tax evasion has become a huge problem whose scale is increasingly admitted.

Out of an estimated 4.2 million potential tax payers in 1986, only 1.1 million paid tax. Many of those who do pay tax are deliberately misclassified, and pay far too little. According to the Karachi newspaper *Dawn*, an estimated Rs 3000 million (150 million dollars) were being paid to tax inspectors annually by rich businessmen. An official report noted in December 1986, "there is no doubt in the minds of the public that most government and semi-government departments are corrupt".

A crisis in the economy

The PPP government is confronted with what some describe as the worst economic crisis yet faced by Pakistan. Foreign debt rose from 3.5 billion to 12.5 billion dollars from 1977 to 1988. As for debt servicing, the relevant figures rose from 310 million dollars annually to 1.2 billion. A large USAID 465m dollar agreement, signed in June 1989, went to help finance overdue primary and higher education programmes, with 100m dollars for private sector housing construction. It was part of a six-year aid package for 4000m dollars, which was approved during Benazir Bhutto's visit to the USA, after she assured the US Congress that Pakistan did not possess, nor intends to make, a nuclear weapon. The nuclear issue still hangs as a cloud over US–Pakistan relations. Under the "Pressler amendment", US law requires as a condition of aid annual certificates by the President of the USA that Pakistan does not have a nuclear weapon.

As far as short term measures are concerned, the government's hands appear to be tied by agreements entered into in 1988 by the caretaker government under President Ishaq Khan. It agreed to borrow one billion dollars over a three year period from the IMF, in return for accepting radical terms recommended for some years by international institutions such as the World Bank and the International Monetary Fund (IMF).

Among the conditions of the IMF standby loan were the ending of generous subsidies on agricultural and other products, big increases in electricity and other utility charges, together with liberalisation of imports. Though postponed for 1989, if implemented in full these measures would increase the rate of inflation, and almost certainly fuel public unrest. Low prices for a range of goods and services have come to be relied upon by the poorer classes, and their abrupt cancellation would be bitterly resented.

PAKISTAN'S LINKS WITH THE GULF STATES

The relationship between Pakistan and the Gulf states developed remarkably during the Zia years. Pakistanis working abroad in well-paid jobs helped to prop up a weak economy, by sending home regular remittances, in particular to the Punjab and NWFP, where most of the workers originated.

At the height of the oil boom, well over two million Pakistanis went to work in the Gulf region, the largest single group of foreign migrant labour in the Gulf, bigger than either Yemenis or Egyptians. Their remittances home provided one of the country's principal sources of foreign exchange, worth between 2.3 and 2.9 billion dollars each year until the mid-1980s. If money smuggled back into Pakistan is included, the true figure, according to some Pakistani sources, may have been closer to four billion dollars annually at its peak in the early 1980s. Even at the official estimates, these remittances accounted for 40 per cent of Pakistan's total foreign exchange earnings at the time, but by 1984 they were four times greater than net aid inflow to Pakistan.

The seemingly effortless rise in annual remittances until 1983 encouraged over-optimism that this bonanza would continue indefinitely. Thus Pakistan's Sixth Five Year Plan (for 1983–88) worked on the false premise that remittances would grow by 10 per cent each year. In fact, remittances declined, because of the numbers of Pakistanis forced to return home with the end of the boom years in the Gulf states.

Official statistics for numbers of Pakistani workers abroad have been vague, or very uncertain, partly because of the undeclared or illegal migrant workers. A 1985 report by the International Labour Organisation (ILO) estimated that in 1983 there were between 1.8 and 2.4 million Pakistanis working in the Middle East region. 59 per cent of these were in Saudi Arabia, with most of the rest in the United Arab Emirates and other small oil-rich Arab states of the Gulf.

"Dubai chalo"

The Gulf represents a contemporary "El Dorado", as the Pakistani anthropologist Dr Akbar S. Ahmed has commented:

> "The saying *Dubai chalo* (let us go to Dubai) – which is the equivalent of the expression 'Westward ho' in Western tradition – has become part of Pakistani culture . . . It signifies the possibility of gathering relatively quick, legitimate, and a great deal of wealth in the Arab states."

Hardly surprisingly the Gulf rapidly became, and still remains, far more important than previous countries for foreign work or settlement, especially Britain and Canada. Both for individuals and the national economy, there have been obvious benefits.

Gulf remittances made a vital contribution to economic growth in Pakistan through the 1980s. According to some economists, GDP growth was raised from a likely level of around two per cent to five per cent. The benefits for ordinary people have been spread wide, with an estimated 10 per cent of Pakistani households benefiting by remittances.

Depressed prices for oil on international markets, and the recession in the Gulf economies naturally had a marked impact on Pakistan too, as more workers returned home, and new work opportunities dried up. From this remarkable work-migration other problems emerged, such as serious distortions of the Pakistani economy – as is also true for those other countries with large numbers of people working in the Gulf, whether Arab or Asian. Most of the money earned by Pakistanis has been spent on imported consumer goods, land and housebuilding, rather than investing in businesses. As little as 10 per cent of the total earnings were being invested productively by returnees from the Gulf, according to a 1982 study by economists based in Lahore.

Rise in inflation

The very scale of funds flowing back to Pakistan contributed to high inflation, especially in land values, running at a rate estimated in excess of 20 per cent through much of the 1980s. The rate of inflation in Pakistan was officially placed at around 4 per cent during 1985–87, and considered a matter of pride by the government. However, independent Pakistani economists assess that for lower income groups, the rate of inflation in basic living costs had reached an annual level of between 10 to 15 per cent during that period.

Shortages of skilled men in many fields became common in Pakistani towns. As a direct result, wages have risen sharply. Although the majority of poorer people finding work in the Gulf states have been unskilled labourers – many of them unemployed, or only seasonally employed, at home – there were also many with skills relevant to the construction industry, such as welding, plumbing and carpentry. It is hardly surprising that such practical vocational skills have since become more highly prized by young men in Pakistan.

At the managerial and professional level, Pakistanis were less numerous in the Gulf than Indians, but proportionately to the pool of available talent, the drain was certainly higher in Pakistan's case. The attraction was not exclusively financial. Some exceptionally well qualified Pakistanis went on to take posts in the Gulf states in the past decade, not only because of superior salaries but because they felt stifled by the political climate in Pakistan.

Social consequences of migrant labour

The drawbacks, however, included some harmful social consequences. They are seen in a spate of medical or psychological symptoms found among a minority of families of the "guest workers". The so-called "Dubai syndrome" undoubtedly stems from the emotional stress caused to male workers, their wives and families alike, by coping with new challenges or personal difficulties arising out of separation for many months or even years at a stretch.

Even if many Pakistanis stay for years in the Gulf, and can feel at home in Dubai and other Gulf towns (where in fact Urdu is very much the *lingua franca*) they are made well aware that they are aliens in states where foreigners are hired for their usefulness to an Arab ruling class.

One side-effect of the Gulf boom from the 1970s was to make labour supply into one of the most profitable activities in Pakistan. It attracted many greedy and unscrupulous contractors. The lure of the Gulf had unfortunately helped swindlers cheat hundreds of thousands of innocent Pakistanis, from villages and towns, desperate to find well-paid jobs in the oil-rich states of the Gulf. The creation of a special Ministry for Emigrant Workers showed the scale of the problem. Fraud by fake job-recruiting agencies had become so common that in 1979 the military government resorted to setting up military courts to deal with the problem, giving out exemplary punishments to detected swindlers.

SUCCESS IN AGRICULTURE

The government's hopes for resolving the serious shortage of foreign exchange are pinned on boosting exports of cotton and textiles, together with rice, wheat and other agricultural products in surplus. Agriculture is the mainstay of Pakistan's export strategy, as well as the backbone of the economy.

Cotton: a key indicator

The country's biggest foreign-exchange earner is the cotton industry. Exports of raw cotton and cotton textile goods from Pakistan did well through the 1980s, and higher international prices have been paid for record crops of cotton. But the future outlook looks far less favourable. The 1989 target set of 8.2 million bales – compared with the previous year's figure of 8.6 billion bales – was not reached, because of damage done in the Punjab by drought and flooding late in 1988. This will make it more difficult for Pakistan to hold onto its share of the world market, let alone to expand it, as hoped by the government. Japan is the country's number one buyer of raw cotton and cotton yarn, but Pakistan also has big markets in the EEC, USSR and many other countries. In addition, there are quite natural fears about maintaining exports of textiles in international markets where the erection of high tariff barriers is growing.

Quite apart from the crops setback, Pakistan's cotton industry was shaken in early 1989 by allegations of large-scale corruption and mismanagement. Private exporters and officials of the state-owned Cotton Export Corporation each alleged that large sums of money were being made illegally in underhand dealings. The PPP government reportedly began an investigation into the scandal, and tried to block gaps in export procedures which could have helped siphon off money to overseas bank accounts. Cotton exports had until recently been a state monopoly.

Outstanding progress in agriculture has taken place since 1977, in spite of periodic setbacks due to drought conditions and pest infestation. Agricultural growth was aided by an unusually favourable weather cycle. Pakistan has not only become more or less self-sufficient in wheat and sugar, among its most important crops, but it has also become a small scale exporter.

The principal cash crop is cotton, followed by rice, for long the largest source of foreign exchange earnings. Records were broken from the early 1980s for all four main crops – cotton, rice, wheat and sugar-cane – in successive harvests, as a combination of agricultural inputs, insecticides and ideal weather conditions yielded rising productivity. Cotton has led the way, with increases due to improved agricultural support services by the government, together with the planting of a new high-yield variety. Records were broken with harvests of 7.76 million bales (1986–87), and 8.9 million bales (1987–88). The yield of cotton per hectare rose in these years too, from 528 kg to 590 kg. Cotton is therefore a key indicator of the agricultural sector. Booming exports of cotton, cotton-based textiles and clothing together provided a major source of foreign exchange, besides employment for millions of families. In Pakistan farmers call cotton by the name "silver fibre", and it is not only valuable to them as a cash crop. The seed from newly harvested cotton is a prized source of vegetable oil – in short supply in Pakistan. Even that part which remains (*khuli*) after pressing for oil is utilised as animal feed on the farms.

Food crops

Total production and yield of wheat, Pakistan's main food crop, has increased due to new varieties of seed. Wheat production, centred in the Punjab, increased from 10.9 million tonnes in 1983–84 to 14.2 million tonnes in 1986–87, an annual increase of 7.5 per cent. Over the same period, yield per hectare increased by 27 per cent to 1880 kg.

Rice production, especially of high-quality basmati rice, rose from 3.3 million tonnes in 1983–84 to 3.5 million tonnes in 1986–87. For a time in the mid-1980s, Pakistan led as the biggest exporter of rice on world markets. However, Thailand soon overtook Pakistan, and in terms of quality improvement and yield, Pakistan's progress has been only moderate.

Mechanisation has steadily increased since 1973, resulting in shrinking numbers of jobs for farm labourers. One of the current problems being tackled is water-logging and salination, which have reached serious levels in many areas of Punjab and Sind, the two most important agricultural provinces.

Foreign markets

A flourishing agriculture has been the key to Pakistan's success in boosting its exports, up to 4.3 billion dollars in 1987–88, from 3.4 billion dollars in the previous year. However, high international prices for Pakistan's bumper cotton crops may well not last much longer. Foreign markets for Pakistan's surplus crops were found in Iran and Bangladesh. Barter and counter-trade deals were also concluded with countries of Eastern Europe, Asia and Africa. The government's new insistence on trading partners with large credit balances taking a minimum proportion of goods from Pakistan helped to increase exports. Imported edible oils formed a major item of barter. Pakistan's imports of various types of edible oils totalled 864 000 tonnes in 1985–86, costing 294 million dollars. Demand rises by 13 per cent each year for Pakistan's state-subsidised edible oil.

THE BIG PUSH FOR ENERGY

Pakistan is promoting one of the most ambitious power expansion plans in the Third World. In an effort to encourage rapid industrialisation, the Bhutto government is relying on a formula of multilateral aid, state backing and private enterprise. Plans for the five years from 1989 aim at 6000 MW of new capacity to be installed, with the goal of tripling total capacity in ten years. Almost half of the budget's development funding is in fact allocated to power and energy.

There are doubts, though, about the success of the government's ambitious strategy. Build-operate schemes on offer were complicated by risks from the unresolved tariff rates to be paid by Pakistan's Water and Power Development Authority (WAPDA). In addition, there were likely to be problems with proposed coal-fired plants, because of the low grade of local coal deposits.

Pakistan's industrial progress has been severely handicapped by inadequate infrastructure. Power shortages made load-shedding very common at peak periods of demand for electricity, especially in Karachi. However, the extension of electricity supply to remote villages took place at an accelerating rate from 1980. In the four provinces, a claimed 3405 villages were connected to the national grid in the year 1986–87 alone, as contrasted with the total of 9560 villages electrified in the 20-year period 1959–1980.

New developments in energy supply

Production of natural gas, centred in Baluchistan, expanded with new discoveries and rose to 402.6 billion cu ft in 1986–87. Gas and electricity together accounted for 76 per cent of total energy consumed by industry by 1983. Changes in the government's policy of holding down gas prices led to increasing substitution in the use of fuels, in favour of oil and coal.

A succession of promising new discoveries of natural gas, oil and coal deposits since 1984 has revived optimism in the energy sector, after many disappointments in prospecting Pakistan's complex geological structures. Pakistan annually imported oil and petroleum products to a value of around 1.5 billion dollars in the early 1980s – the country's major import item. Oil, accounting for 40 per cent of the country's energy needs – cost just over one billion dollars in 1988. As a result of new oil discoveries – all small so far – Pakistan's domestic oil production rose steadily from 1985, reaching 48 000 billion dollars by March 1988. One-third of Pakistan's crude oil requirement was being met by domestic sources in 1988. An oil exploration programme has expanded since 1984, led by 13 companies – nine of them foreign. There were high hopes for offshore oil exploration, with oil rigs being supplied by Canada and the USSR.

The Pipri project

The steel mill at Pipri, near Karachi, is the country's largest industrial complex, employing 19 000 people. It is the major example of Soviet-Pakistani collaboration, and 800 Soviet engineers and technicians were still working there in 1984. Taking almost a decade to bring into production – in 1984 – the steel mill has often been criticised as a white elephant which can never hope to break even, absorbing moreover an unhealthily large part of state investment resources.

The Pipri project had originally been agreed in the mid-1970s, under Z. A. Bhutto. Pakistan's engineering industry is expected to benefit eventually from it by many downstream projects, some of which may also be Soviet-aided. Beset by many technical problems and higher costs than anticipated, nevertheless Pakistan Steel claimed in 1989 that the Pipri mill was saving 150 million dollars annually in steel imports from abroad, with a production of one million metric tons.

Private investment in manufacturing industry remains weak, in spite of incentives offered by the government, whose strategy for industrial growth really depends upon participation by private entrepreneurs. Political uncertainty was a factor which weighed against industrial investments.

One further cause of the disappointing response of private capital was the financial returns and excellent investment potential offered by real estate in Karachi and other cities in Pakistan in this period. Housebuilding in Pakistan, as elsewhere, offered spectacular returns, thanks to inflation and high demand, without risks involved in business ventures.

Conclusion

Benazir Bhutto's government will continue to face major political and economic problems. Beyond the short term, stability in a democratic Pakistan depends on successful modernisation of the economy, a process certain to be obstructed by the divisive forces and vested interests identified in this study.

However, the key to the situation now probably lies with the army. The Chief of Army Staff, General Mirza Aslem Beg, has asserted that he and his army are "soldiers of democracy" and seek no constitutional role. This claim has been viewed with suspicion in some quarters, especially by journalists, who in December 1989 were suddenly overwhelmed by hospitality and freely volunteered information. Bearing in mind the way in which the press was treated during the martial law period, it would be surprising if unease did not prevail for some time to come especially as a debate about the army's role is known to continue in the upper officer echelons.

Within the region progress towards an end of hostilities in Afghanistan would help Pakistan's stability. On the other hand, any tendency to a revival of Hindu fundamentalism in India would set back the rapprochement between the two states started by Benazir Bhutto with Rajiv Gandhi and weaken her position by strengthening Islamic fundamentalist tendencies in Pakistan. A democratic political culture will take time firmly to root itself in Pakistan society: in the meantime major powers with strategic interests in the region need to behave with tolerance and circumspection.

FURTHER READING

Wilfred Cantwell Smith, *Pakistan as an Islamic State*, Shaikh Muhammad Ashraf, Lahore, 1962.

Freeland Abbott, *Islam and Pakistan*, Cornell, New York, 1968.

Peter Hardy, *The Muslims of British India*, Cambridge University Press, 1972.

Inamur Rehman, *Public Opinion and Political Development in Pakistan*, Oxford U.P., Karachi, 1982.

Tariq Ali, *Can Pakistan Survive?* Penguin Books, Harmondsworth, 1983.

Hasan-Askari Rizvi, *The Military and Politics in Pakistan*, 1947–86, Progressive Publishers, Lahore, 1987.

Omar Noman, *The Political Economy of Pakistan*, 1947–85, KPI, London 1988.

Khalid B. Sayeed, *Politics in Pakistan*, Praeger, New York, 1980.

Hamza Alavi, *Class and State in Pakistan*, and *Political Economy of a Praetorian State*, in Hassan Gardezi/Jamil Rashid (eds), *Pakistan: the Roots of Dictatorship*, Zed Books, London, 1983.

Hafeez Malik (ed), *Soviet-American Relations with Pakistan, Iran and Afghanistan*, London, Macmillan, 1987.

Agha Shahi, *Pakistan's Security and Foreign Policy*, Progressive Publishers, Lahore, 1988.

Shahid Javed Burki, *Pakistan under Bhutto 1971–77*, Macmillan, London, 1980.

Lawrence Ziring, *Pakistan: The Enigma of Political Development*, Boulder, Colorado, 1980, and *From Islamic Republic to Islamic State in Pakistan*, in Asian Survey, XXIV, 9 (September 1984).

Lawrence Ziring (ed), *The Subcontinent in World Politics*, Praeger, New York, 1982.

Anthony Hyman, *Afghanistan under Soviet Domination, 1964–89*, Macmillan, London, 1990.

A. Hyman, M. Ghayur, N. Kaushik, *Pakistan: Zia and After*, Asia Publishing House, London, 1988.

Raja Anwar, *The Tragedy of Afghanistan*, Verso, London, 1988.

Olivier Roy, *Islam and Resistance in Afghanistan*, CUP, Cambridge, 1986.

Robert G. Wirsing and James M. Roberty, *The United States and Pakistan*, in International Affairs, London, Autumn 1982.

Jamal Rashid, *Pakistan and the Central Command*, in Middle East Report, Washington DC (July 1986).

Shirin Tahir-Kheli, *The US and Pakistan, The Evolution of an Influential Relationship*, Praeger, New York 1982.

Iqbal Khan (Ed) *Fresh Perspectives on India and Pakistan*, Bougainvillea Books, Oxford, 1985.

Pakistan

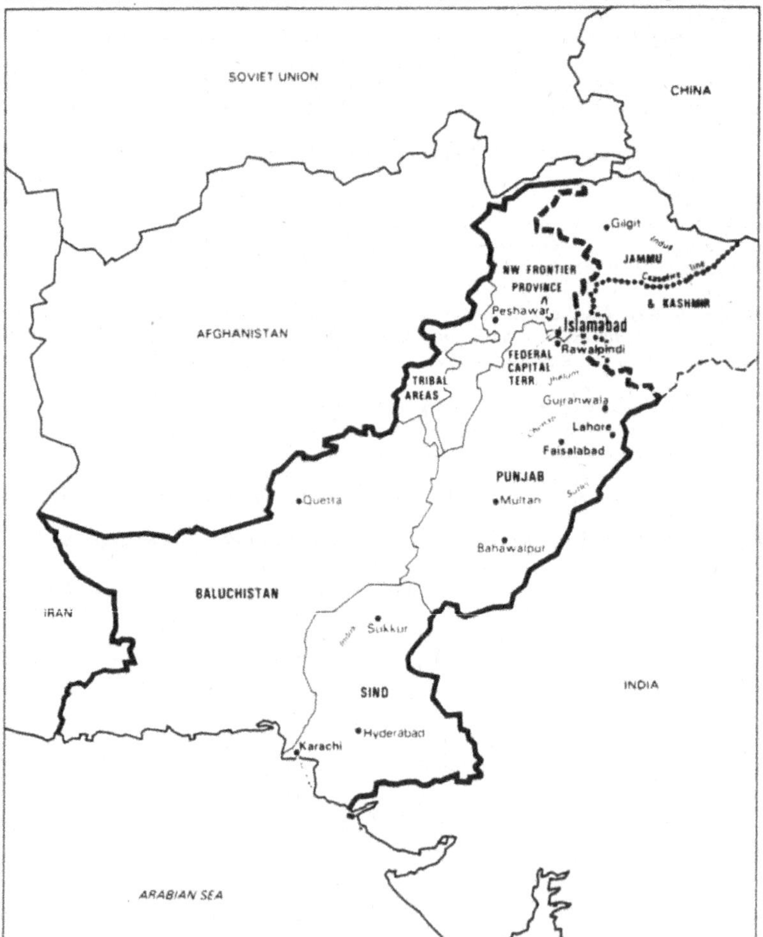

SOVIET UNION
CHINA
AFGHANISTAN
NW FRONTIER PROVINCE
Gilgit
JAMMU
& KASHMIR
Peshawar
Islamabad
Rawalpindi
FEDERAL CAPITAL TERR.
TRIBAL AREAS
Gujranwala
Lahore
Faisalabad
PUNJAB
Quetta
Multan
Bahawalpur
BALUCHISTAN
IRAN
Sukkur
SIND
INDIA
Hyderabad
Karachi
ARABIAN SEA
0 Miles 250
0 Kilometres 400

Map by courtesy of *Control Risks Information Services*

[4]

The Politics of Violence in India and South Asia

Dennis Austin and Anirudha Gupta

Like many regions of the world, South Asia is beset with problems of violence – violence between communities, between citizens and governments and between neighbouring states. There is nothing unusual in that – but India, the dominant power in the sub-continent, is distinct in being a parliamentary democracy of some 40 years standing. Other South Asian countries have not fared so well, although democracy has struggled to re-assert itself in Pakistan under Benazir Bhutto and in Sri Lanka under Ranasinghe Premadasa. Similarly, in Kathmandu, government violence against those demanding change has had to give way to constitutional reforms, while in Bangladesh General Ershad hides behind controlled elections to camouflage the reality of military power – a backhanded tribute to democracy by uneasy soldiers.

The sub-continent is a useful testing ground, therefore, of the relationship between democracy and violence – good and evil – a Manichean view of a problem which seems likely to become a pattern for the 1990s, not only for South Asia but wherever governments are placed uncomfortably between the promise of freedom and the threat of violence.

Is violence evil? One can play with words and argue that violence is defensible in just wars or against tyrants or to protect life and property. But democracy and *political* violence are surely incompatible. Where democracy tries to settle disputes by the peaceful resolution of differences, violence uses weapons of terror to impose its will. The contrast is severe – the ballot box not the gun, not bombs but parliament. If a state is committed to democratic government, do its citizens not have a duty to abide by its rules?

If only all societies and governments would accept the equation! If violence were no more than conflict between individuals, one might hope that democratically enacted laws, liberally interpreted, would deal justly with the offence. A wife murders her husband, and that – unhappily – is that. A burglar steals my goods but commits only a criminal act: there are no political consequences. But suppose a community seeks to suppress, violently, a neighbouring community. The killing of Sikhs by Hindus, or of Hindus by Muslims, or of low-caste labourers by high-caste landlords – such crimes quickly become political. Look at Ulster today. Where violence divides a community along communal lines, the causes of violence become the basis for group loyalties and political action.

And, paradoxically, there are aspects of democracy which feed the violence. Elections can raise the level of conflict to a point where any belief in democracy as a peaceful lever of change is extinguished in the competition which it encourages. *Glasnost* may not only reveal but give heightened expression to the tensions which it is intended to defuse. Gorbachev beware! Already, elections in Eastern Europe have begun to quicken old quarrels of an ethnic, religious and regional character. So, too, as we shall see, in India and the rest of South Asia.

There are comparable effects internationally. Dictators can act without consideration for public opinion, democratic governments are fettered by their electorates. If the Indian government were not subject, democratically, to popular demands over Kashmir and Punjab, it might have a freer hand in the settlement of disputes with Islamabad. As it is, both governments are alert not only to what they see as threats from the Pakistan or Indian army but from those who demand – democratically – a militant stand by Benazir Bhutto or V. P. Singh.

Two questions can be asked about democratic politics in such a context. One is whether democracy in South Asia has been compromised, or endangered, by political violence. The other is whether there are therapeutic qualities in the conduct of democracy by which violence can be tamed and re-directed along peaceful channels of opposition. To these two domestic questions one can add a third: namely, the extent to which democratic governments are the captive of a popular emotion which pushes them towards regional/international conflicts.

What follows is an inquiry into the violence which disfigures South Asian societies and its effect on democratic government in India and its neighbours. We begin with a brief familiar survey of the sub-continent.

SOUTH ASIA

It is not extravagant to speak of a fractured unity to the whole of South Asia. The main fractures came in 1947 when Pakistan was created, then in 1971 between Pakistan and Bangladesh, but the central fact is still the dominance of India – inescapable and disproportionate: 800 million against a combined total of 215 million for Pakistan, Bangladesh, Nepal and Sri Lanka.[1] The effect is plain. Just as there are minorities within the Indian Union which are wary of the majority Hindu population, so there are minority states within the sub-continent which are apprehensive about the power and size of India. And they cannot escape. There is an enforced intimacy among the five states which the South Asian Association for Regional Co-operation (SAARC) attempts to portray. The fact is, however, that the links which bind them together also chafe.

Pakistan, founded for Muslims and now an Islamic republic, exhibits an almost permanent neurosis in relation to its larger neighbour. Despite partition in 1947, there are as many Muslims in India today as there are in Pakistan (minus, of course, Bangladesh), and what happens between Hindus and Muslims in India continually affects relations between Islamabad and Dehli. At the other end of the continent Sri Lanka, too, must live in the giant shadow of its neighbour. The demography of the island, its ethnic geography, amplifies the distrust it has of India's dominance. There is a local Sinhala–Buddhist majority and a Tamil Hindu/Christian minority; but in the wider context of South Asia the position is reversed, for across the narrow Palk strait lies the South Indian state of Tamil Nadu and its 50 million Hindu population, outnumbering the 10 million or so Sinhalese. Little wonder, therefore, that the history of the 1970s and 1980s has been that of violence within Sri Lankan society and tension between Colombo and New Delhi.

The fractured unity of the sub-continent is also a strong element between India and Bangladesh. Bengali is spoken on both sides of what was once undivided India, and Bangladesh was helped to independence from Pakistan in 1971; but relations between Dhaka and Delhi have been soured by quarrels over water resources shared by both states and by the migration of Muslim farmers into India from Bangladesh. Similar problems bedevil ties between India and Nepal. The relationship has been intimate, a little too intimate for the government in Kathmandu, but when it sought to demonstrate its independence by broadening its relations with China, it was quickly made to feel the power of India under a trade embargo.

Separate but related, interlocked but distinct. The five states are linked by language, religious beliefs, social customs, migration and trade as well as politically through SAARC with its headquarters in Kathmandu. Of the links between them, two in particular are a source of friction – religion and migration.

Religion

South Asia shares three of the world's major religions, Hinduism, Buddhism and Islam, and has a substantial Christian minority. There are other faiths – the Sikh religion, for example, Parsees and Jainism. Religion is not a Sunday-go-to-meeting ceremony. It fills men's lives and links them with eternity. But if there is comfort in that, there is also danger. Although millions of Hindus, Muslims and Sikhs live side by side throughout the sub-continent, the fact is that temple, mosque, church, Buddhist *dagobas* and Sikh *gurdwaras* are not only places of worship but rallying centres for political action. Buddhist monks (*Bikkhus*), Hindu priests and Islamic *mullahs* have been extremely militant, less against the sins of mankind than on behalf of their followers who have been willing to kill in the name of religion. They have paid little heed to the warning attributed to the Sikh leader, Guru Gobind Singh: *pap kure parmarath ko, it papan te sabh lajahi*: there is no greater sin than that committed in the name of religion.

Migration

South Asia has been a continent of movement, of cross-border migration and mass exchanges of population in a series of harrowing and violent upheavals. The Punjab is a case in point. Before partition, the province – peacefully administered – was 50 per cent Muslim, 35 per cent Hindu, 12 per cent Sikh. After 1947 the population in Punjab–India was very different – 64 per cent Hindu, 35 per cent Sikh, 2 per cent Muslim. There were further boundary changes in 1966, bringing the Sikh numbers up to 60 per cent by immigration and re-definition (that is by self-identification) and Hindus down to 38 per cent. The Sikhs began to talk of an independent homeland, athough that would still leave about three million Sikhs, out of a total of 13 million in neighbouring states. And so the present troubles began.

Add to this misery, economic pressures of land hunger. When the boundary is moved, it does not bring immediate acceptance. If families are divided, they will travel to meet. If the grass is greener, or thought to be greener, on the other side of the boundary, people will move in search of a livelihood against fierce resistance and conflict between immigrants and residents.

Trans-national conflict

One must also include the themes of this study – violence and democracy. They too are trans-national. Terrorists know no frontiers. They cross the Palk Strait to and from Sri Lanka, they move from Pakistan in and out of the Punjab. Arms, and the drugs which finance their purchase, easily find their way from Kabul to Peshawar, then from the North West Frontier Province into Karachi. And if the traffickers in violence move across the frontiers, so do the ideas which feed the violence, ideas of both right and left – Islamic fundamentalism, Hindu revivalism, Marxist-Maoist beliefs and nationalist convictions.

The political legacy

The five countries of the sub-continent also share a political legacy. British rule left its impress. What the legacy is today remains uncertain: it too is fragmented. Language of course, some social habits and the utilitarian concept of a managed society within a centralised framework of administration.[2] But one can also trace the growth in India among its western educated class of a commitment to representative government and the transmission of such beliefs to a wider electorate. The force of political ideas adapted by India from Britain has shaped a political culture for all to see – in Congress, in the opposition to Congress, in parliament and national elections, in a strong judiciary and a critical press. Democratic institutions in India have been handed down from one generation – fashioned in the nationalist years of opposition under British rule – to the present generation of party leaders.

Some measure of similar beliefs can be found throughout the sub-continent, effective for the present in Pakistan since the election in December 1988 of Benazir Bhutto, struggling for expression in Sri Lanka, Nepal and Bangladesh. The record is examined later, but we turn now to more sombre events, not to democracy but to its dark enemy – violence.

A VIOLENT SOCIETY

Violence in India and South Asia takes many forms. Its mistress is Kali and her devotees.[3] It comes as a shout in the street, the spread of rumour, the sudden looting of shops and the murder of men or women or children; death is by scythe, sword, hand-grenades, sticks, rifles, kerosene. South Asia has not suffered the sustained violence of Cambodia or areas of Central Africa but it has its own pattern of terror, and the statistics are there to read. We quote from Indian sources, but comparable accounts can be given of its neighbours.

Over two days, 12 and 13 January 1990, the *Times of India* reported:

- Violence between army and members of the Jammu and Kashmir Liberation Front, 23 killed, over 100 injured.
- 10 killed in Punjab, including two police constables and a *jawan* (soldier).
- Bomb explosions in Bombay, *dacoit* (gangster) and police violence in Khandar, three dead. *Hartals* (boycotts) *bandhs* (strikes).
- Anti-reservation riots in Bihar, four dead, several injured.
- Disbanding of "Greyhounds" (an anti-terrorist force used by the State Government against Naxalite terrorists) in Andhra Pradesh; anti-Naxalite campaigns to continue by police action and negotiations.
- Terrorist kidnapping in Orissa and West Bengal.
- LTTE (Tamil Tigers) armed clash with Indian army, casualties on both sides.
- Exchange of fire between Indian troops and Pakistan army units in Northern Kashmir.

These were *routine* reports, each day of each week, not descriptions of the frenzy of communal violence, *viz*:

- In a large hall of a Shakurpur camp, housing the Sultanpur victims of carnage, sit a row of women and children huddled together with shock and grief. . . . One household consists of 18 people rendered absolutely destitute without a single earning member left: all four adult males have been murdered. . . . An older woman, who has lost her husband and three sons, gave vent to her grief: "*ab to sabse ac ha yeh hoga ki aap ham sab ko jahar dila dain; ab ham ji nahin sakte: kaise jiyenge, kis ke liye jiyenge?*" (It would be best to give us all poison, for how else shall we live, and for whom?)[4]
- At about four in the afternoon . . . the mob went on the rampage and we were attacked with swords, spears, axes. The victims were chased, rounded up and hacked to death. They tried to cut my leg off, but the weapon was too blunt. Later they brought a sharp sword and severed my foot from the ankle. All the bodies and limbs were thrown into the pond. In all, some 100 were killed. I do not think that more than two or three victims survived.[5]
- Within the past year or so, the brutality of the *Janatha Vimukthi Peramuna* (JVP) has become worse. Knives and swords are used in preference to guns to do the actual killing. Victims are often cut to ribbons part by part, slowly. Very ordinary people like bus drivers, scavengers, small-time shop-keepers and others have been killed.[6]
- The Karachi riots in 1986 were the most violent since partition. Kalashnikovs were openly wielded. People were shot dead without any compunction, their bodies burnt and properties looted.[7]

The Sultanpur victims were among the several thousand Sikhs murdered in the Indian capital in October 1984 after the assassination of Indira Gandhi. The second extract describes the carnage in Bhalgapur, in Bihar, prior to the 1989 election. The third and fourth quotations are from Sri Lanka and Pakistan. Violence and democracy. An elected government, and death by sword, sticks, guns and kerosene.

Democracy: a vulnerable creed

Democracy threatened by violence: the dilemma is to be seen in Eastern Europe and the Soviet Union, and is not altogether new. Very likely we should blame humanity not politics. Perfectibility, Rousseau told the Abbé de Saint Pierre, "is all very well for the children of Utopia but it is useless for the children of Adam".[8] Alas, that it should be so, but the world is peopled by the children of Adam whether they live in a democracy or under dictatorship. There is no perfection and we must scale down our expectations. We have to accept that no state can totally prevent violence by those determined to use it, and that democracy is especially vulnerable.

The problem is moral and practical: moral because violence is inherently repugnant, and practical since no one knows how a democratic government should respond to those who reject its authority. Must it give freedom to its enemies as well as to its friends? If so, might it not fall victim to its own virtues, or can parliaments and elections offer an inoculation against political violence? It was certainly dispiriting in 1989 to record such a high and persistent level of violence during elections in the region's most firmly established democracy, including violence on both sides of the party divide between Congress and its opponents. The chief sufferers, as in the extracts given earlier, were usually the poor, but the poor, after all, are the majority of India's population. And, in fact, violence has no respect for class or caste. Assassination has taken its count of leaders at every level of society.

How should one explain what happens so frequently? Are South Asian societies more violent than their counterparts elsewhere? If one looks at the misery and terror of much of the third world from China to Peru – from Tiananmen Square to *Sendero Luminoso* (Shining Path) – the measure of violence in South Asia may not seem excessive. Indeed, there is a disreputable argument which uses statistics to minimise the suffering: what are 1000 deaths in a city of 10 million or a sub-continent of a thousand million? . . . The answer is plain. Each violent death is a crime, and the suffering it brings is not measurable against any scale of numbers:

> *Action is transitory – a step, a blow,*
> *The motion of a muscle – this way or that. . . .*
> *Suffering is permanent, obscure and dark,*
> *And shares the nature of infinity.*
> (W. Wordsworth *The Borderers, III. 1539*)

Is India prone to violence? A popular image, propagated by Sir Richard Attenborough's film, is of the bravery of the non-violent, exemplified in the life of Mahatma Gandhi, and it is certainly true that the 20th century has been enriched by the moral grandeur of Gandhi; but there is little evidence of the legacy of non-violence today. Even in its own day it struggled to contain the fury of communal rivalry. Perhaps it is that South Asian societies sought to impose on their members the restraints of Buddha or Gandhi precisely because they needed to curb their propensity to violence? Societies frequently protect themselves where they are most vulnerable by evoking mirror images of what they seek to hide. Americans talked most of liberty when they were still a slave society. In similar fashion, Nirad Chaudhuri has derided the notion that Hinduism "is a non-violent creed". The "current belief is that Hindus are a peace-loving and non-violent people, and this belief has been fortified by Gandhism". In reality, says Chaudhuri, "few human communities have been more warlike and fond of bloodshed".[9]

Well, perhaps. The passivity of pre-partition India under Hindu, Muslim or British rule, was always more shadow than substance, and the ferocity of partition in 1947, repeated in 1971, brought to the surface passions which are still running loose. It would be surprising if South Asian societies were exempt from the ill-temper and brutish practice of most of mankind. It is only when one looks at the rivalries of religion, caste, class, regions and sub-nationalities alongside the sustained achievement, at least in India, of democratic government that there is truly "room for wonder".[10]

DIFFERENT FORMS OF VIOLENCE

We must look more closely, if reluctantly, at the several forms of violence. There are many.

Personal violence

Personal violence based on individual crimes as, most typically, on the streets of cities in the United States, is not a South Asian phenomenon except during violence for other ends. For instance, a psychopath was at large in 1989 – the "stone man of Calcutta" whose night-time victims, killed by a blow from a heavy stone, were the pavement dwellers of the city. The nearest parallel is family violence, particularly dowry murders and, more rarely, *sati* – the immolation of widows.

Communal violence

This is the most potent source of conflict and the point at which violence arising from social and religious tension turns into political conflict, *viz*:

(a) Hindu–Muslim hostility. It has a long ancestry and every fear of an indefinite future. "The establishment of British power [transferred] the hatred formerly felt by Hindus for the Muslims to the English, as today with the disappearance of British rule the underlying hatred has again fastened itself on the Muslims".[11] The effect of partition in 1947 and 1971 is there in the two Muslim states which flank Hindu-India; but Hindu–Muslim enmity is endemic within India itself where a substantial, urban-based Muslim population arouses all the familiar tensions of majority–minority hostility. There is said to be an arithmetic of conflict: "those areas which have a Muslim population of more than 15 to 40 per cent tend to be riot-prone [if only because] in a ballot-box orientated democracy, minorities with decisive votes tilt the balance and arouse hostility".[12] But, in fact, communal violence can erupt anywhere, unexpectedly, from seemingly trivial causes, often enough among the poorest of the poor.

In 1989 the focus of Hindu–Muslim conflict in India was the *Babri Masjid* v. *Ram Janmabhoomi* (mosque–temple) dispute in the small town of Ayodya in Uttar Pradesh which threatened to become a major confrontation on the eve of the 1989 election. (The site of the mosque was said to be the legendary birthplace of Rama, and Hindu revivalist groups proposed to lay the brick foundations of a temple within the courtyard of the mosque.) Rajiv Gandhi hesitated between defending Muslim claims to the site and accommodating Hindu demands for a temple. Beset by other problems, he came down on the Hindu side, and the effect was to deny Congress the Muslim vote across a broad swathe of Northern states without, ironically, bringing any benefit from having played a Hindu card.

Enmity between the two communities is not limited to the northern Hindi speaking belt. During the 1980s there was a "sharp increase in communal rioting throughout Karnataka" in central southern India after attempts to impose a Kannada language test for recruits into the State administration. "The Kannada Education Bill was resented because it deprived Muslim institutions of a number of privileges."[13] When riots occurred in Bangalore and Mysore, leaving several hundred dead and injured, there was further provocation: "In many troubled areas in Mysore, saffron flags of the *Vishwa Hindu Parishad* were seen in their thousands – on housetops, autorickshaws and at street corners." The celebrations were for *Sankranti*, a major Hindu festival, but that did nothing to allay fears among the non-Hindu:

> A week long riot saw vehicles burnt, shops looted, houses destroyed, the dead and injured numbering over 250 . . . in savage fighting between Harijans and Muslims in Gandhi Nagar, sparked off by a controversial short story in the *Deccan Herald*, "Mohammed the Idiot", which few could understand and none had read.[14]

Hindu–Muslim violence might truly be said to be immanent – ineradicable and inherent within Indian society – and different in this respect from the political/criminal violence of the cities which is occasional and, often enough, predictable. But because India is a democracy, engaged in competitive politics, the pervasive hostility between Hindu and Muslim is quickly politicised. Of course not all Muslims are united, nor do all Hindus think alike: there are strong local differences. But when party leaders seek to win support from what they believe to be the Muslim or Hindu vote, local communities act out their own fears and the electorate responds to appeals for communal loyalty. There is also a quickening undertow today of militant Hindu sentiment, most obviously represented by the *Bhartiya Janata Party* (BJP), and the reaction of many non-Hindu, excited into action, is to draw protectively together.

(b) A similar phenomenon exists in Sri Lanka where **Tamils** and **Sinhalese**, divided by language and origin, are also separated by religion. The Sinhala majority is Buddhist, Tamils are Hindu or Christian, and for a thousand years or more the two communities lived in uneasy proximity, Tamils in the North, Sinhalese in the rest of the island, but with substantial numbers of both communities in Colombo. Further complications came in the 10th century through the growth of a Tamil-speaking Muslim community on the east coast, and an Indian-Hindu-Tamil population in the central highlands, recruited in the 19th century to work on the tea plantations. One should add those of mixed race (*Burghers*), Malays, and the Veddha forest dwellers who are truly aboriginal. An extraordinary miscellany. Independence in 1948 imposed its own burden of elections, parliaments, and Trotskyist, communist, socialist, conservative, religious-traditionalist and revolutionary parties. It would be silly to say that democracy gave rise to political violence but it is undoubtedly true that the increased violence of the 1950s took political shape from the antagonism between majorities and minorities, so much so that by the end of the 1980s the Tamil bid for some kind of federalism had widened into the demand for *Eelam* – a would-be sovereign enclave.

International tension made matters worse. Tamil Nadu in South India was a major supplier, through Madras, of weapons, training, money and sanctuary for Tamil guerrillas, who were themselves murderously divided between Liberation Tigers, Revolutionary Students, People's Organisations and rival groups. The Sri Lankan army was sent north to try, inefficiently and brutally, to impose its control until the point was reached in 1987 when Ranjiv Gandhi cajoled the former President, Junius Jayewardene, into accepting a Peace Keeping Force for the northern Tamil areas. That too led to violence when the Liberation Tigers turned on the Indian army.

(c) **Hindu–Sikh:** here all the ingredients of communal conflict are present – history, language, religion, economic competition and international rivalry. Hinduism includes the Sikh religion in its pantheon but no government in New Delhi, whether Congress or Janata, is prepared to tolerate Sikh claims for a separate state of Khalistan. Throughout the 1980s violence spread across the Punjab as aircraft were hijacked, bombs were exploded and Sikh terrorists killed or were killed. In June 1984, the government was determined to end the defiance of the Sikh militants in Amritsar where arms and munitions had been stockpiled, and the army was ordered into the Golden Temple under what was termed Operation Bluestar. Casualties in the fighting that followed were heavy on both sides and included three Sikh leaders – Sant Bhindranwale, Amrik Singh and Major General Shubegh Singh, a former general in the Indian army. The militants looked for revenge and in October 1984 Mrs Gandhi was assassinated. The tables were then turned with a vengeance. At the end of October 1984, when news came of Mrs Gandhi's death, "a mob spread to different parts of (Delhi) . . . Sikhs were dragged from buses, taxis, cars, autorickshaws, two wheelers and cycles . . . their vehicles were burnt . . . and at some points frenzied mobs threw their drivers into the flames".[15] Those who tried to act as peace-makers arrived too late:

> As soon as we entered Block 32 we were greeted by a stench of burnt bodies. The entire lane was littered with burnt pieces of furniture, papers, scooters and piles of ash in the shape of human beings. . . . Dogs were on the prowl, rats were nibbling at the still recognisable remains . . .[16]

The violence continues today in the towns and villages of Punjab, the richest, most productive area of India's green revolution, and is not confined to Hindu against Sikh though that is basic to the conflict, or even Punjabi Hindu against Sikh, but Sikh against Sikh. The military traditions and commercial instincts of the Sikh community have not prevented rivalry between local *gurdwaras* (shrines) or within the *Sikh Akali Dal* movement and its numerous splinter groups. When, in 1985, Rajiv Gandhi announced that he had reached agreement with Sant Harchand Singh Longowal over the division of territory between the two rival states of Punjab and Haryana, Sant Longowal was assassinated by terrorists. "The Sikhs", writes Balraj Puri, "are as confused as the rest of the nation is about the Sikh problem" – but that has not stopped the killing.[17]

In the Lok Sabha elections in 1989, the Punjab vote was heavy, suspiciously so, according to those who suspected that coercion rather than commitment lay behind the high turn out for Simranjit Singh Mann and his *Akali Dal* followers. Nevertheless, the defeat of Rajiv Gandhi seemed to open the way ahead. The new prime minister paid an official visit to Amritsar in December, the Sikh leaders came to Delhi. Then nothing. Behind S. S. Mann are the Sikh terrorist groups, behind V. P. Singh is the BJP whose rank and file, if not its leaders, are hostile to compromise. On 3 April 1990 a large bomb exploded at Batala in the Gurdaspur district (a Hindu majority area) which killed over 30 and injured many more. The terrorists are now armed with bombs, land-mines and rocket launchers as well as the familiar Kalashnikov rifle:

> Terrorism is on the increase. Figures of violence show a ten-fold rise over the last year. At the same time, the police harass the innocent. Thus more terrorists are bred.[18]

The abnormality of life in the Punjab is not yet on the scale of Kashmir. Political gatherings have still been possible, under protection, in the early months of 1990. The fact is, however, that the new government in Delhi has drawn back from dialogue. It has refused to allow State Assembly elections to be held and, against the protests of Sikh leaders, it has extended presidential rule in the Punjab for a further six months.

Migrant–local conflict

A community that is poor, living at the edge of subsistence, whether in the countryside or town, will fiercely oppose any encroachment by outsiders. Those that have not, resist the taking away of the little that they have. Similarly, migrants driven by land hunger will struggle to establish even a minimum livelihood when they believe an opportunity to do so exists. Conflict over land or employment widens into communal violence, political reaction and, when frontiers are concerned, into international quarrels. Examples are legion throughout the sub-continent. We note only three.

(a) The frontier between India and Bangladesh has seen open warfare between illegal settlers from across the border and the local Hindu population in Assam. By the end of the 1980s "entire communities had been destroyed. More than 300,000 people had been driven into refugee camps and over 5000 had died".[19] Violence between Assamese and immigrants over who should and should not be registered reached such a pitch in 1989 that no elections could be held in the State.

(b) Sri Lanka has had to struggle with the problem of *internal* colonisation, notably by Sinhalese farmers who began moving into Tamil districts in the north-east of the island, encouraged (it is alleged) by the *United National*

Party (UNP) government in Colombo. The murder of villagers on both sides of the communal divide has been part of the wider violence between Tamil guerrillas and their Sinhala counterparts, part too of the virulent debate between the government and its opponents.

(c) For an urban parallel, one can draw on the account by Asghar Ali of immigrant violence in the city of Karachi. It includes the revealing remark: "When Pakistan was made, we all meant it to be one nation but when our parents came here they found Punjabis, Sindhis, Pathans and Baluchs. The only 'Pakistani' seemed to be the Muhajirs and Biharis" – that is, those who had emigrated to Pakistan from India (Muhajirs) and from Bangladesh (Biharis).[20]

The violence which broke out in October 1986 between these immigrant groups and the local population was as violent as any in the sub-continent. It began with an attack by Pathans on Muhajirs in the settlement known as Sohrab Goth along the Super Highway from Hyderabad to Karachi. No-one quite knew why, but it was probably linked to the endemic war among drug traffickers, slum dwellers and landlords, and local gangs under political direction. The area is very poor, distant from the modern heart of the city, without water or gas or electric light, without schools or clinics. Karachi is now a city of 10 million, full of refugees from North West Frontier Province and from Afghanistan, full also of weapons. In the months that followed the October riots, it was the turn of the Pathans to come under attack. Many were killed – burnt alive in their buses – and their houses destroyed by non-Pathans determined on revenge. The worse affected were probably the Biharis but they were only one of many injured communities.

> The Biharis, as the Urdu-speaking communities from Bangladesh are called, were the worst sufferers. Even now over two *lakhs* of them (200,000) are rotting in refugee camps whom neither Bangladesh is willing to rehabilitate nor Pakistan is willing to accept. . . . The Muhajirs now outnumber the Sindhis, Pathans and Punjabis in the city (but) the hostility they once faced from the Sindhis has now been excelled by the brutality of the Pathans.[21]

Neither Islam nor the common plight of poverty offers any bond of brotherhood between these urban immigrants, many of whom have been settled in Karachi for a generation or more, and whose numbers are constantly being added to by new arrivals from outlying districts.

It is fair to add that India and South Asia are certainly not unique in suffering the violence between strangers and residents. Such conflicts are fabled in history and as old as the enmity of tribe and names:

> And when any of the fugitives of Ephraim said, Let me go over, the men of Gilead said, Are you an Ephraimite? When he said, No, they said unto him, Say now, "Shibboleth", and he said "Sibboleth" for he could not pronounce it right. Then they took him and slew him. And with him died two and forty thousand.[22]

Social conflict

Violence between communities has been matched by violence between social groups – caste and class in particular which, if related, are not to be regarded as identical.

(a) Caste – defines distinctions of birth and (very often) occupation. It is infinitely malleable in the sense of new castes being formed but as an example of bondage to the past it has no equal, though assuaged a little by the associated belief in *karma*, the determination of one's fate by past and present action. The restraints of caste, linked to duty, can be a source of social cohesion, but in a number of Indian states caste rivalry has been extremely violent. In Bihar, it springs from the opposed interests of high caste Rajput landlords, in alliance with *Goondas* (thugs), against low caste tenants and labourers whose cause is espoused by Maoist groups. One night in May 1987, the villages of Dalachak and Badhaura were attacked by almost a thousand men.

> . . . armed with *lathis* (truncheons), spears and guns who pulled people out one by one from their homes, cut them to pieces and threw them into the flames. . . . The killers were shouting slogans like "*Chhotaki Chhechhani ka Badala lenge* – We will take revenge for the Chhokat killings", and "*MCC Zindabad* – Long live the Maoist Communist Centre". They did not use their guns. They preferred the hatchets and sickles to kill.[23]

The assassins came to avenge the killings during the previous month of their own families in the villages of Chhotaki and Chhechhani in the Aurangabad district. Similar murders have taken place throughout Bihar since the early 1970s. As the *Annual Report of the Election Commission* reported in 1986:

> The state is extremely caste-ridden and anti-social elements have been meddling for a long time with elections by using their muscle power.

Caste and politics are woven together with the rural economy, and the killings are well recorded:

1985	May	Aurangabad district – 10 killed in land quarrels
1986	April	Gaya district – 23 killed by police
	September	Aurangabad district – seven "low-caste" farmers killed by Rajputs
		Rhotas district – five "low-caste" killed by Dacoits
	October	Aurangabad district – 11 Rajputs killed by MCC followers
	November	Siwah district – seven killed in land disputes
	December	Bhagalpur district – three women killed by police
1987	April/May	Dalalchak and Badhaura – 54 killed by police

(Taken from the "Calendar of Violence", *Onlooker*, June 1987.)

More recently, caste violence has taken a new turn. At the end of 1989, the new Union Minister for Labour, Ram Vilas Paswan, introduced legislation extending the *Reservation for Scheduled Caste and Tribes Bill* for a further ten years, and strong protests were mounted throughout Uttar Pradesh (V. P. Singh's own State).

"Scheduled castes" are virtually synonymous with Untouchables (*harijans*) and/or "Backward Classes", forming about 16 per cent of the total population in India, rising to 25 per cent in Punjab. The percentage is high in Bihar, U.P., Andhra Pradesh, Tamil Nadu; low in Bengal. Caste Hindus are divided into four main groups but also into several thousand sub-categories, Brahmins ("twice born") at the top. Islam does not recognise caste, Sri Lankan Buddhists have a mild form, the highest caste – *goigama* or farmers – being the most numerous.

Hostility was widespread to any positive discrimination in favour of low caste entrants into the universities and administrative service. Trains were derailed and vehicles burned; when mobs of angry students and their supporters started to throw stones, the police opened fire and demonstrators were killed. The agitation has continued to grow and "threatens to become more violent" between militants and government and "between the various caste groups principally affected".[24]

(b) Class – although caste is not to be confused with class, many of the scheduled castes are poor: the bitter poverty of the city slums and a landless peasantry. Across South Asia an industrial economy has produced not only extremes of urban rich and poor but a rural landscape in which social differentiation has increased in relation to land ownership. The dereliction of life over much of the sub-continent is clear to the most casual visitor. The railway stations of the big cities bear witness to the plight of the homeless; the poverty of the villages, where years of drought emptied the land of crops and cattles, has outlasted decades of development. With the awareness of material want goes a sense of injustice, and that too fuels the violence.

But does India not feed itself, with none of the crippling dependence of Africa or Latin America? Yes: the green revolution has enriched the Punjab and neighbouring states, including a new class of "bullock capitalists" and their intermediaries – *Arhatyas* and *Arhatdars* – who trade between the farmer and the town.[25] All that is true. But alongside those who have grown richer are those who have become poorer.

The picture becomes clearer in miniature, and Dr. Kathleen Gough has given a grim account of village life among landlords, tenants and labourers in the southern state of Tamil Nadu. In one small village, Kirippur, a population of 1055 farmed 648 acres, a village "dominated by caste Hindu landowners". There were 357 Harijans, 685 caste Hindus.

> Throughout the 1970s and 80s the workers of Kirippur and of Thanjavar were in deepening distress. . . . The gap between the richest and poorest had widened . . . partly as a result of the uneven distribution of benefits from the green revolution. In addition to population increase, factors resulting from capitalist development – such as the eviction of tenants, the loss of land by some smallholders and the loss of work by artisans – had swollen the ranks of the property-less labourers.[26]

Farming in such areas is largely paddy, plus rice mills, small sugar refineries and handcrafts. By 1987 – the time of Dr. Gough's story – there had been improvements in schools, roads, street lights, refurbished temples and some privately owned tube wells, but there was still "extreme poverty and malnutrition was widespread". The wealthier 25 per cent of the villagers now owned more land than they had in 1952 or 1976, and her comment is surely right: "the class struggle simmers on in Kirippur with occasional outbursts of violence but the conditions of the workers have not improved."[27]

Here is the raw material of violence and social relationships are changing. Those who were once passive are now active. In earlier times, there was a strong alliance across India between state governments and key figures within the local population – "the small *zamindars* and the upper tenantry . . . as well as among influential merchants and professionals" in the city.[28] Now there is a greater articulation of demands among the rural and urban poor:

> The weaker sections have, however unevenly and imperfectly, tended to develop an awareness of their rights under the law, and have begun to assert themselves, despite pressure from the groups that have long exercised dominance over them. As a result, competition and conflict have quickened, appetites for political spoils have grown among all sections of society and India has become an increasingly lively polity and an increasingly difficult country to govern.[29]

That was written in 1983 and the past seven years have seen an increase in unrest. At one time, South Asia (in Rajni Kothari's phrase) was a "secular order . . . highly differentiated and segmental, and respectful of the autonomy of the sub-systems."[30] Now "there has grown a close link between politics and the other sub-systems. . . . Not only is politics spilling over its boundaries, it is paying for its primacy by carrying an enormous load of expectations."[31]

When such expectations are not met but are still entertained, the result can be a horrifying brutality between those who have and those who demand. In Tamil Nadu, "in Kilvenmani village, 44 *harijans* were burned to death in a conflict between landlords and agricultural labourers."[32]

The violence which comes from these diverse causes might conceivably be kept below the level of politics in a state that was determinedly non-democratic, but in South Asia politics are pervasive. The activity of parties, politicians and elections transmits social conflict into political demands, and the effect is to bring violence into public life as an extension of politics by other means. We turn, therefore, to –

Political violence

Political conflict can be seen in different contexts, ranging from electoral malpractice to state violence and group terror.

(a) Electoral malpractice – that is violence by politicians and hired thugs to intimidate electors or capture polling booths in order to falsify the results. Violence halted the 1989 election in a number of polling stations in Ranjiv Gandhi's own constituency of Amethi; it ran riot in thuggery and murder in several constituencies during State elections in February 1990. The consequences are discussed later, but there is also –

(b) Terrorism – South Asia has always known the danger of terrorist movements which seek to overthrow established structures of authority. The list is long and stretches back in time. There was a tradition of terrorism in Bengal under British rule, borrowing something from Tsarist Russia, something from Ireland. Today there are terrorists in Punjab and Kashmir, the Naxalites (Maoist revolutionists) are still there in West Bengal and Andhra Pradesh, and – most fearful – the JVP in Sri Lanka:

> The election in 1988 was the most violent in the country's history. . . . The JVP was more ruthless than the LTTE (Tamil Tigers) in the use of violence. It murdered more than 800 United National Party and Opposition members and a number of officials.[33]

Murder and intimidation – headless corpses displayed along the main highway from Kandy to Colombo and threats of reprisals against whole families and villages: such have been the hall-marks of a People's Movement.

What do the terrorists want? Some are simply criminals – bandits or gang leaders – who are rationally pursuing an occupation of crime and terror; for others terrorism becomes an obsession, a way of life in which terror is not the means but the end of action. Most, however, are terrorists with a cause – Hinduism, Islam, revolutionary Socialism, communal or caste interests. Some are also proto-nationalists.

(c) Secession: Kashmir, Khalistan, Gorkhaland (for Gurkhas), Assam, Buluchistan, the Hindi areas of Nepal, Eelam. Their proponents draw encouragement perhaps from the creation of Pakistan and Bangladesh although both were part of the turmoil of decolonisation. Kashmir is certainly the greatest danger. Whereas a middle ground of compromise may still be there in Punjab, perhaps even in northern Sri Lanka, the Jammu and Kashmir Liberation Movement is bent on secession:

> A vital difference between Kashmir and Punjab is that normal life in Punjab never comes to a halt. The economy has continued to thrive; a curfew is imposed only occasionally. In Kashmir, the economy is visibly breaking down. Moreover, at the worst of times, 95 per cent of Sikhs never thought of seceding from India [whereas] there is an unprecedented degree of mobilisation of the people of the Valley against rule by India.[34]

The cost has been high – bombs, curfew, assassination, intimidation and a growing refugee population, particularly of Kashmiri Hindus (Pundits) and, ironically, Sikhs. In a "cartographical sense" Kashmir remains with India. There is Ladakh in the north, Jammu in the south and the Indian army along the main lines of control, but "within this circumference lies an island, a virulently non-Indian entity called Kashmir".[35]

And terror begets terror. When men are violent on principle the state will use violence from policy –

(d) State violence: the terrorist drags the government down to his own level. The state turns to oppression and is violently opposed, and a downward spiral of brutality carries society into despair. Look at Sri Lanka and the use of force by the UNP government, including torture and armed vigilantes, or at Nepal when the army fires upon demonstrators, or at Kashmir where

> on 21 January 1990 the police opened fire with automatic weapons on a procession of demonstrators in a narrow street in the Gowkadal area of Srinagar. . . . The militants could not have asked for more. All they now have to do is to keep the pot boiling.[36]

The violence also spreads downwards. The Provincial Constabulary in India, the police in Pakistan and Bangladesh, are notorious for their complicity in local violence. They profit from it. Stories of police involvement are too numerous to be fabricated. "In the resettlement colonies of the city, the police came . . . and directly participated in the violence against Sikhs. . . . In Trilokpuri, the police reportedly accompanied the arsonists and provided them with diesel from their jeeps."[37] That was in Delhi in 1984. And in the villages? In 1987, close to Meerut, the police gave no protection to the surrounding (Muslim) villagers against Hindu extremists:

> What can an innocent person do? If he shuts himself in his house, his house is burnt, if he goes out he is stabbed in broad daylight. If he screams for help, the police fire on him. (*Sunday*, 25–31 October 1987)

Politicians, too, are accomplices. Many have been willing to draw advantage from communal loyalties and to incite communal violence for political gain. What is the *Bhartiya Janata Party* in India but a loose assembly of those who are ready to push Hindu policies – the "rights of the majority" – against the minorities? Behind the BJP stand overtly Hindu parties – the *Shiv Sena* in Maharashtra, the *Vishwa Hindu Parishad* (VHP), the *Rashtriya Seyamsevak Sangh* (RSS), and others. So, too, in Sri Lanka where the adoption of Buddhism as the official religion went hand in hand with the affirmation of Sinhala as the national language, provoking a violent reaction from non-Sinhala, non-Buddhist minorities.

One can sympathise with politicians who are caught up in the democracy of majority versus minority. It is not, says Anita Pratap, "communalism that explained the pro-majority stance of Chief Minister Ramakrishna Hegde's decisions in Karnataka but the exigencies of politics. In view of the intractable caste politics of the State, Mr. Hegde had very little option other than to please the majority community on sticky issues."[38] But there is a more sinister aspect to the politics of accommodation. Politicians do not stop there. They go further. In Ahmedabad, there has been "the politicisation of crime and the criminalisation of politics"[39] through linkages between politicians, gang leaders, drug pedlars, liquor-kings (despite Gujarat being a dry state) and the police. In Karachi, "the Governor of Sind Province was alleged to be in league with the mafia and is said to have received Rs2 *crore* (Rs20 million). He was in Sri Lanka when Karachi was rocked with violence. His absence was not coincidental."[40] *The Report into the Delhi riots* also named names, of MPs, party workers, police and local gangsters who were said to "have paid Rs100 and a bottle of liquor to those involved in the killings".[41]

So much violence – allied to corruption! The sub-continent is truly full of woe. But it is also, primarily of course India, a theatre of peaceful conflict, of elections, parliaments and parties which canvass a huge electorate from villages, towns and cities in the democratic pursuit of political power.

DEMOCRACY

If the prospects for democracy in South Asia are not to be extinguished, the hope must lie with India which stands massively within the Third World as a parliamentary state. We look first, therefore, at the 1989 elections which ended many years of Congress rule.[42]

1989 Elections in India

The details of the election – the ninth since independence – do not obscure the central fact, that the contest was a testimony to a democracy that has no equal. Phrases such as 'the world's largest democracy' roll off the tongue and repeated too often lose their force. But that is what India has become: a continental society whose number of electors – not its population but the electorate – are twice the total population of the United States, whose actual voters outnumber the population of the USSR, and where control of the machinery of elections is an astonishing administrative fact. In the fragmented world of the 1990s small is neither attractive nor sensible. The need is for politics as the art of putting together not breaking apart, and India's achievement is precisely that – holding together, democratically, a very large portion of the globe and almost a sixth of its population.

It used to be said that to attempt to rule India was to govern the impossible. Viceroys acknowledged the problem, prime ministers now complain that their difficulties "dwarf the Himalayas". Well, it is certainly true that no-one in 1989, not even the astrologers, knew which way the electoral wind was blowing. The heat and dust of the campaigns, stirred up by party leaders with their freshly-painted jeeps, chariots, elephants and camels, blotted out the issues between the main contestants. But by the end of October, the picture became clearer. Congress had lost, the Opposition had won. And, on 2 November V. P. Singh was sworn in as India's seventh prime minister.

The pattern of voting was interesting. Rajiv Gandhi's Congress – and the party is very much his – won in the south, lost in the north and lost overall. V. P. Singh and the *Janata Dal* (People's Party) failed to secure a majority in the Lok Sabha but managed to form a government with the conditional support of two other parties, one to the right – the *Bhartiya Janata Party* (BJP), the other to the left – the Communist Party (Marxist) (CPM).

Party	Seats
Janata Dal	142
BJP	86
CPM	32
Congress	193
Communist Party	12
Bahujan Samaj Party	3
Telegu Desam	2
others	56

BSP = pro *Harijan* party
Telegu Desam = regional group, Andhra Pradesh

Congress remains the largest single party in parliament. It won 106 of the 129 southern seats, but only 73 out of 366 seats in the populous northern states plus Delhi, a heavy defeat alongside the landslide victory of 1984 by Rajiv Gandhi in the elections which followed his mother's assassination. The simplest conclusion to be drawn from the pattern of voting was that the electorate wanted a change. Where Congress had been dominant, in the north, it now lost its hold; where, in the south, local parties had been entrenched, they were voted out and replaced by Congress. Only in West Bengal was there continuity, the Communist Party (Marxist) retaining its hold. There was change, too, at the centre. Once the extent of Congress losses was known, Rajiv Gandhi informed the President that he wished to relinquish office. If he had been arrogant in victory after 1984, in defeat he was agreeably magnanimous.

Not everything in the Indian garden of politics is attractive. Anxiety during the election about the Hindu or Muslim vote, or the degree to which politics and violence – criminal violence – had grown together, did not inhibit party leaders from turning such issues to their advantage. The growth in BJP membership must surely be seen as evidence of a move away from secularism, and many Hindu, Muslim and Sikh communities will be fearful. Not the least worrying aspect of the violence in Punjab and Kashmir – the only state in the Union which does not have a Hindu majority – is the loss to India of its claim to be neither Hindu nor Muslim nor Sikh but Indian. Moreover, V. P. Singh cannot move too far from the need for support from the BJP and its aggressive Hindu followers. Admittedly, the safeguards of plurality are still there in the sense that the rivalry of opposed groups is limited by their very number – complexity denies extremism – and there is still a helpful dinosaur quality to Indian politics by which what happens in Orissa takes a very long time to have any effect in Kerala. And, yet, India is now a far more assertive society; its demands are articulated more forcibly today not only *via* television, radio and newspapers, but through the actual institutions of democracy itself – parties, elections, politicians. In this respect, the rise in the level of violence has to be seen as dangerous within its own sphere and a political barometer of the pressures building up in Indian society.

Before testing such conclusions, we must look at India's neighbours. We begin with its least friendly country.

Pakistan

Is Pakistan a democracy? It is certainly more democratic than it was a decade ago, and it would be churlish to deny the title altogether to Benazir Bhutto's government. We ought not to decry the move from military to party rule. There was an election in 1988, there is a civilian government, and the temper of the administration has been much less harsh than that of President Zia-ul-Haq's martial law.

The election itself was born out of violence. President Zia was killed by a bomb explosion on board his aircraft in August 1988 – its culprits are still unknown – and Benazir Bhutto's party took office in November–December. The wheel has turned full circle since the deposition in 1977 (and execution two years later) of Zulfiqar Ali Bhutto. General Zia had begun to move towards a return to civilian rule, but one may readily assume that the outcome of the 1988 election would have been different but for his death.

The results were by no means certain at first. Benazir Bhutto's People's Party, which campaigned very much on the strength of her father's name, was strong in Sind but on a doubtful footing elsewhere. Her chief opponent, Nawaz Sharif's Muslim League, was the directive force behind an Islamic Democratic Alliance – the *Islamic Jamhoori Ittehad* (IJI), the *Jamaat-i-Islami* fundamentalists, and a National People's Party which had broken away from the PPP. There was also strong local support for the *Mohajir Qaumi Movement* (MQM) in the urban settlements around Karachi and Hyderabad:

Party	Seats
PPP	93
IJI	55
MQM	13
Independents	46

The outcome, on a low 42 per cent turnout, was a very qualified victory. The PPP won less than 35 per cent of the vote and control of only two of four provincial assemblies. The electorate, within a divided society, voted in a minority government, whose authority is still overshadowed by the army it was intended to supplant and whose ability to control events is much impaired by the troubled history of the past four decades.

Pakistan, therefore, is an unhappy example of the worst of democracy. Sectional loyalties predominate, and opposition leaders preach a populism which catches at emotive causes – Islam, Kashmir, Punjab, India – while profiting from the violence which feeds on ethnic hostility. Criminal gangs in the slum areas of the cities (the *Katchi abadis*) continue to be allied to politics, and feudal interests in the provinces are too strong for the government to control. Hence the present paralysis at federal and state level. A civil society is not a state, wrote Hegel, when its citizens are loyal only to their Prince. So it is in Pakistan where Benazir Bhutto has had to struggle to form a cabinet and to win votes of confidence from a disjointed society. In time, party leaders may acquire a greater trust in the country's democracy if everything else comes right – peace on the borders, a strong economy and ethnic tolerance. At present, however, there is none of these, only spreading violence and threat of war. The most obvious danger is that both governments, in Delhi and Islamabad, will yield to popular pressure plus army rhetoric over Kashmir and Punjab in a war which will be both futile and destructive. And that, alas, may seal democracy's fate in Pakistan. If the violence of domestic politics does not pull down what is essentially an immature democracy, the violence of war may bring back more militant rulers.

Sri Lanka

Enough has been said of the violence which is tearing the island apart – Tamil against Sinhalese, Sinhalese against Sinhalese, Tamil against Tamil. One would be hard put to say whether the cruelty of Tamil separatists against each other was worse than the vengeance exacted by the *Janatha Vimukthi Peramuna* (JVP) on those, predominantly Sinhalese, who tried to curb their terror. One must count the dead and injured across the whole of Sri Lanka since the early 1980s, including the 1155 killed and 2984 wounded of the Indian Peace-Keeping Force (IPKF) which finally withdrew on 24 March 1990. As it was in 1987, when the IPKF arrived, so it is today. The Liberation Tigers (LTTE) are back in Jaffna and their Tamil rivals have fled to India.

The Indian government had tried to support Tamil rivals to the Tigers, particularly the Liberation Front (EPRLF) under Varadaraja Peramul which had accepted membership of a new North East Provincial Council in Trincomalee. When the Indians withdrew, the anti-LTTE gangs went with them, but not to Tamil Nadu where the Chief Minister, M. Karunanidhi had backed the LTTE. V. P. Singh had to secure a refuge for them further north in Orissa. Such are the convoluted politics in India and Sri Lanka. A final absurdity was the sudden declaration by the Provincial Council on 1 March that it had transformed itself into a national assembly for *Tamil Eelam*, but that was simply theoretical.

President Premadasa's government in Colombo hesitates between using such force as it has against the LTTE and trying to bring the terrorist leaders of both camps within the framework of national politics. An unredeemable tragedy?

And yet there has been a long history in Sri Lanka of elected governments and peaceful change. When Dr. James Jupp called his account of the island's politics, *Sri Lanka, A Third World Democracy*, the title sounded plausible.[43] The problem has been one almost of democratic excess, of leaders wooing a mass following by yielding to its demands. The change is easy to record. Until the mid-1960s, the political balance was between ruling families of right and left within the majority Sinhalese population, represented by the *United National Party* (UNP) and the *Sri Lankan Freedom Party* (SLFP); the Tamil minority in Colombo and Jaffna, also at that time under Anglicised leaders, exerted a pivotal influence (along with the Tamil Muslim community) in the middle of the see-saw. Then came along Solomon Bandaranaike and, after his assassination, his widow, Sirimavo, who built a new following on the cry of "Sri Lanka for the Sinhalese" – religion, language, jobs, land. That alarmed the Tamils who were already aware of a resentment of their disporportionate share of government posts and university places. They too turned to new leaders who raised the level of their demands from a quasi-federalism to "liberation" and, eventually, to that of a separate state – *Eelam*.

Democracy – a somewhat distorted democracy – added its own dangerous ingredient. The balance of left and right, and of Sinhalese and Tamil, was radically upset in July 1977.[44] The UNP under Junius Jayewardene routed the opposition SLFP under Mrs. Bandaranaike and pushed the *Tamil United Liberation Front* (TULF) to the resentful margins of politics:

	UNP	SLFP	TULF	others
Seats:	**139**	**8**	**17**	**2**
Percentage of vote	**51**	**29.6**	**6.4**	**13**

All 17 TULF seats were in the northern Tamil-dominated constituencies.

Jayewardene then set about establishing a Buddhist republic under Sinhalese control, including a new presidential-style republic in 1978. Extremism displaced compromise on both sides. There was a series of horrible murders, bomb explosions, burning of rival villages between Tamils and Sinhalese. The Liberation Tigers of *Tamil Eelam* were born. The *Janatha Vimukthi Peramuna* (JVP) (which had failed to carry through a Maoist-style insurrection in 1971) revived, and used the Tamil revolt to cry vengeance on its own government.

Democracy also came under suspicion. A presidential election in October 1982 brought Jayewardene back to office, but not in such strength as to persuade him to hold parliamentary elections:

Presidential Candidate	Votes Cast	Percentage
J. J. Jayewardene (UNP)	**3,450,811**	**52.91**
H. S. R. B. Kobbekadura (SLFP)	**2,548,438**	**39.07**
Rohanna Wijeweera (JVP)	**273,438**	**4.19**
G. G. Ponnambulam (Tamil Congress)	**173,934**	**2.67**
Others	**75,536**	**1.16**

The *Tamil United Liberation Front* (TULF) refused to take part. Ponnambulam represented the Tamil community in the islands, Wijeweera was the flamboyant JVP leader who was later killed by government forces. The main opposition, the *Sri Lankan Freedom Party*, was in difficulty. Sirimavo Bandaranaike had been deprived of her civic rights – subsequently restored – and the party put up the little known Kobbekadura. The circumstances were favourable, therefore, to Jayewardene and he did well, but not well enough for the UNP which backed away from the elections that were due. Instead, Jayewardene adopted the novelty of a referendum which sought approval in December by 3,141,223 to 2,605,983, but by then accusations of electoral fraud and government intimidation had become widespread.

The island was full of violence. The Sri Lankan army was sent north to suppress the Tamil uprising but, as casualties mounted and a blockade was imposed, Jayewardene was obliged to accept the Indian Peace-Keeping Force of Sikhs, Gurkhas and Madrassis. When it arrived in Jaffna at the end of 1987 it too was opposed. The problem was that, however sympathetic New Delhi might be towards Tamil grievances, it was unwilling to act like Turkey in northern Cyprus: it would not support secession. Hence the ferocity of the Tamil Tiger response. Meanwhile, further south, the JVP continued to murder UNP and SLFP party members, government officials, village headmen and innocent victims of a bloody civil war.

Too little democracy or too much? The present position is hard to assess. After an interlude of some years, elections were held again at the end of 1988 for president and in February 1989 for parliament.[45] The effect of widespread violence could be seen in the low turn out, but considering that the JVP in the south and Tigers in the north were attacking polling stations and voters, the bravery of those who did cast their vote should not be discounted. Amidst accusations of substantial malpractice, Ranasinghe Premadasa – Jayewardene's successor and former prime minister – defeated Mrs Bandaranaike (and a third candidate) for the presidency; the UNP was returned with a majority in the national assembly.[46]

After the elections, the full weight of the Sri Lankan army, plus its private auxiliaries, fell upon the JVP – terror against terror. But Premadasa has tried to talk to the LTTE, hoping (one must assume) to turn terrorists into politicians – democracy transforming violence: but at the time of writing, in the late spring of 1990, the outcome was very uncertain.

The two other states, Bangladesh and Nepal, are differently placed. They are not partial democracies facing violence but autocratic regimes which use violence against those who (often violently) demand reform. Both countries also suffer excessively not from man alone but from Nature – floods in Bangladesh, earthquakes and floods in Nepal.

Bangladesh

General Ershad would like Bangladesh to be a democracy without the inconvenience of any challenge to his authority. He has held elections, but on each occasion the major political parties have refused to take part. That has not prevented the *Jatiya Party*, the General's own creation which appeared in January 1986; from claiming an overwhelming victory in 1988 with 251 seats out of 300 in the national assembly, or General Ershad himself from wanting an elective basis for his rule. Unfortunately, although there are a large number of parties grouped into alliances of various kinds the two main groups, the *Awami League* (founded by Sheikh Mujibur Rahman) and the *Bangladesh Nationalist Party* (brought together by Ziaur Rahman), have so far frustrated the General.

The effect has been a combination of paralysis and frustration in a country which is abysmally poor and likely to become more so under a fast increasing population of over 100 million. Bangladesh is relatively homogeneous, the population 85 per cent Muslim and sharing a common language, Bengali. Yet violence has been a constant attendant, stultifying political life from the inception of the new republic in 1971–72. The register of events is sombre. Within 18 months of independence there was "continuous unrest and violence, and it was officially stated that over 1000 political murders had taken place".[47] The following twelvemonth saw an increase in the killings, particularly among the former "soldiers of the revolution". By 1975, Sheikh Mujibur Rahman was virtually dictator, only to be assassinated in August. Two years later, as was surely inevitable, soldiers took control. Their leader was General Ziaur who had built up the Nationalist Party to legitimise his rule. Then he too was killed in an army mutiny in Chittagong in May 1981. A presidential election brought Mr. Justice Abdus Sattar to office until March 1982 when Lt. General Ershad proclaimed martial law and the resumption of military rule. His justification was to recite his country's ills: "political indiscipline, unprecedented corruption, a devastated economy, administrative stalemate, extreme deterioration of law and order and frightening economic crises".

The rest is the familiar picture of the last decade. There are parties in waiting led by the daughter of Sheikh Mujib and the widow of Ziaur Rahman – the two Begums eager to play the role of Delilah – and there are many who do genuinely want Bangladesh to be a democracy. Through his series of limited elections, President (ex-General) Ershad has tried to edge the republic towards a more liberal framework of control, but terrorism from below and state violence from above have seemingly bound political life to a perpetual wheel of misfortune.

Nepal

As if to illustrate the general theme, the extent of both democracy and violence has increased in Nepal. The inhabitants of this once peaceful kingdom began to demand reforms to an antiquated system of government during the closing months of 1989. They were met by brutality from the army, persisted in their demands, and King Birenda was forced to yield. That brought Nepal close to a party-based democracy under a constitutional monarchy, but it did not end the violence. The police and angry crowds of students again fought out their grievances in Kathmandu in April 1990: six policemen were beaten to death, five students were shot dead, and many injured. Democracy seemed almost to have died an infant death, except that no-one doubted that its demands would be renewed. Those who resist reform have generally been willing to modify their opposition, and those who look for democratic politics are still prepared to work within the traditional framework of authority.

The Himalayan kingdom has been full of such paradoxes.[48] There was an election in May 1986 under the former system of *panchyat* (conciliar) government – king, palace, prime-minister, elected members and voters, but no parties. The election was opposed by all the (prohibited) parties, including the well-established *Nepali Congress*, but that did not prevent the electorate from turning out in very large numbers to vote – between 60 and 80 per cent in the 75 district constituencies – nor individuals from standing – there were over 1500 candidates. Those who were elected professed to be eager to pull down "the fortress of the corrupt *panchas*", but it was the violence in the streets of Kathmandu, and the deaths of those killed when the army fired on crowds, which brought an end to the system. A drafting committee has now been appointed to devise a party-led, cabinet-based form of government.

There is a familiar sociology to both the violence and the democracy. By the 1980s, the old "blend of arbitrary use of Royal power with a benign tolerance of the ambitions of individual politicians and their dependents" was no longer capable (against a background of changes in other SAARC member states) of resisting reform.[49] The introduction of an adult franchise was at first an attempt to limit change. In fact, it opened the way to further demands from a middle class which still had links with the high-caste, patrimonial families of earlier years – the Chhetri, Brahmin and Newar castes. There is now a political elite not only in the higher echelons of the civil service but in a number of private companies. The tally of civil servants increased from 3000 in 1960 to 7000 in 1980; the number of students rose from 2500 to 70,000. If one adds to these social trends an internal migration of almost 1¼ million from the mountainous regions of the republic to the lowland *terrai* – a steady, persistent movement over the past half-century which has given rise to "rich commercial farmers, money lenders, poor tenants and lower-caste landless labourers"[50] – one can understand the ferment of a democratic politics which cannot avoid outbursts of violence. A "caste-ridden, feudal-orientated state" may at first be able to set limits to the competitive politics of a more open society, but the limitations themselves will become, as in Nepal, a source of pent-up violence.

Each of the South Asian states, therefore, must struggle with the relationship between democracy and violence, a relationship made more difficult by the ties between India and its neighbours. There have been times when the scale of the savagery has outrun the capacity of the government to safeguard its citizens. A nation is not governed, observed Burke, which has perpetually to be conquered, and one might add that a society is not governed when its citizens lack the protection of life and property that the state should provide. When, in addition, governments claim to be democratic yet cannot stem the violence which threatens them the contrast is all the more painful. What can they do, and how dangerous is the dilemma?

ANSWERS TO QUESTIONS

One does not have to go to the Lebanon or Ulster or Colombia to see the threat to democracy from violence. All five South Asian states have suffered its effects. Violence may only be the symptom of what induces men and women to adopt its weapons, an index rather than the cause of political discontent. But its effect is measurable, and if the causes cannot be remedied, the damage to democratic institutions will lie in the violence itself. On the other side of the equation, it would be idle to suppose that democracy will improve people's morals, but it may make them better citizens and more willing, for that reason, to accept the legitimacy of a government which has to offer itself for public approval. *Per contra*, it is of course the intention of those who use violence to cancel the equation between citizens and government. And in South Asia? We begin with the damage that is clearly inflicted.

Violence v Democracy

In a broad sense, the aims of all those who turn to violence, other than for domestic or wholly criminal ends, are related. The terrorist seeks to overthrow a government and replace it with an alternative society; the secessionist concurs, though with a particular national end in view; the violence of communal disorder, even when close to frenzy, is rational in wanting to change the balance of power within society, between Hindu and Muslim, Sikh and Hindu, Tamil and Sinhalese. The use of violence by the state is obviously political in seeking to impose its authority by force. Violence is thus woven into politics and will strike at a democratic society where it is most vulnerable.

Elections and parliaments are clear targets. They link governments and society by providing a basis for consent, they hold a watching brief over the liberal aspects of public life. No wonder, therefore, they are attacked, often with a good deal of success. The danger is not only that mechanisms of choice, including elections, may be damaged but that governments, replying to threats, may suspend constitutional rule in favour of coercion: "meeting violence with violence". A number of states during our life-time have taken that route, displacing liberal regimes with totalitarian parties and military junta. Pakistan went that way in 1958. So too did Bangladesh after 1971. The balance in Nepal is still poised, while the venom with which Sri Lankan leaders used counter-terror against the JVP was a frightening example of the readiness of an elected government to repay force with force.

The critical question is how far violence in India has corroded the politics of democratic rule. We look at three areas of danger.

Ungovernability

The obvious cases are Kashmir and Punjab, and the northern districts of Sri Lanka, where the state cannot govern since its writ scarcely runs beyond guarded enclaves. Throughout Kashmir in 1989 there were

> no posters, no party banners or flags, no speeches or election meetings. So successful had

> the militants' call to boycott the polls been that the campaign in the Kashmir Valley was distinguished by its complete absence. The National Conference under Farooq Abdullah was the only party to put up candidates for the three Lok Sabha seats in Srinagar, Anantnag and Baramula. . . . They will be elected unopposed without a single poll rally . . . in a mockery of the electoral process. (*India Today, 30 November 1989*)

The outcome is painfully clear – curfew, censorship, army patrols, assassination, funerals, more violence, longer curfews, the army in control by day, the terrorists ruling by night. A vicious circle develops. Violence cripples public life and opens the way to further terror. In Kashmir it was

> the vacuum created by the collapse of politics through normal means – parties, elections, civil liberties – that terrorism, which is politics by other means, sought to fill. Of course, the training facilities and supply of arms by Pakistan made the task easier. (Balraj Puri, *Times of India, 11 January 1990*, Jaipur)

That may be too simple a view in the sense that, if there were 'normal politics', the outcome would very likely be unacceptable to the government in New Delhi. Ungovernability has to be interpreted in this light, that Kashmir cannot be controlled democratically by India:

> The reins of terror are squarely in the hands of separatists. Through kidnappings, bombings, murders, religious appeals from mosques and censorship . . . the secessionists have virtually achieved the administrative and psychological severance of the Valley from India. . . . In one of the greatest refugee migrations in recent Indian history, some 90,000 Kashmiri Hindus (*pundits*) and other members of the minority community have fled their homes into India. (*India Today, 30 April 1990*)

Similar worries concern the Punjab. "There is no government here, no rule of law," villagers complain. "When posters appear directing shops to close, we all comply. It is not their writ that runs." (Report from Khaled village, *Frontline, 14–27 April 1990*). The Sikh majority has cowed the Hindu minority, the terrorists have subdued moderate Sikh opinion. The nine (out of 13) Lok Sabha seats won by the *Akali Dal* included Simranjit Singh Mann, who had spent the previous three years in prison in Bhalgapur on treason charges relating to Indira Gandhi's murder; Atinderpal Singh of the *Khalistan Liberation Organisation*; Sucha Singh, the father, and Bimal Kaur Khalsa, the widow, of one of Mrs Gandhi's assassins; and Bib Rajinder Kaur from Ludhiana where her husband had been killed during state police action. After the election, Mann was refused admission to parliament since he was carrying a three foot *Kirpan* – the traditional Sikh sword – in a gesture that was more symbolic perhaps than threat . . .

Will the Punjab go the way of Kashmir? There are many who think it will, although negotiations are still in train. It is said that an understanding existed between S. S. Mann and V. P. Singh before the election, on the basis of which the new prime minister went to Amritsar. Then different fears were voiced. In April 1990, the government enacted the Constitution Amendment Bill which extended President's rule (that is, under a Governor appointed by Delhi) for a further six months. The suspicion was that, if elections were held for the Punjab state assembly, the *Akali Dal* (Mann) would not only form the state government but declare its support for *Khalistan*. The Sikh leaders broke off negotiations and the Punjab remains at war with itself and (almost) ungoverned in the worst areas of violence.

The moderating factor in India, looked at nationally, is that Kashmir and Punjab are two states in a union of many. The juggernaut that is political India rolls forward, seemingly regardless, yet alert to all its constituent elements and in no sense willing to abandon any of them. Moreover, the sheer weight of governmental power in Delhi may assert itself in time in the Punjab, if not in Kashmir.

Sri Lanka, however, is a different case. A small island and a unitary republic, wracked by violence. The moderation of earlier leaders who preserved a democratic order by subtle shifts in the balance of ethnic rivalry has been eclipsed by the violence of later years. Today, the hold of the JVP in a number of southern constituencies may have been broken – but only at a terrible price. If the record of counter-terror by the Sri Lankan army and its vigilantes – the "Black Cats" – is added to the atrocities of the JVP the story is grim indeed. There must be a whole generation of young men who have been butchered. Meanwhile, the LTTE is once again in control in the north. Their leaders, Velupillai Prabhakaran and Anton Balasingham, neither look nor behave nor talk like democrats. Nor have they been ready to compromise with Colombo or New Delhi. Are they not ungovernable?

There are those who believe that the government can still summon up accommodatory skills. Professor Kingsley de Silva has pleaded for an understanding of the beleaguered Buddhist majority which is apprehensive of the international dimensions of the island's minorities – Hindu Tamils, Muslim Tamils, Christian Sinhalese and Tamils. Even so (he argues) no government in Colombo has tried to enforce an assimilationalist policy: its leaders have always left room for the management of ethnic rivalries.[51] Other voices are very different. The most erudite exponent of Tamil problems insists that it was in fact the Sinhalese emphasis on a single "land, race and faith (that) split Ceylon into entities. At present this is a state of mind but for it to become a territorial reality is only a question of time".[52]

Well, who can say? Secession would be fraught with difficulty, unless India reversed its stand to extend recognition to a Tamil enclave. At present, Sri Lanka is divided *de facto*. The democracy of elections which has held together the multiple diversity of India has been unable to reconcile political enmities in Sri Lanka or prevent the partition of the island. Better perhaps the larger muddle of a sub-continent than the narrow divisions of a small island?

It would be simple to list other "ungovernable areas" – parts of Bihar, Assam, Haryana, Sind, Baluchistan, though none is so serious as Kashmir, Punjab and Jaffna. We turn, however, to a second danger.

Distortion

If democracy cannot be defeated it can be corrupted. The threat is most evident during elections but it is also pervasive within the politics of the five states. We quoted earlier Asghar Engineer's description of Ahmedabad as being corrupted "by the politicisation of crime and the criminalisation of politics", and explanations are not hard to come by, as in the extraordinary growth of urban ghettos:

> Karachi was a small town in 1947, Lahore really a provincial centre and Peshawar and Quetta small cantonment towns (before) the influx of seven or eight million refugees with very little in common between them. . . . Hence the serious breakdown of law and order, use of drugs, falling education standards and widespread corruption.[53]

Other factors, too. The corrupting effect of violence in India was certainly increased by the harsh emergency measures introduced by Mrs Gandhi and her son, Sanjay. (He was to die later in an aircraft accident in June 1980). It was Sanjay "more than anyone who advised his mother to suspend the constitution, jail her opponents, censor the press and rule by fiat".[54] It was a time when "senior ministers were not the prime minister's colleagues but super-bureaucrats surviving at her pleasure, and when party leaders were loyalists perversely proud of advertising their abject dependence on Indira". President Fakhruddin Ali Ahmed proclaimed a state of emergency on 26 June 1975 on the grounds that India was "threatened by internal disorder"; Mrs Gandhi talked of a "deep and widespread conspiracy" – democracy undermined by the negation of democracy – and locked up her critics.

By the end of the 1980s the criminalisation of politics had to be taken literally. In Uttar Pradesh, Bihar, Haryana and Andhra Pradesh "at least 50 candidates for the Lok Sabha and Assembly seats were facing charges from theft to murder". (*India Today, 30 November 1989*). There was said to be a "veritable industry of violence" trading on communal fears and caste hatred from which politicians and local mafia bosses profited. It was in Bihar in the 1980s that the police, over a four month period, deliberately blinded (with acid) suspected members of a local gang. In such areas the police are lawless, and the Electoral Commissioners in New Delhi were reported as saying that their principal preoccupation was how to meet the danger of intimidation without being able to rely on local forces of order.

Consider, too, the story – a Janata Dal story – of the violence in Haryana, north of the Punjab. Family loyalties in India frequently corrupt political judgement. In 1989 Om Prakash Chautala became Chief Minister, replacing his father, Devi Lal, who accepted office as deputy prime minister to V. P. Singh. Chautala needed a seat in the state assembly and stood for election in November for the Meham constituency. The Electoral Commission annulled the election because of ballot rigging and "booth capturing". His name then went forward in May 1990 for two by-elections – Meham once more and Darba Kalan. The Meham election was again cancelled after the murder of an independent candidate amidst accusations that those responsible were among Chautala's followers. Violence spread through the constituency accompanied by demands, resisted by Devi Lal, for the suspension of the state government and its replacement by direct rule from Delhi.

Kashmir, Punjab, Haryana, to which one can add many other districts. There is no major reason to question the *general* verdict on national elections, yet all violence corrupts and too much violence may one day corrupt absolutely?

A third problem, more difficult to describe but also of long term importance – the erosion or crumbling of democracy.

Erosion

Looking at the world in 1990 one can take some comfort from the resilience of democratic beliefs. But a free society is also a society free to voice its grievances, preferably through the ballot box, but often enough in mass protests. A familiar cycle of events takes shape – popular protest, demonstrations, elections, party conflicts, disorder and violence ending in state intervention. When the level of violence rises too high, and spreads widely, a price is paid in the form of soldiers on the streets, curfews, censorship, summary courts and the transfer of control from local to central government. In this way, violence erodes the institutions of a free society. The electorate grows weary, leaders grow weary, democracy grows weary.

Before and after the 1989 election, reports within India were full of alarm:

> The message seems to have gone out from Punjab, Assam, Kashmir, from Pakistan and even from the LTTE . . . that a few thugs, political vigilantes and religious zealots can hold governments to ransom. . . . Not without reason are criminals being inducted into political parties. Thus the violence once confined to Punjab and Assam has now spread to the point where religious, caste and political differences are subjected to the brutal arbitration of the gun. (*India Today, 15 October 1989*)

Is the picture exaggerated? At present, yes. Outside the troubled provinces, the election was peacefully decided. But there are uncomfortable trends. Politics have become pervasive, violence is now intertwined with politics. Communal violence has always been present – immanent to use the word adopted earlier – shaped by religious festivals and land quarrels, but politics in India are turning such disputes into propaganda. Violence and crime have taken root in the politics of social tension, and wherever there is communal hatred there are politicians willing to benefit, a danger strongly resisted in the days of Jawaharlal Nehru.

Does the fault lie in democracy itself? The state in South Asia is autocratic and authoritarian but it is not, as China is, a commanding power: it is *responsive*. One can call that democratic, but the strength of its virtues is also its danger. Governments, parties and politicians not only respond to local animosities, they have begun to turn them into the stuff of politics. Indeed, there is a case for arguing that governments have been all *too* accommodatory, ready to concede new boundaries and states to linguistic demands in the 1960s and over-eager today to conclude deals with local militant groups, absorbing the poison of violence into mainstream politics.

Democracy v Violence

Poison or inoculation? The question was raised at the beginning whether democratic politics might have a therapeutic quality, transmuting communal violence into political rivalry. The hope of reform is very much alive. Demonstrators call for democracy in Kathmandu and Dhaka, Benazir Bhutto clings to her elected office, Premadasa seems still to believe that there is room for Tamils and Sinhalese within a common parliamentary framework. India, too, while lamenting the violence, holds to elections as therapy: they may raise the political temperature but it is believed that they also inoculate the body politic against worst fevers.

Look, it is said, at the north east. Turn away for the moment from the Punjab and Kashmir. Look at the small hill states – Meghalaya, Nagaland, Mizoram, Tripura, Manipur, Arunachel Pradesh and Assam. In those distant states, one can argue that politics, parties, electioneering, the ethos of parliamentary government and patient negotiations between local leaders, plus intelligent use of the Central Reserve Police, have gradually transformed tribal unions and guerrillas into party factions. Following grants of statehood, the *Mizo National Front*, the *Manipur People's Party*, the *People's Party of Arunchal* and similar groups are now political parties in search of votes. Against the national trend in the north, Rajiv Gandhi's Congress won all 10 seats in six of the seven states in 1989. Was that not the prophylactic of democracy at work against violence?

The exception was Assam and the Nepalese districts of West Bengal. No elections were held in Assam because of arguments over the registration of voters and because of violence by the *United Liberation Front of Assam* (ULFA) against the local *Asama Gana Parishad* (AGP) Ministry. (The initial aim of the ULFA was "to free Assam from colonial rule by India"). The primary issue among all parties has been the intense hostility between local Assamese and the influx of migrants – the "Ali, Coolie, Bengali" settlers, (i.e. Muslims, plantation workers and migrants from Bengal) but talks have long been in progress to curb if not suppress the violence. There are also fair prospects of an agreement between Subash Ghising of the *Gorkha National Liberation Front* (GNLF) and Jyoti Basu, the Chief Minister of West Bengal, backed by officials in New Delhi. Thus time may heal what politics – democratic politics – have begun to mend.

These small north-east states can be seen as responding to, and enlarging, a general trend over the past 40 years. The enduring paradox of Indian politics has been its respect for the maxim – to every action there is an equal and opposite reaction – and the demand for greater autonomy is no exception. It has usually been matched by counter efforts to reinforce existing ties with the Centre. The unrest is tempered by negotiations between parties and leaders with the result that the State achieves a more advantageous position within the Union. That is the history of the *Dravida Munnetra Kazhagan* (DMK) in Tamil Nadu, the *Telegu Desam* in Andhra, and the *Asama Gana Parishad* in Assam. Each started with talk of secession and was then persuaded into State office on favourable terms.

One must not forget, too, the power of the Centre to suspend a State government under rule from Delhi, although arguments which assert that 'the force of democracy in India is in danger of becoming the democracy of force' usually overlook the subtlety of the coercion. A large element of complexity confounds what at first seems simple. The bid for autonomy invariably begins a new cycle of demands within the disaffected State whereby the would-be secessionists are faced either with division within their own ranks, as in the formation of the *All India Dravida Munnetra Kazhagan* (AIDMK), or with the spawning of rival movements, as among the Bodo tribesmen in Assam and numerous local groups in Andhra Pradesh. Agitation then shifts from a centre-state axis to a sub-region/regional conflict, affording New Delhi every opportunity to divide and absorb. It is in the light of a history of tension and adjustment that the claim of democracy to be able to transmute violence into co-operation has to be judged.

Of course, what works for some may not work for all. Kashmir and Punjab are much harder cases than Tamil Nadu and Andhra Pradesh, and negotiations with those who trade in communal violence run the risk not of inoculation but infection. To sup with *Shiv Sena* and the *Vishwa Hindu Perishad*, or with the JVP in Sri Lanka and Islamic fundamentalists in Pakistan, requires a very long spoon. Whether it is easier to counter the violence of political demands than it is to deal with religious, communal and caste/class violence is very much an open question: often enough, as we have seen, they are woven together. But the hope among all those who uphold liberal–democratic beliefs is that many of these conflicts *can* be transformed and reduced to manageable proportions by a therapy of argument and negotiation mediated through democratic institutions.

Is the hope valid? Is democracy stronger than violence, and can one look forward to the triumph of parliaments and elections over the corruption and erosion caused by violence? No. Both are part of the political landscape of South Asia. We can be more hopeful about India than about its neighbours, but the violence which stains political life has its origins in the grievances with which democratic politics must also contend – grievances which do not seem likely to be remedied in the present condition of the sub-continent. Evil and good; violence and democracy. As in the Manichean universe, where light and darkness struggled against each other and neither prevailed, so in the political universe of South Asia, democracy and violence are forever locked in conflict. There has never been a linear movement from darkness to light but only a contraction and expansion of democratic forms.

We should note that both are subtle adversaries. The chief danger from violence is that it will infect not only society but the state which then becomes its instrument. But democracy, too, has its strengths. One might even argue at least for India, that so large and complicated a society can *only* be governed democratically: that India must either be democratic or cease to be India. In this sense, democracy too is assured. The sentiment is comforting until one remembers the other half of the equation. For if indeed democracy is the necessary condition of India's survival, violence will certainly be its inseparable companion. All the evidence of this essay forces us to that conclusion.

Envoi

There was a third question to ponder – whether democratic governments make peaceful neighbours. The picture from South Asia is not encouraging. It is in fact alarming. If governments were fully responsive to popular pressure, India and Pakistan would already be at war. In practice, the question cannot be divorced from India's belief in (and Pakistan's apprehension of) India's role as a regional power: but that calls for its own inquiry.

APPENDIX: SRI LANKA 1990

The main focus of the essay is India but Sri Lanka in 1990 is a very representative example, a sad example, of the undermining of democracy by violence. The tragedy is not only the ungovernability of parts of the island but the corruption of democratic life, and an erosion of belief in the validity of elections, parliaments and parties. In the struggle between violence and democratic institutions success has been more on the side of terror – LTTE, JVP, the state itself – than on the side of political freedom and civil liberty. And yet, astonishingly, as in some Latin American countries today, elections have been held which cannot be dismissed entirely as facade although they were undoubtedly flawed. A parliamentary framework still exists in Sri Lanka, and at the lowest level of hope one suspects that politicians are simply not capable (yet) of perverting the electoral system beyond all bounds. The electorate is certainly willing to vote, and those who do brave the polling booth must retain some belief in the meaning of what they do. Whether from the colonial past, or out of regard for Sri Lanka's regional standing, or because of a widespread belief in the world today in the virtue of reform, something of the ethos of parliamentary rule is still discernible, if only in the strength of the protests against its betrayal and (occasionally) in the unease of some members of the UNP over the worst excesses of its rule.

Look, for example, at the *Report* by the much respected Suriya Wickremasinghe, secretary of the Civil Rights Movement in Colombo.[1] It was compiled after the December 1988 and February 1989 elections which saw the return of Premadasa as president and the UNP as the majority party in parliament:

Presidential Election	**Votes**	**Percentage**
Ranasinghe Premadasa	2,569,199	50.4
Sirimavo Bandaranaike	2,289,868	44.9
Ossie Abeygoonesekera	235,719	4.5

Parliamentary Elections	**Votes as percentage**	**Seats**
United National Party	50.7	125
Sri Lanka Freedom Party	31.8	67
United Socialist Alliance	2.9	3
Sri Lankan Muslim Conference	3.6	4
Mahajana Eksath Peramuna	1.7	3
Various rival Tamil parties	7.3	23
Others	1.3	—

Note: the percentage poll was 55.3 per cent in 1988, 63.6 per cent in 1989, the latter being the first parliamentary election since 1977.

The holding of the two contests, one must assume, was not only to retain the UNP in office but to do something to repair the basis of parliamentary rule. The *Civil Rights Report* stresses the need "to restore faith in the democratic process among those who have lost it, and to create it in the minds of the younger generation who have grown up without ever having gained it". But the *Report* also makes two serious allegations:

(1) "Both the Presidential Election of December 1988 and the General Election of 1989 were gravely affected by violence in the country; they were also marred by blatant instances of misuse of power by the ruling party." And

(2) "The one-sided news and views expressed in the state-controlled press, radio and television, the paucity of genuine news, and the pitiful absence of any real, lively debate on the issues of the day . . . does not mesh with the concept of the democratic process in which all are free peacefully to question authority, and which those wielding the gun are now so earnestly being invited to join."

And the gun, or worse, is still very much in use. The *Report* lists familiar horrors – the "17 dead bodies found at Anuradhapura . . . ascribed to the 'Black Cats' and popularly believed to be perpetrated or condoned by agents of the State. The dead include Stanley Wijesundera, former Vice-Chancellor of the University of Colombo, shot dead in his office, M. Panchalingam, Government Agent Jaffna . . . J. M. D. Bandare, a leading lawyer . . . and countless others, un-named and unknown except among their own families. . . . Eye-witnesses have told me that they saw 'dogs devouring charred bodies of persons killed by setting fire to tyres hung round their necks'. . . . The country continues to be engulfed in violence [and] the Presidential Election and Parliamentary General Election have not brought the return to normalcy that many had hoped for."

Well, one could add other accounts to the *Report*.[2] But in the Sri Lankan world of the 1990s it is still an open question which will triumph – good or evil, democracy or violence.

NOTES TO APPENDIX

[1] *Civil Rights Movement of Sri Lanka, Report, 1 May 1989, "Instilling Faith in the Democratic Process".* (Colombo, 1989)

[2] eg Janaki Perera, *The Subversion of the Electoral Process in Sri Lanka* which carries extracts from the *Report of the Non-Governmental Observer Group* from SAARC countries, *Amnesty International*, books, journals and local newspaper accounts. The 30 page inquiry is a detailed criticism of the 1988 presidential election. (Colombo, n.d.)

NOTES TO TEXT

[1] India 792,986,000, Pakistan 89,729,000, Bangladesh 94,651,000, Sri Lanka 15,416,000, Nepal 15,738,000.

[2] See Eric Stokes. The Indian Civil Service "became a system which harmonised a strong executive with the rule of law. In the sixties and seventies of the nineteenth century there eventually emerged a structure which substantially realised James Mill's ideals of Indian government". *English Utilitarians and India*, p. 180, OUP 1959.

[3] Kali, wife of Siva, goddess of destruction and death, known as Durga, Bhawani, Parvati, etc. "Her idol is black, with four arms, and red palms to her hands. Her eyes are red, and her face and breasts are besmeared with blood. Her hair is matted, and she has projecting fang-like teeth, between which protrudes a tongue dripping with blood. She wears a necklace of skulls, her earrings are dead bodies, and she is girded with serpents. . . . The goddess also of smallpox and cholera." *Encyclopaedia Britannica*, 11th Edition, 1910–11, Vol. 15–16.

[4] "Who Are the Guilty?" *Report of a Joint Inquiry into the Riots in New Delhi*, 1984, p. 18.

[5] "Violence in Bhalgapur" *Surya* December 1989.

[6] Bruce Matthews "The Janata Vimukthi Peramuna", *The Round Table*, No 312, October 1989, p. 434.

[7] Asghar Ali Engineer *Ethnic Conflict in South Asia*, p. 10 Ajanta 1987.

[8] See Robert Wokler, "Rousseau's Perfectabilian Libertarianism" in Alan Ryan (ed.) *The Idea of Freedom*, OUP, 1979, p. 233.

[9] Nirad C. Chaudhuri, *The Continent of Circe*, London, Chatto & Windus, 1965, pp. 97–98.

[10] The phrase concerning Delhi and India attributed to Babur, the first Mughal emperor. See Stuart Webb, *Room for Wonder, Indian Painting during the British Period 1760–1880*. New York, Rizzoli, 1978, frontispiece.

[11] Nirad C. Chaudhuri, *The Autobiography of an Unknown Indian*, London, Hogarth Press, 1951, reissued 1987, pp. 407–8.

[12] Engineer, pp. 3–4.

[13] Anita Pratap, "An Anger Rising from Insecurity", Engineer, p. 86.

[14] V. N. Subba Rao, "A Moment's Madness in the City of Palaces", Engineer, pp. 92–3. Karnataka has some 11 per cent of its population Muslim, about the national average for India; but the Muslim community is *urban* based: – Hyderabad 38 per cent, Mysore 27 per cent. It is estimated that over 30 per cent of Muslims live in the towns and cities of India.

[15] *Report of a Joint Inquiry into the Riots in New Delhi*. There was no remorse among the attackers. "It was significant that wherever we went, we did not find any grief on the faces of those who were participating in the looting and burning. Attempts to pacify them by the peace marchers met with derisive laughter. Listening to their raucous exultation and looking at their gleeful faces, one would have thought it was a festival, but for the arson and loot that was going on." (p. 4)

[16] *ibid*, p. 5.

[17] Balraj Puri, "Punjab Accord and After", Engineer, p. 105.

[18] *Frontline 14–27 April 1990.*

[19] Peter Lyon, *Annual Register 1983*, p. 261.

[20] Balraj Puri, "Ethnic Dimension of Subcontinental Muslims", Engineer, p. 164. See, too, Harapradad Chattopadhyaya, *"Internal Migration in India: A Case Study of Bengal*, K. P. Bagchi, Calcutta 1987.

[21] *ibid*, p. 166.

[22] Judges, XII.

[23] *Sunday 23–31 October 1987.*

[24] *India Today 15 January 1990*. "Anti-Reservation Stir".

[25] See Khadija A. Gupta, forthcoming study. New Delhi, 1990.

[26] Kathleen Gough, *Rural Change in South-East India 1950s to 1980s*, OUP, Bombay 1989.

[27] *ibid*, p. 524. Land reform acts helped to promote the green revolution, together with hybrid high-yielding seeds, fertilisers, pesticides, irrigation pumps, tube-wells, tractors etc. Paddy yields increased through double cropping. But the effect (says Dr. Gough) has been to widen the gap under credit arrangements – "they favoured the rich and mulcted the poor".

[28] Gyanendra Pandey "A Rural Base for Congress – The United Provinces 1920–40" in D. A. Low (ed.), *Congress and the Raj*, Heinemann, London, 1977, p. 218. See, too, Max Harcourt, "Kisan Populism and Revolution in Rural India", *loc cit*, p. 315.

[29] James Manor, "Anomie in Indian Politics", *Economic and Political Weekly*, May 1983.

[30 & 31] A. Nandy, *At the Edge of Psychology*, Delhi, 1980, quoted in J. Manor, *loc. cit.*

[32] Gough, p. XVI.

[33] S. W. R. de A. Samrasinghe, "Sri Lanka's Presidential Elections" *Thatched Patio*, Colombo 1988–89. See Appendix: "Sri Lanka 1990".

[34] Shankar Jha, "How To Save Kashmir", *Sunday Observer* (Delhi) 15 April 1990.

[35] *India Today, 30 April 1990*, special issue: Kashmir Valley.

[36] Shankar Jha (n. 34).

[37] *Report of Inquiry into Delhi Riots*, p. 21.

[38] Anita Pratap, in Engineer, p. 87.

[39] Engineer, p. 13.

[40] *ibid*, p. 10.

[41] *Report, Annexure IV.*

[42] What follows is discussed in greater detail in D. Austin & A. Gupta, 'India's Ninth General Election', *Round Table 1990*, pp. 137–146.

[43] See James Jupp, *Sri Lanka: Third World Democracy*, London Frank Cass 1978.

[44] Discussed at greater length in D. Austin & A. Gupta, *Lions & Tigers – Sri Lanka Crisis*, Conflict Study 211, Institute for the Study of Conflict, London 1988.

[45 & 46] See Appendix: "Sri Lanka 1990".

[17] See *Annual Register 1973*, p. 295.

[48] Anirudha Gupta, "Post-Election Politics in Nepal" in *International Studies* 24, 2 (1987). New Delhi, Sage.

[49 & 50] *ibid*, p. 99–100.

[51] K. M. de Silva, *Managing Ethnic Tensions in Multi-Ethnic Societies: Sri Lanka 1880–1985*, University Press of America, 1986. Ch. XXII. Conclusion.

[52] A. Jeyaratnam Wilson, *The Break-up of Sri Lanka. The Sinhalese-Tamil Conflict*, London, C. Hurst, 1988.

[53] Akbar S. Ahmed, "Identity and ideology in Pakistan: an Interview". *Third World Quarterly*, October 1989, p. 55.

[54] Quotations from Inder Malhotra, *Indira Gandhi: A Personal & Political Biography*, London, Hodder & Stoughton, 1989.

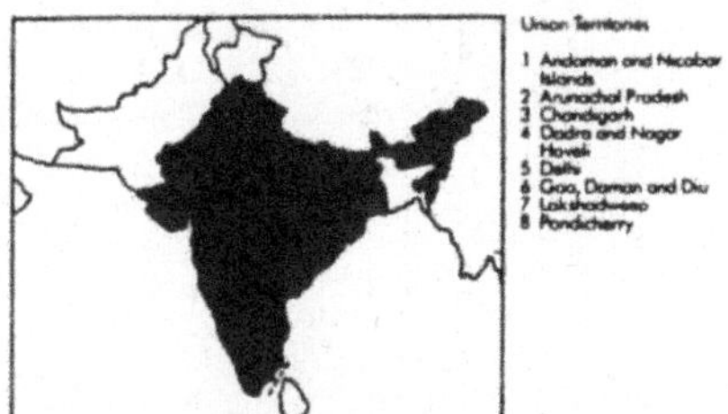

Union Territories

1 Andaman and Nicobar Islands
2 Arunachal Pradesh
3 Chandigarh
4 Dadra and Nagar Haveli
5 Delhi
6 Goa, Daman and Diu
7 Lakshadweep
8 Pondicherry

India

Map by courtesy of *Control Risks Information Services*

[5]

The Mongolian Revolution of 1990 Stability or Conflict in Inner Asia?

Marko Milivojević

INTRODUCTION

In September 1990, the first coalition government in Mongolia's history was formed during an historic session of the Great People's *Hural* (GPH). The newly elected Chairman of the Presidium of the GPH, Punsalmagiin Ochirbat, represented the ruling Mongolian People's Revolutionary Party (MPRP), whose General Secretary, Gombojavyn Ochirbat, was excluded from the presidency by a new residence rule.[1] The new Vice-President, Radnaasurengiyn Gonchigdorj, leader of the newly formed Social Democratic Party (SDP), also became ex-officio Chairman of the recently reconstituted and influential Little *Hural* (LH), a permanent standing parliament with strong powers for supervising the executive, determinating government expenditures and initiating new legislation.[2]

The LH, working through the Council of Ministers and various state committees, was also given a special responsibility to oversee the transition from a centrally planned to a market economy from early 1991 onwards. After 70 years of communist misrule by the MPRP, which has left Mongolia economically backward and stagnant, this immense task will be far harder to carry out than the political transition from dictatorship to democracy which took place in 1990: a political revolution that was completed in a remarkable six month period that culminated in Mongolia's first free and fair elections in July 1990.[3]

Although these historic elections were won by the recently reformed MPRP, the opposition Coalition of Democratic Forces (CDF) did very well indeed by polling just under 40 per cent of the popular vote, with a voter turnout of over 90 per cent.[4] However, because of Mongolia's first-past-the-post electoral system, the CDF gained less than 20 per cent of the 430 seats in the GPH.[5] Although disappointing, this was no disaster, given the fact that the 53-seat LH was the source of all real power in Mongolia. Here, because of a complicated system of proportional representation based on party-preference votes, the CDF gained 40 per cent of the seats.[6]

Consequently, the leaders of the CDF – made up of the Mongolian Democratic and National Progress Parties (MDP/NPP), and the SDP – were in a good negotiating position when a MPRP–CDF coalition government was subsequently formed, with control of the crucial chairmanship of the LH going to the SDP of the CDF.[7] In this regard, the MPRP, which only formally renounced its claim to a monopoly of political power in March 1990, needed the CDF more than Mongolia's new democratic forces needed the communists, reformed or otherwise. To its credit, the CDF leadership decided that the need for national unity necessitated a coalition with the communists at the present time.

Concomitant with this political process is a marked resurgence of pan-Mongol nationalism and an associated revival of Buddhism, which together are presently focused on two crucial issues. Firstly, the world's six million or so Mongols are divided between Mongolia (2 million),[8] China (3.5 million resident in the Inner Mongolian Autonomous Region and Sinkiang),[9] and the Soviet Union (around 700,000 resident in the Buryat-Mongol, Tuva and Kalmyk Autonomous Soviet Socialist Republics,[10] which are all sub-units of the Russian Soviet Federative Socialist Republic); secondly, Mongolia's 70-year subservient position in the Soviet empire in Inner Asia.

Presently, this empire is on the verge of economic and political collapse. Having largely left the East European states to their own devices in 1989, Moscow did the same to its oldest and most reliable ally in 1990.[11] This development explains why the MPRP régime, created and sustained by the Soviet Union for 70 years, collapsed so quickly when challenged by Mongolia's new democratic forces.[12] A collapse that has enabled Mongolia to begin to find its own political destiny in Inner Asia, ridding itself of its long standing subservience to Moscow.

The Mongols, a proud people with a very strong national tradition, have long resented their unequal relationship with Moscow. In Mongolia, there is now a barely concealed xenophobia about all things Russian, focused on the 50,000 or so Russians and other Slavs resident in the country.[13] It is only a matter of time before these expatriates are forced out by local hostility, as is already happening in neighbouring Soviet Tuva, where an exodus of Russians is now underway.[14] Formerly part of Mongolia, Tuva may once again be reunited with the old country.

This is the dream of all pan-Mongol nationalists, who would also like to see the Soviet Buryat-Mongol territories reunited within a reconstituted Greater Mongolia. The latter is no longer as fanciful as it once seemed, given the strong influence of recent events in Mongolia on the Soviet Union's Mongols, and the continuing collapse of the Soviet empire. In Tuva, where the locals outnumber the Slavs by a factor of two to one, popular support for reunification with Mongolia is already strong.[15] In the Buryat-Mongol territories, however, the situation is more complicated, as the Mongols are a minority in their own autonomous republic, with local Slavs outnumbering them by a factor of two to one.[16]

To the south, in China's Inner Mongolian Autonomous Region (IMAR), pan-Mongol nationalism and loyalty to the Buddhist faith have been strengthened by recent developments in Mongolia. Here, however, the Mongols face immense obstacles to reunification within a reconstituted Greater Mongolia, which did not differentiate between Outer and Inner Mongolia.[17] Outnumbered by Han Chinese by factors of anywhere between 10 and 20 to one (depending on the location), the Mongols are a very small minority in an autonomous area that is theirs in name only.[18] Politically, they are kept in an iron grip by the Han-dominated communist régime in Beijing.

For this régime, increasingly repressive since the Tiananmen Square massacre of 1989, democracy and a nationalist resurgence in nearby Mongolia are nightmares that might spread into China itself through the Mongols of the IMAR.[19] For the Mongols, fear of the Han Chinese has been central to their national tradition for centuries. It is, in essence, a hatred fully reciprocated by the Han – arising out of a great and historically justifiable fear of complete annihilation as a people when confronted by the world's most numerous ethnic group. For Mongolia, the threat posed by China is still real, which makes it vital that it finds new allies in the West and East (notably Japan),[20] now that it has begun to break away from the Soviet empire in Inner Asia.

THE LEGACY OF COMMUNISM

The end of the ancien régime

In December 1989, at the very end of the Year of Revolutions in Central-Eastern Europe, a Mongolian Democratic Union (MDU) was founded in Ulan Bator. The leader of its co-ordinating council was a 27-year-old academic, Sanjaasuregiyn Dzoring, who was to play a pivotal role in bringing about the end of the *ancien régime* in his country. What made the first significant challenge to the MPRP in decades doubly remarkable was that it was favourably reported upon by the media in both Mongolia and the Soviet Union.[21]

This strongly suggested that the work of the MDU's founders initially enjoyed the support of reformist elements in the MPRP, whose then General Secretary, Jambyn Batmonh, had belatedly introduced a policy of *perestroika* in 1988, following pressure from Moscow. During January 1990, however, a number of large pro-MDU demonstrations in Ulan Bator and Darhan showed that Dzoring's democratic forces were not interested in reforming a one-party communist dictatorship, but in getting rid of it completely in favour of a multi-party democracy. This became even clearer the following month, when the MDU became a political party, the MDP, which was committed to democracy, a smaller state bureaucracy, a free market economy, the elimination of Mongolia's large foreign debt, respect for human rights, and freedom of religion.[22]

Concomitantly, other political parties, such as the NPP and the SDP, were founded in Ulan Bater, where large demonstrations were staged almost daily, thereby placing immense public pressure on the MPRP régime to concede the demands of the country's democratic forces. Demands that enjoyed significant popular support throughout Mongolian society, including the 90,000 members of the MPRP, whose leaders were thus obliged to rule out the use of force from the very beginning of the crisis that confronted them. This became a matter of public record in February, when the Minister of Public Security, Lt Gen Jamsranjab, said that under no circumstances would lethal weapons ever be used against peaceful demonstrators.[23]

Those demonstrators scored their first major victory in March, when Batmonh and his entire Politburo resigned at an historic MPRP Central Committee Plenum, which also agreed to end the party's monopoly of political power, and to separate the new General Secretary, Ochirbat, from the office of President. The following month, during the MPRP's first ever Extraordinary Congress, a *de facto* election campaign began, with the new party leadership promising, *inter alia*, to establish a multi-party democratic system of government; to replace central planning with a market economy; and, to pursue an independent and non-aligned foreign policy.[24]

For the MDP, which held its first Congress in April, the more the MPRP régime conceded, the more changes it demanded, and the larger its demonstrations became. On 27 April, for example, upwards of 40,000 people demonstrated in the largest such gathering in the history of Ulan Bator. Such tactics, devised by a well-organised and self-confident democratic movement, proved to be highly effective. A week before this large rally, for example, the Ministry of Public Security was abolished altogether, to be replaced by two smaller state police and security directorates.[25] Such changes meant that the end of the *ancien régime* was becoming increasingly irreversible.

The greatest opposition victory came in May, when further popular demonstrations, hunger and labour strikes all over Mongolia finally forced the MPRP régime into serious negotiations with the MDP and its allies within the framework of a Consultative Council, whose agenda was the political future of the country. So great was this crisis that President Ochirbat, then on an ill-timed state visit to China was forced home prematurely to handle it at an historic session of the GPH,[26] which introduced a number of constitutional amendments, as well as new legislation, so as legally to entrench the country's new multi-party democratic system of government; reconstitute and empower the LH (abolished in 1949); and schedule elections for July 1990.

What followed – elections, round-table negotiations, government formation – was as peaceful, civilised and politically effective as the remarkable popular revolution that made it all possible.[27] All of which was in marked contrast to the political prospects of the Mongols of both the Soviet Union and China. In the former, Gorbachev's failing *perestroika* remained only a meaningless slogan in Tuva and Buryat-Mongolia, where local hostility to the Russians and all their works is now intense. The logic of this is reunificiation with Mongolia if time and opportunity allows it in the future. In the latter, Tiananmen Square has been followed by political repression throughout China, whose Mongols must perforce suffer and wait for better times and political opportunities in the difficult years ahead.

A Pan-Mongol national resurgence

In July 1990, on the occasion of Mongolia's National Day, President Ochirbat appeared in public wearing Mongolian national dress. This highly symbolic act, which earned Ochirbat much popular support, is thought to have been an important factor in the GPH's decision to re-elect him to the post of President in September. During the same National Day celebrations, the traditional sports festival was started by a grand parade of horsemen dressed like warriors from the time of Genghis Khan, whom all patriotic Mongols revere as the father of their nation, and its most famous son. Held in Ulan

Bator's central stadium, the parade was rapturously and emotionally received by all present.[28]

A year earlier, however, things were very different. Then, as a policy of half-hearted *glasnost* was gradually adopted by the MPRP régime, it was still possible only tentatively to suggest that Genghis Khan (1162–1227), conqueror of the world (including Russia and China), was perhaps not just the ruthless and blood-thirsty feudal tyrant of MPRP propaganda since the late 1920s.[29] Forced upon the Mongols in order to confirm the prejudices of the Russians, whose own historical memory of the so-called Tatar Yoke (1240–1480) is highly selective, this view of Genghis Khan was somewhat distorted, failing as it did to mention his considerable positive achievements.[30]

It was also an affront to the national pride of all Mongol patriots, whose historical memory of the great Khan and his empire is absolutely central to pan-Mongol nationalism and its vision of a reconstituted Greater Mongolia, which would reunify the Mongol nation after centuries of division and domination at the hands of the Russians and Han Chinese. Yet in the Mongolia of the MPRP, where pan-Mongol nationalism was denied and reviled for decades, nothing remained to evoke the Khan's memory. Only once, in 1962, was there an attempt to change all this by the erection of a monument at the birth-place of Genghis Khan on the occasion of the 800th anniversary of his birth. Soviet objections scuppered the entire enterprise, thereby showing that communism and nationalism were irreconcilable in Mongolia.[31]

Only in 1990, with the collapse of the MPRP régime and the democratisation of Mongolia's political life, did pan-Mongol nationalism, and its historical memories, resume their rightful place in the nation's public life. For the anti-communist opposition, which adopted the image of Genghis Khan as its symbol, the struggle for democracy, national self-determination and the rehabilitation of the great Khan were all inextricably connected, given the nature and past record of the MPRP régime. At a large opposition rally in Ulan Bator in March 1990, for example, the speaker who got the most applause was Dojo Dorje, a film maker, who proposed that Genghis Khan's *yurt* (tent) be recreated in the capital, and further monuments to his memory be built at his birth-place on the Onon river in north-eastern Mongolia.[32]

For the MPRP régime, forced to change radically in order to survive politically, the best and most obvious way to retain power was to join its opponents on the nationalist band-wagon. During the course of 1990, therefore, decisions were taken to, *inter alia*, honour the memory of Genghis Khan (the 750th anniversary of the publication of his first biography, *The Secret History of the Mongols*, was celebrated); rewrite the official histories of Mongolia and the MPRP, so as to produce more historically credible accounts of a highly distorted past;[33] reintroduce the old Mongolian script, which was abandoned in 1941 in favour of Russian Cyrillic, by 1993 at the latest; and, even encourage some of the milder pan-Mongol initiatives, such as the Hearth of the Mongols voluntary society.[34]

The latter, by aiming to strengthen links between Mongolia and all the Mongols beyond its borders, touched upon the dilemma at the heart of contemporary pan-Mongol nationalism. Though the wish to see the reunification of the Mongols was on everybody's mind in Mongolia, this issue had to be handled very carefully and selectively by the government in Ulan Bator, so as to avoid provoking its neighbours. This was especially true of China, whose own rulers have played the pan-Mongol nationalist card in the past, so as to bring about a pre-1911 union of Inner and Outer Mongolia within China. After the communist victory in 1949, for example, Beijing had a large mausoleum for the alleged remains of Genghis Khan built in Ordos, near the IMAR capital, Hohhot. The old Mongolian script was also retained by China's Mongols.[35] Beijing's use of the pan-Mongol card failed, but it would be greatly angered if Ulan Bator tried to play it in some overt way in relation to Inner Mongolia. Moscow would react likewise in relation to Tuva and Buryat-Mongolia. Presently, therefore, Ulan Bator can only hope for better relations with its neighbouring compatriots; a reconstituted Greater Mongolia, or the complete reunification of the Mongol nation, will only come about upon the collapse of both the Soviet and Chinese empires.

Permanent economic stagnation

In March 1990, the Presidium of the GPH passed a decree that removed all restrictions on the number of livestock that an individual could privately own. An earlier decree, passed at the very end of 1989, annulled the hated law on the obligatory procurement of meat, wool and milk at low state-fixed prices from the owners of private livestock.[36] The former decree, passed in the very month when the old communist leadership resigned, is thought to have won the MPRP the July election, when Mongolia's politically significant rural population of livestock herdsmen and farmers largely voted for Ochirbat's party and its new enthusiasm for a free market economy.

There is now general agreement that the former system of collectivised agriculture, which was adopted in 1955–60, has been a total failure. The so-called agricultural associations, which account for over 80 per cent of the nation's livestock herd, have proved incapable of boosting overall livestock numbers to any great extent over the last 30 years. In 1989, the livestock herd stood at 24.6 million; in 1960, the figure was 22.3 million. The highest figure ever recorded, 27.5 million in 1941, was never reached again after 1960.[37] Only a free market economy, where incentives exist and private initiative is encouraged, can change this state of affairs.

Bringing this about is a vital task, given that agriculture (livestock herding, crop growing and forestry) is still the main economic activity in Mongolia. It is marked by stagnation and backwardness, with relatively low and declining output, abysmally low productivity, and consequent shortages throughout the entire country, which cannot now feed itself. The small industrial sector, largely concerned with processing agricultural products, is in a similar state, which fuels inflation as too much money seeks too few goods. The crucial mining sector, which now accounts for around half of Mongolia's export earnings, suffers from a chronic shortage of capital.

Consequently, living standards are relatively low, with an estimated GNP per capita of 600 US dollars in 1988.[38] Present shortages and inflation mean that living standards are now falling in real terms. Unemployment, estimated at around 27,000 in 1989, is now rising, and will rise even further in the short-term as a free market is introduced, and the large state bureaucracy reduced. Worsening labour unrest is already a serious problem, following the creation of a Free Trade Union Movement (FTUM) out of the discredited remnants of the old official unions in March 1990.[39] Political strikes helped bring down the MPRP régime; future governments could suffer the same fate.

Externally, Mongolia's immediate economic prospects are dire. Its entire economic infrastructure, and well over 90 per cent of its foreign trade (down by 60 per cent during the first quarter of 1991), is entirely dependent on the visibly collapsing Soviet Union, which is now both economically unable and politically unwilling to continue the indefinite financing of Mongolia's large trade deficits. In this regard, Mongolia's total debt to the Soviet Union stood at just under 19 billion roubles (around 15 billion US dollars at the official dollar/rouble exchange rate) in 1990.[40] Nobody pretends that Mongolia has the economic means even to service, let alone repay, this vast foreign debt.

Politically, Mongolia's foreign debt is now a highly charged issue. It is an intolerable provocation to every Mongol nationalist, given the commonly held view that the so-called Soviet investment in Mongolia has only benefited Moscow, and that the Russians have taken far more out of Mongolia than they ever put into it. This perception even influences MPRP régime policy. In March 1990, for example, Mongolia suggested that the Soviet Union drop all its creditor debt claims on the country.[41] For Moscow, committed to free market trade with its former COMECON satellites as of 1 January 1991, (Mongolia joined in 1962) such ideas are totally unacceptable. In February 1991, the two sides reportedly reached a basic agreement on the terms of settlement of the debt when the Prime Minister, Dashiyn Byambasuren, visited Moscow.

Such issues, plus the continuing collapse of the Soviet economy, means that Mongolia must, as a matter of the greatest urgency, seek new trading, investment and financing opportunities in the West, Japan, South Korea and China. Prospects are good in the long-term. Japan, the regional economic superpower, is very interested in Mongolia's immense mineral resources, which include coal, iron ore, tin, copper, gold, silver, uranium, manganese, tungsten and molybdenum, plus some oil/oil shale, and immense amounts of timber.[42] The country also has vast agricultural potential. Hitherto, communist dogma, subservience to Moscow and lack of capital meant that most of this economic potential remained unrealised. If politics allows it, all this will change for the better in what promises to be a far more economically prosperous future for Mongolia.

A cultural reincarnation

In June 1990, the Mongolian Religious Democratic Party (MRDP) was founded in Ulan Bator. Two months earlier, in April, the recently formed Mongolian Union of Believers (MUB) presented a petition to the GPH, which was asked to adopt a number of measures to promote the Buddhist faith in

Mongolia. At the same time, Buddhist Monk Sugaryn Dagvadorj became the new Hambo Lama (Father Superior) of the country's only functioning monastery, Ganden, in Ulan Bator. These three events, though unconnected, reflected a remarkable wider revival of Buddhism during Mongolia's Year of Revolutions.[43]

The power of this revival, after over 50 years of total war against religion by the MPRP régime, indicates that the vast majority of Mongols – communists included – are still true believers in a unique and spiritually rich mixture of lamaistic/tantric, or yellow hat sect (Tibetan), Buddhism, and indigenous "shamanism", animism and ancestor worship. The lamas and monasteries of the former were destroyed by the communists in the 1930s, but this did not lessen popular faith in its teachings and practices. The relative invisibility of the latter enabled it to survive all the persecutions by the communists over the last half century.[44]

The evil nature of this persecution, involving both ethnocide and genocide, makes it one of the worst crimes of the MPRP régime. Only now, when the actual past of Mongolia is being reclaimed by its people, is the full extent of these horrors becoming apparent. During the 1930s, for example, 75,000 monks (a whole social group, or over 10 per cent of the population at the time) were exterminated on the orders of Stalin.[45] All but four of the country's numerous monasteries and temples were destroyed, including the oldest, Erdeni (1586); at the old site of Karakorum, the capital of the Mongol Empire. A whole culture, centuries in the making, was annihilated, so that the "religion" of communism might thrive.

The ferocity of this secular religion towards the true faith was in inverse proportion to the absolute power and influence of lamaistic Buddhism in pre-communist Mongolia. Co-ruled by an aristocracy and a succession of Javzundamba Khutagts, or reincarnated Living Buddhas, the pious Mongols' veneration of their god-kings matched that of the Tibetans towards the Dalai and Panchen Lamas. The eighth and last god-king of Mongolia, the Bogd Khan (1878–1924), was largely responsible for bringing about the country's independence from Manchu China in 1911.[46] He ruled it until his death, although his power was only nominal following the communist takeover of 1921.

The MPRP régime let his position die with him, and 67 years later a key religious question for all Mongols is whether they will ever regain a spiritual leader through the ninth reincarnation of the late Bogd Khan. Rumours abound about the possible existence of just such a reincarnation in either Tibet or India. After over 50 years of spiritual and cultural impoverishment under communism, Mongolia certainly needs such a leader to help direct its people towards a better future, which past experience shows cannot be reached by political and economic means alone.

Regardless of whether such a messiah reappears, the power and influence of religion is bound to grow in Mongolia. It is now a living faith, and not the dead museum piece that the communists and some in the West thought it to be.[47] This has important political implications, given Mongolia's quasi-theocratic past, and the close historical and present associations between, on the one hand, pan-Buddhism and pan-Mongol nationalism, and, on the other, between Mongolia and Tibet. As regards the latter, it is now only a matter of time before the Dalai Lama visits Mongolia again.[48]

In this regard, any overt Mongol–Tibetan alliance would greatly concern the communist dictatorship in Beijing, whose own political and religious persecution of its Mongol population in Inner Mongolia has been as bad as anything that took place in Mongolia and the Soviet Union in the past. There, as in Tibet, anti-religious policies were ruthlessly implemented, reaching a frenzy of destruction during the so-called Cultural Revolution (1966–69), which seemed ethnocidal and genocidal in intent and practice.[49] China's Tibetans and Mongols have still not fully recovered from the horrors of that period.

In the Soviet Union, the same anti-religious repression that swept through Mongolia during the 1930s was applied with even more ruthlessness in the Kalmyk republic, Tuva and Buryat-Mongolia, where only one monastery, Ivolga near Ulan Ude (capital of the republic), was left standing. As in Mongolia, however, the Buddhist faith survived to renew itself during the 1980s.[50] A similar process took place in China following the Cultural Revolution.

A STOLEN PAST

The rise and fall of the *Pax Mongolica*

Continuously inhabited since the earliest days of prehistory, the Mongolian Plateau steppelands, and the warlike nomadic warriors that lived there, first came to historical prominence in about the fourth century BC, when the Huns began to create a great tribal empire in what is now Mongolia. Following several centuries of war with China, the Hun empire broke up, with the northern Hun tribes migrating westwards, where they appear in Europe in the fifth century AD as the Huns of Attila (406–453), who changed the course of European history.[51]

In Mongolia, the Geougens, later known in Europe as the Avars, were displaced by the Turks, whose various steppe empires lasted from the sixth to the ninth centuries AD. They were followed by the Khitans, a Mongol people from Manchuria, who created the Chinese Liao dynasty (987–1125). Like all their predecessors since the building of the Great Wall of China (214 BC), the Liao controlled Mongolia by divide and rule tactics, although their sources recorded the existence of a shadowy tribal power later known in Mongol tradition as "Nation of all the Mongols." Their successors, the Chin dynasty (1125–1234), played the same game even more ruthlessly.[52]

Thus, the world a certain Temüjin was born into in 1162 was one in which the Mongol tribes were both divided amongst themselves and dominated by China. His father, a minor clan chieftain, was murdered by rival Tatars during Temüjin's adolescence. Thereafter, great political astuteness and success in tribal warfare enabled the young warlord to get himself proclaimed in 1206 as supreme ruler of the "Nation of all the Mongols" with the rank of Khan and the title of Genghis (meaning a large body of water, or ocean),[53] a name which well described what he aspired to become: conqueror of the world.

What followed next, the creation of Genghis Khan and his successors of the largest continuous land empire in world history, put half the known world under Mongol control. At its height, during the reign of Genghis Khan's grandson, Kublai Khan (1260–94),[54] the Mongol Empire extended from Eastern Europe and the Middle East in the west to Korea and China in the east, and from southern Siberia in the north to Tibet in the south. Only the sudden death of Genghis Khan's son, Ogedei, in 1241 saved western Europe from the fate that befell the Russians a year earlier.

Yet despite its undoubted achievements, the *Pax Mongolica* could not survive the ultimate contradiction between the nomadic life of plunder from which it arose, and the pleasures of permanently ruling, and hence being absorbed by, the sedentary civilisations which it conquered. When Marco Polo met Kublai Khan in 1275, for example, he was clearly more Chinese than Mongol. Superior military power and organisation, which certainly enabled the Mongols to create the *Pax Mongolica*,[55] could not in itself resolve the fatal contradiction that lay at its heart, and hence perpetuate it for any significant period of time. In 1386, the Mongol Empire began to die, with the loss of China to the Han Ming dynasty.

Thereafter, the Mongols reverted to internecine strife, anarchy and political marginalisation during the 15th and 16th centuries. Towards the end of the latter, during the reign of Altan Khan (1543–83) in Ordos, Tibetan Buddhism began gradually to supplant "shamanism", thereby strengthening an older Tibetan–Mongol relationship going back to the time of Genghis Khan. This development, initially pan-Mongol in intent, failed to unify the divided Mongols in the face of growing Manchu power in China from 1644 onwards. The Chahar Mongols of what then became Inner Mongolia fell to Beijing first, followed by the Khalkha Mongols of Outer Mongolia (1691), whose princes opted for submission to the Manchu Emperor rather than accepting Oirat (western Mongol) hegemony as the price of pan-Mongol unity. The Oirats were finally conquered by the Manchus in 1759.[56] The northern Buryat Mongols became part of the Russian Empire during the century prior to 1727, when the present border between Russia and China's province of Outer Mongolia (then including Tuva) was finally determined.[57]

Henceforth, the Mongols were to remain divided between two declining empires. The worst of the two, that of the Manchu Ching dynasty (1644–1911), kept its Mongols in a state of stagnation, economic decline and, until the late 19th century, isolation from the rest of China. Once the latter policy was changed, leading to increasing Han colonisation into Inner and Outer Mongolia, local conditions became intolerable.[58] This situation, coupled with the political prescience of the Javzundamba Khutagt, was to lead directly to Mongolia's revolution of 1911.

Independent Mongolia

The political prescience of the Javzundamba Khutagt, a Tibetan with a rare understanding of the Mongols, was shown as early as 1900, when he sent a secret mission to the Tsarist government in St. Petersburg asking for Russian help for his people to win independence from the dying Manchu Empire in China. No help was forthcoming. Prior to the Russo-Japanese War of 1904–05, when the Tsarist Empire suffered defeat abroad and revolutionary upheaval at home, Mongolia was secondary to Manchuria in Russian Far Eastern strategy. After the war, however, Mongolia was divided into two spheres of influence in a number of secret treaties between Russia and Japan.[59]

With most of Mongolia now in the Russian sphere of influence, the second Mongol mission to St. Petersburg in July 1911 was far more successful than the first. Yet it was only a relative success.[60] Because of its secret diplomacy with Japan, Russia would only agree to support the autonomy and not the independence of Outer Mongolia, which was subsequently formalised in the 1912 Russo-Mongolian Treaty and the 1915 Tripartite Treaty between Russia, China and Mongolia. International political factors thus cut short the wider pan-Mongol aspirations of Mongolia's leaders, but they also brought about international recognition of the *de facto* independence of Outer Mongolia: an independence that was formally proclaimed in December 1911, following a revolution in Mongolia.

This revolution, the first in the modern history of Asia, predated the one that ended the Manchu dynasty and established a republic in China in 1912. And unlike the phoney communist revolution of 1921, which in fact was only a Soviet military invasion, the one of 1910–11 enjoyed widespread popular support, given the intense local hatred of the Han Chinese and all their works. Its leader, known as the Bogd Khan after independence was proclaimed, wielded legitimate authority. He also had the genuine affection of his subjects.[61] The contrast with the communist carpet-baggers of 1921 could not have been greater.

For the communists, the only permissible history was the one manufactured by themselves, with 1921 as Year Zero. The actual past was falsified out of existence. The events and historical personalities of the 1911 revolution, even more than those of the more distant Genghis Khan period, were twisted and distorted out of all recognition by ideologues in the service of an antagonistic foreign power. Thus, in the communist view, the motives and actions of the Bogd Khan and his government had nothing whatsoever to do with a genuine patriotism in extremely difficult circumstances, but were purely to be explained in terms of class greed, corruption and even treason.[62]

Following the Chinese invasion of Mongolia in 1919, for example, the totally isolated Bogd Khan government was forced into an agreement with the Republic of China, whereby Outer Mongolia's autonomy under the 1915 Tripartite Treaty was terminated. A clear case of class greed, according to later communist accounts,[63] which fail to explain what other options were available to those who signed the 1919 agreement at a time when Russia's earlier protectorate over Mongolia no longer existed. To sign was certainly capitulation; not to sign would have risked an even worse occupation régime.

Such difficult dilemmas require historical understanding, not prattle about class origins, which was as absurd as it was dishonest.

Early in 1921, in a development that was ultimately to seal Mongolia's fate for the next 70 years, the wider progress of the Russian civil war swept the hated Han Chinese out of the country for good. The Mongols' new liberator, Baron Ungern-Sternberg, was a White officer of psychopathic tendencies. Thinking himself a reincarnation of Genghis Khan, the Baron hoped to liberate Lenin's Russia with help from Japan. When he attempted to do so in May 1921, the Red Army invaded Mongolia, seizing Urga (later Ulan Bator) in July of the same year. A new Mongolia was thus born.[64]

Contrary to later propaganda claims, the role of Mongolia's handful of communist revolutionaries and fellow travellers in these events was entirely marginal, and completely subordinate to Soviet security interests and rigid Comintern control.[65] The MPRP, founded in March 1921 on Soviet territory, set up a provisional government and army in the same month on Comintern orders. This, of course, far exceeded the mandate given to the revolutionaries by the Bogd Khan, whose political realism again manifested itself when he authorised a secret mission to Soviet Russia in the summer of 1920. Though ultimately politically fatal to the Bogd Khan, this apparently selfless decision was as sincere in its desire to help the Mongols as all its precursors since the birth of modern Mongolia in 1911.

Soviet Mongolia

Having gained control of Mongolia – the Comintern's only success in the entire inter-war period – Moscow's first order of business was to grab Tuva, formerly Uryanghai, and turn it into a nominally independent satellite state, which was later formally annexed by Stalin in 1944.[66] This caused considerable resentment in both Tuva and Mongolia, where pan-Mongol nationalism, Buddhism and loyalty to the memory of the late Bogd Khan defined the nation's political and social life until the late 1920s. The MPRP régime, though under the control of imported Russians and Russified Buryat Mongols, was regarded as politically unreliable by the Comintern, whose continuing purges of the party began as early as 1922.[67]

Real power was with the Red Army occupation forces in Mongolia, the Soviet-controlled GVO (secret police), and, from around 1926 onwards, the Revsomols (Mongolia's Komsomols), whose young Jacobins were used by the Comintern against the more moderate elements of the MPRP.[68] A little earlier, in 1924, the ground had already been prepared for this new radical policy, with the promulgation of Mongolia's first constitution (a copy of the 1918 Russian republic's constitution) following the death of the former Bogd Khan in May of that year.

In late 1928, at the Seventh MPRP Congress, Stalin's new policy line in the Soviet Union was adopted by Mongolia's communists. In 1929, the native aristocracy was wiped out under the direction of Khorloin Choybalsan, an unsavoury character with an GVO/NKVD background. Concomitantly, and especially after the Eighth MPRP Congress in 1930, a full-scale anti-religion campaign got underway, culminating in the almost total destruction of the Buddhist Church in the late 1930s. Even worse, a ruthless collectivisation of all Mongolia's herdsmen was attempted with predictably disastrous consequences for the country's primitive nomadic economy. The number of livestock, for example, plunged from 23.4 million in 1930 to 16 million in1932, leading to famine and civil war.[69]

The 1932 nationwide uprising, which very nearly toppled the MPRP régime, was violently suppressed by Soviet military and NKVD forces drafted in from the Soviet Union. Though later written out of the MPRP's official histories, this seminal development convinced Stalin that chaos in Mongolia could give the Japanese – in neighbouring Manchuria since 1931 – a pretext to invade the country. Collectivisation was therefore abandoned in Mongolia in 1932. Over 30 years were to pass before it was finally carried out in the late 1950s. In Tuva and Buryat-Mongolia, however, collectivisation was fully implemented in the early 1930s, although resistance to it was as intense as in Mongolia, where Soviet policy was to maintain a stable, reliable and militarised buffer state against Japanese expansionism from Manchuria and Inner Mongolia.[70]

In 1934, Stalin's Great Terror began in the Soviet Union, spreading to Mongolia in 1936, when Choybalsan became Minister of Internal Affairs. Over the next three years, as Choybalsan's power increased, the entire leadership of the MPRP and the Mongolian People's Army (MPA) was purged. Thus, by the time of the promulgation of the country's second constitution (a copy of Stalin's of 1936) in 1940, the MPRP had been entirely remade in the Stalinist image of its counterpart in the Soviet Union. A year earlier, Choybalsan, a Soviet agent from the very beginning of his career, gained supreme power, which he was to exercise until his death in 1952.[71]

The full human cost of these terrible events is only now becoming clear, after being covered up for decades by the MPRP régime. In March 1990, for example, a series of TV documentaries by Doj Dorje claimed that over 100,000 Mongols had been killed in Mongolia and the Soviet Union during the 1930s. According to this source, 75 per cent of the victims were monks; the rest being ordinary herdsmen, party members, army officers and intellectuals. An incredible one in ten Mongols perished at this time.[72] Underpopulated Mongolia is still living with the demographic consequences of this man-made disaster.

During the Second World War, when Mongolia was ruthlessly exploited to aid the Soviet war effort, the Volga Kalmyks were singled out and especially cruelly treated for their alleged pro-Axis sympathies. Only half those deported to Siberia in 1943 survived to see their nation rehabilitated in 1958.[73] In Mongolia, Choybalsan ruled a country that was getting poorer under a régime of virtual Stalinism. It was not until 1948, or over 25 years after the so-called revolution of 1921, that the first Five Year Plan was introduced to develop the country's economy. And it was not until well into the 1950s, when Beijing's new communist régime began to send substantial economic aid to Mongolia, that the Soviet Union did the same. At the beginning of that decade, in 1952, the deceased Choybalsan was replaced by Yumjaygiyn Tsedenbal, MPRP First Secretary since 1940, and the chosen heir of Mongolia's Stalin.

Continuously in power until 1984, when he was forcibly deposed on Andropov's orders, Tsedenbal died in disgrace in his Moscow exile in April 1991. As the former head of the *ancien régime* he was hated and despised in Mongolia. All its failures, which are as varied as collectivisation, the 1960 constitution, and total subservience to Moscow during the Sino-Soviet dispute (1960–84), are his ultimate responsibility. However, many others were to blame as well, including Tsedenbal's chosen successor, Jambyn Batmonh, who was forced to resign in March1990 precisely because of his earlier close links to Mongolia's Brezhnev.[74]

Such politicians belonged to a past Stalinist Soviet Mongolia that ended with their passing from the political stage in 1990. The political future, though likely to be defined by a reformed MPRP in at least the short-term, really belongs to a new and unprecedented generation of up-and-coming democratic leaders, such as Vice-President Gonchigdorj, and the MDP leader, Dzoring, who is now also Chairman of the Parliamentary Union. They are far removed in every way from their Stalinist predecessors.

Moscow's puppets

If the shadowy Damdiny Sukhebator (1893–1923) – the so-called Mongolian Lenin of later MPRP propaganda – is disregarded,[75] then only two men ruled Soviet Mongolia for nearly 50 of its 71 years of existence. The first, Choybalsan (1895–1952), was Mongolia's Stalin; the second, Tsedenbal (1916–1991), was Mongolia's version of Brezhnev long before that Soviet leader came to power in 1964. Tsedenbal's successor, Batmonh (1926–   ), was a bird of the same feather as his old chief, despite an attempt at Gorbachev-style reform from 1988 onwards. And all three men, from first to last, were Moscow's puppets.

Born into humble circumstances and educated in a monastery until 1912, Choybalsan was one of the very few Khalkha Mongols who taught themselves Russian at an early age.[76] His unique fluency in this language ensured him important, though often covert, positions in Mongolia's communist movement, which he helped found in 1919–20. Closely connected to the Comintern representative in Irkutsk (Boris Z. Shumyatsky, 1886–1943), who master-minded the Soviet takeover of Mongolia in 1921, Choybalsan was almost certainly recruited as an agent of the Soviet secret police, then the CHEKA, as early as 1920. Two years later, he helped set up the GVO, Mongolia's secret police. Only somebody who had made a Faustian bargain with Moscow would have been trusted with such important work.

It was this secret GVO/NKVD career that explained his rise to power in the 1920s and 1930s. He was far more than the simple soldier he often pretended to be, although his military career was an important aspect of his life from the earliest days of the MPA in 1921. In 1924, after attending a military academy in Moscow, he became MPA Commander-in-Chief. In 1929, he came to political prominence, but was not to hold any high office until becoming Interior Minister in 1936. By 1940, he was simultaneously Prime Minister, Minister of the Army, MPA Commander-in-Chief (with the title of Marshal), Foreign Minister, and Interior Minister.[77]

Though regarded as a mass murderer of his own people during the 1930s, Choybalsan is now credited by some for persuading Stalin not to annex Mongolia during the wartime period, and 1944 in particular, when Tuva was annexed. At that time, when Soviet power and prestige were immense, Stalin could easily have done this. No major foreign power would have lifted a finger to save Mongolia. The fact that Stalin ruled out the annexation option, which was a real possibility during the war, was almost certainly due to his view of Choybalsan as an ultra-loyal, reliable and tested puppet who was incapable of becoming any sort of threat to Moscow.

Choybalsan wanted Mongolia to exist, albeit under total Soviet control. His successor, Tsedenbal, had only one ambition in his now infamous career: to see his country become the 16th union republic of the Soviet Union. What made such treason particularly obnoxious was that Moscow, though certainly willing fully to integrate Mongolia into its union, did not want actually to annex the country.[78] That drastic option was ruled out by Stalin during the war, and has never been on Moscow's agenda during the post-war period.

It is this, plus the manifold failures of his old régime,[79] that accounts for the intense hatred the late Tsedenbal still inspires in Mongolia. His Russian widow, Anastasya Filatova, is hated even more. The MPRP, though still top-heavy with Tsedenbal stooges, dumped him in April 1990, when he and his spouse were kicked out of the party, stripped of all their official honours, and crucified in the media.[80] Only his death a year later ended the vexed issue of his possible extradition, when even worse indignities could have followed, including indictment for crimes such as fraud allegedly committed by him and his wife in the past. Hopefully, the people he tormented for so long will one day find it in their hearts to forgive and forget an old man who ended his days sick, senile, disgraced and far from home.

AN EXTERNAL ENVIRONMENT IN FLUX

Inner Asia's pivot and pawn

Sandwiched between the Soviet Union and China in Inner or High Asia,[81] Mongolia – a vast country of just over 600,000 square miles – occupies a pivotal geopolitical position that figures prominently in the national security interests of both its neighbours. For the Soviet Union, control of Mongolia has guaranteed the security of its vital Irkutsk–Ulan Ude–Chita "Baikal corridor", through which runs the Trans-Siberian railway. For China, the loss of control over Outer Mongolia in 1911 entailed a considerable strategic weakening, given the proximity of Beijing to Mongolia, which borders Sinkiang, Inner Mongolia and Manchuria.

Historically, the strategic importance of this area derived from its millennial role as the "heartland" of warlike nomadic tribes who rode out of its endless and poor steppelands to plunder and conquer the rich sedentary littoral civilisations of China, the Middle East and Europe.[82] With the decline of Mongol power, Greater Mongolia, the core of its old empire, was divided between its two stronger neighbours during the 17th century. In such a situation the fate of the Mongols was to become mere pawns in a wider Great Game in Inner Asia.

Only in 1911, when the wheel of history began to turn in China, were the Mongols of Outer Mongolia able to proclaim an independent Mongolia with assistance from Russia. A decade later, following the effective end of independent Mongolia at the hands of the Chinese in 1919, only Soviet Russia could ensure the country's survival. For Moscow, strategic considerations led to the invasion of Mongolia in 1921, and largely determined future Soviet policy towards the country, China, and, more distantly, Japan. The creation of a communist society was a secondary matter, with strategic needs often over-riding ideological considerations. Thus, the 1921 Soviet–Mongolian Treaty of Friendship did not preclude an agreement on Outer Mongolia (a name accepted by Moscow) with the Kuomingtang government in China in 1924.[83]

Similarly, collectivisation was abandoned in Mongolia in 1932 because of a greater strategic need to check Japanese expansionism, as it spread into Manchuria (1931) and then, by stages, into the whole of north China (1937) and Inner Mongolia (1938). Following numerous incidents on the Mongolian–Manchurian border, Moscow invoked the relevant clauses of the 1936 Soviet–Mongolian Protocol of Mutual Assistance to use its military forces to defeat a limited Japanese invasion of Mongolia at Nomonhan in the summer of 1939. Though a great victory, whose strategic consequences were to be global,[84] it was a Russian enterprise, with the MPA acting as a mere auxiliary to the Red Army. Politically, Nomonhan finally scuppered Japan's inept playing of the pan-Mongol national card from Inner Mongolia, where many Mongol nationalists hoped that Tokyo would deliver them from the Han Chinese and Russians alike.

It was not to be. At the end of the Second World War, when the Soviet Union invaded Manchuria and Inner Mongolia through Mongolia, the Mongols of that nominally independent country were again haggled over by their two neighbours. Typically, China only agreed to recognise Mongolia in 1946 within the context of a codicil attached to a Treaty of Friendship and Alliance signed with Moscow in the summer of 1945.[85] This enabled Stalin to stop pretending that China had any sovereign rights in Mongolia, which entered into a full state Treaty of Friendship and Mutual Assistance with the Soviet Union in 1946.

Renewed and expanded upon in 1966, and renewed again in 1986, the Soviet Union's extensive mutual assistance commitments towards Mongolia guaranteed the country's security throughout the post-war period. A period in which Mongolia's external environment changed from extremely close Sino-Soviet relations in the 1950s, which allowed Mongolia to adopt a more balanced foreign policy between its neighbours, to the momentous split between the two communist giants, which lasted from 1960 to 1984. Appalling Sino-Mongolian relations were the result of this split.[86] Thereafter, another change took place, with a growing Sino-Soviet *rapprochement* during the 1980s.

The positive spin-offs of this change included the withdrawal of Soviet military forces from Mongolia, closer Sino-Mongolian bilateral relations, and, up to 1989 at least, the prospect of closer links between Mongolia and the Mongols of Inner Mongolia. Presently, though relations with Beijing remain uncertain, Mongolia has an unprecedented opportunity to change its foreign policy in a quite fundamental way, so as finally to end its role of pawn in the Sino-Soviet relationship. Other options are now being considered in Ulan Bator.[87] If handled properly and effectively, Mongolia may well have a pivotal role to play in the area in the future.

The Moscow–Ulan Bator Axis

In March 1990, a Soviet–Mongolian Protocol on the complete pull-out of all Soviet military forces from Mongolia was signed in Ulan Bator.[88] Under this agreement, 27,000 troops (one tank; one motor rifle division) left Mongolia in May 1990, leaving one incomplete motor rifle division of around 10,000 troops, which will be finally withdrawn over an agreed period in 1991–92. The protocol also agreed that the MPA would have no need of any Soviet military advisers after 1992.[89] Under earlier agreements dating back to 1987, Moscow had gradually reduced its military forces in Mongolia by around 50 per cent from a baseline of 65,000 troops (five divisions) and 90 combat aircraft in 1987.[90]

Brought about by Gorbachev's desire to effect a *rapprochement* with Beijing, this Soviet withdrawal ended a 70 year foreign military occupation of Mongolia, which every Mongol patriot could not but resent. Officially, Soviet military forces were based in Mongolia from 1921 to 1925, from 1936 to 1956, and from 1966 to 1990. Unofficially, there has been no year since 1921 when some Soviet military and para-military (secret police) forces have not been in the country. At no time has the MPRP régime had any control whatsoever over the operational deployment of these forces on its territory, which the Soviet military regarded as one vast militarised base for the forward defence of southern Siberia.

It was also an ideal spring-board for invading China. During the 1930s and 1940s, the Japanese threat in China prompted Moscow to build a rail and road network in Mongolia. It was clearly designed to serve Soviet military requirements then and thereafter. In 1945, vast Soviet military forces moved out of eastern Mongolia into southern Manchuria, whose star prize, Port Arthur, had been lost by Russia to Japan in their war of 1904–05. The Japanese Kwantung Army was utterly destroyed in a classic Soviet *blitzkrieg* campaign.[91] In 1969, when Moscow and Beijing came to the very brink of war, the Soviet garrison in Mongolia stood at over 100,000 troops, including fixed and mobile intermediate ballistic missiles with nuclear and chemical warheads.[92]

Thereafter, though the threat of a Sino-Soviet war abated, Mongolia remained a perennial apple of discord between Moscow and Beijing. In 1978, the Chinese government formally stated that all Soviet military forces in Mongolia would have to be withdrawn before any improvement in Sino-Soviet relations could take place.[93] Though Brezhnev's successor, Andropov, made some moves to effect a real reconciliation with Beijing (such as dumping Tsedenbal), it was not until Gorbachev's 1986 Vladivostok speech that it became clear that Moscow would indeed pull out of Mongolia in the wider strategic interest of a Sino-Soviet *rapprochement* that culminated in Gorbachev's visit to China in 1989.

Politically, Moscow's primary objective in Mongolia was to maintain its stragetic interests in the country, which had to be kept under a permanent military occupation as a result. This, of course, necessitated gaining and permanently retaining full control of Mongolia's domestic political life and its foreign policy. The methods used varied over time. During the 1920s and 1930s, the permanent purge and terror were the norm. Thereafter, as a new generation stepped into the shoes of yesterday's purge victims, more sophisticated methods were required. Tsedenbal's *nomenklatura* was educated and trained in the Soviet Union, so as to be more Russian than Mongol. The result of that was a mongrel ruling class made up of confused and alienated people who were strangers to the class they claimed to represent.

Following Mongolia's revolution of 1990, it is clear that communism has very shallow roots among the Mongols. A 70-year experiment that was total nonsense even by the so-called historical laws of Marxist dogma, whereby communism is reached after socialism and capitalism, which Mongolia by-passed altogether.[94] In this regard, it is highly doubtful whether Moscow's ideologues ever took Mongolian "communism" entirely seriously. The MPRP, whose name does not even include the word "communist" in it, has contributed nothing to communist theory, and its influence on the world communist movement has been virtually nil. In 1990, Moscow washed its hands of the whole sorry farce.

Economically, Moscow's propaganda concealed a ruthless type of neo-colonialism, whose primary objective was maximum plunder at minimum cost. From 1921 to 1948, nothing was done by Moscow to develop Mongolia's economy, which even supplied goods gratis to the Soviet Union during the Second World War (in the First World War, the Tsar of Russia paid in gold). Thereafter, following large-scale Chinese aid during the 1950s, Moscow financed steady economic development, albeit at the price of a large foreign debt and the imposition of a flawed economic system that was a failure in the long-term.

Investment priorities were also biased to first serve Soviet interests. The vast Erdenet copper-molybdenum works is the prime example of this. Its large capital costs added to Mongolia's foreign debt, while its entire output of 20 million tons of concentrates is exported to the Soviet Union to help service that very same foreign debt. After processing the Erdenet concentrates, the Soviet Union sells some of the finished raw materials on the world market for high prices. Mongolia gets nothing for its wealth.[95] Such ruthless swindles explain why the Russians are hated so much in Mongolia at the present time.

Beijing's Mongolian problems

In May 1990, President Ochirbat visited China for the first Sino-Mongolian summit in 28 years. Though both over-shadowed and then cut short by Mongolia's revolution, Ochirbat's visit was nevertheless an historic milestone in his country's difficult relationship with China. The summit's agenda concentrated on bilateral economic co-operation, although the Beijing régime – having imposed a complete media black-out on events in Mongolia during 1990 – went out of its way publicly to "advise" its Mongol guest to maintain a so-called "stability" in his country.[96] Such advice was not wanted. Other sensitive issues, such as pan-Mongol nationalism, were avoided altogether, although they were implicit in Ochirbat's leaving China via Hohhot, capital of the IMAR.

Historically, the loss of Outer Mongolia in 1911 was something that China never really accepted. Only in 1946 did Beijing agree to recognise Mongolia. In 1947, when Stalin could have allowed Choybalsan to annex Inner Mongolia, Mao-Tse-Tung's communists founded the IMAR well before the People's Republic of China (PRC) came into existence two years later. The IMAR was clearly designed both to prevent Ulan Bator doing this in 1947, and to create a pan-Mongol card for Beijing to play against Mongolia in the future. In the early 1950s, Mao reportedly asked Stalin for permission to re-annex Mongolia in return for full Chinese participation in the Korean War.[97] China's invasion of Tibet was the precedent for this proposal, which Stalin rejected. This rebuff, however, only served to make Mao even more determined to regain Mongolia during the 1950s.

A change of tactics was required. Following the signing of a Sino-Mongolian economic and cultural co-operation agreement in 1952, Beijing made available large amounts of economic aid, including around 10,000 workers, to Mongolia. Modern Ulan Bator, for example, was largely built by the Chinese at no cost to Mongolia. Though not unwelcome to those in the MPRP régime who wanted to pursue a more even-handed foreign policy towards Moscow and Beijing, these subtle Chinese moves began to alarm the Russians. The famous Bulganin–Tsendenbal joint statement of May 1957, which was clearly anti-Chinese, reflected this new mood.[98]

However, it was not until the Sino-Soviet split began in earnest in the early 1960s that Beijing's new strategy towards Mongolia collapsed altogether, as Tsedenbal leapt onto Moscow's side in the great schism of communist history. This seems to have surprised the Chinese. Domestically, Mongolia's collectivisation campaign was greatly influenced by Mao's "Great Leap Forward" of 1958–59. Externally, a Sino-Mongolian Treaty of Friendship and Mutual Assistance was signed in 1960, followed by a border demarcation treaty in 1962, when Tsedenbal actually visited Beijing.[99] Yet when it came to the crunch – Moscow or Beijing? – there was no real choice as far as Tsedenbal was concerned.

Thereafter, and especially during and after the so-called Cultural Revolution (1966–69) in China, Sino-Mongolian relations were to be even worse than those of its two neighbours towards each other. In 1969, when Mongolia's embassy in Beijing was attacked by a mob of Red Guards, Tsedenbal freely confessed – to an American journalist – that he hated the Han Chinese even more than did the Russians.[100] Such racial hatred was fully reciprocated by the Chinese, who unleashed a Great Han campaign against the Mongols of the IMAR during the Cultural Revolution. This frenzy of violence and destruction, which Inner Mongolia has yet to fully recover from, gave China's bilateral relations with Mongolia a particularly bitter twist.

In 1967, as virtual civil war raged in Inner Mongolia, the creator and leader of the IMAR, Ulanfu (1906–88), or Ulanhu to use the Mongol rather than the Chinese pronunciation, was toppled from power in Hohhot by Red Guards.[101] His crime, promoting local nationalism, had been official policy in the 1950s. Such largely imaginary treason was harshly punished by Red Guard terror throughout the IMAR, which was itself drastically truncated to a third of its former size in 1969. This meant that most of China's Mongols were henceforth outside the so-called autonomous region that was only nominally theirs anyway.

Although Ulanhu was rehabilitated in 1973,[102] Mao's communists had proved to be just as committed to a Great Han unitary Chinese state as their Kuomintang predecessors. The so-called "autonomy" they offered to China's ethnic minorities was a sham. Fear of ethnic minority revolts and, after 1989, democracy, prompted the Beijing régime to use the harshest methods of control in its borderland areas. The 1990 revolution in Mongolia has worsened the already bad situation of China's Mongols. Only the collapse of communism can change this situation for the better.

Mongolia's other options

In April 1990, Mongolia established full diplomatic relations with South Korea, and sent a high-level governmental delegation, headed by the Chairman of the GPH, to Japan, where it was received by Prime Minister Toshiki Kaifu, and leading figures from the country's top industrial and financial institutions. The previous month, in a historic development, Mongolia's Prime Minister, Dumaagiyn Sodnom, also visited Tokyo, where Kaifu and, even more importantly, Emperor Akihito, were among his hosts. The Emperor was invited to visit Mongolia, which was immediately granted most-favoured-nation status (MFNS) in a new Japanese–Mongolian trade agreement.[103]

The summer witnessed further historic changes in Mongolia's foreign policy, as it moved out of the constrictive and dreary Sino-Soviet ghetto it had been imprisoned in for most of the 20th century. In July, for example, Mongolia applied to join the International Monetary Fund (IMF), whose seal of approval it would need before being able to borrow badly needed foreign exchange in Western and Pacific financial markets. In February 1991, Mongolia became a member of the IMF, the World Bank and the Asian Development Bank.[104] An earlier Law on Foreign Investments was designed to attract foreign direct investment to help develop the country's under-capitalised economy.

Further trading and other commercial opportunities were created in August, when the US Secretary of State, Mr James Baker, arrived in Ulan Bator for the first such visit since Mongolia and the United States established diplomatic relations in 1987. Important bilateral agreements were signed, including one that would in time pave the way towards MFNS for Mongolia in the United States. Mr Baker also publicly praised the July elections and met CDF opposition leaders.[105] In January 1991, President Ochirbat visited the United States (the first such visit by a Mongolian head of state), where he met President George Bush, signed a trade agreement, and met senior officials from the IMF and World Bank. Similar initiatives were taken by European diplomats in Ulan Bator, where the crucial European Paris–Bonn axis was taken to its logical conclusion in the form of a joint Franco-German embassy in the city.[106] Earlier in the year, Mongolia established full diplomatic relations with the European Community (EC).

A solid foundation was thus laid for further improving relations with the world's three economic power centres. Japan, for reasons of geography, history and economy, will play the leading role in Mongolia's continuing *rapprochement* with the non-communist free world, and its related search for new foreign policy options to guarantee its future security, national independence and economic prosperity. Tokyo's interest in Mongolia goes back a long time. The first militaristic bid for influence (1907–45) ended in disaster in Manchuria in 1945, but not before many Mongols had been strongly attracted by Japan's seeming support for pan-Mongol nationalism as a weapon against both the Han Chinese and the Russians.

The second, and as yet purely economic, bid for influence has only now begun, although Japan and Mongolia established diplomatic relations as far back as 1972. Politics, specifically Mongolia's role as a pawn in the Sino-Soviet dispute, prevented this opening from developing into a full relationship. This, of course, was part of an older story of political and economic isolation. From 1911 to 1946, for example, Mongolia had diplomatic relations only with Tibet (1912),[107] the Soviet Union (1921), Tuva (1926), and China (1946). Because of a US veto after the war, membership of the United Nations (UN) did not come until 1961, after which various Western countries, such as the United Kingdom (1963), extended diplomatic recognition to Mongolia.[108]

Presently, Mongolia perceives itself as being a developing country of great economic potential;[109] part of the Inner Asian–Pacific region and century; a model for peaceful change in the stagnant pond that is Asian communism; and capable of moving from being the pawn to the pivot of Inner Asian affairs. An ambitious vision to be sure, but not an impossible one by any means. Mongolia's external environment has changed out of all recognition in recent years. The Cold Wars between the Soviet Union and the West, and the Soviet Union and China, are now over. Communism has collapsed worldwide. The Soviet empire is disintegrating; the Chinese could go the same way if central communist control collapses, as it invariably will sometime in the 1990s. Other foreign policy options are thus now open to Mongolia.

Interesting new ideas are now being floated in CDF circles in Ulan Bator. One, to give Mongolia some form of internationally recognised and guaranteed (by the UN Security Council) permanent neutrality, could become politically possible soon. Mongolia will be free of all Soviet military forces in 1992.[110] The 1966 Soviet–Mongolian mutual assistance treaty, last renewed in 1986, could be terminated by mutual agreement. China, though presently ruled by an unstable régime, has no treaty claims on Mongolia, and could be persuaded to support such an idea. Anything is now possible in Inner Asia, whose continuing state of flux has yet to play itself out into a new order in the region. Mongolia's new allies in the West and East Asia should act accordingly, as they have everything to gain by so doing. And their gain is Mongolia's too.

A HOPEFUL FUTURE

The need for change

In February 1990, the last statue of Stalin, a huge bronze monstrosity in the centre of Ulan Bator, was taken down.[111] Demanded by the democratic opposition from the very first, this act was highly symbolic, as the new political and social forces of the present decisively rejected those of a discredited and failed past. Even more so than in the Soviet Union, the institutions, political methods and falsehoods of that Stalinist past were kept going for what seemed like an eternity by old, tired and senile men such as Tsedenbal.

A *nomenklatura* that has left Mongolia with a flawed political economic and social legacy will take the remaining decade of this century properly to resolve. Tsedenbal's successor, a half-baked reformer trying to reform the unreformable, could not do this, being part of the very problem which he was trying to solve. A totalitarian and bureaucratic system of government that was stagnant in intent and practice was hated by the people it claimed to represent. At best, its absurd and meaningless rituals elicited popular indifference. In the summer of 1988, for example, an unprecedented opinion poll revealed that only 20 per cent of those polled were satisfied with the work of their GPH deputy; 40 per cent did not even know who their so-called representative was.[112]

The most negative consequence of this flawed political legacy was a backward and stagnant economy. Following Gorbachev's example in the Soviet Union, Batmonh fondly imagined that the country's economy could be improved without fundamental political change in 1988 and 1989.[113] Yet such political change was the prerequisite for any lasting economic turn-around in Mongolia. During 1990, this view was largely held by government and opposition alike. There was no real disagreement about the need for change, which everybody agreed had to come, given the manifest failure of past political methods and policies. The only differences were over what sort of change should be introduced, its timing and management.

Given the almost complete capitulation of the MPRP to the democratic opposition, however, these differences became less important as Mongolia's revolution gathered momentum. In this regard, there was a virtual consensus of opinion from the very beginning about the need for a free market economy, a more open and democratic system of government, and a new foreign policy. Before May 1990, when the GPH formally introduced a multi-party democracy, the crucial argument was between reforming a one-party communist dictatorship and going far beyond it in favour of what was in the end agreed upon. The democratic opposition won this argument hands down.

Now in government, the CDF represents the present and the future in Mongolia. The leaders and members of its political parties are extremely young, born for the most part after 1960. They are thus highly representative of Mongolia's largely young population, 75 per cent of which is under the age of 35.[114] Inspired by sophisticated urban intellectuals like Dzoring, this new generation is more urban than rural (a 50/50 ratio in Mongolia). It is educated and intensely curious about the outside world and its own past. Its thirst for new ideas, views and fashions is insatiable. During the 1990 revolution, for example, new opposition newspapers typically had print-runs of 50,000–200,000 copies, which is remarkable for a country of only two million people.[115]

Though proud of its own national and cultural traditions, Mongolia's new generation is resolutely modern in such areas as popular music, where Western rock and roll influences are very strong. Mongol rock and roll groups, such as *Honkh* (The Bells), sang and inspired large numbers of young people during the 1990 revolution.[116] It is this mixture of traditional and modern, coupled with a serious commitment to civilised political, economic and social change, that now defines Mongolia's new generation, which is a credit to its country and parents.

This phenomenon cannot but affect the MPRP, whose older leaders are now being replaced by a younger generation of politicians whose political outlook is dominated by the events of 1990. Outside Mongolia, the same phenomenon cannot but profoundly affect the younger Mongols of both the Soviet Union and China. In the latter, of course, evil old men massacred the flower of Beijing's youth in 1989, so as to briefly delay the inevitable end of themselves. A similar situation exists in nearby North Korea, whose deranged Pharaoh dreams and plans for immortality. Change will come to both these countries when their old dictators die. Mongolia, meanwhile, has made this generational shift, and is now on the road long ago taken by Japan and South Korea, a road which will take it to a better future.

Political and economic prospects

Though the historic elections of July 1990 were free and fair under the specific circumstances under which they were held, the MPRP régime had undoubted advantages over the CDF. Politically, the country's distorted electoral system favoured the MPRP, as did electoral laws that gave 2,000 rural residents a seat in the GPH, whereas 10,000 urban voters were required to get a seat in the same place. The CDF was strongest in the cities; the MPRP in the rural areas. In addition, lack of money, time and organisation prevented the CDF from putting forward far more candidates than it did for the 430 seats of the GPH.[117]

Now that the CDF is in a coalition government, the next election in Mongolia in 1995 will be very different from the one of 1990. Electoral and consitutional reform is now on the political agenda in the country, and the MPRP cannot hope to disregard the views of its coalition partner on such fundamental issues. The CDF's *de facto* control of the crucial LH rules this out in any event. In this regard, the first order of business is a new constitution, as the present one, promulgated in 1960, has been amended extensively during 1990. That constitution is one of the symbols of Mongolia's discredited Stalinist past. Its worst articles, such as the 82nd (which guaranteed the MPRP's monopoly of power up to March 1990), have been amended by the GPH,[118] but the entire edifice is too much associated with the MPRP to survive much longer in Mongolia's new democratic political landscape.

The CDF is already thinking of the 1995 election, which it is convinced it will win outright, thereby pushing the MPRP out of power and into political marginality in the late 1990s. Its credible performance in 1990, when the odds were stacked against it, bear this out. Presently, however, a coalition with the MPRP is necessary in the interests of national unity, which the country's immense problems demand. Politically, the most immediate and crucial problem is both to cut and properly control the country's inert and bloated bureaucracy, which experience suggests will do everything in its power to preserve itself. The MPRP also has a vested interest in the *status quo* surviving, as there are no votes in job cuts. To date, only minor cuts have been made, but harsh and worsening economic realities mean that difficult decisions in this area cannot now be avoided much longer.

In the short-term, these economic realities are worsening by the day due to the unstoppable collapse of the Soviet Union. Already endemic food and consumer goods shortages are now being compounded by short-falls or even complete non-delivery of essential Soviet supplies of oil, machinery and spare parts. The oil issue is now critical – literally a matter of life or death, given the harshness of Mongolia's climate and the vast size of the country. In November 1990, for example, Ulan Bator experienced its first heating and electricity cuts, which continued throughout the winter.[119] Further chaos will spread throughout the entire economy, and its industrial sector in particular, as Soviet machinery wears out or breaks down due to shortages of crucial spare parts. The urban areas, where 50 per cent of the population lives, will be particularly badly affected. The already creaking infrastructure of over-crowded Ulan Bator, where one in four Mongolians live, could collapse altogether.

Government exhortations – such as the one made in November 1990 by Prime Minister Dashiyn Byambasuren – for people to stop hoarding essential goods and work harder will not have much impact on this worsening situation. The black market, a barometer of wider economic and social conditions, is presently booming in Mongolia. In January 1991, rationing for meat, milk, butter, flour, rice, liquor, green tea and vegetable oil was introduced in all the major cities, following panic buying in Ulan Bator. Anti-social behaviour and crime – particularly theft, juvenile delinquency, alcohol-related violence and speculation – is on the increase. A sinister new development is intimidation and violence (mostly beatings) against the Russians in Mongolia. This could lead to dangerous international complications if it is not stopped. Prospects are not good. The state police and the judicial system are both discredited, demoralised and in urgent need of reform.

As in Central-Eastern Europe at the present time, these social and economic problems pose a threat to Mongolia's continuing political democratisation.

The complete transition to a free market economy will cause even more problems in at least the short-term, while its advantages will not come about until well into the 1990s. In this regard, Mongolia now requires immediate economic assistance, including emergency food aid, which was formally requested of the international community by the government in May 1991.[120] The Soviet Union cannot provide anything other than modest debt relief and promises about sticking to its contracts as regards deliveries of oil and other vital goods. Its promises are virtually worthless at the present time. The same is true of China. Only the West and Japan can now help Mongolia.

The Mongol Question in Inner Asia

Like the Koreans to the east, the Mongols remain a divided nation at a time when other nations, such as the Germans and Yemenis, have reunified themselves. Even more so than is the case in Korea (divided only a generation ago), the long division of the Mongols is the source of permanent sorrow and pain in the heart of every pan-Mongol nationalist patriot. Time has not deadened but intensified it and it resulted in an extraordinary explosion of feeling during the course of Mongolia's revolution of 1990.

Though certainly democratic in form, that revolution's essential content was and remains pan-Mongol nationalism, whose agenda is dominated by national self-determination and reunification; the public reclamation and celebration of Mongolia's actual and stolen past; and the reincarnation of suppressed cultural traditions, of which the Buddhist faith and pan-Buddhism are the most important. That essential content defines what all Mongols are. Soviet communism attempted but failed to change such fundamental aspects of the Mongols' self-identity. And like the Tsarist system it replaced, the Soviet Union supported the division of the Mongols in Inner Asia for its own selfish strategic reasons.

This division permanently denied the reconstitution of a Greater Mongolia, which was as important as independence itself to the Bogd Khan's government in 1911 and thereafter:[121] a division that was entirely due to the Mongols' two powerful neighbours, and not to themselves. Their pan-Mongol nationalism could never accept this division. Nationalism has proved to be remarkably resilient during the 20th century, when it was ferociously attacked in the Soviet Union and Mongolia in the 1920s and 1930s, and permanently suppressed thereafter. Manipulated by Japan in China in the 1930s and 1940s, it was briefly used by the Chinese communists in the 1950s, only to be attacked by them during the 1960s and thereafter.

Presently, following Mongolia's revolution of 1990, pan-Mongol nationalism in Inner Asia is stronger than it has ever been in its entire modern history. Its present epicentre is, of course, Mongolia itself, but its influence is also strong in Tuva, Buryat-Mongolia and Inner Mongolia, where in fact it largely originated, and where it survived the longest during this century, due to favourable circumstances such as the weakness of China, the power of Japan, and the ambitions of Mao.

The Mongol question now has the potential to become the cause of possibly serious regional instability and insecurity for both the Soviet Union and China. For Moscow, already confronted with secessionist nationalist revolts in its Baltic, Moldavian, Transcaucasian and Central Asian borderlands, Tuva and Buryat-Mongolia could be the next areas to go the same way out of its visibly disintegrating empire.[122] Beijing's empire, though seemingly stronger than that of Moscow, could follow in the not-too-distant future. Its two other Inner Asian borderland areas, Tibet and Sinkiang, have been in a state of semi-permanent revolt for decades.[123] Inner Mongolia, because of its proximity to Beijing and the large number of Han Chinese in the area, cannot as yet go the way of Sinkiang and Tibet, but may well do so if favourable circumstances occurred in the future due to events in China proper.

In this regard, the present régime in Beijing is fearful of a collapse of communist power throughout China, which could then revert to the sort of implodent chaos that existed in the country prior to 1949. China's vast borderlands – making up 60 per cent of its territory, but only 6 per cent of its population[124] – would then go their own way, with Inner Mongolia being reunified with Mongolia proper. Such a scenario, though improbable at least in the short-term, cannot be ruled out altogether in the longer-term. The present régime will last only as long as the very old men that dominate it. Mongolia cannot feel entirely safe until they are dead or out of office, expecially now that its axis with Moscow is coming to an end.

For the new government in Ulan Bator the Mongol question in Inner Asia is fraught with dangers. Given the strength of pan-Mongol nationalism domestically, its claims cannot be entirely ignored, nor pushed too hard for fear of what may follow from both its two neighbours. To do nothing is almost as politically dangerous as doing something. Finding a balance between these two points will not be easy, but one will have to be found if the volatile Mongol question in Inner Asia is to be kept at least stable in the short-term future.

The role of the West and Japan

After having forced the MPRP regime into negotiations with the democratic opposition in May 1990, S. Dzoring, and another MDP leaders, went on their first foreign tour to the former communist countries of Central-Eastern Europe. The purpose of the tour was to learn from the experiences of Democratic Forum in Hungary, Civic Forum in Czechoslovakia, New Forum in East Germany, and Solidarity in Poland.[125] Later the same year, in September, Dzoring was elected Chairman of the influential Parliamentary Union of the GPH, which maintains contacts with various foreign parliaments and governments.[126]

At that time, every Western government would have received him had he been inclined to pay a visit; in May, he would not have been given the time of day, let alone received in an official capacity. That explains why he went to Central-Eastern Europe, where he was well received by former dissidents who themselves had bitter experience of being ignored by Western governments in the past. Such governments did little to topple communism and advance the cause of democracy in Central-Eastern Europe during the so-called *détente* era. In the case of Mongolia, far removed in Inner Asia, they did absolutely nothing. From 1921 to 1961 – when Mongolia joined the UN – the country simply did not exist as far as Western policy-makers were concerned.

Thereafter, as Mongolia was gradually recognised diplomatically by more and more Western countries, things began to change slowly in areas such as Mongolian–European trade. Politically, however, Western indifference or hostility helped to keep Mongolia trapped within its communist ghetto in Inner Asia. American diplomatic recognition, for example, was withheld until as recently as 1987. The country was also poorly served by the few people who bothered to write about it in the West. These largely consisted of fellow travellers, such as the late Owen Lattimore;[127] officially-approved hacks connected to various friendship societies in the West;[128] and, the odd journalist, who most typically "covered" Mongolia from either Beijing or Moscow. Scholars of genuine integrity and knowledge, such as Charles Bawden (UK) and Robert Rupen (US), were rare, and not at all welcome in Ulan Bator under its former régime.[129]

This rather abysmal Western record in Mongolia contrasted sharply with the enthusiasm of the Mongols for Western political, economic and cultural models during Mongolia's revolution of 1990. Clearly, the Mongols feel that the West has much to offer, both with regard to the transition to a free market economy, and the democratisation of the country's system of government. Foreign support of the latter is particularly important at the present time, given the lack of any real democratic tradition in Mongolia's history. More immediately, however, Mongolia needs emergency economic assistance from Western governments and multilateral agencies, followed by long-term private capital investments, credits and technology transfers. Only time will tell if all this will be forthcoming.

An even greater commitment will be required from nearby Japan, whose future role in Mongolia will no doubt be commensurable with its immense economic power in the region. Korea, which will almost certainly be reunified sometime during the 1990s, has a similar role to play in Mongolia. Across the Pacific, the United States is now committed to a new and more intensive relationship with Mongolia, following decades of mutual hostility and indifference. Similar goodwill emanates from the European Community, whose member states are now expected to match Japanese investment in Mongolia's rich mineral resources.

The new role of the West and Japan in Mongolia should also concern itself with the country's external security, as it moves away from Moscow towards an uncertain future where the great imponderable is, of course, China. In this regard, present Western and Japanese appeasement of the dictators in Beijing is bad news for Mongolia. Presently, it remains highly vulnerable to threats and intimidation from China, whose unstable rulers cannot be trusted not to use such methods against Mongolia in the future. Should such a scenario unfold, the West and Japan should not abandon Mongolia to the fate that befell Tibet in 1950, and which now awaits Hong Kong in 1997.[130]

In this regard, the idea that Mongolia should adopt an internationally recognised and guaranteed permanent neutrality merits serious consideration. The UN, once again a serious international forum, could play a major role in redefining Mongolia's international status. With good will among all concerned, such a settlement on Mongolia is politically possible. Mongolia could only gain by such a development, which would both formalise Ulan Bator's new foreign policy of *de facto* neutrality between Moscow and Beijing, and allow it freely to pursue other foreign policy options in the world beyond Inner Asia. For all who wish Mongolia and the Mongols well in the years ahead, such a foreign policy transition is devoutly to be wished for and supported if it ever becomes a political reality.

NOTES

[1] Unrelated to President Ochirbat, G. Ochirbat had lived in Prague for five years prior to becoming General Secretary of the MPRP in March 1990. See "Mongolia", *Eastern Europe Newsletter* (London – hereafter EEN), Vol. 4, No. 19, 24 September 1990, p. 7. In February 1991, at the 20th MPRP Congress, he was replaced by a younger man, Budragchaagiyn Dash-Yondon.

[2] Created along with the GPH in 1924, the LH was abolished in 1949, and then reconstituted with new powers at a session of the GPH in May 1990. See "Mongolia: Political Reforms", *Kessing's Record of World Events* (London – hereafter KRWE), Vol. 36, No. 5, May 1990, p. 37454.

[3] According to the 20 foreign-observer groups present, there was no cheating by the MPRP-controlled National Election Commission. The main problem was the confusion caused by an electorate unfamiliar with the complexities of a genuine election. See Marguerite Johnson, "Mongolia: Democracy Gets a Chance", *Time*, 13 August 1990, p. 19.

[4] "Mongolia: Multiparty Elections", KRWE, Vol. 36, Nos. 7/8, July 1990, p. 37610.

[5] The MPRP, with 60 per cent of the popular vote, won 340 of the 430 seats in the GPH. See *ibid.*, p. 37610.

[6] "Opposition Polls Strongly Against Communists in High Turnout for Mongolia's First Free Election", *The Guardian*, 31 July 1990.

[7] Outside the CDF, there are a number of other parties, including the Mongolian Party of Free Labour and the Mongolian Party of Greens (MPG), plus some influential pressure groups, such as the Mongolian Union of Students. See KRWE (May, 1990), *op. cit.*, p. 37454, and "Mongolia: The Party's Last Gasps", EEN, Vol. 4, No. 8, 16 April 1990, p. 7. The three CDF parties, plus the MPG, all hold portfolios in the Cabinet formed in October 1990, and finally confirmed by the LH the following month, with Dashiyn Byambasuren (MPRP) as Prime Minister, and Davaadorjiyn Ganbold (NPP) as Vice-Prime Minister. See "Mongolia: Formation of a New Cabinet", KRWE, Vol. 36, No. 10, October, 1990, p. 37777.

[8] 1989 census. See Academy of Sciences, Mongolian People's Republic, *Information Mongolia* (Oxford: Pergamon Press, 1990), p. 55.

[9] Estimates of China's Mongol population vary from this figure to over four million. The true figure is not in the public domain, as China's 1990 census does not present data on ethnic minority numbers.

[10] Presently, the Mongol populations of these three ASSRs are as follows: 350,000 (Buryat–Mongol, plus its two associated national areas to the east and west of Lake Baikal), 200,000 (Tuva), and 150,000 (Kalmyk). The Tuvinians, a Turkic-Mongol people, were part of Mongolia prior to 1921; the Kalmyks, originally from western Mongolia, live in European Russia along the Volga river to the north-west of the Caspian Sea.

[11] Jasper Becker, "Mongolia Saddles Up for its Second Revolution as Russians go Home", *The Guardian*, 6 April 1990.

[12] EEN (16 April 1990), *op. cit.*, p. 7.

[13] This expatriate community, which may be as large as 100,000 people if all dependents are included (or 5 per cent of the total population of Mongolia), is hated for its racist arrogance, high living standards, access to flats in over-crowded urban areas, and ubiquity in Mongolia. It also enjoys *de facto* extraterritoriality; its military component is a law unto itself and beyond any Mongol control.

[14] According to Soviet reports, around 3,000 people left in the first half of 1990. See Ann Sheehy, "Russians the Target of Interethnic Violence in Tuva", *Radio Liberty Report on the USSR* (Munich), Vol. 2, No. 37, 19 September 1990, p. 16.

[15] This demographic fact also accounts for the particularly violent nature of Tuvinian nationalism at the present time. See *ibid.*, pp. 13–14.

[16] The other Soviet Mongol population, the Kalmyks, account for around 50 per cent of the total number of people resident in their autonomous republic on the Volga.

[17] These are simply Manchu administrative divisions used when Mongolia was part of China from 1691 to 1911.

[18] The IMAR of the 1947–69 period was roughly the same as the old Manchu province of Inner Mongolia; the smaller IMAR of the post-1969 period, however, contains only around half of China's 3.5 million Mongols. With a total population of 21 million in 1988, the local Mongols were outnumbered by Han Chinese by an average factor of 12:1. See *Whitaker's Almanack 1990* (London: Whitaker's, 1989), p. 741.

[19] In February 1990, a Hong Kong-based Chinese émigré publication, *Tang Tai*, reported that Beijing had adopted a policy of "being inwardly tense and outwardly relaxed" in the IMAR, in response to events in Mongolia. See BBC Monitoring Service, *Summary of World Broadcasts*, Part 3, Far East (Reading – hereafter SWB), FE/0685–B2/5, 10 February 1990.

[20] Plus South Korea, with whom Mongolia established diplomatic relations in April 1990. A Mongol–South Korean Friendship Society was founded the following month, as was a Mongol–Japanese Society (18 years after diplomatic relations were established between the two countries). See Radio Ulan Bator in English 0910 gmt 15 May 1990 (SWB, FE/0767–A3/5, 18 May 1990).

[21] For the latter reports, see *Komsomolskaya Pravda* (13 December 1989) and *Isvestiya* (14 December 1989) – SWB, FE/0642–B2/B3, 18 December 1989.

[22] "Mongolia: Strengthening of Opposition Movement", KRWE, Vol. 36, No. 2, February 1990, p. 37247.

[23] Radio Ulan Bator in English 0910 gmt 9 February 1990 (SWB, FE/0687–B/5, 13 February 1990).

[24] "Mongolia: Extraordinary MPRP Congress", KRWE, Vol. 36, No. 4, April 1990, p. 37374.

[25] "Mongolia: Anxious Moments", EEN, Vol. 4, No. 9, 30 April 1990, pp. 7–8.

[26] "Mongolia Leader Returns as Government Wavers", *The Guardian*, 7 May 1990.

[27] In this regard, Mongolia now regards itself as a model for other Asian communist countries to follow. This has implications for China, North Korea, Vietnam, and the rest of Indochina, plus even the Soviet Union, which is more an Asian country than a European one.

[28] Nick Middleton, "Genghis Back in the Saddle", *The Independent*, 29 July 1990.

[29] To suggest otherwise – that the period of Genghis Khan was a Golden Age, for example – was to be guilty of "bourgeois nationalism" and other such "crimes". See Academy of Sciences, MPR, *The History of the Mongolian People's Republic* (Cambridge, Mass.: Harvard University Press, 1976), p. 498.

[30] According to Mongolia's main biographer of Genghis Khan, Professor Natsaglery, these include: unifying the Mongol tribes into a nation, creating the first world empire that linked east and west, encouraging trade along the Silk Road, and religious tolerance. See Jasper Becker, "Glasnost Finds a Place in History for Genghis Khan", *The Guardian*, 3 August 1989.

[31] Charles R. Bawden, *The Modern History of Mongolia* (London: Kegan Paul International, 1989), pp. 417–19.

[32] Jasper Becker, "Civilised Revolution Hails Spirit of Genghis", *The Guardian*, 26 March 1990.

[33] "New Political Thinking Permits Rewriting of Party History", Radio Ulan Bator in English 1200 gmt 29 January 1990 (SWB, FE/0676–B/2, 31 January 1990).

[34] "Society for Strengthening Expatriate Links With Historical Motherland", TASS in Russian for abroad 1232 gmt 12 February 1990 (SWB, FE/0706–B/3, 7 March 1990).

[35] Bawden, *The Modern History of Mongolia*, *op. cit.*, p. 417 (Ordos) & 422 (old Mongolian script).

[36] Radio Ulan Bator in English 0910 gmt 21 March 1990 (SWB, FE/0726–B/2, 30 March 1990) for the 1990 decree; Radio Ulan Bator in English 0910 gmt 24 January 1990 (SWB, FE/0673–B/2, 27 January 1990) for the 1989 decree.

[37] The herd consists of sheep (the most common: 14.2 million in 1989), goats, cattle, horses and camels. For the 1989 figures, see *The Europa World Year Book 1990*, Vol. II (London: Europa Publications, 1990), p. 1776; for the 1960 and 1941 figures, see Alan J. K. Sanders, *Mongolia: Politics, Economics and Society* (London: Frances Pinter, 1987), p. 91.

[38] *The Europa World Year Book 1990*, *op. cit.*, p. 1774. Arriving at the true figure is virtually impossible due to the largely fictional nature of the MPR's economic statistics in the past.

[39] "Free trade Union Movement Formed", Radio Ulan Bator in English 0910 gmt 13 March 1990 (SWB, FE/0713–B/3, 15 March 1990).

[40] *The Europa World Year Book 1990*, *op. cit.*, p. 1775.

[41] "Mongolia to ask USSR to annul credit debts", Radio Ulan Bator in English 0910 gmt 8 March 1990 (SWB, FE/0715–A2/3, 17 March 1990).

[42] W. E. Butler, *The Mongolian Legal System: Contemporary Legislation and Documentation* (The Hague: Martinus Nijhoff Publishers, 1982), p. 523.

[43] For the MUB, see "Union of Believers Petitions for Religious Worship", Radio Ulan Bator in English

0810 gmt 9 April 1990; for the new Hambo Lama, see "New Head of Mongolian Buddhists", TASS in English for abroad 1135 gmt 12 April 1990 (both in SWB, FE/0743–B/7, 20 April 1990).

[44] Walther Heissig, *The Religions of Mongolia* (London: Routledge & Kegan Paul, 1988), p. 45.

[45] Jasper Becker, "Buddhism Survives Stalin's Massacre", *The Guardian*, 18 April 1990.

[46] Sechin Jagchid & Paul Hyer, *Mongolia's Culture and Society* (Boulder, Col.: Westview Press, 1979), p. 338.

[47] Larry W. Moses, *The Political Role of Mongol Buddhism*, Indiana University Uralic Altaic Series, Vol. 133 (Bloomington, Ind.: Asian Studies Research Institute, Indiana University, 1977), p. 263.

[48] His last visit, in 1979, was to attend the Fifth Asian Buddhist Peace Conference. Though this event was a MPRP propaganda exercise to score points against Beijing, it did give international recognition to the Dalai Lama, who entered Mongolia via the Soviet Union. It was hard to tell who was using who during the 1979 visit. See Robert A. Rupen, "Mongolia", in Richard F. Staar (ed.), *Yearbook on International Communist Affairs 1980* (Stanford, Cal.: Hoover Institution Press, 1980), pp. 284–85.

[49] Jane T. Dreyer, *China's Forty Millions: Minority Nationalities and National Integration in the People's Republic of China* (Cambridge, Mass.: Harvard University Press, 1976), pp. 210–14.

[50] Hans Bräker, "Buddhism in the Soviet Union: Annihilation or Survival?", *Religion in Communist Lands*, Vol. 11, No. 1, Spring 1983.

[51] Stuart Legg, *The Heartland* (London: Secker & Warburg, 1970), p. 149.

[52] This dynasty was created by the Juchen, a people ethnically related to the Manchus in Manchuria. See David Morgan, *The Mongols* (Oxford: Blackwells, 1986), p. 47.

[53] For the 1206 *quriltai*, a great meeting of the Mongol tribes, see paragraphs 202–34 of the Khan's first biography, *The Secret History of the Mongols* (1240), trans. Francis W. Cleaves (Cambridge, Mass.: Harvard University Press, 1982),pp. 141–71.

[54] Whom the great Venetian traveller, Marco Polo (1254–1324), first met in 1275, and whom he served in various capacities for nearly 20 years. Marco Polo's famous *Travels* are the best Western primary source of the Mongol Empire's Gold Age.

[55] For this, see Leo de Hartog, *Genghis Khan: Conqueror of the World* (London: I. B. Tauris, 1989), Chapter 5 (The Mongol Army).

[56] Their descendants, the Kalmyks, fled from the area to escape Manchu persecution. They settled along the Volga river in European Russia.

[57] By the Sino-Russian Treaty of Kiakhta. For this, see W. A. Douglas Jackson, *The Russo-Chinese Border-Lands*, 2nd. Edition (Princeton, NJ.: D. Van Nostrand, 1968), p. 138.

[58] Extensive Chinese money-lending activities, which created heavy local indebtedness, was another source of anger. For this, see M. Sanjdorj, *Manchu Chinese Colonial Rule in Northern Mongolia* (London: Hurst, 1980), Chapter 7 (The Role of Chinese Money-Lending Capital in Khalkh).

[59] Four such treaties were signed between 1907 and 1916. The dividing line between the two spheres was the Peking meridian. For this, see Thomas E. Ewing, *Between the Hammer and the Anvil: Chinese and Russian Policies in Outer Mongolia, 1911–1921*, Indiana University Uralic Altaic Series, Vol. 138 (Bloomington, Ind.: Asian Studies Research Institute, Indiana University, 1980), pp. 21–22.

[60] For this, see Urgunge Onon & Derrick Pritchatt, *Asia's First Modern Revolution: Mongolia Proclaims its Independence in 1911* (Leiden: E. J. Brill, 1989), p. 77.

[61] *Ibid.*, p. 117, for a brief biographical sketch of the Bogd Khan.

[62] Only those of the "right" class origins were later turned into "heroes" for the communist pantheon. Commander Damdinsüren, who drove the last Chinese troops out of Mongolia in 1912, is one example. For this, see *Mongolian Heroes of the Twentieth Century*, trans. Urgunge Onon (New York: AMS Press, 1976), Chapter 3.

[63] *The History of the MPR*, *op. cit.*, p. 62.

[64] For this, see Peter Hopkirk, *Setting the East Ablaze: Lenin's Dream of an Empire in Asia* (London: John Murray, 1984), pp. 146–51. The mad Baron was shot by the Bolsheviks in September 1921.

[65] Mongol national pride and the MPRP's claim to legitimacy meant that these harsh facts could never be accepted. A fictional "history" of 1921 was thus produced. See George G. S. Murphy, *Soviet Mongolia: A Study of the Oldest Political Satellite* (Berkeley, Cal.: University of California Press, 1966), p. 2.

[66] For Tuva, see Robert A. Rupen, "The Absorption of Tuva"; for Mongolia, see Thomas T. Hammond, "The Communist Takeover of Outer Mongolia: Model for Eastern Europe"; both in: Thomas T. Hammond (ed.), *The Anatomy of Communist Takeovers* (New Haven, Conn.: Yale University Press, 1975).

[67] Dogsomyn Bodo, the régime's first Prime Minister, was shot in August 1922; Danzan, a prominent MPRP leader, met the same fate in August 1924. Pan-Mongol nationalism got both of them killed. For this, see Robert A. Rupen, *The Mongolian People's Republic* (Stanford, Cal.: Hoover Institution Press, 1966), p. 32.

[68] For this, see Robert A. Rupen, *How Mongolia is Really Ruled: A Political History of the Mongolian People's Republic, 1900–1978* (Stanford, Cal.: Hoover Institution Press, 1979), p. 42.

[69] Walter Kolarz, *The Peoples of the Soviet Far East* (Hamden, Conn.: Archon Books, 1969), p. 136.

The Mongolian Revolution of 1990 31

[70] For this, see Trevor N. Dupuy *et al.*, *Area Handbook for Mongolia* (Washington, DC.: U.S.G.P.O., 1970), p. 68.

[71] As with Stalin, Choybalsan acquired a hideous personality cult, which began around 1941. For this, see Victor P. Petrov, *Mongolia: A Profile* (London: Pall Mall Press, 1970), p. 60.

[72] Jasper Becker, "Mongolia Purge Put at 100,000", *The Guardian*, 23 March 1990.

[73] In December 1943, the Kalmyk ASSR was dissolved, and its entire Kalmyk population was deported to Siberia and Central Asia. Of the 130,000 people deported, only half lived to return home in 1958. For this, see Aleksandr M. Nekrich, *The Punished Peoples: The Deportation and Fate of Soviet Minorities at the End of the Second World War* (New York: Norton, 1978), Chapter 3, and pp. 142–46.

[74] He served Tsedenbal as Chairman of the Council of Ministers (Prime Minister) from 1974 to 1984. See Bogdan Szajkowski (ed.), *Marxist Governments: A World Survey*, Vol. 2 (London: Macmillan, 1981), p. 520. G. Ochirbat, former MPRP General Secretary, also served in Tsedenbal's GPH Presidium, but was sacked after a quarrel in 1982.

[75] An example of this absurd propoganda is Sh. Nachukdorji's *Life of Sukhebator*, which is translated in Owen Lattimore, *Nationalism and Revolution in Mongolia* (Leiden: E. J. Brill, 1955), Part II.

[76] See A. J. K. Sanders, *The People's Republic of Mongolia: A General Reference Guide* (London: Oxford University Press, 1968), p. 172.

[77] See *Mongolian Heroes of the Twentieth Century*, *op. cit.*, p. 207.

[78] Khrushchev rebuffed Tsedenbal on this issue in the 1950s and 1960s. See Peter Popham, "Coming in from the Cold," *The Independent Magazine*, 21 April 1990, p. 25.

[79] His only success, if that is the right word was to survive as long as he did. For this, see Robert A. Rupen, "Yumjagiyn Tsedenbal: Soviet Mongolian Puppet," in Rudger Swearingen (ed.), *Leaders of the Communist World* (New York: Free Press, 1971), Item 24, pp. 414–23.

[80] "'Unen' Reports Tsedenbal and Spouse Deprived of Orders and Titles", TASS in Russian for abroad 0205 gmt 20 April 1990 (SWB, FE/0744–B/1, 21 April 1990).

[81] This high plateau also includes Sinkiang and Tibet to the south. For this, see W. G. East & O. H. K. Spate, *The Changing Map of Asia: A Political Geography*, 4th Edition (London: Methuen, 1966), pp. 295–98.

[82] For this, see Stuart Legg, *The Heartland*, *op. cit.*, Chapter 2 (Heartland and Littoral).

[83] A Sino-Soviet Non-aggression Pact followed in 1937. It was rumoured to contain secret clauses pertaining to Mongolia. For this, see G. M. Friters, *Outer Mongolia and its International Position* (Baltimore, Md.: John Hopkins University Press, 1949), p. 351.

[84] The Nomohan defeat led Japan to avoid war with the Soviet Union during the Second World War, thereby saving Stalin from a two-front war that he would have probably lost in 1941. For this, see Philip Snow, "Nomonhan – The Unknown Victory", *History Today*, Vol. 40, July 1990.

[85] The codicil also contained a non-interference pledge as regards Sinkiang, occupied by the Soviet Union for most of the 1930s and 1940s. This was traded for Chinese recognition of Mongolia. For the 1945 Treaty, see Raymond L. Garthoff (ed.), *Sino-Soviet Military Relations* (New York: Praeger, 1966), pp. 203–05.

[86] Culminating, in 1979–83, in the expulsion to China of most of Mongolia's small (7,000 people) Han community. For this, see Alan J. Day (ed.), *China and the Soviet Union, 1949–84* (London: Longman, 1985), pp. 154–56.

[87] Such as some form of internationally recognised and guaranteed permanent neutrality.

[88] "MPR–Soviet troop Withdrawal, Agreement Reached", TASS World Service in English 0850 gmt 2 March 1990 (SWB, FE50704–A2/1, 5 March 1990).

[89] For the former, see "Details of Second Stage of Soviet Troop Withdrawal from Mongolia", ADN (E. German News Agency) Report (SWB, FE/0757–i, 7 May 1990); for the latter, see "No More Need for Soviet Military Instructors", Radio Ulan Bator in English 1200 gmt 3 March 1990 (SWB, FE/0706–A2/1, 7 March 1990).

[90] For this, see Marko Milivojević, "The Mongolian People's Army", *Armed Forces*, Vol. 6, No. 12, December 1987.

[91] The race for Port Arthur was the key to the entire Manchurian campaign. For this, see Malcolm Mackintosh, *Juggernaut: A History of the Soviet Armed Forces* (London: Secker & Warburg, 1967), pp. 260–68.

[92] T. N. Dupuy, *Area Handbook for Mongolia*, *op. cit.*, p. 433.

[93] A. J. Day, *China and the Soviet Union, 1949–84*, *op. cit.*, p. 151. This precondition was the first of four, the others being Soviet military forces on the Sino-Soviet border and in Afghanistan, and Vietnam in Cambodia.

[94] MPRP ideologues would have made Marx spin in his grave. For an example of their nonsense, see B. Shirendyb, *By-Passing Capitalism* (Ulan Bator: M. P. R. State Publishers, 1968).

[95] The Erdenet operation began in 1978. For this, see A. J. K. Sanders, *Mongolia*, *op. cit.*, p. 106.

[96] "'Ming Pao' Calls Beijing Selfish for Demanding Stability in Mongolia", *Ming Pao*, Hong Kong, 7 May 1990 (SWB, FE/0758–A3/1, 8 May 1990).

[97] For this, see M. T. Haggard, "Mongolia: The First Communist State in Asia", in Robert A. Scalapino (ed.), *The Communist Revolution in Asia: Tactics, Goals, and Achievements*, 2nd. Edition (Englewood Cliffs, NJ: Prentice-Hall, 1969), p. 109.

[98] The statement publicly reaffirmed the importance of the Ulan Bator–Moscow axis to both its signatories. For this, see Robert A. Rupen, "The Mongolian People's Republic and Sino-Soviet Competition", in A. B. Barnett (ed.), *Communist Strategies in Asia: A Comparative Analysis of Governments and Parties* (London: Pall Mall Press, 1963), p. 265.

[99] This was followed by a 1964 protocol listing border posts. For this important treaty, which was not actually implemented until the 1980s, see Alastair Lamb, *Asian Frontiers: Studies in a Continuing Problem* (London: Pall Mall Press, 1968), p. 200.

[100] Harrison E. Salisbury, *To Peking and Beyond: A Report on the New Asia* (London: Arrow Books, 1973), p. 239.

[101] For this, see Paul Hyer & William Heaton, "The Cultural Revolution in Inner Mongolia", *China Quarterly*, Vol. 36, October–December, 1968, p. 124.

[102] He rose to the office of Vice-President before his resignation in 1988. For this, see John Gittings, "Ulanhu – or fu: Mongol Party Man", *The Guardian*, 16 December 1988.

[103] For the April 1990 visit, see "Mongolian Leader in Japan Says Foreign Policy Unchanged", Kyodo News Agency, Tokyo, in English 1416 gmt 2 April 1990 (SWB, FE/0731–A3/2, 5 April 1990); for the March 1990 visit, see "Mongolian Premier in Japan", Kyodo News Agency, Tokyo, in English (i) 1133 gmt, (ii) 1157 gmt & (iii) 1436 gmt 1 March 1990 (SWB, FE/0704–A3/1, 5 March 1990).

[104] "Application to join IMF", KRWE (July, 1990), *op. cit.*, p. 37610, and "Mongolia Becomes IMF's 155th Member", *IMF Survey* (Washington, D.C.), 4 March, 1991 (Press Release 91/6, 14 February).

[105] M. Johnson, *Time* (August, 1990), *op. cit.*, p. 19.

[106] "Paris and Bonn to Strengthen Links with Joint Embassy in Mongolia", *The Guardian*, 14 October 1988.

[107] U. Onon & D. Pritchatt, *Asia's First Modern Revolution*, *op. cit.*, Appendix 1. The 1912 Treaty with Russia established a protectorate over Outer Mongolia; it did not diplomatically recognise an independent Mongolia. The Mongols have never forgotten this, and many now would like to thank Tibet for giving them recognition in 1912 by recognising the Dalai Lama's Tibetan government-in-exile in India. This would infuriate Beijing, but it would greatly aid the Tibetan cause internationally if it ever took place.

[108] Entry to the UN was the turning point in increasing the legitimacy and security of Mongolia. See Paul Hyer, "Mongolia's Measured Steps", *Problems of Communism*, Vol. XXI, No. 6, November–December 1972, p. 33.

[109] In 1989, for example, Mongolia rejoined the Group of 77, which is connected to UNCTAD. For this, see *The Europa World Year Book 1990*, *op. cit.*, p. 1775.

[110] Mongolia's own armed forces have also been cut by around 13,000 troops in 1990, with further cuts made in 1991. By 1992, the present MPA of around 20,000 troops will be cut even more to leave a purely token border guard. The para-military forces of the defunct Ministry of Public Security were abolished in 1990. For the present MPA, see International Institute for Strategic Studies, *The Military Balance, 1990–91* (London: Brassey's for the IISS, 1990), p. 171, and Marko Milivojević, "The Mongolian People's Army: Military Auxiliary and Political Guardian", in Shirin Akinar (ed.), *Mongolia Today* (London: Kegan Paul International, 1991),

[111] M. Johnson, *Time* (August, 1990), *op. cit.*, p. 19.

[112] Richard F. Staar (ed.), *1989 Yearbook on International Communist Affairs* (Stanford, Cal.: Hoover Institution Press, 1989), p. 243.

[113] His idea of political change was a game of bureaucratic musical chairs, which began in 1987. See *The Annual Register: A Record of World Events 1987* (London: Longman, 1987), p. 113.

[114] 42 per cent of the population was in the 0–15 year age range in 1989. Mongolia has one of the youngest age structures in the world. See *Information Mongolia*, *op. cit.*, p. 54.

[115] Sales of such newspapers provided the CDF parties with most of their income in 1990 and thereafter. See Tim Malyon, "Freedom Spreads Among The People of Genghis Khan", *Independent on Sunday*, 24 June 1990.

[116] For this, see Jasper Becker, "Mongolia is Getting Back onto the Ancient Silk Road", *The Guardian*, 28 March 1990, and "Mongolians in Steppe with British Rock Scene", *The Guardian*, 8 August 1989.

[117] Of the 800 candidates on election day – themselves reduced from over 2,400 in primary elections held on 22 July – 628 were MPRP, plus 16 from the pro-MPRP Revsomol. The CDF accounted for 91 (MDP: 68, SDP: 18, NPP: 15); the rest being independents. Most MPRP candidates were thus unchallenged. See "Mongolia: Multiparty Elections", KRWE (July, 1990), *op. cit.*, p. 37610.

[118] This infamous article did not, however, actually proscribe other political parties, as is also the case in the 1977 Soviet constitution. See Robert A. Rupen, *Mongols of the Twentieth Century* (Hague: Mouton, 1964), Vol. 1, Appendix II (MPR 1960 constitution), p. 424, for article 82.

[119] For this, see *The Guardian*, 15 November 1990.

[120] The request was made by the National Development Minister, Jamiyangin Batsuri, who also asked

for badly needed medicines. See Simon Ling, "Mongolia rations meat as herds fall", *The Guardian*, 17 May, 1991.

[121] U. Onon & D. Pritchatt, *Asia's First Modern Revolution*, *op. cit.*, p. vii.

[122] The fact that they are not full union republics, but part of the Russian republic, slightly complicates the issue, but not by much.

[123] In March 1990, for example, Beijing staged a large military parade in Lhasa to intimidate its inhabitants, following protests against the Han occupation of Tibet in 1989. See "Chinese Show of Force Chills Tibet", *The Guardian*, 9 March 1990. The following month, an armed uprising of Turkic and other Muslims in Sinkiang was ruthlessly crushed by Chinese security forces. See "China Admits Torture and Death in Prisons", *The Guardian*, 30 April 1990.

[124] J. T. Dreyer, *China's Forty Millions*, *op. cit.*, p. 3.

[125] "Mongolian Democrats Visiting Eastern Europe to Study Elections", ADN in German 1051 gmt 24 May 1990 (SWB, FE/0777–A2/2, 30 May 1990).

[126] EEN (September, 1990), *op. cit.*, p. 7.

[127] 1902–90. Author of many books on Mongolia, such as *Nationalism and Revolution in Mongolia* (1955), which are generally favourable to the MPRP régime and its highly distorted version of Mongolia's history.

[128] Such as the Anglo-Mongolian Society in the UK, whose own Foreign Office supports such so-called "friendship" activities in Mongolia. It is questionable whether the Mongols need such "friends" at all.

[129] Both authors of standard works on Mongolia: Bawden, *The Modern History of Mongolia* (1968/1989); Rupen, *How Mongolia is Really Ruled* (1979). Now that the classic works of Robert Conquest are being published in the Soviet Union, it would be fitting if Bawden and Rupen appeared in print in Mongolia in the future. This will almost certainly take place soon.

[130] Or annexation, followed by the destruction of a whole society, with nothing been done by the Western appeasers of Beijing in Europe and the United States, where the events of 1989 are now forgotten, and business as usual is the name of the game.

SELECTED READING LIST

•Academy of Sciences, Mongolian People's Republic, *Information Mongolia* (Oxford: Pergamon Press, 1990).

•Shirin Akiner (ed.), *Mongolia Today* (London: Kegan Paul International, 1991).

•Charles R. Bawden, *The Modern History of Mongolia* (London: Weidenfeld & Nicolson, 1968; Kegan Paul International, 1989).

•Leo de Hartog, *Genghis Khan: Conqueror of the World* (London: I. B. Tauris, 1989).

•Walther Heissig, *The Religious of Mongolia* (London: Routledge & Kegan Paul, 1980).

•Sechin Jagchid & Paul Hyer, *Mongolia's Culture and Society* (Boulder, Col.: Westview, 1979).

•David O. Morgan, *The Mongols* (Oxford: Blackwells, 1986).

•Urgunge Onon & Derrick Pritchatt, *Asia's First Modern Revolution: Mongolia Proclaims Its Independence in 1911* (Leiden: E. J. Brill, 1988).

•Robert Rupen, *How Mongolia is Really Ruled: A Political History of the Mongolian People's Republic, 1900–1978* (Stanford, Cal.: Hoover Institution Press, 1979).

•Alan J. K. Sanders. *Mongolia: Politics, Economics and Society* (London: Frances Pinter, 1987).

MONGOLIA

0
400
MILES
N
W
E
S

Russian Soviet Federative Socialist Republic
Ust-Orda Buryat-Mongol National Okrug
Khangais Mountains
Kentai Mountains
Aga-Buryat-Mongol Autonomous Oblast
Irkutsk
SOVIET UNION
To Moscow
Novosibirsk
Trans-Siberian Railway
Nomonhan(1939)
Lake Baikal
Chita
Khabarovsk
Kyzyl
Ulan Ude
Sukhbaatar
Borzya
Moron
Hovd
Erdenet
Darhan
Choyr
Ulan Bator
Choybalsan
Altay
Manchuria
Urumqi
Harbin
Sinkiang
Saynshand
MONGOLIA
CHINA
Great Wall
Dalandzadgad
Inner Mongolian
Autonomous Region
Hohhot
Altai Mountains
Beijing
Tuva Autonomous Soviet
Socialist Republic
Gobi Desert
Yellow Sea
P'yongyang
NORTH KOREA
Buryat-Mongol Autonomous Soviet
Socialist Republic
Port Arthur
Seoul
SOUTH KOREA
Karakorum(ruins of Genghis Khan's
old imperial capital)
Pacific Ocean
Vladivostok
1947–1969 area(1,);post-1969 area(2,)

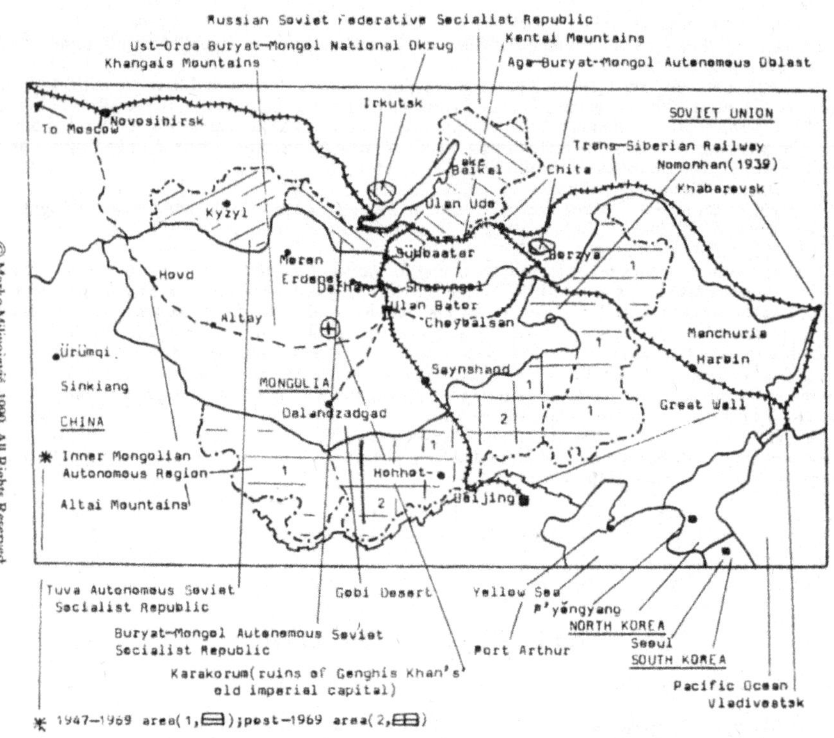

[6]

The Continuing Conflict in Kashmir Regional Detente in Jeopardy

Iftikhar H. Malik

For millions of Indians, Pakistanis and Kashmiris, the unresolved dispute over the former princely State of Jammu and Kashmir (hereafter simply Kashmir) has turned out to be an enduring conflict. In an atmosphere of mutual distrust, India and Pakistan, since their independence in 1947, have already fought three wars besides ongoing skirmishes over Siachin Glacier. Both the countries claim Kashmir on respective historical grounds and even the UN, despite its early prompt initiatives, has not been able to resolve this major bone of contention. With appalling poverty and underdevelopment, South Asia is home to one-fifth of humanity. Its inter-state relations have, however, been largely governed by hostility rather than cordiality. Desire for co-operation has always been vetoed by forces of confrontation and polarisation.

In the main Kashmir Valley itself, since 1989, the wide-ranging rebellion against the Indian government has put added strains on precarious bilateral relations besides costing more than 12,000 Kashmiri lives. The intermittent cases of gang rape and serious human rights violations perpetrated by security forces have added to Muslim Kashmiris' sense of alienation. While the world media occasionally give out details of the multi-dimensional conflict, the Kashmiris in diaspora complain of a global indifference to their plight. The human rights organisations have mostly not been allowed to investigate the events on their own, while India routinely accuses Pakistan of carrying on a proxy war in its northern, vulnerable flank by abetting the militants.

The present Kashmir uprising, sometimes called Kashmiri *Intifadeh*, has added a new vital factor to the entire conflict as some of the Kashmiri groups are already talking of a third option – an independent Kashmir. At a time when the forces of regionalisation and global co-operation are winning, the rise in ethno-regionalism in South Asia has put the regional detente in jeopardy. In the case of Kashmir itself, the state, rather than comprehending the dilemma, seems to have opted for coercion and repression. Thus, the Kashmir conflict, in its entirety, turns out to be a cohesive case-study in growing ethno-nationalism and its ramifications for inter-state relations.

THE KASHMIR REGION

Land-locked between the Himalayas and Karakorams and divided between two belligerent South Asian neighbours, Kashmir, consists of about 86,000 square miles with an estimated population of 12m. Surrounded by Pakistan, China and India, Kashmir is the source of the river-system creating a life-line for Pakistan with a major significance for the Indian Punjab and the adjoining territories. With many of its traditional routes leading through Pakistan,

Kashmir still shares most of its borders with the former,[1] though two-thirds of its territory since 1947 has remained under Indian control. In simple statistics, Kashmir is territorially larger than 68 countries of the world and more populous than 90. Within the State – created in the 19th century with the sale of the territory by the British to a chieftain – there is considerable ethno-religious plurality, further augmented by diversified historical traditions. The predominantly Muslim Valley with a population of 7m consists of a mere 10 per cent of the entire territory, and lies in the middle of the former princely State whereas 2.5m inhabitants live in Azad Kashmir and Northern Areas (including Gilgit, Hunza and Baltistan) indirectly administered by Pakistan. In addition to these predominantly Muslim areas, Ladakh, the biggest land-mass in the State, accounts for a little more than 130,000 inhabitants with a slight Buddhist majority, while in southern districts in Jammu province, with migrations in 1947 and subsequent developments, Hindus make a visible majority. While the Chinese claim suzerainty over Aksai Chin, two thirds of the State, both in terms of area and population – the Valley, Ladakh and Jammu have been under Indian control since October 1947. According to the 1941 Census, out of a total population of 4,021,616 the Muslims and Hindus accounted for 3,100,000 and 809,000 respectively. Yet, despite successive demographic changes and political divisions, as is obvious in the following table, Kashmir has remained an overwhelmingly Muslim majority area, and the total ratio of Muslims especially in Indian-held Kashmir is still around 65 per cent.

TABLE 1

POPULATION OF THE INDIAN-CONTROLLED KASHMIR, 1981
(in millions and percentage)

REGION	POPULATION	TOTAL	MUSLIMS	HINDUS	OTHERS
Valley	3,134,904	52.35	94.96	4.59	0.05
Jammu	2,718,113	45.39	29.60	66.25	4.15
Ladakh	134,372	2.24	46.04	2.66	51.30
TOTAL	**5,987,389**	**100**	**64.19**	**32.24**	**3.57**

Source: Government of India, *Census of 1981*.

It is equally important to note that there are 1.5m Kashmiri refugees living in Pakistan while some 300,000 are settled in the United Kingdom and another 150,000 around the world. This is not to say that a multi-faceted issue like Kashmir may be seen simply in the light of the religious composition of its population, though religion-based identity certainly remains one of the most vital determinants in various crucial developments varying from the Jihad Movement of 1931 in the Valley, party-politics in the State and the rest of South Asia all through the subsequent decades to the partition of the sub-continent itself. Notwithstanding a rhetorical emphasis on supra-religious *Kashmiriat*, the post-1989 defiance in Kashmir is in fact a totally *Muslim* uprising against a government commonly perceived as alien. The retaliation by the Indian security forces – comprising of regiments from areas other than Kashmir with an overwhelming non-Muslim composition – against the Kashmiri militants, has degenerated into a religious hatred against the Muslims. By building massive momentum through *yatra* and other similar strategies, the parties like the Bharatiya Janata Party (BJP) have successfully cashed in on existing anti-Muslim and anti-Pakistan sentiments. Similarly, in Pakistan and other neighbouring Muslim communities, Kashmir conflict, at a massive level, is frequently perceived as a continuous victimisation of the Muslim people.

Sale of the territory

The land of Kashmir, otherwise extremely rich in scenic beauty and natural resources, has presented a sorrowful story of grief and pathos since the 19th century. After an uneasy Sikh rule, the territory equal to the size of the United Kingdom, was sold to a Hindu Dogra chieftain for a paltry sum of 7.5m rupees. The sale was conducted subsequent to the British conquest of the Punjab through the Amritsar Treaty of 1846 signed between the British East India Company and the Maharajah – himself a man of dubious character and shadowy background. The ludicrous sale of such a vast area with a predominant Muslim majority was justified by the Viceroy, Lord Hardinge, in his correspondence with Queen Victoria, as a means of recouping the losses in the Sikh Wars.[2] Since 1846, the predominantly Muslim region has languished in abject poverty and destitution and rarely witnessed sustained periods of peace. Despite an overwhelmingly Muslim population, the State under the Dogra rule of a century, never had a single Muslim prime minister.

Because of the speed of events just before independence, the future of princely states did not receive sufficient attention by the government and the main Indian political parties. For a long time, the princes had successfully quarantined themselves against any "outside" influence through an autocratic grip on their subjects.[3] In 1947, while surrendering its paramountcy over the princely states in the sub-continent, the British Government in India advised their rulers to accede to one of the two new successor states. Their decision was to be based on the obvious geographic, cultural, economic and demographic considerations. Certainly Kashmir, as a predominantly Muslim territory, contiguous to Pakistan ("K" stands for Kashmir in Pakistan) was supposed to join that country but its ruler, Maharajah Hari Singh dithered, triggering a number of revolts across the State. His own sense of insecurity caused by regional revolts was made use of by the ambitious new leadership in Delhi who drew up an Instrument of Accession facilitating the advent of Indian troops into the State apparently to defend him against the tribal invaders from the Frontier province of Pakistan. The Instrument carried the commitment of a "reference to the people" – making the whole arrangement provisional.[4] The Maharajah whose ancestor had acquired Kashmir in the mid-19th century as a personal fief "was arm-twisted into acceding to India".[5] The Indian official view on the accession has been a constant rebuttal of Kashmiri and Pakistani stances. It simply takes the accession as final and legal: "Kashmir's accession to India took place under circumstances over which the Government of India had no control . . . Kashmir's status as an integral part of India should not, therefore, be questioned".[6]

Pakistanis have looked at the Kashmir dispute as a well-orchestrated effort to strangle their country at its inception. The discretionary changes on the Boundary Award, stoppage of water supply and assets and intransigence on the future of princely states like Kashmir and Hyderabad in the wake of the world's largest migration, left lasting scars on the Pakistani mind.[7] "The origin of the Kashmir dispute lies in the hasty and surgical partition of India and Mountbatten's biased role in securing accession from most of the States for India disregarding, if need be, the principles he himself laid down governing the process of partition".[8] Many Pakistani writers, while studying the constitutional aspects of the issue, are at pains to quote extensively from Nehru on his emotional attachment to Kashmir.[9] While to certain Pakistani intellectuals, India's reluctance in reaching an agreement on Kashmir with Pakistan reflects her desire to hegemonise the South Asian region,[10] to others the Kashmir issue needs to be seen in a larger perspective of South Asian security especially in the context of the rising tide of ethno-nationalism.[11] Pakistanis, like the Kashmiris, bemoan the UN's inactivity and the policy of appeasement pursued by the Western powers especially at a time when the former Soviet Union supported India in her claims on Kashmir. To some of them, the recent upsurge in the Valley is essentially of indigenous origin but has been largely influenced by both regional[12] and extra-regional developments in the recent past.[13]

HISTORICAL ORIGINS

The consolidation of the authoritarian Dogra rule on the State, characterised by routine massive human rights violations, alienated the predominantly Muslim population, many of whom sought refuge in British India. Many British administrators in India over the successive decades criticised the Maharajah's oppressive policies towards his Muslim subjects including the intermittent massacres in Hunza, Nagar and elsewhere, yet the acquisition of Gilgit for strategic purposes – financed largely by the State's money – superseded such reservations. In 1925, the semi-autonomous *jagir* of Poonch was also ceded to the Maharajah whose coercion and waywardness had left no soft corner for him among the Muslim Kashmiris. The Muslims, despite being a numerical majority, had been continuously deprived of their socio-political and economic rights, while on the other hand, the Pundits and Dogras monopolised the power.[14]

It was in 1931 that the Kashmiri Muslims seriously began the protest movement, popularly known as the *Tehreek-i-Jihad*, culminating in massive massacres by the security forces which hastened the establishment of the Glancy Commission.[15] Whereas the Commission recommended a number of fundamental reforms in the system, the movement itself catapulted several Kashmiri leaders including Mir Waiz Yusuf, Chaudhary Ghulam Abbas and Sheikh Abdullah onto the political scene. During the 1940s, when Sheikh Abdullah from the platform of his National Conference pursued his pro-

Indian National Congress policies by striking a closer friendship with Pandit Nehru, Chaudhary Ghulam Abbas, Mir Waiz and many other distinguished Kashmiri leaders strengthened their ranks and files in the Muslim Conference. M. A. Jinnah, who specially visited Kashmir in 1944 to reconcile the parties, was thwarted by Sheikh Abdullah inviting Jinnah's disapproval of his policies.[16] Jinnah asked the Kashmiri Muslims to lend their support to the "Muslim Conference alone".[17] Jinnah's visit had helped the Muslim Conference in stealing a march over the National Conference, as it "injected new life and authenticity" into the former.[18] Jinnah was well aware of segmentary politics within Kashmir and felt apprehensive of Abdullah's inclinations towards the Indian National Congress.[19] Nehru certainly considered Abdullah to be an asset for Indian Government as he confided in Mountbatten as early as 17 June 1947 in a secret memorandum. On the other hand, many contempories felt that Abdullah was not playing a fair game. His own friend and the editor of the *Hamdard*, P. N. Bazaz challenged his right to accede to Kashmir while accusing him of "opportunism".[20]

The Boundary Commission

Within Pakistan there has been a persistent consensus both among the elite and the masses that the Boundary Commission led by Sir Cyril Radcliffe has been responsible for most of the Indo-Pakistan discords with Kashmir heading the list. Pakistanis have maintained all along that last-minute changes were made in the Boundary Award due to personal manipulation by Lord Mountbatten, Nehru and their confidantes to suit the Indian geo-strategic imperatives in the region. The cession of Muslim majority areas in Ferozepur and Gurdaspur (in eastern Punjab) to India at the last moment was explained in terms of Indian designs on Kashmir. Even long after the Radcliffe Award, such questions were raised not only in the Pakistani and British press but, as contemporary classified official documents reveal, inter-departmental concerns dogged officials in the British Foreign Office, the Commonwealth Relations Office and their diplomatic missions in the region.[21] Radcliffe's secretary, Christopher Beaumont, in an interview in February 1992, authenticating Pakistani suspicions, seemed finally to confirm that the Boundary Award was unduly manipulated by Mountbatten at the behest of Nehru. Rao Ayer, the assistant secretary to the Commission, and the Maharajah of Bikaner along with V. P. Menon played a crucial role in influencing the British official decisions at that fateful juncture in Indo-Pakistan relations.[22] Even Mountbatten and his British aides knew that Menon was "the trusted confidant of Vallabhbhai Patel".[23]

The geo-political considerations of the Political Department in the British Indian government radically differed from the principle of partition since they visualised Kashmir's integration into the Indian union. Developments like the change of prime ministers by the Maharajah, visits to Srinagar by Mountbatten, Gandhi, Kripalani, Nehru, and V. P. Menon, and the release of Sheikh Abdullah from jail following a compromise with the ruler, have caused a number of unanswered questions about the role played by Lord Mountbatten,

Congress leadership (both Nehru and Patel), the Maharajah and Sheikh Abdullah in the entire imbroglio.[24] Patel had openly said in Mussoorie long before the British departure from the sub-continent: "Kashmir remains within the Indian Union even if a division of India and partition of Punjab takes place".[25] Even before partition, the roads, wireless and military communication between India and the State were upgraded and Madhopur was already buzzing with Indian military presence.

It is ironical that on 17 October 1947 the Maharajah of Patiala deputed into Kashmir one mountain battalion and a battery of artillery from his troops, which by then were technically part of the Indian Army. The Patiala infantry battalion had been sent to guard the Maharajah's winter palace in Jammu and a battery of Patiala mountain artillery was ordered to protect Srinagar airport. On their arrival in the Valley, Brigadier Sen and Major Palit, the Indian military commanders, were surprised to find the troops already there. On the other hand, Jinnah, voicing Muslim optimism felt: "Kashmir will fall into our lap like a ripe fruit".[26] On 26 October 1947, the new Prime Minister of Jammu and Kashmir, M. C. Mahajan, formerly of the Punjab High Court, visited New Delhi to seek Indian assistance against the Poonchi rebels who, on 24 October 1947, had formally declared the establishment of Azad Jammu and Kashmir. Both Nehru and Menon informed Mahajan that Indian assistance would be conditional both on the Maharajah's accession to India and on his agreement to entrust his government to Sheikh Abdullah, recently released from detention. Mahajan agreed to both the terms subsequent to Indian military intervention. According to his own account, he refused to return to Jammu until he had been informed by his airport manager that the Indian troops had already landed in Srinagar. On 26 October, V. P. Menon had been able "to squeeze" the accession from the Maharajah as he boasted the same evening before the British Deputy High Commissioner, Alexander Symon:

> " V. P. Menon was back in his Delhi home late on the evening of that same Sunday, 26 October. Alexander Symon, Britain's Deputy High Commissioner, joined him for a drink a few minutes after his return. Menon was jubilant. He poured them each a stiff drink. As they sat down, an enormous smile spread across his face. He raised his glass to Symon. Then he pulled a piece of paper from his jacket pocket and waved it gaily towards the Englishman.
>
> 'Here it is', he said. 'We have Kashmir. The bastard signed the Act of Accession. And now that we've got it, we'll never let it go.' "[27]

The Muslim revolt in Poonch merits a special note as it was originally an autonomous *jagir* and 60,402 Poonchis of the Pathan Sudhan tribe had seen action in the Second World War. In the spring of 1947 the Maharajah dismissed them and instead started "importing Sikhs and Hindus" to man his troops. The Poonchis expressed their protest by initiating a "No-tax campaign".[28] The news of Muslim massacres in Jammu, Patiala, Kapurthala and elsewhere further infuriated them and, in a state of despondency, they began their war of liberation:

> "Within a period of about 11 weeks starting in August, systematic savageries, similar to those launched in East Punjab and in Patiala and Kapurthala practically

eliminated the entire Muslim element in the population amounting to 500,000 people. About 200,000 just disappeared, remaining untraceable, having presumably been butchered, or died from epidemics or exposure. The rest fled destitute to the West Punjab."[29]

The growing Poonchi resentment against the Dogra dynasty fuelled by strong feelings of solidarity with the co-religionists was apparent to outside observers in the area.[30] By the summer of 1947, the Poonchis, led by young activists like Abdul Qayyum Khan had taken up arms and began an advance on Srinagar. After liberating Mirpur and adjoining areas in Poonch and Jammu sub-divisions, they announced the establishment of the government of Azad Jammu and Kashmir, headed by Sardar Ibrahim, a Kashmiri barrister.

ACCESSION, THE UNITED NATIONS AND PLEBISCITE

The Government of India presumably raised the Kashmir dispute before the United Nations to score a moral victory over Pakistan but ended up committing itself before the world body to a plebiscite in the state. In the same letter, from Lord Mountbatten, in his capacity as Governor-General of independent India, which accepted the Maharajah's request for accession, a committment for ultimate reference to the people had been made. The Security Council, while asking both the contenders for cessation of hostilities,[31] endorsed the existing Indian commitment for a general plebiscite and appointed a United Nations Commission for India and Pakistan (UNCIP) to decide the modalities. The Indian Government felt that by getting Pakistan declared as the aggressor, its own position would be strengthened and a limited franchise (not exceeding 7 per cent of the then total population in the State and that with an overwhelmingly urban Hindu majority) would guarantee a decision in its favour. However the contemporary secret British and American assessment held "that Kashmir would go to Pakistan under a fair plebiscite except perhaps for the Hindu majority district in the extreme south".[32]

India expressed serious reservations on the appointment of Admiral Nimitz as the UN Plebiscite Administrator and despite numerous UN calls for a plebiscite, it preferred to evade the issue. Even the tangible proposals by Sir Owen Dixon, the UN mediator on Kashmir, put forward in the summer of 1950, stipulating regional plebiscites and partitions and originally accepted by Pakistan, could not make any headway in New Delhi. In 1950, Sir Owen was so exasperated that, in one of his secret letters, he even accused Nehru of "downright lying".[33] Eighteen years on, the Indian Defence Minister, Krishna Menon, when asked by a journalist why India had consistently refused to agree to carry out the promised plebiscite in Kashmir, replied: "Because we would lose it. Kashmir would vote to join Pakistan, and no government responsible for agreeing to the plebiscite would survive."[34] Subsequent mediatory efforts by UN emissaries like General McNaughton, Frank Graham and Gunnar Jarring proved equally fruitless.

The Indo-Soviet entente

The Soviet Union, which had earlier remained aloof from Indo-Pakistan conflict, was now intent upon using its veto more often on Kashmir. The Indo-Soviet Entente had earnestly begun at the Bandung Conference, consummated by Nehru's visit in 1955 to the former Soviet Union. The Soviet press hailed the Indian prime minister as "one of the most outstanding statesmen of the age". In November–December 1955, both Nikolai Bulganin and Nikita Khrushchev reciprocated by undertaking a detailed visit to India. Khrushchev, during a special tour of Srinagar, declared that "the question of Kashmir as one of the constituent States of the Republic of India has already been settled by the people of Kashmir".[35] In 1962, it was again the Soviet veto which torpedoed the Security Council resolution on Kashmir. It is quite true that by 1955, both India and Pakistan were receiving military assistance from the contemporary global powers and the dispute itself became a casualty of the cold war. It is sad to note that for 17 years the UN had not been able to achieve any major progress on the dispute adding to the regional frustrations. Nehru's visit to Pakistan in 1960 to sign the Indus Basin Water Treaty raised hopes for a possible solution to this enduring flash-point, yet on his return to Delhi the Indian Prime Minister started denigrating Pakistan for its alliance with the Western countries. To him, an "aligned" Pakistan and "non-aligned" India could not be equated. Soon, the China factor deflated India's pronouncements on non-alignment though she was already receiving military assistance from the Soviet Union and economic assistance from the West. Pakistan viewed this assistance with concern reckoning to be its ultimate target since, to her, the Chinese threat to Indian integrity was merely an inflated myth. In such an atmosphere the marathon Z. A. Bhutto-Swaran Singh parleys in late 1962 and early 1963 proved futile, with India accusing Pakistan of developing a new anti-India axis.

In December 1963, the *Moee-i-Muqqaddas*, the Islamic relic – a hair from the head of the Prophet deposited at the shrine of Hazrat Bal in Srinagar – was found to be missing, causing quite an agitation in the Valley. It was eventually found restored to its place but only after adding to Kashmiri separatist sentiments. In an atmosphere of tension, Jayaprakash Narayan, the veteran Indian socialist leader, published two articles in *The Hindustan Times* questioning India's claims on Kashmir's integration within the Indian Union on the basis of suspicious elections of 1957 and 1962. Criticising the rationale of holding on to Kashmir to deter India's disintegration, Narayan found it ill-conceived and advised the Indian leadership not to ignore Pakistan's genuine sensitivities on the issue. He differed from the official view of extricating Pakistan from the Kashmir question and felt that any amicable solution would result in a closer friendship between the two neighbours. He advised India to show statesmanship by undertaking an initiative in this direction.[36]

The 17-day war

Sheikh Abdullah's visit to Pakistan in May 1964 soon after his release from Indian incarceration, ended abruptly with the demise of Nehru. By then, some members of the Pakistan Government were exasperated by the Kashmir stalemate. In particular, an overestimation by Pakistan's Foreign Office of indigenous resentment in the Valley betrayed an inflated assumption that the Kashmiris were ripe for rebellion. The break-up of the hostilities this time did not remain confined to the State itself. On 6 September 1965, after a threat by Prime Minister Lalbahadur Shastri, Indian military crossed the international borders and invaded West Pakistan. The Kashmir dispute was certainly the major cause of the 17-day war which ended with UN intervention and Soviet arbitration in Tashkent. Kashmir was once again responsible for the outbreak of Indo-Pakistan hostilities in 1971, and an ongoing high-altitude war over Sicahin Glacier since 1984.

Both the Tashkent Award of 1966 and the Simla Agreement of 1972 underlined the need to settle the Kashmir issue through negotiations though nothing concrete has transpired yet. Exasperation with the UN, continued economic stagnation, emergence of a new generation of assertive Kashmiris, growing religious *rhetoric* in the Indian body politic, rise of the BJP as a ruling party, Afghan resistance, Iranian revolution and the eventual break-up of the former Soviet Union have been the major catalysts for the Kashmiri defiance which began in earnest in 1989, taking everybody by surprise. It appears that the Kashmiris have taken affairs into their own hands and belied their longstanding reputation for submissiveness. Unlike earlier phases, the new era in Kashmir hinges on the Kashmiri initiative itself.

REGIONAL DIMENSIONS

The Kashmir dispute[37] has proved again and again to be the main bone of contention between the two South Asian neighbours for almost half a century. Pakistan takes the view that the Simla Agreement of 1972 recognises not only the existence of the dispute but the urgent need to resolve it. On the basis of

TABLE 2

THE BALANCE OF INDIAN AND PAKISTANI ARMED FORCES

Category	**India**	**Pakistan**
Total Armed Forces	1,262,000	550,000
Army	1,100,000	500,000
Navy	52,000	20,000
Air Force	110,000	30,000
Total Reserve Forces	Not known	513,000
Army	490,000	500,000
Navy	?	5,000
Air Force	?	8,000

Source: International Institute for Strategic Studies, *Military Balance, 1990–1991*. (London, 1990).

the UN resolutions Pakistan accordingly presses the Kashmiri right to self-determination.[38] The Indians feel that the Simla Agreement of 1972 has superseded the UN role in the issue and accuses Pakistan of internationalising it.[39] They also point out that the Pakistani ruling elite use Kashmir to divert attention from domestic issues. Thus the claims and counter-claims continue, resulting in an ever-growing arms race on the sub-continent, as is clear from the statistics in Tables 2 and 3.

TABLE 3

MAJOR MILITARY WEAPONS

Category	India	Pakistan
MBT	3,150 (+500 in store)	1,850
T55	800	50
T72/-M1	700	—
Ch.Type-59/69	—	1,300
Vijayanta	1,700	—
PT-76	100	—
Naval Bases	7	1
Submarines	19	6
Carriers	2	—
Destroyers	10	3
Frigates	20	10
Amphibious	10	—
Naval Air Craft	41	5
Helicopters	73	10
Aircraft	833	470
Armed Helicopters	12	—

Source: *Ibid.*

South Asia today remains one of the most heavily indebted, immensely impoverished ethnically divisive and volatile regions of the world, as is clear from the following two tables:

TABLE 4

SOUTH ASIA ON HUMAN DEVELOPMENT INDEX
(Ranking in 160 Countries)

Country	Rank Number	Value
Sri Lanka	75	0.665
Pakistan	120	0.311
India	123	0.308
Bangladesh	136	0.186
Afghanistan	157	0.069

Source: United Nations, *Human Development Report 1991.*

TABLE 5

REGIONAL DISTRIBUTION OF POVERTY, 1985–2000
(in millions)

Region	**1985**	**2000**
South Asia	500	350
Sub-Sahara	175	250
East Asia	225	50
Europe, M. East	50	50
Americas	75	50

Source: The World Bank, *Human Development Report 1990*, and *Human Development Report 1992*.

According to the UN, there are altogether 1,200m individuals in the developing countries who live below the income level commensurate with essential food requirements, with India, Bangladesh and Pakistan making almost half of the total.[40]

Benazir Bhutto, the then prime minister of Pakistan, speaking in London on 7 July 1989, explained that Pakistan was concerned about the Indian arms build up which had followed accusations that Pakistan was helping Kashmiri separatists. She suggested direct talks on Kashmir and arms control.[41] But the Bhutto-Rajiv Gandhi talks in Islamabad on the latter's short visit to Pakistan on his way back from Europe in July, made the Indo-Pakistan divergences more public without helping any resolution of the Kashmir dispute. Gandhi rather focused on Pakistan's nuclear programme instead of any further talks on Kashmir itself.[42] By August, the guerrilla activities in Kashmir had increased within the Valley, with India criticising Pakistan for training and harbouring the Kashmiri separatists. The rhetoric for war multiplied in the wake of increased repression by the security forces with the Kashmiri policemen playing a reluctant role. In a few months, "a previously vague and somewhat lethargic Kashmiri yearning for religious and economic security has been transformed into a heavily-armed guerrilla struggle, aimed at separation from India . . . At a time when Rajiv Gandhi, the Indian Prime Minister, and Benazir Bhutto, Pakistan's Prime Minister, are pledging friendship to each other, Indian accusations that the latest trouble has been provoked by renewed Pakistani attempts at destabilisation have been decidedly hollow".[43] The deterioration in Kashmir came to a head in December when the Kashmiri activists kidnapped the daughter of Mufti Saeed, the interior minister in the newly-installed government of V. P. Singh. Rubaiya Saeed was finally released on 13 December by her kidnappers in exchange for the freedom of five Kashmiri detainees. The release of fellow activists was celebrated throughout the Valley giving more momentum to the separatist movement. On the one hand, for V. P. Singh, Kashmir, like Punjab, demanded an urgent solution to alleviate the Hindus fears of non-Hindu separatism, on the other hand most of the Kashmiris, wanted either complete independence or annexation to Pakistan through a plebiscite.[44] Such a concession to a Muslim-majority state is unlikely ever to be acceptable to Indian Hindus – either the secularists or the fundamentalists. New Delhi's two-pronged approach since early 1990 has been to use state coercion (scorched-earth policy) on the Kashmiri activists simultaneously with political and military pressure on Pakistan.

Continuing defiance

As 1991 wore on, it appeared that the Indian troops and militant elements within Indian society were getting jittery over the persistent defiance in the Valley. The Kashmiri revolt, despite state-led coercion, went on unabated. As late as April 1992, security forces were raiding towns such as Sopore, Baramula, Srinagar, Handwara, Kupwara, and Anantnag looking for suspects, commonly derided as Pakistani agents or infiltrators. On 16 April, 200 Kashmiris from Sopore were arrested besides women being verbally abused. Four days later, in the same town, 40 civilians were killed while demonstrating against violations of human rights. The troops fired on the peaceful protesters indiscriminately, while during a similar demonstration by women in Srinagar on 28 April 1992, five civilians were killed in the "crossfire". In retaliation against a guerrilla attack on the Faisal Camp, the Indian security forces killed three civilians and gutted several shops and houses in Baramula. It happened barely a week after the Lal Bazaar Tragedy when 90 Kashmiris lost their lives as a roof collapsed. They had gathered to mourn a family death. Given the persistent guerrilla activities, Governor Saxena, in an interview with the Voice of America on 29 May, dismissed any possibility of sending Indian forces back to barracks.

Massive demonstrations, prolonged curfews spreading over weeks and the break-up of the entire political and administrative machinery of state cannot simply be attributed to the machinations of a foreign power. The very fact that the issue has not only survived over four decades but has emerged strongly once again bringing both countries to the brink of war, underscores the regional dynamics of the problem. Despite five meetings between the prime ministers of both sides and six meetings between their foreign secretaries no new ground has yet been broken.[45]

KASHMIRI ETHNO-NATIONALISM

There are four major types of ethnic movement in contemporary South Asia:

1 **Autonomous:** the Sikhs and Tamils provide the best examples where the major goal is to have maximum cultural, political and economic autonomy just short of total independence, making ethnicity (sub-national?) a case of majority-minority relationship.

2 **Situational:** in such a case, politicised ethnicity aims at ensuring proper economic, cultural and political rights in a given national set-up. It may arise from an influx of population from outside using slogans like "sons-of-soil" to emphasise native rights. Assam, where the main focus is on nativism, is a good example.

3 Parallelist: Sindh offers such a case, where indigenous Sindhis find themselves in a "nut-cracker situation" due to the influx of "outsiders". Simultaneously, the former immigrants from India, find themselves losing their cultural and politico-economic power to other rivals including Sindhis, Punjabis and Pushtuns. Here the reluctance of various ethnic groups in accepting pluralism turns out to be the main issue.

4 Separatist/Secessionist: the movement in Kashmir is a case in point. Here all the major movements listed are working to consolidate ethno-nationalism with the main Valley becoming the focus of the movement led by Muslim activists. Earlier, former East Pakistan was a similar case study in separatism but in this case religion played an altogether different (integrative?) role.

The separate Kashmiri identity is substantiated on the basis of geographic, linguistic, historical and religious differentiation. However, *Kashmiriat*, as pronounced mainly by Jammu and Kashmir Liberation Front (JKLF) premises on a supra-religious ethnic identity, independent of both India and Pakistan.[46] It is not irrelevant to mention here that Sheikh Abdullah occasionally vacillated between such a state and separate identity within a secular India. However, Abdullah and his ambiguous relationship with India, do not carry any weight today either with JKLF or pro-Pakistan Kashmiris. On the other hand, every other Kashmiri activist group in the Valley takes Islam as the basic component of ethnic identity and aims at reuniting Kashmir with Pakistan. With the rise of revivalist parties like the BJP, religion has created a larger and more vocal dimension in Indian political rhetoric.[47]

Kashmiri Muslims are united in their feeling of separateness from India in the way that Jammu's Hindus or Ladakhi Buddhists feel "different" from them. They believe their political agenda to be outside the uneasy Hindu-Muslim relations in India and do not wish to add any strain on them.[48] They believe that their independence would neither alter the main course of this relationship nor challenge Indian secularism, since Kashmir, given its credentials as an outstanding case on UN agenda and its recognition through Article 370 in the Indian constitution, allows for such a decision.[49] Moreover, India might, in the face of the heavy defence expenditure and the opprobrium attracted by evident human rights violations, find it eventually convenient to relinquish Kashmir. In that sense, a regional negotiated consensus might avert the repetition of the tragedies of 1947 when the British left the sub-continent. At another level, many Kashmiris wonder why they must be kept hostage as a guarantee of India's secularism which, in any case, is under severe strain due to rising Hindu fundamentalism and the growing partisan character of the state itself.[50] The *ekta yatra* (unity march undertaken by the BJP) of 1991 and successive unarmed marches from Azad Kashmir to cross the LOC (Line of Control) in 1992 have substantially intensified Kashmiri ethno-nationalism.

For many Kashmiris in diaspora, the Kashmir issue has provided a means of articulating their own ethnic identity. In plural and multi-cultural societies like the UK and USA, recent Kashmiri efforts at lobbying public opinion through the media, petitions, publications, seminars, conferences and marches have rallyed support for their cause. They received a major boost for their efforts in early March 1992 when the European Parliament took the unprecedented decision of calling upon the United Nations Security Council to resolve the Kashmir dispute by explicitly mentioning the Kashmiris' right to self-determination. However, despite JKLF's call for a secular, united and independent Kashmir, for many Kashmiri Muslims, union with Pakistan through a fair plebiscite, remains the ultimate ideal.[51]

Northern Areas and Azad Kashmir

The politico-administrative status of Northern Areas both before and after 1947 has been to some extent ambivalent. Overwhelmingly Muslim, yet belonging to different linguistic families and regional identities, the inhabitants of Baltistan, Hunza, Gilgit and adjoining territories, have been considered part of the entire State by some observers.[52] Divided into semi-autonomous principalities, they resisted the Dogra authority from Srinagar which usually retaliated with large-scale repression carried out by special military expeditions. The acquisition of Gilgit by the British and then its return to the Maharajah on the eve of independence added another complexity to claims and counter claims on Northern Area. Concurrently, these regions had been able to wrest their independence from the Maharajah through armed rebellions, followed by declarations to join Pakistan. While India considers them part of Kashmir and thus controversial, Pakistan has maintained their special administrative and political status by avoiding a policy of integration. Azad Kashmir governments time and again have demanded the integration of these districts into Azad Kashmir on the basis of historical claims. In fact, the Northern Areas remained aloof from political, cultural and economic life in Jammu, Valley and Poonch. The only uncertain link among these diverse areas was through Pothowar, the neighbouring Pakistani region thus leaving the areas mutually exclusive from Srinagar; nor did the Maharajah enjoy any sovereignty over these territories. The inhabitants of Northern Areas question all such claims and demand to be treated like other districts in Pakistan, enjoying full political and electoral rights.

Economic activity

The Karakoram Highway (KKH) has intensified economic and commercial activity in the region, by opening these scenic areas to the rest of the country. In addition to a booming tourist and hotel industry, the development work both by the government and the private sector has changed the socio-economic contours of the Northern Areas. Similarly, Azad Kashmir has been economically and culturally a beneficiary of its closer and enduring relationship with Pakistan. A small territory with an economy in deficit, Azad Kashmir's links with Pakistan have nevertheless afforded job opportunities and mobility for Azad Kashmiris, in some cases better than those of their Pakistani counterparts. Pakistan's spending on the four districts of Azad Kashmir has been lavish, resulting in better road infra-structure and improved facilities in education, health and administration. Pakistani support has meant that a massive number of Azad Kashmiris have been able to migrate to the United Kingdom, the Gulf and elsewhere making Mirpur and Kotli more prosperous towns than many in Pakistan. These Kashmiris have the best per capita income and a high level of literacy compared with the ordinary citizens in Pakistan. There has been a rapid and fruitful transformation from a backward, land-locked personal fiefdom of Poonch to a more prosperous, forward-looking and mobile international community. The Azad Kashmiris, despite their share of South Asian poverty, have achieved relative stability and prosperity in cities like Bradford, Luton, Slough, Birmingham, Islamabad, Rawalpindi and Karachi. The economic and cultural transformation of Northern Areas and Azad Kashmir, together with greater mobility than ever before in the region, has created an ambitious middle class, eagerly involved in its quest for identity in a plural region.

GLOBAL DIMENSIONS

The South Asian sub-continent may be regarded as a non-priority region in the global political and economic sphere yet its importance is vital in regional development. The Soviet intervention in Afghanistan, revolution in Iran, dissolution of the Soviet Union and emergence of independent Muslim republics, the Gulf crisis and economic recession world-wide have left their crucial imprints on the South Asian political and economic scene. The Kashmir question may not be a direct threat to world peace but the military cost to the whole of South Asia at the expense of human needs and the risk of nuclear confrontation certainly have serious implications outside the region. Kashmir remains one of the few oldest unresolved items on the UN agenda, beside posing a serious question of human rights.[53] In the complete absence of a political mechanism, Indian control over a defiant, homogenous population in the Valley, equally suffers from practical and moral difficulties.[54] A number of the Indian intelligentsia are questioning the validity of Indian control and the resultant policies in Kashmir. "Opposition elites" in India believe in good-neighbourly relations based on mutual co-operation in South Asia.[55]

VIOLATIONS OF HUMAN RIGHTS

Reports of intermittent incidents of gang rape, arson and murder have caused an uproar amongst various opinion groups. Commenting on one march, Gerald Kaufman, the former UK Shadow Foreign Secretary, urged the international community to help settle the Kashmir conflict: "The raising of the Indian flag by the Hindu 'unity convoy' in Srinagar, the predominantly Muslim capital of Kashmir, has brought the expected and inevitable response from Kashmir 'militants'. The outcome, as all too often expected in Kashmir, has been yet further death and bloodshed more among members of both communities".[56] An American commentary, while reviewing the human misery in the State, observed:

> "The Muslim majority of the Kashmir region is now pitted against the entire Hindu India nation. Ironically, the free press of India was the first to document in detail

the systematic attempts at repressive military measures to subdue Kashmir rebel actions that are even condoned by special legislative measures by the Indian parliament.

"In this active rebellion, up to 30,000 people have been killed by a regional military and paramilitary force fluctuating between 350,000 to 430,000 in just the last two years. Torture, gang rape and various other heinous acts are commonplace by uniformed members of the security forces. Only a fraction are being documented by a small element in the India press, some of whom have been killed or imprisoned, with even groups like Asia Watch and Amnesty International being denied access to the region."[57]

Fact-finding missions

The Indian press and human rights organisations have frequently carried news of human rights violations perpetrated by Indian security forces in the Valley though in general, the Indian media have reported the official version of events.[58] A seven-member fact-finding delegation of the Indian People's Front (IPF) visited the Valley in the third week of June 1990 and on their return submitted a detailed resumé of numerous violations of a serious nature and found the situation "approaching a point of no return".[59] The Committee For Initiative on Kashmir sent a team of four women to the State in June 1990 to investigate the impact of oppression on the lives of the people, especially women. In their *India's Kashmir War*, they found both Muslims and non-Muslims "filled with fear and insecurity" and "women had become a particular target for the security forces. The method and manner of attack on women had a definite pattern. It was almost as though the attacks were premeditated – as evident from the numerous case histories of torture and molestation that we have collected and adduced in our report."[60] Such reports were submitted following the reprisals by security forces on processions taking place soon after the murder of Maulvi Mir Waiz in May 1990. In another report on paramilitary vendettas, Yusuf Jameel, a correspondent for the BBC and various Indian and international newspapers, reported: "More than 170 families were rendered homeless in Odina and Vittamagam villages, about 25 km west of Srinagar, where CRPF personnel ran amok on Sunday, torching houses, cattle-sheds and grain stores".[61] *The Kashmir Massacre* was a similar report submitted by the Punjab Human Rights Group in 1990 purporting to investigate the circumstances leading to the death of Mir Waiz and its consequences.

The resurgence of Kashmiri disenchantment with Indian rule was reflected in reports carried in the world press which took Indian security forces to task for carrying on heinous human rights violations.[62] It was felt that the Kashmiri activists clearly enjoyed a massive support and were "likely to be around for some time. A walk through the narrow alleys of Srinagar shows how uniformly committed Kashmiris seem to be. Toddlers flash victory signs and chant, 'Indian dogs go home!' and 'We want freedom!' An elderly woman confronts an Indian soldier beneath her window with cries of 'Murderer! You rape our girls, you shoot our boys. God will punish you.' For the average Kashmiri, the violence is becoming a way of life."[63]

A leading English newspaper published a report on a grave human tragedy in Poshpura in late February 1991 when "more than 800 Indian soldiers sealed off Kunan Poshpura and herded all the men out on to an icy field. While the men stood shivering in their bedclothes, under guard, the soldiers allegedly went from house to house, raping the Muslim girls and women. Villagers claim that nearly 80 women were raped before the soldiers, members of the 4th Rajput rifles, cleared out at dawn.

"The incident only came to light several days ago, after a copy of the district magistrate's report to Kashmir's chief commissioner was leaked to the press."[64]

Human rights groups and Kashmir

Various organisations, both Indian and international, have brought out special studies on the gruesome violations of human rights in the State, especially after 1989. It is important to note that organisations such as Amnesty International have not been allowed into the Valley itself, but they have still attempted to investigate and record serious violations. These have included arson, gang rape, cold-blooded murders of civilians through indiscriminate shooting, lynching, numerous kinds of torture such as drilling various parts of the human body, skin burning, hanging upside down and amputations, kidnaps and incarceration – all, without any judicial recourse. Amnesty International, in its recent report on India, has enumerated patterns of torture in various regions in the country. Torture in cases of counter insurgency is common in the areas where "political groups are actively seeking independence or increased autonomy" and where the security forces have been empowered under the Terrorist and Disruptive Activities (Prevention) Act (TADA) to arrest and detain for one year for investigation. The detainees held under TADA are commonly denied bail. The report quotes a number of cases of torture from the State with extensive human rights violations "attributed to the Indian army, and the paramilitary Border Security Force (BSF) and the Central Reserve Police Force (CPRF)". *India: Torture, Rape & Deaths in Custody* also documents the means of torture in such cases.[65]

The Co-ordination Committee on Kashmir (CCK), a human rights group in India, sent its four-member team into the Valley in May 1992 to investigate the violations of human rights. Led by V. M. Tarkunde, a senior advocate of the Supreme Court of India and a known jurist, the team included Balraj Puri, a well-known Jammu-based writer and political activist and N. D. Pancholli, the general secretary of the KCC. The fourth member, Mrs. Sulochana Shikhare, is also an active member of the People's Union of Civil Liberties (PUCL) involved in a number of social causes. 83-year-old, Mr. Tarkunde, a retired judge of the Bombay High Court, had co-founded the PUCL and Citizens Forum for Democracy (CFD) along with the late Jayaprakash Narayan (JP). Justice Tarkunde had visited Kashmir heading a similar representative team of four Indian human rights groups from 9 to 13 March 1990, followed by another extended visit from 28 March to 25 April 1990. His early report on Kashmir, appearing in 1990, established numerous cases of gross violations and recorded strong anti-India feelings in the Valley.

Kashmir 1991 is a report based on a fact-finding mission to Kashmir by an independent human rights group called Physicians for Human Rights (UK) which documented the health consequences of the civil unrest and the actions of the police and military in Kashmir. This was in response to widespread concern about medical and human rights violations after the official retaliation at civil unrest in the state, although the immediate cause was a letter from Professor Abdul Ahad Guru, head of the department of surgery at the Institute of Medical Surgery, Srinagar.[66]

The Asia Watch Committee, led by Sidney Jones, published its recent report: *Human Rights in India: Kashmir Under Siege*, in May 1991 simultaneously from Washington DC and New York. The report, at the very outset, revealed that:

> "Indian army and security forces operating in Kashmir have consistently violated the provisions of Common Article 3 and customary international humanitarian law by engaging in the summary executions of suspected militants, 'reprisal killings' of civilians, torture, rapes and other assaults on civilians and captured combatants. Security legislation authorising the security forces to shoot to kill and protecting themselves from prosecution has facilitated such abuses. The security forces have also engaged in the wanton destruction and looting of civilian property, primarily by burning down residential neighbourhoods in retaliation for militant attacks."[67]

As a consequence of various reports on human rights abuses in India in general and in Kashmir in particular, Representative D. Fascell, Chairman of the Congress Committee on Foreign Affairs and Representative Gus Yatron, Chairman, Subcommittee on Human Rights and International Organisations, sent an urgent letter to the Indian Ambassador to the United States. "Forms of torture employed include burning victims with hot irons, gang rapes of girls and women and indiscriminate beatings. After reading Amnesty's report, reports from other human rights organisations as well as the State Department's human rights reports on India for 1991, we can only conclude that torture committed by government authorities is taking place in India on a regular and systematic basis."[68]

KASHMIR AT THE CROSS-ROADS

In any realistic resolution of the Kashmir conflict, the larger interests of the Kashmiris must receive priority. For a long time, rather than being the focal point, they were simply regarded as a side-issue. Yet, it is the Kashmiris who, for generations, have continued to suffer from decisions made about them without consultation. The sale of the entire territory to one individual committed generations of Kashmiris to a sub-human bondage which found no redress even in 1947 when the rest of South Asia was jubilant over independence. The Maharajah and a few capricious individuals once again decided the fate of millions of Kashmiris as if they did not exist. History had come full circle. All the legal and political sweeteners given by New Delhi through its surrogates left nothing but a bitter taste for the Kashmiris who instead took up arms defying the myth of their traditional submissiveness.

The Muslim Kashmiris do not want to have anything to do with India. "More and more honest Indians now realise the untenability of keeping

Kashmir under indefinite occupation. A former Indian minister, George Fernandes, then with temporary responsibility for Kashmir, admitted after a fact-finding visit that even trees and stones were opposed to Indian presence."[69] The world has to come to grips with the realities in Kashmir where the prospects of maintaining even a repressive peace are negligible.

After the Kashmiris, it is Pakistan which has suffered the most in post-1947 developments. To Pakistanis, Kashmir is not merely an issue of territory, it is a reminder of an "incomplete" Pakistan and is a restatement of all the massacres and injustices. Kashmir is economically and psychologically the jugular vein of Pakistan, which unlike any other nation, has faced the severest challenges to its very existence since its inception. Its sense of despondency over Kashmir due to India's insistence on forestalling the plebiscite and a continued history of mistrust and skirmishes with its giant neighbour have not only tested its steadfastness but have reaffirmed its position as the major party in the dispute. Pakistan cannot be sidelined in any resolution of the crisis and though it continues to favour a UN style of solution has, over the years, reiterated a willingness to negotiate over other possible solutions.

There is no doubt that India, not simply because of its size and resourcefulness, holds the pivotal position in the resolution of the conflict over Kashmir. India's insistence on holding on to Kashmir has not helped in any major economic or geo-political sense. It has rather dented its own stance on decolonisation and human rights. Equally, within the country itself, it has created a moral dilemma besides exacerbating inter-religious tensions. India's own priorities lie somewhere else and not in policing the region. Similarly, its obstinacy on an otherwise human issue has added to suspicions and fears amongst smaller neighbours. A bold initiative on Kashmir, involving both give-and-take, would certainly help to demilitarise the region, stabilise movements and processes for democracy and development, and augur well for more than 1bn people in the region with the world's largest concentration of poverty.

KASHMIR: THE PROGNOSIS

The Kashmir conflict, despite its longevity, is not an intractable case and a genuine and bold initiative both at the regional and extra-regional levels, might result in a surprising consensus if the will to co-operate can be generated. At the moment, the following scenarios are possible:

1 Stalemate: there could be an enduring no-win situation and a continued stalemate on the sub-continent. A centralised Indian authority, superimposed by an overwhelming number of troops using coercion and temptation seems to be the favourite short term/long term Indian policy posture. Such a scenario, modelled on India's policy in the Punjab is meant to exhaust the activists in the long run in a quarantined situation. Pakistan would have to be kept engaged under pressure in Sindh or through a low-intensity conflict somewhere else. This policy is largely a stop-gap arrangement and premises Kashmir as a "lost" case. In addition, it warrants increased global attention to India's violations of human rights adding pressure to it besides damaging its prestige as a democracy. In terms of cost/benefit analysis, Kashmiri Muslims and Pakistan might be the eventual winners in the long term.

2 Gradual disengagement: such a strategy might operate only after India's acceptance of the erosion of its authority in the State simultaneous with a willingness for an honourable demilitarisation in the Valley by entering into negotiations with some willing partners from amongst the guerrilla groups. Such a situation could lead to restoration of electoral politics to ward off world criticism and to begin a dialogue for a solution within the Union. At present this does not seem to be a possibility. Pro-establishment Kashmiri Muslims have already fled for safer havens and there is no substitute cadre available to enter into negotiations with New Delhi. The favourite and perhaps India's only major ally in the state, Dr. Farooq Abdullah, lives in hiding in the United Kingdom and under the circumstances would not risk his life.

3 All-out war: India, in a hot pursuit, or sheer frustration, might attack Pakistan or Azad Kashmir to push Pakistan for a final resolution of the crisis on her own terms. This threat was possible in the early months of the movement when Pakistan feared a military offensive.[70] However, now such a dramatic development is not likely with the nuclear threat from both sides added to global condemnation.[71]

4 Expulsion of Muslims from Kashmir: the BJP and many other Hindu organisations have been advocating ethnic cleansing by raising slogans like: "Pakistan Yaa Qabrisitan!" (Pakistan, or graveyard). Such a scenario is presumed through the abolition of Article 370 in the Indian Constitution and by dint of "Kapurthalisation" of the Muslims in the Valley and surrounding areas in the State.

5 Bilateral agreement: India and Pakistan, despite various meetings at prime ministerial and diplomatic levels, have not been able to have a meaningful, direct and open dialogue devoted to Kashmir like the Paris Talks over Vietnam. Indian insistence on Kashmir being a "domestic" issue does not allow such parleys to take place since New Delhi does not like appearing weak to powerful sections in society. Any argument stipulating civil war and balkanisation has not been put to the test and bureaucratic inertia has permeated bilateral relations. In the spirit of the Simla Agreement of 1972, India and Pakistan can initiate a dialogue so as to end the only remaining cold war in the world. Such bilateral discussions can begin at the behest of some global arbiter as a mutually agreeable third party.

6 Confederal arrangement: this stipulates a confederal arrangement for the whole of South Asia but given the SAARC experience it looks more like an ideal than a reality.

7 Creation of numerous smaller states: this again is based on a concept like that of Western Europe, under which South Asia may be divided into smaller, manageable units, sharing natural resources, defence, economy and communications, and governed through treaties. Geographic and ethnic homogeneity might decide the demarcation of such smaller independent states. Such a solution itself might prove a problem raising the spectre of unending population transfers, the rise of religious and sectarian dissensions and vast differences over already scarce natural resources.

8 UN arbitration: it is not easy to be dismissive towards the UN role which seems to have been reinvigorated with a new era in global politics. UN resolutions on Kashmir are part of international obligations and commitments and the very presence of the UN observers on LOC besides Kashmir's inclusion as an unresolved dispute in the annual report by the UN Secretary-General justify an assertive UN role in the resolution of the crisis. The UN-led plebiscite, administered through a non-partisan mechanism, still remains a valid option. In this context, given the respective geo-political and ethnic interests of the parties involved, the Dixon Formula of 1950 could form a reasonable beginning. Through such a mechanism, stipulating regional plebiscites and partitions, the inhabitants of the entire State can decide about their future. One cannot dismiss the ethnic and cultural diversity in the entire State which allows sufficient justification for a Dixon-type solution. After all, as the contemporary documents now reveal both parties had agreed to the Formula in 1950 and it was Nehru who dithered at the crucial moment.

9 Jointly-administered Kashmir: an autonomous Kashmir with checks and balances prohibiting the settlement of non-natives in the State yet under joint Indo-Pakistani guarantees is sometimes presented as another viable option.

10 Independent Kashmir: such a scenario or "third option" projecting a secular and independent state, has been obtaining more currency in recent months but given the regional imperatives it may not appear convincing and pragmatic enough to many. The geo-political interests of the neighbouring countries like China, India and Pakistan have to be considered. They would not like to see a new, independent state on their borders, with conflicting ethno-religious loyalties.

11 Trieste-type solution: such a solution for Kashmir was explored by the American strategist, Selig Harrison at the international Kashmir seminar in Oxford in June 1990,[72] followed by a similar proposal by Kuldip Nayar, a well-known Indian journalist and former Indian High Commissioner in London.[73] More recently, Harrison put forward his views in an article in a journal, as he noted: "As the first step towards a solution of the dispute over Kashmir, India would have to split the state, integrating most of Jammu and Ladakh with the Indian Union while giving special autonomous status to a new state in which the Kashmir Valley would be united with the sizeable pockets in Jammu and Ladakh. India could then offer to give this new state far-reaching autonomy as part of a Trieste-type solution under which Pakistan would grant the same degree of autonomy to Azad Kashmir." Both India and Pakistan would look after defence, foreign affairs, communications and currency while withdrawing their troops from the territory under UN-supervised arrangements. It further suggested: "The present Kashmir cease-fire line would become an international border. As in the Trieste settlement, it would be a porous border, with Kashmiris free to travel back and forth without Indian and Pakistani visas. Islamabad would retain Gilgit, Hunza, and Baltistan, thus maintaining its access to China." But to Harrison, the main opposition would be from India, fearful of autonomy movements elsewhere, though he himself is not convinced by the argument. "India, however, shows no signs of moving in this direction. Indian policy is to crush the insurgency militarily before pursuing a political solution." He expects Kashmiris, especially in JKLF eventually to agree to the arrangement.[74] It might, however, be some time before there is any major debate on these and related proposals, though urgency to resolve the conflict has never before been so manifest.

NOTES

[1] Mr. N. C. Chatterjee, the Hindu Mahasabha MP, had observed in an article: "The geographical situation of the State was such that it would be bounded on all sides by the new Dominion of Pakistan. Its only access to the outside world by road lay through the Jhelum Valley road which ran through Pakistan, via Rawalpindi. The only rail line connecting the State with the outside world lay through Sialkot into Pakistan. Its postal and telegraphic services operated through areas that were certain to belong to the Dominion of Pakistan.

"The State was dependent for all its imported supplies like salt, sugar, petrol and other necessities of life on their safe and continued transit through areas that would form part of Pakistan." Even the tourist traffic and the timber trade, the two main sources of Kashmir's economy were via the Jhelum Valley Road. Quoted in Sheikh Mohammad Abdullah, "Kashmir, India and Pakistan", *Foreign Affairs*, 43, (3), April 1965, p. 528.

[2] See Hardinge to Queen Victoria, 18 February 1846, in A. C. Benson and Viscount Esher, eds., *The Letters of Queen Victoria. A Selection of Her Majesty's Correspondence between the Years 1837 and 1861, Volume II, 1844–1853*, London, 1908, pp. 73–74.

[3] Even Lord Mountbatten, the last Viceroy, did not formulate any clear policy on the future of these states until very late and that too: (a) predicated on the lapse of paramountcy and, (b) persuasion to join either of the two new states. See, W. H. Morris-Jones, "The Transfer of Power, 1947", *Modern Asian Studies*, XVI, 1982, 1–32.

[4] Sheikh Abdullah believed that the "accession was to be purely provisional and temporary until the will of the people could be ascertained through a referendum". See Sheikh Mohammad Abdullah, *op. cit.*, p. 529. Another Indian specialist also considered the accession both "provisional and conditional". See, A. G. Noorani, *The Kashmir Question*, Bombay, 1964, p. 34.

[5] "Kashmir. A Lifetime ago", *The Economist*, 31 October 1992.

[6] Jyoti Bhusan Das Gupta, *Jammu and Kashmir*, The Hague, 1968, p. ix.

[7] For a first-hand account on the Radcliffe Award, see Chaudhri Muhammad Ali, *The Emergence of Pakistan*, New York, 1967.

[8] Pervaiz Iqbal Cheema, *Pakistan's Defence Policy, 1947–58*, London, 1990, p. 38.

[9] S. M. Burke, *Pakistan's Foreign Policy: An Historical Analysis*, Karachi, 1990 (revised edition), p. 21.

[10] See K. Sarwar Hasan, *The Strategic Interest of Pakistan*, Karachi 1954; ed., *Documents on the Foreign Relations of Pakistan: The Kashmir Question*, Karachi, 1966; also Z. A. Bhutto, *The Myth of Independence*, London, 1969.

[11] Iftikhar H. Malik, "Ethnicity and Contemporary South Asian Politics: The Kashmir Conflict as a Case Study", *The Round Table*, 322, 1992, 203–214.

[12] See, Iftikhar H. Malik, "The Kashmir Dispute: A *Cul-de-sac* in Indo-Pakistan Relations?" in Raju G. C. Thomas, ed., *Perspectives on Kashmir*, Oxford, 1962.

[13] Mushahid Hussain, "The Kashmir Issue: Its New International Dimensions", in *ibid.*

[14] The best example was Sheikh Abdullah himself, who despite an MSc from Aligarh Muslim University, at the most acquired a very ordinary, junior teaching position in the State. For more on long-standing Muslim backwardness, see Prem Nath Bazaz, *Inside Kashmir*, Srinagar, 1941, pp. 100–101.

[15] For an Indian viewpoint, see, Sisir Gupta, *Kashmir: A Study in India-Pakistan Relations*, London, 1967.

[16] On Jinnah's visit to Kashmir, see, M. Y. Saraf, *Kashmiris Fight for Freedom*, Volume 1, Lahore, 1977, pp. 622–638; and, K. H. Khurshid, *Memories of Jinnah*, Karachi, 1990, pp. 5–17.

[17] See his statement in *Dawn* (Delhi), 25 July 1944.

[18] Josef Korbel, *Danger in Kashmir*, Princeton, 1966 (revised edition), p. 21.

[19] For the developments on the events, see Ian Copland, "The Abdullah Factor: Kashmiri Muslims and the Crisis of 1947", in D. A. Low, ed., *The Political Inheritance of Pakistan*, London, 1991, pp. 218–254.

[20] See, Prem Nath Bazaz, *Truth About Kashmir*, Srinagar, 1950, pp. 4–5.

[21] See DO/35–3054, *The Punjab Boundary Award*, Public Record Office (PRO), Kew, London.

[22] See, Simon Scott Plummer's interview with Christopher Beaumont, *The Daily Telegraph*, 24 February 1992.

[23] Alan Campbell-Johnson, *Mission With Mountbatten*, London, 1953, p. 85.

[24] For an excellent study, see Alastair Lamb, *Kashmir: A Disputed Legacy, 1846–1990*, Hertingfordbury, UK, 1991, pp. 101–145.

[25] *The Times of India*, 29 May 1947.

[26] While the events took a different and equally difficult turn, an ailing Jinnah was deeply dismayed as he observed: "We have been put on the wrong bus". Quoted in Chaudhri Muhammad Ali, *op. cit.*, p. 297.

[27] Larry Collins and Dominique Lapierre, *Freedom at Midnight*, London, 1975, p. 356.

[28] Korbel, *op. cit.*, p. 55.

[29] Ian Stephens, *Pakistan*, London,1963, p. 200.

[30] John Richard Symonds, a British youth involved in the Quaker-sponsored social activities in the area, himself witnessed such developments. *The Statesman*, (Calcutta), 4 February 1948.

[31] The hostilities over Kashmir, confined to the State itself, went on with varying intensity until the beginning of 1949, when the Ceasefire finally took place. However, it is interesting to note that the British officers had made it clear to both the countries that in case of a direct Indo-Pakistan war they would refuse to participate.

[32] Memorandum of Conversation by the Assistant Chief of the Division of South Asian Affairs (Ray Thurston), 10 January 1948, *The Foreign Relations of the United States (FRUS), 1948*, Washington, D.C., 1975, pp. 276–278. The memorandum was based on a secret meeting held in Washington D.C. including senior British and American officials like Lord Ismay, Philip Noel-Baker, Lovett (Under-Secretary of State), and L. Henderson.

[33] UK High Commissioner (New Delhi) to Commonwealth Relations Office (London), 3 August 1950, in *DO/35/2048, KASHMIR*, PRO, London. During that period, Sardar Patel, reflecting Indian policy, wrote to Pandit Nehru: "It appears that both the National Conference and Sheikh Sahib are losing their hold on the people of the Valley and are becoming somewhat unpopular . . . In such circumstances I agree with you that a plebiscite is unreal."

[34] Arthur Bernon Tourtellot, "Kashmir: Dilemma of a People Adrift", *Saturday Review*, 6 March 1965, quoted in Khalid B. Sayeed, *The Political System of Pakistan*, Boston, 1967, p. 266.

[35] Quoted in M. S. Rajan, *India in World Affairs* 1954–56, London, 1964, p. 319

[36] See J. P. Narayan, "Our great opportunity in Kashmir", *The Hindustan Times*, 20 April and 14 May 1964.

[37] For a discussion on Indo-Pakistan relations, see Iftikhar H. Malik, "Indo-Pakistan Relations: A Historical Reappraisal. Lost case or turning point?" *Contemporary South Asia*, 1, (1), 1992, 127–142.

[38] Para 4 (ii) of the agreement signed between India and Pakistan mentions "a final settlement of Jammu and Kashmir" as one of the outstanding issues. Basing its case on Para 1 (i), Pakistan stresses that the UN Charter "shall govern" Indo-Pakistan relations without making the dispute simply a bi-lateral issue outside the UN.

[39] It is curious to see that in view of a Kashmiri determination to cross the Line Of Control (LOC) from the Pakistani side in February 1992, India itself approached the ambassadors of five permanent UN member states to exert pressure on Pakistan to dissuade the Kashmiris from undertaking the march. See "Volte-face by India on UN in Kashmir", *The Independent*, (London), 8 February 1992. Even long before the Simla Agreement, the Indian Government, while trying to avoid its pledge for plebiscite in Kashmir, occasionally gave out as if the bilateral talks were "the only solution". Ministry of Information and Broadcasting, Government of India, *Kashmir 1947–1965. Speeches and Statements of Mr. M. C. Chagla*, New Delhi, 1965, p. 102.

[40] United Nations, *1992: Human Development Report*, Oxford, 1992, p. 176.

[41] Jeremy Gavron, "Bhutto seeks arms talks with India", *The Daily Telegraph*, (London), 8 July 1989.

She quoted the instances of India's controversial role in Sri Lanka and her blockade of Nepal and urged for "confidence-building measures" in her forthcoming meeting with Rajiv Gandhi on his stop-over in Islamabad on 17 July on his way from Paris.

The skirmishes over Siachin glacier in northern areas since 1984 were being extensively reported in the press then and given the situation in Kashmir and its spill-over on Indo-Pakistan relations, the world leaders and press predicted another war in the sub-continent. Despite the amassing of the troops on the borders, the area commanders on both sides, maintained direct links with each other. Equally, both the sides did not want war yet that is never enough deterrence in case of South Asia. For details on Siachin conflict, see Christopher Thomas, "Warriors in an ice wilderness", *The Times, (review)* 9 September 1989. Also, *The Guardian*, 11 July 1989.

[42] Anatol Lieven, "Islamabad visit fails to solve dividing issue", *The Times*, 18 July 1989.

[43] Tony Allen-Mills, "India and Pakistan play Kashmir charades", *The Independent*, 10 August 1989. The Western media began to pick up news on turbulence in the valley acknowledging the fact that it was a keystone to Indo-Pakistan discord with the latest movement, among other factors, being prompted by the "inefficient and incapable" administration led by Farooq Abdullah propped up by Rajiv Gandhi's Indian National Congress. "New Troubles in Kashmir", *Newsweek*, 28 August 1989. India became the focus of international media due to violence within the country beside its worsening relations with neighbours. See the leader, "Mr. Gandhi's painful lesson", *The Independent*, 19 September 1989.

[44] Derek Brown, "Kidnap victim freed but Kashmir problems linger", *The Guardian*, 14 December 1989. All the five prisoners belonged to the Jammu and Kashmir Liberation Front (JKLF) and the deal had been negotiated through Farooq Abdullah on the persuasion of the central government represented by I. K. Gujral, the Indian foreign minister and Arif Mohammad Khan, the minister for transport. Soon after their release the Pakistani flag was hoisted on major buildings in Srinagar and other towns in the valley to show solidarity with the nationalist movement. *The Independent*, 14 December 1989.

[45] Derek Brown, "Kashmir shooting puts talks in doubt", *The Guardian*, 4 August 1992.

[46] Such an issue came out into the open with the JKLF-led march on 11 February 1992, meant to violate the Line Of Control leading to a few casualties caused by Pakistani security forces while stopping the marchers. To Pakistanis, who always contested the bona-fides of the LOC, such an emotional step would have entailed large-scale killing of Kashmiris, given India's threat to the effect, and might have even led to a full-fledged war. While Kashmiris complained of Pakistani use of force, the world felt that a tragedy had been averted. However, it was certainly a difficult decision for Pakistan to shoot at fellow unarmed Kashmiri marchers and for many JKLF supporters and some foreign observers the demand for a "third option" seemed more convincing: "Torn between the claims of Pakistan and India, it is blindingly obvious that what Kashmiris want is independence", observed a leading British daily. See Derek Brown, "And divided, they fought", *The Guardian*, 15 February 1992.

[47] Here religion does not essentially mean "fundamentalism", rather it stipulates a generic *Muslim* identity as we see in case of Bosnia, where it meant a general ethnic identification without any theological or communalist connotations.

[48] It has been established beyond any doubt that the uprising in Kashmir has not taken a usual communal pattern with Muslim Kashmiris killing Kashmiri Pundits. The Kashmiri Hindus migrating to Jammu and New Delhi largely did that in the initial stages due to pressure tactics by the then governor, Jagmohan, who aimed at discrediting the movement by depicting it as a typical Hindu-Muslim disharmony created by Pakistani "agents".

[49] For more on this, see Iftikhar H. Malik, "Ethnicity and Contemporary South Asian Politics: the Kashmir Conflict as a Case Study", *The Round Table*, 322, 1992, 203–214.

[50] Based on interviews with Kashmiris in diaspora both in the UK and the USA, during 1990–1992.

[51] It was revealed in a number of interviews with Kashmiri leaders in Pakistan, United Kingdom and the USA. Many Kashmiris in the Valley feel that an independent and secular Kashmir is just an unattainable ideal. After the Soviet retreat from Afghanistan, the pro-Pakistan elements within the Kashmir resistance have gained prominence. However, they are quick to point out that war of liberation for Kashmir is not an inter-religious battle rather a resistance against an illegal occupation. They harbour no ill-feeling against the Indians as such but feel that their struggle is against the official policies.

[52] Leo E. Rose, "The Politics of Azad Kashmir", in Raju Thomas, ed., *op. cit.*

[53] Christopher Thomas, "Indian army uses torture in Kashmir". *The Times*, 12 November 1991.

[54] The Indian security forces applied in the Valley, belonging to different religio-ethnic stocks, have failed to establish any common grounds with the locals. The latter are rather perceived as secessionists and Pakistani agents co-operating with India's Muslim enemies across the LOC. Such a demonisation results in severe backlashes and massive violations of human rights.

[55] Gupta, *op. cit.*

[56] Gerald Kaufman, "Slaughter in mountain paradise", *The Guardian*, 27 January 1992.

[57] Andy Messing Jr., "Hidden Conflict in Kashmir", *The Washington Times*, 5 February 1992.

[58] *The Tribune*, (Chandigarh), 25 May 1990.

[59] The report suggested the immediate abandoning of "totally counterproductive strategy of state

terrorism" which had questioned externalisation of the issue: "But all the same, the unrest in the Valley cannot be dismissed as the handiwork of a handful of subversives aided and abetted by Pakistan. In essence it remains a mass political upsurge with everybody speaking in the same voice: 'We want Azadi'." From "Press Handout" of the IPF, 25 June 1990.

[60] For details, see *Kashmir Imprisoned*, July 1990.

[61] "Three villagers were gunned down and two others thrown into blazing houses: one was roasted alive but the other escaped with third degree burns on his right arm. The security forces used molotov-cocktails in their orgy of arson, the villagers told this correspondent when he visited the two villages today. He found the terror-stricken villagers scavenging among the still-smouldering houses for whatever few belongings they could recover." *The Telegraph*, (Calcutta), 1 July 1990.

[62] "Srinagar presents the looks of a ghost city invaded by bunkers and soldiers with their fingers on the trigger. 'In the streets remain only stray dogs and Indian dogs, people are afraid'", launches a doctor from Sopore, another city of the Valley strongly affected by the Movement.

"The situation deteriorates every day. People are killed at random since Kashmir was decreed 'zone of troubles' in the beginning of July', says Omar Farooq, son and successor of the religious chief of the Valley murdered in May last by persons unknown." *Le Soir*, (Brussels), 13 August 1990. While reporting on curfews and massive demonstrations, another newspaper wrote: "The capital of the 'Indian Switzerland', long ago the paradise of the tourists, has the look of an occupied town which inhabitants have all escaped. Not a civil on the street, hundreds of the souvenir shops and others had the blinds closed." *The Star*, (Port Louis), 29 July 1990. A Portuguese newspaper found the behaviour of the Indian troops "shames democracy and leaves indelible scars on the soul of Kashmir". "War Without An End in Kashmir", *Diario de Noticias*, (Lisbon), 13 August 1990.

[63] *Insight*, 20 August 1990.

[64] Such brutalities by the security forces and soldiers have been a common way of life since the defiance began in 1989. At the most the military authorities claim to carry out their own inquiries, if they are unable to lay the blame on an adverse propaganda. *The Independent*, 19 March 1991.

[65] Amnesty International, *India: Torture, Rape & Deaths in Custody*, London, 1992, pp. 18–20. The report appeared in March and the Indian High Commission in London, at first refused to comment on it and later took refuge in procedural mazes.

[66] Physicians for Human Rights (UK), *Kashmir 1991*, London, 1991, p. 9.

[67] Human Rights Watch, *Human Rights in India: Kashmir Under Siege*, (An Asia Watch Report), New York, Washington DC, May 1991, p. 5.

[68] Representatives D. Fascell and G. Yatron to Mr. Abid Hussain, 2 April 1992.

[69] This was stated by Ghulam Muhammad Safi, leader of the Hizbal Mujahideen in an interview in London. *The Impact International*, (London), 10 July–13 August 1992, p. 11.

[70] See "Kashmir and the Bomb", (editorial), *The Washington Post in IHT*, 5 May 1992; also "End Kashmir's Misery", (editorial), *The New York Times*, 22 March 1992.

[71] See, Sumit Ganguli, "Avoiding War in Kashmir", *Foreign Affairs*, 69, (5), 1990–1.

[72] The seminar took place in late June, 1990, at Queen Elizabeth House, Oxford, and was attended among others by academics, diplomats and media men from the sub-continent, USA and the UK. The Indian officials somehow felt that even such an academic activity might further internationalise the issue.

[73] Kuldip Nayar, "Kashmir: A Way Out", *The Hindustan Times*, 15 July 1991.

[74] Selig S. Harrison, "South Asia and the United States: A Chance for a Fresh Start", *Current History*, 91, (563), 1992, p. 102.

USSR
AFGHANISTAN
Cease-fire line, 1949
Roads
Mountains
25,868 ft
KARAKORAM RANGE
28,250 ft
CHINA
Gilgit
R. Indus
R. Indus
26,660 ft
DEOSAI MOUNTAINS
Kargil
Leh
Srinagar
23,403 ft
Islamabad
Rawalpindi
Punch
ZASKAR MOUNTAINS
Vale of Kashmir
R. Indus
14,238 ft
Jhelum
Sialkot
Jammu
21,376 ft
R. Jhelum
INDIA
Pakanthot
CHINA
PAKISTAN
Amritsar
Lahore
Jullundur
Simla

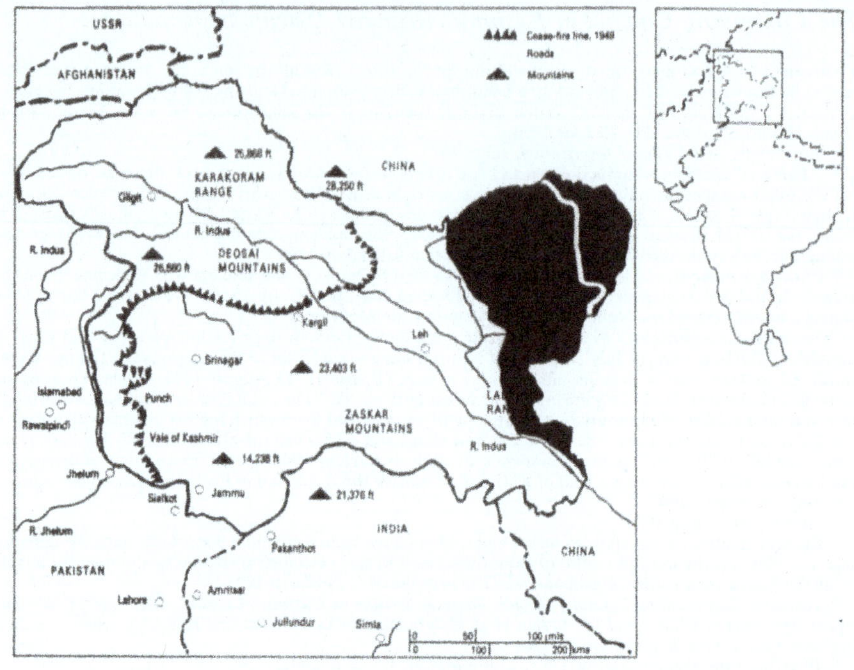

Kashmir

[7]

Combating Terrorism in Punjab

Indian Democracy in Crisis

Manoj Joshi

1992 saw a significant turnaround for the situation in India's troubled Punjab state which had been racked by a decade-long militant movement demanding a separate nation for India's 17m Sikhs. The movement was characterised by terrorist action such as assault and intimidation, the murder of individuals and planned massacres in Punjab as well as in other areas such as Delhi, the neighbouring Haryana State and the Terai region of Uttar Pradesh. It was accompanied by the assassination of political activists and leaders, media workers and Government officials. It spared neither high nor low: a retired Army Chief and a serving Prime Minister also fell victim. An official estimate at the end of 1991 put the total killed at 14,462.[1] Another 3,500 died in 1992.

The causes of the problem are complex—history, misperceptions, changing socio-economic trends, political and economic dynamics and so on. However, it is likely that political management of the State by Indira Gandhi since the early 1970s characterised by attempts to outflank the religious platform of the Akali Dal, and manipulation of the rules governing centre-state relations combined with the Akali's own political dynamics, dominated as they are by religious politics, led to the tragic momentum of events in the 1980s.

The major cause for the terrorist upsurge in the late 1980s and early 1990s was *Operation Bluestar*, the Army's assault on the Sikh "Holy of Holies," the Golden Temple in Amritsar in June 1984, and the accompanying *Operation Woodrose*, which alienated even moderate Sikhs. This led first to the assassination of Indira Gandhi and then the massacre of Sikhs in Delhi and other areas in northern India. Following *Bluestar*, many supporters of the militant Sikh leader Bhindranwale fled across the border and with encouragement from Pakistani officials organised themselves to mount a bigger challenge to the Indian control of the State.[2] This process was assisted by the enhanced sense of bitterness that Sikhs all over the country felt towards the Congress party and the Indian State because of the anti-Sikh pogrom of November 1984.

The involvement of Pakistan has been a complex process. Punjab has been a border state, divided in 1947 under the Radcliffe Award, a partition that saw one of the largest transfers of population in history accompanied by the killing of hundreds of thousands of people on either side. There is sufficient evidence to show that from 1985 onwards Pakistan began facilitating terrorism, if not directly aiding and abetting it.

The militant-terrorist movement has seen a number of ups and downs since 1983. There were periods when the security forces had the upper hand and others when the terrorists seemed to hold sway. A common theme of missed opportunities runs through these years: the negotiations between Indira Gandhi and the Akalis before *Operation Bluestar*, the Accord of 1985 between Rajiv Gandhi and the moderate Sikh leader, Harchand Singh Longowal (subsequently assassinated by Sikh extremists) and the positive climate after *Operation Black Thunder* in the summer of 1988. Are we witnessing another false dawn?

Table 1: Index of terrorist activity 1986–89: deaths and arms recoveries.

	1986	1987	1988	1989
AK rifles	–	73	398	295
Handguns	584	1097	809	635
Other rifles, guns	155	425	373	300
RPG–7	–	–	20	28
LMB/GPMG	–	3	9	17
Remote control devices	–	–	–	–
Explosives	–	–	–	–
Radio sets	–	–	–	1
Persons killed (police)	562 (42)	1005 (95)	2050 (110)	1320 (152)
Terrorists killed	78	328	373	699

Author's note on sources: Much of the data in this and subsequent tables is compiled from a variety of Government sources which have been attributed wherever possible. Some of the data is from confidential official sources. In some cases the figures of weapons or those killed may not reconcile for a particular period because they have come from two different sources. But I believe that the differences are not significant.

EARLY ATTEMPTS TO DEAL WITH THE PROBLEM

In the post-*Operation Bluestar* period, Government strategy varied. It began with the carrot, embodied by the Rajiv-Longowal Accords, but with the latter's assassination and the combined militant-terrorist assault on the Barnala Government, it reverted to the stick. The Akali Dal, the main party representing the dominant Jat Sikh peasantry of the State was unable to capitalise on the Rajiv-Longowal accords because of factionalism, endemic to the party, and its political dynamics, dominated by the SGPC and the Sikh faith. By 1990, not only had the party made itself irrelevant, but the whole structure of religious politics of the Akalis had been turned topsy-turvy. Beginning with the strategy of compelling the SGPC and the Sikh high priests to move along their chosen path, the militants at one point actually took over the priesthood themselves.

Between 1986 and 1989, the situation went precipitously downhill with killings, extortion and assaults becoming more and more common.[3] By the end of 1989, besides attacks on unarmed civilians, militants were able to carry out strikes on the security forces, the paramilitary as well as the Army, especially in the border areas. Government policy was to treat it as a "law and order" problem. The team of Governor S. S. Ray, who had crushed the Naxalite uprising in Bengal, and "supercop" Julio Riberio, were given a more-or-less free hand.[4] Although the situation became worse, there were episodes like that in the Golden Temple following the declaration of Khalistan in April 1986 or *Operation Black Thunder* in May 1988 when the police scored decisive victories only to be let down by the lack of any complementary political effort.[5]

By 1990, the Central Government in New Delhi had attempted a variety of means to control the problem but nothing seemed to work. Localised successes like *Operation Black Thunder* could never become synchronised to political initiatives which may have resolved the situation. Instability in Delhi following the Bofors scandal and the approaching General Elections compounded the problem.[6]

Year by year, the quality of weaponry and training of the terrorists seemed to improve. Between 1985 and 1986 murders and even massacres were carried out with .455 pistols with Indian-origin rifles and sten-guns, and from 1987 onwards AK-47s started appearing. 1988 began with attacks on the security forces with RPG-7 rockets besides well co-ordinated and highly damaging bomb blasts. Later, terrorist equipment was standardised to versions of the AK rifles, General Purpose Machine Guns (GPMGs) and explosives, with some sophisticated "add-ons" and accessories such as night-vision equipment, Dragunov sniper rifles, Kenpro transceiver sets and so on.

Since the source of supply for all this was in Pakistan, the Government also attempted to take up the issue of cross-border support with the Pakistani authorities. Within weeks of *Black Thunder*, armed with interrogation reports of terrorists captured in the Golden Temple, Indian officials gave their Pakistani counterparts a 21-page dossier outlining their case. The Pakistanis denied everything and called for joint patrolling on the border, a proposal which later turned out to mean "co-ordinated" patrolling by the respective border police, each on their own side of the border.[7] This document was updated and presented to Pakistan in May 1990 as well, to little or no effect.[8]

A third prong of the effort, an indicator of the failure of other steps, was the initiation of the fencing of the border of Punjab with Pakistan. A fence comprising a triple row of barbed wire, floodlit at night, was begun in late 1988. It was a short distance behind the "zero" line, (the actual border marked by pillars) since there is cultivation to that point. Gates controlled by the border police were also installed.

The fourth, and potentially most important strand was to allow Punjab to participate in the General Elections of November 1989. Towards this end, Manjit Singh of the AISSF and Simranjit Singh Mann were released as well as a number of others held since *Operation Bluestar*. There was a sweeping success in the elections by the terrorists/militant sponsored candidates who won the bulk of the 13 Parliamentary seats in the State. Among those elected to Parliament from Punjab were Simranjit Singh Mann, a former police officer who had become an ardent supporter of Bhindranwale, and now an advocate of an independent Punjab and heading the "United" Akali Dal and Attinder Pal Singh, once accused of involvement in the assassination of Indira Gandhi, and now leader of the Khalistan Liberation Organisation and charged with having illegally visited Pakistan several times. Another winner was Bimal Khalsa, the widow of an assassin of Indira Gandhi. This piquant situation, probably unparalleled in the annals of terrorism, led to a collapse of the police effort.

THE WORSENING SITUATION: TERROR

By the beginning of 1990, things were desperate in the State. A marked feature was the criminalisation of the militant movement. This was reflected by figures that showed that proportionately more and more Sikhs were being killed as compared to Hindus. This meant that the movement was consuming those very people on whose behalf it was supposed to be fighting.[9]

In terms of terrorism and its tools—murder, threat, extortion and domination by fear—the years 1990 and 1991 were the worst years in Punjab.[10] They were so even in the blunt arithmetic of the human toll. In the period 1981 to 1989, 5,521 people including policemen were killed by terrorists. But in just two years, 1990 and 1991, more than 6,000 were killed. The figures are even more revealing if we look at the breakup of the number of police personnel killed. Some 451 had been killed in the 1981 to 1989 period. But in 1990 alone some 493 Punjab Police, paramilitary, home guards and special police officers were killled and in 1991 another 480.[11]

Not only were police personnel targeted, but members of their families as well. In 1991, 133 members of families of police personnel were shot dead. In some instances entire families—men, women and children—were wiped out. In early 1991, as part of a package to negotiate with militants, the tough Punjab Police Chief K. P. S. Gill was eased out. In February, a carefully planned bomb blast nearly took the life of the new Police Chief D. S. Mangat. By that time the police had just about given up active counter-terrorist operations.

In December 1990, to retrieve the situation, the Army had been sent in under *Operation Rakshak I* but *Rakshak I*'s aims were limited to the three border districts of Ferozepur, Amritsar and Gurdaspur. The task was firstly to seal the border (which meant carrying out patrols and maintaining checkpoints behind the BSF and secondly assist the police and paramilitary in anti-terrorist operations in those border districts and restore the lost authority of the State. The operation coincided with the appointment of General (Rtd) O. P. Malhotra, the former Army Chief, as Governor of the State—a signal, somewhat confusing, of hard-line intent.

Gill's removal and Malhotra's appointment worked against each other and indicated the ambivalence of the Government in dealing with the situation in a tough fashion. One senior police officer believed that this was the crucial issue. Punjab Police officers and their personnel were affected severely by the double-edged sword. On one hand, the terrorist attack on the families of "active" police officials was an obvious disincentive for activity. On the other, police personnel were affected by the prevailing political uncertainty: they could not be sure, given the various moves being made, as to whether or not they would have to deal with some of the militants/terrorists as ministers in the near future.

Edicts issued

In 1990, the militant ideologues, especially the Babbar Khalsa, and the Panthic Committee led by Dr Sohan Singh attempted to restore the ideological justification for their movement by issuing *diktats* demanding conformity to a new set of social codes. These included demands that school uniforms should be in particular colours of religious significance as well as the banning of skirts for girls. A school headmistress was shot for not enforcing the changeover in early January 1991. The other "edicts" related to the promotion of Punjab and Punjabi language and Sikhs in the media as well as in the workplace, a ban on the consumption of alcohol, cigarettes and meat and ostentation in weddings.

To enforce the edict that banks must favour Punjab in terms of their credit/deposit ratios, transactions and use of Punjabi, terrorists set fire to 31 branches of various banks operating in Punjab in one day, on 21 October 1991. Five days later, the Director of Punjab Health Services, Dr Bachitar Singh, and six other doctors were shot dead, allegedly for promoting family planning amongst Sikhs.

Another effective terrorist operation was in the coercion of the media. Many journalists had been killed in the period from 1981 to 1989 but the brunt was borne by newspaper deliverymen who were gunned down for delivering certain papers. Many of these *diktats* came out as advertisements that the newspapers were compelled to print on the pain of death. The "code of conduct" for the media demanded that the terrorists be called "militants" and honorific titles like "Bhai" (Brother) be used before their names.[12] In the mid-1990s according to the editor of a prominant English daily published out of Chandigarh, the campaign of intimidation and forced publication of their "press notes" had reached a point where "the militants very nearly captured the government without wasting bullets".[13]

The Government of India itself admitted that "the courts and judicial system have been subjected to intense pressure by terrorists with the result that their functioning has been severely affected".[14]

Geographical expansion

By late 1990 another feature was noticeable. The geographical area affected by terrorism expanded. In Punjab itself it spread from the border and earlier core areas of Amritsar, Gurdaspur and Ferozepur and Faridkot districts, to Sangrur, Barnala, Ludhiana and Ropar and to a slightly lesser extent Jalandhar and Patiala.[15]

There was expansion across India as well. There were reports of large sums of money being extorted from the prosperous Sikh communities in Bombay, Indore, Raipur, Jabalpur and Bhopal or shelter from the farmer communities of Rajasthan, Madhya Pradesh and Uttar Pradesh in the name of the *Panth*. The police pressure on the Punjab border, or the good pickings to be had from extortion, were only the partial reasons for this. The main reason was the psychological domination that the terrorists were able to enforce, based on the sense of grievance perceived by the Sikh society at large, focusing primarily on the anti-Sikh massacres of November 1984. A major reason for the ease of these operations was that in comparison to Punjab, the level of policing was quite poor.[16]

In early 1991, there were two incidents—on the Bengal-Bihar border and in Gujarat—when militants were gunned down by the police, indicating that they had the ability to act far afield from Punjab and that they had built up a national network of harbourers, sympathisers and supporters.[17] There were early signs of activity in the Bombay area as well. There was a bomb blast on a local train in April 1991 and in January 1992 there was a shootout in which two terrorists were killed. On 16-17 October 1991 there were two massive bomb blasts in the town of Rudrapur in the Terai region of Uttar Pradesh during a Hindu festival killing 60 people. On 5 December in four strikes in two different States, Haryana and Uttar Pradesh, terrorists gunned down 54 people.[18]

With the Punjab border becoming difficult, attempts were being made to develop alternate routes for arms supplies. As the work on the border fencing, begun in April 1988, progressed, Punjab militants began to look at routes in Rajasthan and Gujarat. Officials believe that this activity began in earnest in 1990. The first routes were explored south of the Ganganagar area and for this special teams were deputed. Some 23 intruders were apprehended in 1991. In late 1991, an attempt was made to develop the sea route via Jakhau in Kutch.

In 1988 and 1989 four trans-border clashes had been reported in Rajasthan, all in the Ganganagar district, proximate to Punjab where many Sikh farmers reside. In 1991 there were 77 encounters in the Rajasthan border in which 57 infiltrators were killed, of these, the police estimate, 15 had militant-terrorist links and one was even equipped with a bullet-proof vest and a night vision device. 109 assault rifles, 55 pistols, 6 LMGs and 145 kg. of explosives were seized.[19]

Terrorists in control

By the end of 1991, then, the militants had through their terrorist actions paralysed the police and administration, coerced the media and overawed the local population. Their "social reform" campaign had extended their ideological sway over the remaining institutions. The divide between Punjab and the rest of India was increasing. The fiasco of the election had disastrous effects on an already difficult situation. The cancellation of the elections in June 1991 led to Gen Malhotra's resignation and the Army withdrew within days of this.

The aborted *Rakshak I* operation led to a resurgence of terrorism, now across the lengh and breadth of Punjab. Immediately the terrorists began to strike at the police to prevent them from maintaining the momentum. The strikes were aimed at police personnel's families—43 of them were killed in September alone—and succeeded in bringing police operations to a virtual stand-still. Extortion and kidnapping became common and intelligence reports indicated a surge of trans-border movement, often in connivance with the BSF. Recruitment to terrorist ranks went up and migration of Hindus from the vulnerable areas increased sharply. Industry too, began to take the first tentative steps to move out of the State.

However much India may have wanted it, the option of taking the war to the terrorist sanctuaries was not considered realistic, even when the situation in Kashmir deteriorated at the end of 1989 and early 1990. Since war was ruled out, a defensive strategy was adopted which meant trying to stop the infiltration from across the border. In Kashmir it meant no cultivation in the 5 km zone to the border with patrolling and free-fire ambushes in this area. In Punjab it involved night curfews and special passes for those cultivating land across the fence up to the "zero line".[20]

But under the surface, and this is really evident in retrospect, the high-point of the terrorist sway also marked the beginning of the end. The depredations against their own supporters, looting and murder had led to a collapse of support for the militancy.

The people were not yet willing to speak, for that could mean not just death but the elimination of entire families. They kept their mouths shut, but they had stopped cheering the militants. Their problem was: who to trust? When the Punjab Police acted it was with a harsh hand and often entire families would be rounded up for questioning and worse. Then there was fear, justified in some cases, that the lower ranks of the police were riddled with terrorist sympathisers.

THE WORSENING SITUATION: POLITICS

The November 1989 election coincidentally also inaugurated a period of profound political instability in India as a whole. Rajiv Gandhi was defeated and replaced by V. P. Singh who headed an unstable coalition that came apart in less than a year. This led to a minority Government supported by the Congress which lasted for another six months before elections were called in May 1991.

The new Governor, N. K. Mukharji, sent by the V. P. Singh Government in December 1989 was an advocate of a "soft" line. He was succeeded after six months, in June 1990, by an even "softer" person, the Gandhian, Virendra Verma. Six months later, in December, Gen Malhotra was sent in.

The Chandrashekhar Government attitude towards tackling the Punjab militancy was not clear. Even though it sent the Army in, it had also eased out Gill as the police chief. In early 1991, Chandrashekhar made a controversial effort to negotiate the settlement of the Punjab problem with the "United"

Akali Dal headed by S. S. Mann. However little or nothing came of this. Chandrashekhar spoke of negotiating unconditionally with the militants and even amending the constitution itself. There were claims that some terrorists had met his Minister of State for Home Affairs, Subodh Kant Sahay.[21]

One problem in negotiating with the militants was that there was no one organisation that could be considered representative. Groups like that led by original Panthic Committee founder and Chief of the BTFK, Gurbachan Singh Manochahal, were willing to participate in the electoral process.[22] But there were other, more powerful, forces such as those led by the rival Panthic Committee headed by Dr Sohan Singh who opposed any deal with the Government or elections. Another wing of the militant movement, the Babbar Khlasa had initially hedged its bets and created a front organisation, the Babbar Akali Dal under the leadership of Kartar Singh Narang, but this group eventually boycotted the 1991 elections.

Elections of 1991

The substantive line-up of candidates some fronting militant groups in the 1991 elections again indicated that the electorate in Punjab was willing to overcome its fear of terrorists. Among the candidates were Bimal Khalsa and, Karamjit Singh, under arrest for an attempt on Rajiv Gandhi in 1986. Manochahal had given his conditional support to the election process by allowing his supporters to stand. As many as three *Lok Sabha* and 24 *Vidhan Sabha* candidates had been killed in a bid to postpone their election (elections are countermanded in any constituency where a candidate dies) and elections to 16 seats were cancelled. Adding to this were other incidents of violence, for example 74 passengers travelling in trains were gunned down. But the assassination of Rajiv Gandhi panicked the bureaucracy in Delhi which postponed the elections on the morning of 20 June when polling was about to start.

The victory of the Congress-I in the elections was the next critical input into the Punjab situation. Unlike V. P. Singh and Chandrashekhar who had no political base in the State, the Congress was very much present in Punjab, and its leadership now became a factor in Central Government calculations. Of considerable importance was the attitude of this party towards militancy/terrorism. For historical reasons, including Mrs Gandhi's assassination and its terrible aftermath, the party was an unrelenting opponent of the militants, and, unlike V. P. Singh and Chandrashekhar, it could not brook the idea of negotiating a settlement with any branch of the movement. They had only one alternative—to strike hard at the terrorist and carry out elections.

Conventional wisdom in New Delhi was that the solution to the Punjab problem lay in carrying through elections to the State Assembly which had to be held by February 1992. But given the spread of terrorism across the State, the only way that elections could be held was to send in the Army once again, this time under *Operation Rakshak II*. The Army move began on 15 November 1991, and operations commenced from 1 December.

Table 2: Index of terrorist activity 1990 to 15 March 1993: deaths and arms recoveries.

	1990	1991	1992	1993
AK rifles	646	475	479	131
Handguns	556	789	542	79
Other rifles, guns	405	833	1118	186
RPG–7	33	23	45	11
LMG/GPMG	50	33	26	2
Remote control devices	11	–	–	–
Explosives kg	390	202	1604	197
Radio sets	4	3	10	6
Persons killed (police)	2849 (506)	3161 (495)	1520 (251)	231 (14)
Terrorists killed	720	1494	2109	258

THE 1992 WATERSHED

The elections

The enthusiasm for elections displayed by the Punjab electorate in the summer of 1991 was apparently viewed with alarm by the terrorist leadership and their backers in India and abroad. So a major effort was launched to ensure that the postponed elections were not held at all.

The elections were held in February 1992 in a climate of tension, fear and unprecedented security precautions. The mainstream Akali Dal boycotted the polls, senior intelligence officials claiming that many of them had been coerced into doing so.[23] Joining them were the Bharatiya Kisan Union (BKU), a well-off farmer's organisation, as well as groups associated with some militant factions close to Manochahal who had been willing to contest in 1991. With this the main forces representing the disaffected Jat Sikh peasantry were out of the elections. The Congress, the Bahujan Samaj Party and the Communist parties had a relatively limited support base among the Jats and the other segments of Sikh community. The Bharatiya Janata Party's appeal to the Hindus was substantial in some of the northern districts of the State as well as in its urban centres. With the boycott, the campaign became mainly urban. The Congress had secured a three-fourths majority in the *Vidhan Sabha* with just 9 per cent of the votes. It was clear that the Hindu voters had preferred to trust the Congress party over what may have been their ideological choice, the BJP. The Congress, both in the State and the Centre, were quite happy at the outcome. The minority Narasimha Rao Government got 12 MPs it desperately needed and the State Congress got a government it may have found impossible to obtain, minus the Akali boycott.

Early reports of the election and its outcome obviously questioned its legitimacy. Comparisons with the consequences of similar elections in Kashmir and Assam were there. There appeared to be no desire on the part of the officials, however, to inflate the figures of votes polled which was some 23.91 per cent, one-third of the 1989 turnout. The elections outcome reflected a communal divide with the bulk of the Jat Sikhs boycotting the election.[24]

The Central Government's own handling of the elections was not without an element of opportunism since the Prime Minister needed the Punjab seats to shore up his status in Parliament.[25] No effort was made to help the Akalis take courage into their hands and participate through some concession or political gesture. The one or two groups which did try slowly dropped off. Emboldened by the plight of the Akalis, the militant organisations now moved to co-opt them. Master-minded by Kartar Singh Narang of the Babbar Akali Dal, a closed-door meeting of the Akalis and overground militants constituted a new unified Shriomani Panthic Action Committee comprising Narang himself, Prakash Singh Badal, Baba Joginder Singh, the father of Sant Bhindranwale, Manjit Singh of the AISSF. The Akalis lost their "moderate" moorings and were now captive to militant logic, if not its means. The Babbar Khalsa also floated another front organisation, the *Babbar Sikh Vidhyarti Jathebandi* to organise the youth. Buoyed by the ease with which the moderates fell into their hands, the terrorists moved to fight their final offensive.[26]

The terrorist offensive

Given the scale of the security forces' deployment in the State, the terrorists' task was undoubtedly daunting. But the ground had been well prepared; the police had been coerced into inactivity, the populace was even more scared and there was no shortage of arms and ammunition. Additional shipments had been sent in through Jammu and Kashmir and the Rajasthan/Gujarat border. The KCF (Panjwar), for example, reportedly obtained five shipments of weapons each with 16 AK-47s, a number of light machine guns, ammunition and explosives through a new route on the Rajasthan border. Manjit Singh alias Lal Singh who had come into the country in late 1991 had brought in arms via Gujarat and opened a channel to supply the KLF.

The successful installation of a Congress Government was a direct challenge to the militants and it had to be discredited. So the first thing to do was to assert their authority by making good their promise to kill the first five voters in three separate places. Thirteen people were killed in these incidents.

The second was to ensure that the Congress Government remained unstable by a campaign of boycott and coercion. A "directive" circulated to the Punjab bureaucracy by the Babbar Khalsa in early March contained 10 points to implement the programme of making the Government non-functional. It warned officials not to implement government orders on the pain of punitive measures; no bureaucrat was to implement the Sutlej-Yamuna Link canal project which would provide Sutlej waters to Haryana; any officials who participated in the Indian national functions would have their legs chopped off. Finally, the circular demanded that all government transactions be carried out in Punjabi from 17 March.[27]

On 10 March, a little after sunset, six terrorists attacked the Indian Acrylics Fibre Plant near Sangrur and killed 15 non-Punjabi engineers who were getting the Rs. 200 crore plant ready for production. Later in the month two terrorists struck at a crowded locality of Fieldgunj in Ludhiana mowing down 30 people. On 25 April two teachers in the Punjab University Campus at Patiala were gunned down to underline the message that all work should be done in Punjabi. But the attacks reached their peak in May when nine people were killed by a bomb blast in Gurdaspur on 2 May, 10 in Bhatinda on 10 May, 12 when an attempt was made on the life of a minister by a bomb-blast on 9 May and on 23 May a former MP, Hakim Singh, was assassinated along with 14 others in different parts of the State. The attacks on government officials indicated the careful planning behind this new campaign. On 6 May the State Excise Commissioner A. K. Misra was gunned down in Patiala, on 10 May the scene shifted to Delhi where the Union Agricultural Prices Commission (APC) Chief, Dr. Devendra Tyagi, was killed in a locality which houses senior Government of India officials. Later in the month M. L. Manchanda, an All India Radio (the State-owned national radio) engineer was kidnapped, killed and his beheaded body found on 27 May. A week later, on 4 June, a zonal officer of a nationalised bank was shot dead in Jalandhar district.

The aim of these killings was clear—to drive home the "social-reform" and "political" message of the militants through terror. The APC Chief was gunned down to show that Punjab's farmers were not getting a good deal from the Central Government organisation which fixes support prices for agricultural products. The Excise official was killed to underline the anti-alcohol and anti-tobacco message, and the junior AIR official beheaded to emphasise the "code of conduct" to official media.

THE COUNTER-OFFENSIVE

The Army in Punjab

The Indian Army is no stranger to Punjab: 8 to 10 per cent of its soldiers come from that state and soldiering has been considered an honourable tradition there. As a strategic border area the State has had a major complement of the Army deployment, especially since it is located in an area that has seen major military action in the 1965 and 1971 wars with Pakistan.

One of the Army's five regional commands, the Western Command, is located near Chandigarh and the main defensive deployments on the Indo-Pakistan border in Punjab focus on the 10 and 11 Corps headquartered at Bhatinda and Jalandhar respectively. While the Army holds the border in Kashmir, in Punjab the border is manned by the Border Security Force which uses high observation towers spaced at a distance of 200 to 500m, patrolling the distance between them. Behind this line and some 0.5 to 5 km away is the Army's first line of artificial defences called ditch-cum-bunds (DCBs).

Army units are located anywhere up to 20 to 30 km away. In times of tension each battalion may rotate one company on its normal DCB frontage.

The Army was first deployed in Punjab in the dramatic and tragic circumstances of *Operation Bluestar*, launched to clear Sant Jarnail Singh Bhindranwale and 300 militants entrenched in the Sikh "holy of holies", the Golden Temple at Amritsar. In that unfortunate operation, the Army lost not just 87 men and officers, but its enormous prestige in the minds of the Sikhs. There were mutinies and desertions from several Sikh units. Immediately after this it launched *Operation Woodrose* to clear the rural areas surrounding the Golden Temple of alleged militants. The heavy-handed approach alienated many rural folk and the scattered leadership of the militants was able to utilise this sense of grievance into urging the youth to flee to Pakistan where they were converted into hard-core militants.

In the 1985 to 1990 period, the Army stayed away from the terrorist-police battle but ensured that its own soldiers and installations were secure. But there were occasional run ins and even fire-fights between militants and the Army, a development obviously considered alarming by the latter.

Under *Rakshak I* the Army role was limited to sealing the border and assisting the police to fight terrorists in the border areas. This was perceived as important by the Army because these were potential operational areas for any possible war with Pakistan. In early 1990 with the Kashmir rebellion at boiling point, the two sides had indeed come close to war. So the Army saw its participation in *Rakshak* as part of an effort to improve its own operational posture.

But the three-division operation was not well received by the people, and the Army, for its part too, was not well-prepared for the task since it was called in in some haste. In addition the operation had some unintended results. Its intensity in the border areas, forced the terrorists to move to other areas of the State and thus actually expanded the base of the terrorist operations.[28]

Once elections were called the Army was in a dilemma. In the very area it was operating many of the candidates were supported by the terrorists/militants and indeed many were said to be militants themselves. The result was a slackening of effort.

In the light of the experiences of *Rakshak I*, *Rakshak II* was designed to be an all-encompassing operation involving the Army not just in the State of Punjab but deployments in the border stretching down to the sea in the Rann of Kutch.

In Punjab, the Army was the key component in blanketing the State with security personnel. In addition to its 120,000-odd personnel deployed for the operation, there were 53,000 Punjab Police, 28,000 Home Guards, 10,000 Special Police Officers and 70,000 paramilitary personnel by the time of the peak deployment in February 1992.[29]

The operation's tasks were firstly to assist in preventing trans-border movement of terrorists and arms; secondly to aid civil authorities in their anti-terrorist operations, enhance the sense of security amongst local people and restore the authority of the State; thirdly to undertake civic actions to develop local contacts and lastly to create conditions for a free and fair election.

The main deployment of the Army was in the rural area. Its task was not just physical but psychological.[30] It gained dominance of the area by aggressive patrolling, especially at night. It provided manpower for the police "cordon and search" operations, and, when required, firepower. Police personnel were not then accustomed to take on the GPMGs by some terrorists, and were not trained to assault terrorists sheltering in sugar-cane fields or built-up bunkers in some farm areas. The Army evolved a system of Quick Reaction Teams (QRTs) which would be hooked to the police wireless net and whenever there were reports of a fire-fight the teams would be in a position to help within 15 minutes anywhere inside the State.

Civic action was seen as a key component of their operations. Army teachers restarted schools, their medical personnel fanned out into the country-side to provide much needed relief for villagers and Army personnel cleared drainage systems and canals and so on.[31] Part of the overall goal was to restore the image of the Army that had been destroyed by *Bluestar*.

To incorporate lessons from *Operation Rakshak I*, the Army altered its tactics in policing the border areas as well as in the conduct of operations with the paramilitary forces. The gates in the fencing were closely watched. BSF posts suspected to have been "sold out" were placed under the Army's command and aggressive patrolling was carried out by mobile formations between the BSF posts and the DCBs. Each of the 900 border villages was put under surveillance and the entire area placed under a dusk to dawn curfew which meant any untoward movement at night could be presumed to be hostile.[32]

Towards this end the Army committed not only 10 and 11 Corps but 1 Corps as well. This Corps is a strike formation built around an armoured division which can be deployed anywhere along the front with Pakistan. It is normally headquartered at Mathura, south of Delhi, but for *Rakshak II*, it shed its armoured division and came with its remaining formations, minus their heavy weaponry to take up the security responsibilities of the south-eastern districts of Punjab. It was headquartered at Patiala. Another strike formation, 2 Corps, headquartered nearby at Ambala retained its military operational posture.

Through their peak period between the end of November 1991 and June 1992 when 1 Corps had returned to its normal stations, the Army had participated in some 1334 operations as a cordoning force, besides carrying out 121,465 patrols, roughly 600 to 700 patrols a day. Each brigade had responsibility for an area 100 sq km. Less quantifiable was the efficacy of sealing the borders, but certainly the impact was substantial. The Army's own actions resulted in the killing of 120 militants, the arrest of 175 and the surrender of 56 plus the capture of 56 AK-47 assault rifles.[33] As Table 4 shows, 13 Army personnel had been killed in these operations between February and August 1992.

The Police Reorganisation

Among the hard-line measures compelled on the Government was the return of K. P. S. Gill as State police chief in December 1991.[34] With the aid of the Army, a major retraining programme was undertaken and in the first instance 20,000 Special Police Officers and 9,000 Punjab Police and Paramilitary Forces, constables were instructed for 4 to 10 weeks in various operational tactics. The Punjab Police itself was overhauled and two new commando battalions were organised, equipped with AK-47 rifles. Again with the aid of the Army, security plans were drawn up for large cities infected by terrorism. The police did not have the staff skills required to draw up plans for cities of the size of Ludhiana so this was done by the Army.

By 1991, the police in Punjab had gone into a shell, content to do static duty and guard the VIPs. The induction of massive Army manpower freed the police to do the "police work" required to track down individual gangs and killers. Small teams of 15 or so persons headed by senior officials were set up systematically to track down specific targets. Surprisingly this had not been done in the past and there were circumstances in which people often got through the net because the police were not aware of who they were.

Table 3: Terrorist killings (including policemen) and terrorists killed in 1992–1993

month	terrorists	others including security personnel
January	80	110
February	51	186
March	157	226
April	195	188
May	182	165
June	236	119
July	234	102
August	200	171
September	218	71
October	178	84
November	166	53
December	182	44
January '93	103	9
February '93	107	4
until 15 March	48	8

Former police chief Julio Riberio was said to have instituted the "bullet for bullet" strategy, another name for a shoot-to-kill tactic which in one phase was manifested the "escape" of arrested militants/terrorists and in others of "encounters" where arrested terrorists were shot after interrogation and an encounter subsequently fabricated.[35] The police were reacting to the fact that not only were constables or officers involved in arresting, interrogating and torturing a marked person, but their own families were also implicated. No one was immune: for example D. S. Mangat, who headed the police force in the State in 1991 had lost a son in one such encounter in 1986. There have been instances where the two sides played the same brutal game. In retaliation for attacks on one police officer with a particular reputation for brutality, female relatives of the chief suspect were "liquidated".[36]

But Riberio had simply coined the phrase. The policy was more the creation of K. P. S. Gill who served as Additional Director-General of Police with Riberio and later as the D-G. The Punjab Police had instituted a system of rewards which could be as high as Rs. 10 to 30 lakhs for tracking down and eliminating individuals or gangs of terrorists. This "bounty hunting" system may have provided the police with some "incentive" but it also resulted in excesses and as in its Western-movie counterpart, a "bring him back dead rather than alive" policy. The Army, for its part, made it clear from the outset that it would have nothing to do with rewards.

This situation was the inevitable result of the collapse of the judicial system and the targeting of the families of police personnel. While the Central Government frequently made pious declarations about its determination to insist on human rights' observance, the reality was that they had no answer to the real problems faced by the men in the field. For them, the leadership of people like Gill who would shield his personnel "right or wrong" was a morale sustainer.[37]

Turning the tide: Army–Police operations

The Army–Police partnership was to have very important consequences. The Army enabled the police to break the prevailing fear psychosis which was affecting the police forces as well. Second, it opened up the information channels. From 1989 to 1991 the peasantry had been ground between the mill-stones of the police and the terrorists, and they were unwilling to give information. But the Army presence changed that and information began to flow.

According to a senior Army officer, April 1992 was the watershed when they broke the power of the militants in the Tarn Taran area. It was only by June, with the "winning side" clearly established, that the Army began operating on "information based" strikes as against general sweeps.

Tables 2 and 3 show that the February to May 1992 period, was the most intense both in terms of what the security forces lost and the losses the terrorists suffered. Qualitatively, according to a senior police officer, the most important development was the elimination of the BTFK (Sangha) group's influential Ludhiana district chief Rachpal Singh Chandran. It also lost other "Lt Generals" like Sukhram Singh Mazhabi in Patiala, Jaspal Singh Pala and Devinder Singh in Khanna and Jagdish Singh Disha in Hoshiarpur. Other groups too lost "Lt Generals" notably the Khalistan Commando Force.[38] But the major breakthrough came with the elimination of the Khalistan Liberation Force (KLF) Chief, Gurjant Singh Budhsinghwala, who was shot following the police raid on his hideout in Ludhiana's upper middle-class Model Town locality on 29 July.[39] Three days after Budhsinghwala's killing, his successor, Navroop Singh Dhotian was also eliminated.

On 9 August the police had an even bigger success when Sukhdev Singh Dasuwal, the legendary Chief of the Babbar Khalsa, was shot dead when the police, forewarned of his efforts to attend Budhsinghwala's death ceremonies, managed to detect and shoot him. He was one of the oldest surviving militants, active since the late 1970s and his activities had made him a hero of the militant movement. In both cases it seems that the two leaders were sheltering in urban areas, a technique that has both advantages and disadvantages—witness the capture of Shining Path leader Abimael Guzmán, in Peru. They were also involved with women, and in the case of Dasuwal, the police made much of the fact that this reputedly ascetic leader was living with a woman who was not his wife.

The terrorist counter-attack

Although the terrorists had lost some of their top guns by July 1992, it was the death of "Generals" like Budsinghwala and Sukhdev Singh which struck home since they headed the most active groups at the time. A major fear for them was over the exact circumstance of a terrorist/militant's death. If he had in fact been previously arrested, tortured and then killed, the possibility that he had talked could not be ruled out. The militants and their handlers in Pakistan could not afford the police to gain the upper hand for fear of a domino-type collapse. So they carried out a precise, desperate and ruthless counter-attack. A savage strike was launched against the families of police personnel. Of the 171 persons killed in August, 35 were security personnel and 63 members of their families. But this proved to little avail.

The watershed event was the fallout of the hanging, on 9 October, of Sukhdev Singh alias Sukha and Harjinder Singh alias Jinda, a leader of the KCF convicted for the assassination of the former Indian Army Chief A. S. Vaidya in 1986. From the time their death sentence had been confirmed in July, the Akali-militant grouping made their death penalty a political issue. When the sentence was carried out, they called for a three-day general strike. This was a major test of wills between the State Government and the militant-Akali combine and when it fizzled out after the first day, it was clear that a qualitative change had indeed occurred in the State.

So the "encounter" on 15 October near Kang Rain village near Phillaur, in which Talwinder Singh Parmar, of the Babbar Khalsa International, and two Pakistanis were killed almost appeared like an anticlimax but it was not. According to senior intelligence officials, he was a far bigger "catch" than Budhsinghwala or Sukhdev Singh Dasuwal. A Canadian citizen, he was the mastermind behind the fund-raising operations of the Babbar Khalsa

International as well as a link between the movement and the Pakistani Inter-Services Intelligence.[40]

There is little doubt that by the end of the year, despite retaliatory strikes against "soft" targets such as large numbers of farm labourers unprotected in isolated farm houses, that the militant groups were in disarray and recruitment was down though weaponry was not yet scarce. By the end of the year other top militants like Dharam Singh Khastiwal of the Babbar Khalsa and Nishan Singh Makhu, who headed his own KLF faction, had been eliminated.

For many in India, the real watershed was the death in an encounter on 28 February 1993, of Gurbachan Singh Manochahal, the Chief of the BTFK, erstwhile self-declared Jathedar of the Akal Takht, the person who played a key role in eroding Barnala's elected Akali Ministry in 1986. He was alone and no longer a major actor when the light machine gun position of the Indian Army's *Rashtriya Rifles* shot him as he sought to escape an encirclement.[41]

Table 4: Number of security personnel killed in 1992–93.

Month	PP	CRPF	SPO	PHG	BSF	Army	Other	Total
Jan.	13	–	1	1	–	–	–	15
Feb.	21	–	8	5	–	1	–	21
March	10	–	3	2	1	2	–	18
April	27	2	1	9	4	6	1	50
May	15	1	–	4	6	1	5	32
June	8	2	1	3	3	2	–	19
July	4	2	1	–	–	2	1	10
August	15	3	5	4	7	1	–	35
Sept.	9	3	2	2	–	–	–	16
Oct.	9	1	1	4	–	–	2	17
Nov.	9	2	–	–	–	–	–	11
Dec.	5	1	1	–	–	–	–	7
Jan.	4	–	1	–	–	1	–	6
Feb.	–	–	–	2	–	–	–	2
March	2	1	1	2	–	–	–	6

PP=Punjab Police; CRPF=Central Reserve Police Force; SPO=Special Police Officer; PHG=Punjab Home Guards; BSF=Border Security Force.

The change

By the end of October 1992 many seasoned observers of the Punjab scene were agreed that the situation there had turned for the better. The writer

Khushwant Singh, who had been a tough critic of the militants and of the Congress Government's handling of the Punjab situation wrote a two-part piece in *The Times of India* describing what he saw four days after the hanging of Sukha and Jinda. He called the change "dramatic" and said that the terrorists were responsible for their own unpopularity in the countryside where they were viewed as nothing but common criminals.[42] Similar sentiments were penned by V. N. Narayanan, the editor of the leading English daily from Chandigarh and an acute observer of the Punjab scene.[43] In an interview in *Frontline*, the former Chief Minister Surjit Singh Barnala was quite precise in his description of improvement in the situation "insofar as law and order are concerned".

Media persons, who travelled through the state have also reported on the transformation that has occurred. This is manifested in movement of night traffic on the roads, and an overall atmosphere of normality. The sound of revelry and celebration at festivals and weddings confirms this as well as the general tenor of life which pays little heed to the "social reform" code insisted on by the militant *diktat* of 1990 to 1991.

Why did militant terrorism fail?

While the demand for Khalistan and an independent Punjab kept on recurring, the goals of the militant-terrorist movement were quite incoherent. The strategy was to "cleanse" the state of a minority *a la* Serbia today or West Punjab *circa* 1947. The plan seemed to be that through selective massacre, the 7m to 8m Hindus would be shocked into leaving the State and in the violent aftermath, a similar number of Sikhs resident in other Indian States would be forced to move in.

But the conception was erroneous since it was based on a false reading of Sikh history and a lack of understanding of the symbiosis that existed between the two communities. Activities of fundamentalists on both sides have strained the relationship between the two faiths over the past century with some lurid propaganda for and against both. The relationship between the two communities has been the cause of heartburn among the ideologues of Hindu and Sikh fundamentalism but it is deeply embedded in the Sikh faith as well as Punjabi culture. Inter-marriage, the custom of the eldest son of some families becoming a baptised Sikh and so on, resulted in terrorist crimes affecting people on both sides of the divide which the terrorists sought to create.[44]

The policy of massacre of Hindus severely strained the ties, but could not break them. Attempts to give the movement "purity" through campaigns (backed by the gun) against tobacco, alcohol, eating meat and so on, created even greater alienation between the militant-terrorists and the people of the State, Hindus and Sikhs.

A significant aspect of the criminalisation was the assault on women. Rape, molestation and extortion by groups claiming to be fighting for the "cause" also became a common feature. In retrospect this was the beginning of the end since this process not only alienated those who sheltered the terrorists, whose daughters and daughters-in-law were raped, but also the women themselves, who had been the ideological cutting edge of the movement after *Operation Bluestar*.[45]

The veneer of religion wore thinner and thinner between 1986 and 1989. Terrorists did not hesitate to assault women, extort money and kill not only Hindus but Sikhs as well. Figures available indicate that notwithstanding well-publicised massacres of Hindus, the bulk of those killed were Sikhs. The means adopted to break the Hindu-Sikh links broke the militants instead. In the end, it was the Sikh dominated Punjab Police that defeated the Sikh terrorists.

In this event, the Army, the ruthless police policy and the induction of a popular Government all played an interlocking role in transforming the situation. With hindsight, it seems that the installation of a Congress government, with however many questions about its legitimacy, was an important development. This is not only because political activity opened clogged channels of communication, but because the State Chief Minister and his political team had the benefit of independent and authoritative access to the Central Government which belonged to the same political party and which was committed to fight militant terrorism for historical reasons, not least because of the pathological hatred exhibited by the militants towards the Gandhi family.

The other advantage of a Congress Government was that it came to power with a clear-cut view that it would not compromise with terrorists. Security officials led by Gill, sought a "hands off" policy from various administrations but the only one that gave *carte blanche*, and could have given it, was the Congress Government of Beant Singh.

Had any Akali faction come to power, and this was a clear lesson of the Barnala period from 1985 to 1987, it would have come under immediate and intense pressure, ideological or otherwise, to ease off the battle against the militants, release detainees, transfer police officials and so on. National Opposition groupings had also shown between 1990 and 1992 that they suffered from the illusion that they could negotiate with the militants without crushing terrorist violence.

Role of the Army

The Army's role was that of a catalyst and therefore appears both important and unimportant. But whether or not the counter-offensive could have been effective minus the Army is a moot point.[46] In October 1992, the Punjab Police Chief K. P. S. Gill noted "Operation Rakshak II was sophisticated, low-key and well-planned. The result is that the Army is today looked upon as a friend of the people. It has also helped us out in a lot of places and nowhere has it been accused of excesses or over-reaction."[47] This statement, almost an understatement, says it all. The Army's role was to make collaboration with the security forces easy again and to reassure people who had been terrorised into silence but could not quite trust the police. Throughout the summer of 1992 there was a debate over the continued use of the Army in

Punjab. The conventional wisdom of Army Headquarters in Delhi has always been that the Army should avoid such "aid to the civil power" roles. However, this was overruled by the political authorities. The Western Army Command and its field formations, however, saw the importance of the continued deployment of the Army in Punjab.[48] Punjab is their operational area in times of war and they would not like to see their efforts of *Operation Rakshak* fritter away.

Revitalisation of the Police

If the Army presence was the catalyst, the main element was the revitalisation of the Punjab Police. Armed with draconian laws, assisted by the Army and a friendly political dispensation, the Police, led by Gill, eventually turned the tide. There is little doubt that this was done with scant respect for the niceties of the law of the land or consideration for human rights. It was a tooth and claw battle in which the Police emerged as winners. Despite the media hype, Gill's leadership requires some comment. He was able to take a united force into battle and carry out a brutal campaign in such a way that very few of the practical implications of the "shoot-to-kill" policy became publicly known.[49] But this was also because the police were largely able to ensure that while they did on occasion kill innocent people, by and large their targets were the guilty. However, the worst affected were the so-called "harbourers" and relatives of the terrorists who might themselves be victims but were put through torture and interrogation. In the rough and ready culture of Punjab, people find nothing extraordinary in the implementation of the maxim: "those who live by the sword shall perish by the sword," especially as terrorists put themselves outside the canons of civilised behaviour through their own actions. Notwithstanding the scale of the violence, the situation has not been as bad as in Argentina and Chile. To a large degree this has been because the freedom of the Press has mostly been maintained and newspapers have reported excesses when they have come across them.[50]

Another generalised reason for the failure of terrorism in Punjab was that it was unable to dent the ability of the multi-national and multi-ethnic Indian State to win any battle of attrition. Punjab was a big problem in one sense, but it is a small state compared to others in India. Over the years, the massacres and depredations kept on receding into the back pages of the newspapers.[51] In Punjab and other areas affected, despite death and destruction, life carried on as before and people just rationalised their predicament – a comment, perhaps, on South Asian cultural mores.

THE FUTURE

The internal aspect

The surviving generals of the "movement" are Paramjit Singh Panjwar (KCF), Daljit Singh Bittoo (SSF), Wadhawa Singh of the Babbar Khalsa, Dr. Sohan Singh, head of the Panthic Committee and Wassan Singh Zaffarwal (Old

Panthic Committee). There are questions about the whereabouts of Panjwar, who is variously described as being in the US or Pakistan, as well as the chief of the New Panthic Committee, Dr. Sohan Singh, who is suspected to have passed away since he has been aged and ailing for some time. Wadhawa Singh is reportedly hiding out in Uttar Pradesh, as is Daljit Singh Bittoo.[52]

The rapidity of the collapse of the movement has panicked the surviving terrorists who cannot now depend on their harbourers, who have been, more often than not, victims themselves. Some have been lucky to have been merely assaulted, others have had their women raped and murdered. So there is little love lost and in the changed circumstances information is flowing to the police.

A third key leader still at large is Wassan Singh Zaffarwal the master-logistician of the movement. He has in the main resided in Pakistan and organised operations from a safe-house there. He is the head of one of the Panthic Committees and his main influence is due to his ability to supply weaponry to the various groups besides his links with the Pakistani intelligence officials.

Most officials seem convinced that terrorism will not revive in Punjab. But notwithstanding the successes in Punjab there have also been worrying developments related to the links forged by the various militant-secessionist groups across the country. These have been allegedly encouraged by the Pakistani Inter-Services Intelligence, but partly caused by the failures of the Indian political-administrative system that has frequently allowed problems to fester so creating a base of grievances upon which structures of terrorist-militant movements are built.

There are two sides to the situation in Punjab – the availability of recruits and access to weapons. A remarkable aspect of the movement was the fact that 70 per cent of the hardcore terrorists came from 220 of Punjab's 13,000 villages and most of these were near the border with Pakistan. But many of the equally dangerous "non-hardcore" came from across Punjab, lured by the "gun-culture" which is linked to the warrior tradition of the Sikhs.[53]

Nearly 6,000 terrorists described as "hard-core" and "non-hardcore" died in the 1981 to 1992 period and 20,000 were arrested.. Only in the last six months of 1992 was there a reported fall in the recruitment of militants. Currently some 650 remain, divided in 90 or so gangs.[54]

The availability of weaponry has been a difficult factor to assess. The BSF argues that the border is sealed tight for obvious reasons, but ground information suggests that, although more dangerous, attempts to cross the border continue: all it has meant is a higher premium for the product. Corrupt border officials and security personnel on both sides are part of this nexus and as recent incidents have shown there are still instances where major shipments are let through by the connivance of officials.[55]

Although fencing and floodlighting of the border has taken place to a considerable distance – extending even to Rajasthan – the border is not impenetrable. Only 433·9 km of the 554 km of the Punjab border with Pakistan has been fenced and floodlit as well as electrified in some sections. Some 150 km runs along the turbulent Ravi river creating several enclaves on either side, and the riverine terrain makes it impossible to fence and floodlight completely. Dense fog in winter when the elephant grass is high or storms in the monsoon assist crossings. Reports of crossings even on the fenced and floodlit portions lower down in the Ferozepur area are not uncommon.

Nevertheless, with the fencing and the occasional intervention from the Army, militants have found the Punjab border too lethal and so other routes have had to be opened. Nepal has been one convenient place to operate from because the Indo-Nepalese border is not policed and no travel papers are needed for Indian and Nepalese citizens to cross the border. There is a direct flight from Karachi to Kathmandu and while weapons may not move through it is convenient for the top operatives. In August 1992, Jammu and Kashmir militants who entered India by this route were held in Delhi following the arrest and interrogation of a member of their company who had proceeded directly to Srinagar. Parmar and his associates were reported to have used this route as well.

India has a 512 km border with Pakistan in the Gujarat state of India and 1335 km in Rajasthan. The border comprises a swamp (Rann of Kutch) in the southern extremity with a number of creeks and desert in Rajasthan. People living in this area often have kinship ties across the border. Smuggling is a way of life and the region has been a major drug route for bringing opium and heroin to the Indian ports of Kandla and Bombay for transhipment onwards.

But the routes are not necessarily across land borders. The March 1993 Bombay bomb blast investigations have shown with what impunity a huge shipment of arms and explosives was unloaded in a coastal village. Some of the explosive was used for the Bombay blasts.[56]

Customs officials believe that modern ports also aid the smuggler/terrorist. The large container terminals in Bombay, Kandla (in Gujarat), Goa, Cochin, Vishakapatnam and Calcutta create problems for the Customs at the best of times. Individual containers cannot be checked and bribery is effectively used to persuade the inspectors to look the other way. A major proportion of Indian goods traffic moves over the road system and many of the truckers are Sikhs who have links with villages in Punjab. Terrorists have sought to use this to their advantage.

Militant ethnic and religious links

An alarming development has been the links that are emerging between some Muslim fundamentalists and the Sikh terrorists. In the past there has never been any significant involvement of Indian Muslims in subversive activities despite the fact that several well-known smugglers in the Rajasthan, Gujarat and Bombay areas are Muslims. Events in the past four months have changed this. The participation of Muslim gangs in the Bombay blasts once again underlines how easy it is to sow seeds of subversion in a failed political culture made worse by administrative and police incompetence.

Muslims in Kashmir have been in rebellion for some time now. But theirs is as much an ethnic revolt as a religious fundamentalist one and the worsening communal climate in India marked by anti-Muslim rhetoric and riots is bound to exacerbate this trend.

The Secretary-General of the Student's Islamic Movement of India (SIMI), Tahir Jamal, was arrested for assisting Manjit Singh, wanted for the bombing of the Air India Boeing 747 which took the lives of 329 people. Singh came to India as an ISI operative. A Bhopal Forest Service Officer Nur Mohammed was also arrested for being a conduit for the supply of explosives to the Sikh militants.

Karim Hussain, a smuggler from Hadgam village in Mehsana district confessed that Pakistani authorities had put him in touch with Manjit Singh some time in early 1991. He said that the sack-loads of weapons were delivered by Pakistani officials near the border and then broken down to camel loads which he then brought across to India. There were estimated to be some 350 AK rifles, 40 RPG-7s, 100 Light machine guns and 5 MMG/HMGs. Some of the arms seized from Ahmedabad were worth Rs. 2 crores. Apparently a Border Security Force Sergeant had been suborned to enable the crossing to take place. Intelligence officials believe that there have already been contacts between the Kashmir militants and their Sikh counterparts pushed by their ISI "handlers." The two states are adjacent to each other and even in troubled times civilian truck traffic operates freely. There have been reports of arms supplies being made to Punjab via Baramulla in Kashmir. In early December 1992 Nishad Ahmed Shaikh, a top functionary of the fundamentalist group Hizbul Mujahideen, a leading insurgent organisation in Kashmir, was arrested in Jalandhar in Punjab.

With definite information of the efforts being made to link up the Kashmir and Punjab movements, the Indian Government is now clearly worried that this process can have wider ramifications if links are formed between various movements inimical to the Indian State. These range from the Punjab groups, North-eastern insurgents, the LTTE, the United Liberation Front of Assam, the Jammu and Kashmir militants and so on. Such links can provide synergy, with groups helping each other out in some specific way such as with funds, training, supply routes, and sanctuary. A more alarming aspect of this is the belief that much of the co-ordination is being done by Pakistan.[57]

The Pakistani hand

Pakistan's hand in the Punjab situation is something that Indians take for granted. The truth depends on your point of view. If you believe that hundreds of AK rifles, handguns, machine guns and explosives can cross your border without the connivance of your Government, then there is a problem. But there is more to it than that. To those who want to protect the reputation of Pakistan, and until early 1991 this meant most western governments, these activities did take place, but the Government had no hand in them, or they were outside their control.

For obvious reasons the precise nature of this intervention is difficult to substantiate. The Pakistani hand was first hinted at in the White Paper on the circumstances that led to *Operation Bluestar*. According to Indian intelligence officials from April 1985 Pakistani intelligence began to think of ways of stoking the embers in India. But the "hand" as such became evident only between 1986 and 1987.

The Government of India's case, as detailed in the documents given to the Pakistanis in 1988 and 1990 and the pamphlet of 1993, *Facets of a Proxy War*, is presented through what has appeared in the Pakistani media, through statements by Pakistani leaders, interrogation reports and detailed reports of trans-border encounters. Some of the information also comes from monitoring telephone calls and the last-named document also listed commonly connected numbers in Lahore which are called by terrorists through international subscriber dialling systems.

One manifestation of this is seen if we compare Tables 1 and 2 and observe how the quality and quantity of weaponry changed over time and also retained a certain standardisation. The absence, for example, of any SAM missiles seems to indicate a higher level of control than is otherwise obvious.

Police officials also say that when they captured Malkiat Singh Ajnala and Nirvair Singh after *Operation Black Thunder* they were surprised to find that the two were nothing but semi-literate peasants and not the "master brains" of the Panthic Committee as previously thought. They argue that the real brains of the movement reside in Pakistan. Some are Pakistani and others are Sikhs like Zaffarwal and Sattinderpal Singh Gill and other expatriates from Canada and the UK.

Given the nature of the involvement, much of the evidence of the Pakistani hand is necessarily circumstantial. Some of this was first given to Pakistani officials in 1988 and then again in 1990. The 1990 document outlined the Pakistani involvement in Punjab and Kashmir based on information gleaned from "interrogation of important extremists," especially those captured following *Operation Black Thunder* in 1988 when the police drove them out of the Golden Temple through a siege. Also cited were documents recovered from terrorists killed in encounters especially before or after border crossings.

The document also listed foreign (non-Indian) Sikhs who had visited Pakistan. These were in the main Babbar Khalsa International leaders like Talwinder Singh Parmar and Gurdip Singh Sibia of Babbar Khalsa UK who surrendered in August 1992. He admitted that he had crossed over from the Gujarat border and had been living in Pakistan for the past 18 months. Another group was the International Sikh Youth Federation which has branches in the UK, Canada and Germany.

In these talks, Indian officials also gave their Pakistani counterparts a list of four or five top names like Wassan Singh Zaffarwal, Sukhdev Singh Dasuwal, Gurbachan Singh Manochahal etc who were alleged to be residing in Pakistan. They noted that any true expression of Pakistani good-will would be the return of any one or all of these as wanted terrorists. The Pakistanis denied that any of these persons were in Pakistan.[58]

Many Indian officials believe that the Pakistanis are working to a "K-2" (Kashmir-Khalistan) plan and intend to use every possible means to encourage the secessionist movements in India. The ISI has considerable experience in covert operations, and it has certain in-built advantages in this area. Moreover there is no problem with motivation. The Sikh sense of grievance with India is considerable. They do not have to pay for the movement since it has access to substantial funds from the UK, Germany, Canada and the US. In the main no training has to be undertaken since their major strikes are on "soft targets". What the Sikh militants have needed of Pakistan, and what it has provided, is sanctuary and a base from which low-intensity conflict can be carried out against India. There is sufficient leverage in the hands of the ISI through resident militants and through the control of the flow of weaponry which must go through with the aid of the Pakistani border police and Army.[59]

The fencing of the border and the two *Rakshaks* have created problems as have the more intensified patrolling including the use of night-vision devices. While crossings are still carried out by individuals, larger efforts such as sending across arms have become difficult so the effort seems to be to encourage the supply through Jammu and Kashmir where the mountainous terrain makes interdiction much more difficult. Weapons to the Kashmiri militants which have been supplied in far greater quantity than in Punjab are free, though the Sikhs are charged for them.

Western Sikh communities

Another web of external involvement runs through the Sikh communities of the UK, USA, Canada, Germany and elsewhere. Living in distant lands and facing the pressure of maintaining their cultural identity, expatriate communities tend to be conservative and sometimes fanatical. Many of the Sikh communities abroad date from early this century. They are also affluent and have thus provided a major source of funding for the militants. The most prominent of the groups is the International Sikh Youth Federation, as well as the Babbar Khalsa groupings and the Dal Khalsa which have branches in the US, the UK, Canada and Germany. They were the first proponents of Khalistan and they have since provided volunteers like Parmar himself, some other members of his family and Gurdip Singh Sibia, and Manjit Singh.

These people have also provided expertise in weaponry gained through training in mercenary schools in the US or in the use of electronic equipment like wireless sets and remote switching for explosives whose use is not illegal in their countries of residence. They have also supplied equipment such as specialised radio sets, rubber dinghies, and heavy-duty bolt cutters to the militants in Pakistan for use in India.

More than money and equipment, foreign leadership provides ideological fervour which is absent in India. Many of these leaders have the least to lose since they are not directly involved in the struggle and so they tend to be the least compromising and not open to any but the most extreme settlement. Pakistan provides the important interface for the activities of these non-Indian Sikhs to support terrorism in India. Through this process it has also gained invaluable leverage to control the movement in India.

The prominent personalities and groups are well-known since they have figured in the media. There are many others, especially those from the UK and Canada who have been active in support of the terrorists and have travelled to and from Pakistan. From an Indian point of view the attitude of western governments seemed ambivalent until recently. The question remains whether they see India's problems in terms of their own global perspective on terrorism.

PROGNOSIS

Given the very recent turnaround in the Punjab situation, definitive conclusions cannot be drawn. The victory against terrorism is only one part of the solution of the overall Punjab problem. The biggest challenge is to bring the Akalis into the mainstream of political life. The Punjab crisis is to a considerable degree an outcome of the Congress Party's strategy to marginalise the Akalis begun in the mid-1970s. Today with the Congress in the saddle, the party continues to work on that agenda which may be fine for the State organisation, but could prove costly for the country.

The ideological confusion of the Akalis led first to their temporising with the militants and later being swallowed up by them. Throughout 1992 the militant-Akali nexus appeared strong. There were the Hola Mohalla celebrations at Anandpur Sahib from 17 to 19 March and later the efforts to make an issue of the execution of the death sentence on Harjinder Singh and Sukhdev Singh, killers of the former Army Chief Gen A. S. Vaidya.[60] Efforts by the party in early 1993 to present a united front are not yet quite credible. Their demand for the release of Ranjit Singh, convicted for the assassination of Baba Gurbachan Singh, the head of the Nirankari sect, points to militant pressures within. Ranjit Singh was declared Jathedar of the Akal Takht in 1990.

The future depends to a considerable degree on the finesse with which the success gained by the security forces in the field is buttressed by moves on the political chessboard. If the policy of pushing the Akalis to the wall is continued, or if the Akalis undertake policies that keep them on the extreme fringe, normality cannot be achieved. The Centre has an important role in this. It can restrain the State Congress party's more partisan enthusiasm and it can also move fast on the fulfilment of the Rajiv-Longowal Accord which still forms the political basis of any settlement. The key stumbling block is not the transfer of Chandigarh, or the sharing of the river waters, or even more autonomy though there are problems there, but the punishment of people who massacred more than 3,000 Sikhs in Delhi and other parts of India following the assassination of Indira Gandhi in 1984. More than any other act, even *Operation Bluestar*, it was this which alienated the Sikhs from India.[61]

Separation of religion and state

The Centre can also make a positive contribution by initiating steps that will ensure the separation of religion and the state in India in general, and Punjab in particular. The political-cultural climate in the country following the destruction of the Ayodhya mosque make this an opportune moment. The role of the SGPC or Temple Management Committee is sanctioned by an Act of Parliament and can therefore be guided by it. The SGPC has played a questionable role in Punjab politics in the past 30 years because it controls the vast resources, running into crores of rupees, that come in as donations. In the period we are looking at, it has blatantly used the Jathedars of the various Sikh shrines, including the highest, the Golden Temple, (who are appointed by the SGPC) for partisan political ends. Effective legislation can be passed to ensure that it does not destabilise Punjab politics and sticks to its main task – managing the Sikh holy shrines.

Although this study is confined to the past two or three years, even a cursory glance at the history of what has happened in Punjab will show that none of it was inevitable. Nothing need have happened as it did. Most of the key events occurred because of poor decisions, incorrect assumptions and ill-motivated goals. Modernising politics in the State is the key goal, but it cannot be done in isolation from events in the rest of India.

A passing glance at the causes of the problems in Assam in the 1980s, Tamil Nadu in 1989 to 1990, Darjeeling in 1988 to 1989, and more recently developments in Ayodhya and Jharkhand show to what extent they were created by the political-bureaucratic mismanagement of the mandarins and their political masters in New Delhi rather than through any intrinsic, intractable element.

The most portentous crisis now, once again the result of a failure of the instruments of government, is the one created by the destruction of the Babri Masjid (Mosque) in Ayodhya on 6 December 1992 by a crowd of Hindu fanatics led by the right-of-centre Vishwa Hindu Parishad and the Bharatiya Janata Party. This event has left India's 110m-strong Muslim community deeply humiliated. It was this sense of grievance that seems to have motivated the shocking series of bomb blasts that hit Bombay on 12 March 1993.[62]

Parliamentary democracy undermined

In the 1970s and 1980s radical changes occurred in the relationship between the Centre and the culturally and ethnically diverse Indian states. They did not want independence but would have liked substantial autonomy befitting regions as large as individual European nation states. The Government of Indira Gandhi, in attempting to retain effective control of the system, resisted this tendency and in the process undermined the authority of the major national institutions, such as parliament, the civil service, the police, judiciary and the intelligence service.

Whereas in 1971 Mrs. Gandhi and her party won a sweeping election victory, the quick elections of 1989 and 1991 have now shown that the electorate is unwilling to give categorical verdicts as it used to in the past. It could be argued that India has entered into the era of coalition governments, suited for the factional nature of its politics. The other more obvious reason may be that no party, national or regional, is finding it possible to meet the competing demands they themselves are generating through the no-holds-barred appeal to the electorate. The Indian political system has become fragmented, corrupt, incoherent and incompetent.

Implications of military intervention

In these circumstances, the use of the central paramilitary forces and the Army in ever increasing intensity has serious implications for India's democracy in the medium term. Since *Operation Bluestar* in 1984, the Army has been a fixture of the internal security scene. The Army leadership has been reluctant to participate in such operations but they have no alternative but to act when ordered. In recent times the Army has been called out three times in Punjab, twice in Assam and has been effectively participating in operations against militancy in Kashmir since late 1990 and early 1991 as well as being deployed on occasions to quell other disturbances.

The enormous powers of arrest, detention and seizure assumed by the police and security forces have implications for the whole country. The free hand given to the Punjab Police may become a "model" for application elsewhere, and, more dangerously, everywhere in the country. Unchecked by a political system which is itself in a state of profound crisis, it could mean the collapse of democracy such as witnessed in Sri Lanka in the 1980s.

The present trends in the world – the collapse of the Soviet Union, the Yugoslav death-dance, the "velvet" split of Czechoslovakia – indicate that all multi-national and multi-ethnic states are under severe pressure. A great degree of political skill is needed to deal with such problems, not just strong armies and a tough police force. The need for a leadership which is able to put across a transcendent vision to meet, with sensitivity and skill what can really be termed the "political-cultural" needs of their people. This means breaking the present cycle of the making and unmaking of problems and encouraging rather the evolution of a political culture that instead of being divisive and destructive, insists on players who play by the rules.

NOTES

[1] Ministry of Home Affairs, *Agenda: National Integration Council Meeting, 31 December 1991* (New Delhi, Government of India Press, 1991) Annexure–I. This figure breaks up to 10,029 civilians, 1,424 policemen and 5,009 terrorists/militants killed.

[2] Almost all the major leaders of the terrorist-militant groups have been from the border areas, Labh Singh, Manochahal, Aroor Singh, Avtar Singh Brahma, Sukhdev Singh Dasuwal, Gurjant Singh Rajasthani, Harjinder Singh "Jinda", Manbir Singh Chehru, Wassan Singh Zafarwal, Paramjit Singh Panjwar and so on.

[3] According to a Government of India document, there were some 129 mass killings in the 1981–June 1992 period. In many instances Hindus, who are a minority in the State, were the target, but later Sikh families, if they happened to be on the wrong side of the terrorists for a variety of causes, were also targeted. See "Pakistan Aided Terrorist Activities," a pamphlet which is part of a collection *Facets of a Proxy War* (Government of India [Ministry of External Affairs], n.p. n.d. [1993]).

[4] Among the tactics taken up was the use of vigilante groups. While Police Chief Riberio defended these as using terrorist victims to attack terrorists, others saw great danger in using such elements. See Vipul Mudgal, "The Underground Army," *India Today* (Delhi) 15 September 1988, pp. 74–77 outlines a

story of a "cat" as some of these underground operatives are described, who shot two senior police officers who were his "controllers".

[5] See Special Feature on Julio Riberio and the Punjab situation in *Frontline* (Madras) 27 December 1986–9 January 1987. This includes an interview with him as well as an assessment of the situation by Manoj Joshi.

[6] *Operation Black Thunder* is the name given to a police action where the Golden Temple was freed from the control of terrorists through a siege where police marksmen using special sniper rifles and night-vision equipment forced the surrender of some 47 terrorists holed up in the *Darbar Sahib*, the Sikh "Holy of Holies." They killed 20 in the siege lasting several days without sustaining any loss themselves.

[7] Manoj Joshi, "The Pakistan Connection," *Frontline* 28 May–10 June 1988, pp. 13–15 discusses this.

[8] [Ministry of Home Affairs, Government of India] *Involvement of Pakistan in terrorism in Jammu & Kashmir and Punjab* (From May 1988 to April 1990) (mimeo n.p. n.d.) The document shows 14 transborder incidents between May and December 1988 (2 in Rajasthan), 40 in 1989 (2 in Rajasthan) and 13 between January and May 1990. A typical clash listed shows a party of four is trying to cross the border when it is challenged by the BSF. A 2½ hour fire-fight ensues and 2 of the intruders are killed and 2 flee. They leave behind 2 AK-47s, 2 AK-74s, 1 RPG-7, 1 GPMG, 4 pistols, ammunition, 10 half-kilo packets of explosives, cordex wire, detonators, and Indian and Pakistani currency.

[9] See *Agenda* n. 1 Annexure II which shows that Sikhs were indeed the main victims of terrorism. Of some 10,000 people killed by terrorists between 1981–1991, some 6,000 were Sikhs and 3,700 Hindus.

[10] For an account of the conditions in late 1990 and early 1991 see Shekhar Gupta, "Punjab: The Rule of the Gun," *India Today* 15 January 1991, pp. 24–34.

[11] See *Agenda* n. 1 Annexure I.

[12] A Special Correspondent, "Punjab's winter of despair," *Frontline* 8–21 December 1990, p. 5. For the first time, the magazine deemed it prudent not to name the correspondent who had written the piece to prevent him from being targeted by the terrorists.

[13] V. N. Narayanan, "A weathercock in the wind," *Seminar* (Delhi) No. 398 October 1992, p. 43.

[14] See the National Integration Council document cited above, p. 8.

[15] Many reasons have been ascribed for this. The most common one is that the Army *Operation Rakshak I* in November 1990 was confined to the border areas, compelling terrorists to seek shelter inland. When they realised how easy it was to operate there, and how good the pickings were from these richer agricultural and industrial areas, they stayed on and established local roots.

[16] Dilip Awasthi, Terrorism: Expanding Turf," *India Today* 30 September 1991, pp. 74–75.

[17] This was also linked to money from extortion being channelled to other parts of the country in terms of land and property purchases as well as acquisition of assets like trucks and taxis. Some of this was linked to terrorist activity, but a lot of it was plain loot being laundered.

[18] Madhusudan Srinivas, "Spreading fear: Extremist violence in U.P., Haryana," *Frontline* 21 December–3 January 1992, pp. 22–23.

[19] This information was given to me by Mr. Amitabha Gupta, Inspector-General of the Border Security Force looking after the Rajasthan-Gujarat border. Mr. Gupta also told me that in 1992, because of the 245 km. of fencing completed in the Anupgarh-Ganganagar area, the recoveries were smaller – 14 AK rifles, 62 pistols, 4 Light machine guns/general purpose machine guns, 5 anti-tank mines and 120 kg. explosives. There were 39 encounters on the border in which 17 intruders were killed of which 4 were Punjab related. The Army *Operation Rakshak II* also reduced the infiltration, at least in the first six months of the year. See also Manoj Joshi, "The Last Frontier: Policing the porous border in Rajasthan," *Frontline* 18–31 July 1992, pp. 58–68.

[20] Rajya Sabha unstarred question number 1084 of 3 March 1993 notes that 433.92 km (of 554 km) in Punjab and 332.72 km (of 1335 km) in Rajasthan have been completed and that there are no plans to fence the remaining areas of Rajasthan because of the terrain or Gujarat (512 km).

[21] Sahay's attempts to contest from a Punjab constituency in the 1991 elections seems adequate proof of this since he is from Bihar. See also Kanwar Sandhu, "Sudden Eclipse: Mann being marginalised," *India Today* (New Delhi) 15 March 1991.

[22] See Kanwar Sandhu's interview of BTFK Chief Manochahal in *India Today* 15 September 1991, pp. 43–44. This is the only recorded interview of its kind with one of the terrorist/militant "Generals". Manochahal pointed out that one reason for his position was that "The 1985 and 1989 elections taught us that people wanted to exercise their vote. We have not been able to prepare them [the people of the State] to boycott the polls."

[23] A senior Intelligence official told the author that in late 1991, when the decision to hold elections was announced, the principal leaders of the terrorist groups met in Pakistan and decided on a joint strategy to ensure a boycott. Among the participants were Sukhdev Singh Dasuwal of the Babbar Khalsa, Panjwar of the KCF, Zaffarwal who had his own faction of the KCF, and Bittoo of the AISSF. Panjwar came back in early January 1992 and warned leaders of the Manjit Singh faction of the AISSF, which was participating in the elections in 1991, to stay off. Mann was warned of dire consequences over the telephone and he immediately joined the boycott.

[24] Yogendra Yadav, "Who won in Punjab: Of the real contest," *Frontline* 28 March–10 April 1992, pp. 122–126.

[25] The Congress was a minority Government assisted by a number of allies. The possibility of winning 12–13 Punjab seats was a welcome shot in the arm, which did not make his Government a majority one, but reduced the "blackmail" potential of his smaller allies.

[26] At the *Hola Mohalla* celebrations in Anandpur Sahib town, the Shiromani Panthic Committee passed six resolutions calling for the militant-Akali nexus to fight for a sovereign Sikh State. See Ramesh Vinayak, "Punjab: A Separatist Surge," *India Today* 15 April 1992, p. 50.

[27] Venkitesh Ramakrishnan, "Fear and a farce: Militants strike, Government flounders,"*Frontline* 28 March–10 April 1992, p. 121. In 1988, the head of the Bhakra-Beas Management Board, B. N. Kumar had been assassinated. Earlier in a spectacular action the Bhakra canal had been breached. These actions to prevent "Punjab's waters" from being given to others had a special appeal to the peasantry notwithstanding the fact that most of Punjab land, unlike other States, is irrigated and some areas even waterlogged.

[28] Senior Army officials who talked to this writer have had no doubts in their minds that the Punjab militancy was nothing but a Low Intensity Conflict directed against India.

[29] For the numbers involved see V[enkitesh] R[amakrishnan], "The Zero Story: Fear Keeps the Voter Away," *Frontline* 29 February– 13 March 1992, p. 125.

[30] An Army official involved in the planning and execution of the Operation noted that the Army's internal "terms of reference" were also clear cut. The Army would claim no monetary rewards, all press-releases would be through the Punjab Police who were free to claim what credit they wanted. "The uniqueness of the Punjab model," he noted "is that the Army has acted to build up the Police and Administration, and to restablish the authority of the State as such. We did a lot of fighting, but we are happy when people term it as the 'Government's success' not the Army's."

[31] Manoj Joshi, "Fear in the Fray: Elections amid security," *Frontline* 15–28 February 1992, pp. 4–10.

[32] Maj. Pravin Sawhney (Rtd) "Plugging the Dyke: Operation Rakshak in Punjab," *Indian Defence Review* (Delhi) April 1992, p. 101.

[33] B. R. Jaitley's report of a press briefing by Lt. Gen. B. K. N. Chibber to press persons in *Indian Express* 5 June 1992. Gen. Chibber was the 11 Corps Commander headquartered at Jalandhar and is currently Chief of Staff of the Western Army Command.

[34] Army officials stress the importance of inter-personal relations in joint operations. Thus a senior officer told me that while the Army had excellent co-ordination with the Punjab Police when Gill was Director-General, the situation was reversed when he was removed in early 1991.

[35] The policy came into operation sometime in late 1986. At the time Mr. Riberio told the author that he was under enormous pressure from his force. In 1987, there were several "escapes" of leading terrorists earlier reported arrested: Roshan Lal Bairagi on 2 January, Manjit Singh involved in the Khudda massacre the next day, Roshan Lal Bairagi on 2 January, Manbir Singh Chehru on 14 October, Aroor Singh on 30 October, Tarsem Singh Kohar on 14 November.

[36] Kanwar Sandhu, "Hitting Home: Militants target policemen," *India Today* 15 November 1991, p. 75.

[37] See for example, Kanwar Sandhu, "Punjab Police: Uniformed Brutality," *India Today*, 30 September 1989, pp. 34–36. The officer concerned in this episode, Gobind Ram was subsequently targeted by the terrorists and killed in a bomb blast.

[38] Ludhiana Police Chief S. Chattopadhyaya told the author in an interview in March 1993 that the Chandran gang was the fastest growing one and had reportedly been trained by the LTTE in the sophisticated use of explosives. Its elimination was in many senses fortuituous, he said.

[39] According to a senior Army official the author talked to, his elimination was the result of the interrogation of Manjit Singh alias Lal Singh, on July 16 in Bombay. But Ludhiana police chief Chattopadhyaya claimed it was on the basis of information received.

[40] Manoj Joshi "The Turnaround: Positive signs in the troubled State," *Frontline* 7–20 November 1992, pp. 26–27.

[41] Kanwar Sandhu, "G. S. Manochahal: How the trap was laid," *India Today* 31 March 1993, pp. 124–125.

[42] Khushwant Singh, "Punjab Today–1" and "Punjab Today–2" in *The Times of India* (Delhi) 27 October 1992 and 28 October 1992.

[43] V. N. Narayanan, "Punjab: the qualitative difference," *The Tribune* (Chandigarh) 27 October 1992.

[44] The Sikh faith was a syncretic creed that emerged in the 16th century. It was monotheistic and sought to straddle the space between Hinduism and Islam. Until June 1992, there were 129 mass killings taking the lives of over 1,000 people. One feature of these was the singling out of Hindus whether they were travelling in buses, trains or in their place of residence or business. [Ministry of Home Affairs], "Pakistan's aided terrorist activities,"*Facets of a Proxy War*.

[45] See Ramesh Vinayak, "Punjab: Sexual Terrorism," *India Today* 31 December 1992, pp. 90–95. A senior police officer told this writer that raping girls belonging to upper-caste Jat Sikh families was a perverted "empowerment" process for the lower-caste Ramgarhiya or Mazhabi Sikhs. See also Kanwar Sandhu's report, "Spawning rampant criminality," *India Today* 15 October 1990, pp. 48–49.

[46] A senior Army official told me that the bulk of the ground assault against the terrorists in 1992 were done by the Army. "They (the police) used to run away as a GPMG opened up," said one officer. Another recounted the manner in which the Army first obtained the trust of the locals and then "[re]-introduced" the police to them. In a conversation, Punjab Police Chief K. P. S. Gill said such charges were malicious gossip and that not a single episode of the type described ever took place.

[47] "We are nearing normality," Interview with K. P. S. Gill, *Frontline* 7–20 November 1992, p. 29.

[48] This was stated in no uncertain terms by Army officers in the Command that the author spoke to and the only public comment emerged from the Western Army Commander, Lt. Gen. B. C. Joshi who when talking to newsmen the day his appointment as the Chief of the Army Staff was announced said that the secret of the Army's success was the low profile it adopted. Vivek Sharma, "Joshi lauds Army's role in Punjab."*Tribune* 11 April 1993.

[49] In an interview Gill noted: "My orders to my officers are clear-stay within the law. Still, if an officer has done something wrong, it is between him and his maker." He also went on to point out that the "bullet-for-bullet" policy was enunciated by his predecessor to ensure that the Punjab Police stood up and fought. "We have refined the policy. We made the message clear: you shoot us, we shoot at you. And then you have one option: surrender, or die. We declared open season on terrorists." *India Today* 15 April 1993.

[50] Kanwar Sandhu, "Punjab Police: Official Excesses," *India Today* 15 November 1993. This gives an excellent outline of the police policy and excesses or Navneet Grewal, "Watery Graves for Punjab militants,"*Pioneer* 26 and 27 March 1992.

[51] A remarkable aspect is the absence of "management" of the media by the Government. Undoubtedly individual correspondents did use "planted" stories, but there was never a concerted effort. In fact until mid–1992, the fear of terrorists ensured that they had a much better press than they deserved. Attempts to restrict the media failed even at the time of *Operation Bluestar* since media personnel could visit Punjab, where restrictions prevailed, but file their stories from neighbouring States.

[52] A number of leaders are hiding out in various parts of the country. Some of the terrorists used their ill-gotten gains to acquire enormous property in other parts of the country, others passed it on to relatives. But they are being systematically hunted. Apparently the Punjab Police have set up a "missile" (?) squad to track down these people. See "Top KCF militant killed in encounter," *Statesman* (Delhi) 29 March 1993.

[53] A senior police official who had served through the disturbances in the border areas saw terrorist recruitment in sociological terms as well. He pointed out, in a conversation with the author in March 1993, that many terrorists came from the non-Jat groups, usually the underclass who saw the gun as a means of empowerment. A perverse aspect of this "empowerment" was the rape of girls belonging to the dominant and higher caste Jat peasantry carried out by some of these terrorists. "Operation Healing Touch launched," *Tribune* 12 April 1993.

[54] Manoj Joshi, "Receding Terror", *Frontline* 23 April 1993, p. 62.

[55] According to a Government pamphlet, in 1991 29 AK-47 rifles, 5 AK-74s, 23 AK-56s, 2 GPMGs and 77 handguns were seized. [Ministry of Home Affairs], "Arms Supply from Pakistan and Narco-Terrorist Links," *Facets of a Proxy War* (New Delhi, Government of India [1993]).

[56] Smuggler "landing agents" Mustaq and his associates received 138 cartons comprising of over 5,000 kg of explosives, 200 AK-47 rifles, 250–300 pistols/revolvers, detonators, and ammunition. "Government convinced of ISI hand in Bombay blasts," *Hindustan Times* (Delhi) 4 April 1993.

[57] Subhash Kirpekar, "Chavan fears more trouble from Pak," *Times of India* 7 June 1992.

[58] See *Involvement of Pakistan in Terrorism in Jammu & Kashmir and Punjab* cited above; for Sibia's confession see Chandan Mitra, "Confessions of an ex-terrorist," *The Hindustan Times* 22 August 1992; "Over 70 militants surrender in Punjab" *The Hindu* 12 August 1992.

[59] The Indo-Pak border, especially in Punjab, is not a place that can be breached without official connivance. It is densely populated and cultivated to the "zero line" and any movement of vehicles on people carrying sacks of rifles for example, cannot escape the eyes of the locals or the police. As it is, the zone 30 km to the border is considered a primary security zone with a heavy deployment of the Army as well. Nevertheless, because of the tight Indian security net, a high-level of co-ordination is required. That may have been the reason that Parmar and the two Pakistanis, Inthikhab Ahmed Zia, and Habibullah came to India in October 1992 and were shot in the Kang Rain incident. Pakistan has claimed that Zia was an Administrative Officer in a private hospital and had travelled to India via Nepal on a valid visa. There was no comparable information on Habibullah, and in fact, the Pakistani protest referred to him as an "alleged Pakistani national." Indian officials noted that the visa application of the two seemingly unconnected individuals was in the same hand-writing and Zia had claimed to be in the construction and building business.

The arrest of Manjit Singh alias Lal Singh on 16 July 1992 by the Bombay police threw invaluable light on the systematic Pakistani aid to efforts being made to develop other routes for weapons and explosives supply. His arrest was a coup as important as the elimination of Parmar. Manjit had developed close links with Pakistani officials who had reportedly whisked him out of Canada where he was wanted as a suspect for the bombing on the Air India aircraft that took 329 lives in 1985. He had lived in Pakistan since then. He entered India in November 1991 as "Mohammed Iqbal" on a Pakistani passport accompanied by a Pakistani ISI operative who had since returned. He had apparently been taught the rudiments of Islam and to imitate the movements of the namaz or prayer so that he could easily merge into the Muslim areas of Aligarh where his base was to be set up.

[60] Ramakrishnan, "Fear and a farce," cited above p. 120.

[61] There are problems here since many of the ruling Congress were party to the events. Prime Minister Rao, for example, was the Home Minister.

[62] While the Babri Masjid was not a special shrine for the Muslims, the manner in which the issues have been posed meant that the destruction of the Mosque was tantamount to a defeat for the Muslim community as such. See also Manoj Joshi, "An Explosive Mix: Of men and motives," and "A familiar link; Another ISI action?" *Frontline* 9 April 1993, pp. 115–117.

FURTHER READING

Brass, Paul R. *The Politics of India since Independence* (Cambridge University Press, 1990) Part IV vol. 1 of The New Cambridge History of India.

Grewal J. S., *The Sikhs of the Punjab* vol. II.3 of the New Cambridge History of India, (Cambridge,1990).

Kapur, Rajv A. *Sikh Separatism: The Politics of Faith* (London, 1986).

Kohli, Atul, *Democracy and Discontent: India's Growing Crisis of Governability* (Cambridge University Press, 1990).

Kumar, Pramod et. al. *Punjab Crisis: Context and Trends* (Chandigarh, Centre for Research in Rural and Industrial Development, 1984).

Naipaul V. S. *India: A Million Mutinies Now* (Calcutta, Rupa, 1990).

Singh, Khushwant, *A History of the Sikhs* (Delhi, Oxford University Press, 1991).

Singh, Khushwant, *My Bleeding Punjab* (Delhi, UBS Publishers, 1992).

Singh, Gurbir, Series of four articles, "Sikhs, Akalis and the Panth," *Tribune* (Chandigarh) 2–5 November 1992.

Seminar publications, "Understanding Punjab: A Symposium on rethinking a persistent problem," *Seminar* (New Delhi), No. 398, October 1992.

Surjeet, Harkishan Singh, *Deepening Punjab Crisis: A Democratic Solution* (New Delhi, Patriot, 1992).

Tully, Mark and Satish Jacob, *Amritsar: Mrs. Gandhi's Last Battle* (London, Jonathan Cape, 1985).

GLOSSARY

Akali Dal — The Akali Party, which is broken into a number of factions, is recognised to be the main party representing the Jat peasantry in the State.

Akhand Kirtani Jatha — Literally a hymn group. Founded by Bibi Amarjit Kaur, it contributed to the early growth of militant ideology. Some of its members became leading terrorists but the group itself has been confined to spreading its message of austere and strict Sikhism. There were personal differences between this group and that of Bhindranwale, some were doctrinal and some based on the Bibi's contempt for that leader.

All India Sikh Students Federation — Originally the students' front of the Akalis later taken over by the terrorists as two factions, one led by Daljit Singh Bittoo, a ranking terrorist, and the other by Manjit Singh.

Babbar Khalsa or Babbar Khalsa International — One major autonomous wing of the militant movement. It goes back to the days of Bhindranwale, but it had doctrinal differences with him and the Taksal. It was led by Sukhdev Singh Dasuwal from the early 1980s until in August 1992 he was discovered and shot. It has had links with the Babbar Khalsa groups in the UK, the US and Canada. Dasuwal and Anokh Singh, another leader, learnt to handle explosives in Pakistan in early 1984. Their main effort was originally directed against the "heretical" Nirankari sect. The main international organiser for the group was Talvinder Singh Parmar though he had by the time of his death broken away and founded his own group called Azad Babbar Khalsa or Independent Babbar Khalsa.

BSF — Border Security Force, a paramilitary force set up to guard the Indo-Pakistan border. It is also used for internal police duties. It has over 100 battalions including some light artillery.

BTFK — Bhindranwale Tiger Force for Khalistan founded by Gurbachan Singh Manochahal, a former Army man, and a key player in the militancy in the 1985–89 period. He was shot dead in early 1993. He was originally in the KCF but then founded his own group. But this group has two wings, one led by Rachpal Singh Sangha who broke away from Manóchahal. Later this spawned another group headed by Rachpal Singh Chandran, which was decimated along with its leader in early 1992. It was then the fastest growing group and there were reports that its personnel had received training from the LTTE on the use of explosives.

CRPF Central Reserve Police Force, originally set up in 1939. It is more than 100,000 strong and has 124 battalions which can be deployed anywhere in India at the request of the State Government to assist the local police.

Centre The Indian Union Government.

Crore Indian measure signifying 10 million.

Damdami Taksal A religious school where Sikh priests were trained. Headquartered at Chowk Mehta, near Amritsar. Jarnail Singh Bhindranwale was its chief and now it is headed by Baba Thakkar Singh. It played a key role in the militancy in the late 1980s, but has now reverted to its original role as a religious school.

ISI Pakistan's powerful Inter-Services Intelligence which is controlled by the Army. It played a major role in the not-so-covert war against the Soviets in Afghanistan and has since turned its attention towards subversion in India by supporting Sikh militants and Kashmiri secessionists as well as a variety of other groups.

ISYF International Sikh Youth Federation, a group based in the UK, Canada and Germany, promoting terrorism in India.

Jat Sikh A cultivator caste, numerically and politically significant, known for its warrior traditions. Though not known for any special religiosity, they have been the true sinews of the militant-terrorist movement.

KCF Khalistan Commando Force, a major terrorist group founded by Manbir Singh Chehru alias Gen. Hari Singh. Taken over by Labh Singh, following the latter's arrest in late 1986. Now divided into two factions, one led by Wassan Singh Zaffarwal, who resides in Pakistan and the other by Paramjit Singh Panjwar who is a nephew of Labh Singh who was killed in July 1988.

KLF	Khalistan Liberation Force was founded by Aroor Singh of the original Panthic Committee Avtar Singh Brahama who was shot trying to cross the border in July 1988. Since then led by Gurjant Singh Budhsinghwala whose most daring act was to gun down two senior police officers in Patiala in December 1987.
Khalistan	Land of the Khalsa, the independent nation comprising the Indian state of Punjab and some other areas of the country claimed by militants. The call for converting the militant movement for a fight to obtain Khalistan was given by the original Panthic Committee comprising Manochahal, Aroor Singh, Dhanna Singh, Wassan Singh Zaffarwal and Gurdev Singh on 29 April 1986 from the Golden Temple.
Lakh	Indian measure signifying 100,000.
Lok Sabha	The Lower House of the Indian Parliament.
MLA	Member of Legislative Assembly of any State.
MP	Member of Parliament belonging to either house of Parliament.
Militant/terrorist	In current Indian custom these two terms are used almost interchangeably. "Militant" is most often used for those fighting the state or its symbols; "terrorist" for those who kill unarmed innocents for political effect.
Panthic Committees	Five member group first set up in early 1986 by Gurbachan Singh Manochahal and Wassan Singh Zaffarwal to form a united front of different terrorist groups. Later it divided into factions. The one led by Dr. Sohan Singh, former chief of the Punjab Health Services is the strongest. Dr. Sohan Singh is either dead or living in Pakistan. This group was supported by most of the major terrorist organisations. Its ideological stance has made it the most uncompromising in its demand for a theocratic state of Khalistan.
Panth	The Sikh message and the path to god.
Rashtriya Rifles	National Rifles, a paramilitary organisation of ex-Army men under the command and control of the Army set up in 1990. There are six battalions currently but the Army wants at least 90.

Rajya Sabha Upper House of Parliament.

Special Police Officers Vigilante-style civilians who deputise as officers in Punjab. They are provided with guns and some training. Many of them belonged to the Mazhabi Sikh community and their recruitment, initiated by Police Chief K. P. S. Gill was to ensure that they had channels of activity other than to join the terrorists.

SGPC Sikh Gurudwara Prabandhak Committee, or Temple Management Committee which is headed by G. S. Tohra and is a powerful element in Akali politics because of the control of patronage obtained from the massive money offering to the Golden Temple.

Vidhan Sabha The State Assembly.

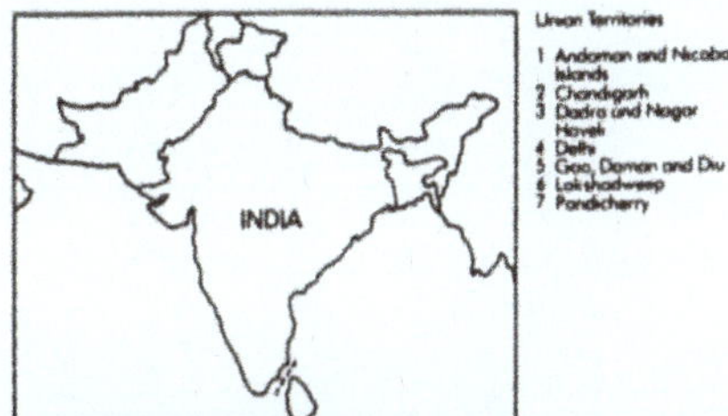

Union Territories

1 Andaman and Nicobar Islands
2 Chandigarh
3 Dadra and Nagar Haveli
4 Delhi
5 Goa, Daman and Diu
6 Lakshadweep
7 Pondicherry

India

Map by courtesy of Control Risks Information Service

[8]

Japan: Hesitant Superpower

Brian Bridges

In May 1993, a few days after a Japanese policeman on duty with the United Nations peace-keeping operations in Cambodia was killed in an ambush, one member of the Japanese Cabinet commented that Japan was prepared to "sweat" but not to "go to the extreme of shedding blood" to maintain peace in foreign lands.[1] While his remarks were quickly disowned by the prime minister, who refused to withdraw the Japanese contingents from Cambodia, they nonetheless epitomised one strand of Japanese opinion about how Japan should act in the international arena. Indeed, the Japanese approach to the UN Cambodian operation, the first occasion since the Second World War for Japanese ground troops, or Self-Defence Forces (SDF) as they are correctly called, to serve overseas, has not been untypical of the hesitancies and inconsistencies which characterise the Japanese search for an international role.

For Japan has become a paradox to the outside world: a massive economic power, which even in its current slowdown has shown more resilience than most Western economies, but yet a faltering and, at times, even immobile force in political and security affairs. Japan is a major trader and overseas investor, the world's largest creditor nation and provider of development aid, and increasingly an innovator in new technologies. It alone accounts for roughly 15 per cent of the world's Gross National Product (GNP). This has given the Japanese a basic confidence in their economy – and its ability to survive "crises" such as Gulf War-associated oil price rises or the current "high yen" – but this has not been translated into any confidence over handling a higher political profile in international affairs.

However, the Japanese are well aware that their formidable economic stature brings forth increased responsibilities as well as growing demands from the outside world that Japan should do more. Through to the mid-1980s, as some senior Japanese diplomats certainly contend, Japan ran a comparatively successful, low-risk, low-cost foreign policy – heavily reliant on US patronage and concerned primarily with the business of doing business. However, the passive, essentially reactive, foreign policy of the past four decades or so is no longer feasible in the more complex post-Cold War environment.

Change in Japanese defence and foreign policies usually comes slowly and incrementally. Change is undeniably taking place – in that Japan is involved in actions and operations that would have been impossible even five years ago – but the pace and direction are still uncertain. This is even more the case as a result of the July 1993 Lower House elections, which marked the first step in what will surely prove an agonising restructuring of the Japanese political system. As Japan enters a new era of coalition government, the awkwardness of uncertainty abounds.

This study discusses the main elements of Japan's political and economic system which underpin and can either promote or inhibit its international role as well as the crucial perceptional issues of how the Japanese feel about themselves and the outside world. It examines the state of the vital US-Japanese relationship, Japan's regional aspirations, its defence posture, and its non-military contributions to the international order. The study also considers how far the Japanese are able and willing to move into a more balanced and proactive role in the "new world order".

POLITICAL PAROCHIALISM

At the July 1993 G-7 Economic Summit in Toyko Japan missed a golden opportunity to show authority amongst a G-7 group which was crying out for dynamic leadership. For prime minister Miyazawa Kiichi was distracted by being in the middle of an election campaign in which his party was clearly heading for its worst performance in nearly four decades. Once again, for Japan, domestic political introspection overshadowed foreign policy aspirations. Much of the blame for this must be laid at the door of the Japanese political system.

Japan has been ruled by one party, the Liberal Democratic Party (LDP), for nearly four decades, a political longevity without parallel amongst industrialised countries. Belying its name, the LDP is a conservative, top-down dominated amalgam of factions which often appear to function almost as separate parties within a party. One key element in its survival has been the LDP's ability to incorporate into a kind of "grand coalition" new groups and sectoral interests. The blurred and fuzzy ideology of the LDP has helped. So, too, has the penetration of party structures by interest groups, so that the "politics of interest" dominate over the "politics of ideology".[2]

This has meant that the politics of money have become pervasive. Pork-barrel patronage and gerrymandering have been much in evidence; the spoils of public expenditure, such as procurement or subsidies, have been recycled back to the LDP in the form of financial contributions. Unsavoury underworld connections have developed. Consequently, in recent years, the LDP has been wracked by a series of financial scandals. Of these, the most serious have been the Recruit Cosmos insider-share dealing scandal in 1988–89 and the Sagawa Kyubin gangster-linked corruption affair, which emerged in mid-1992 and is still running. The Recruit scandal claimed the scalp of the then prime minister as well as several cabinet members and helped to contribute to the LDP losing, for the first time ever, its majority in the Upper House in the July 1989 elections.[3] The current Sagawa scandal first destroyed the influence of the party's kingmaker, Kanemaru Shin, and then brought about the LDP split which heralded the end of its singular domination of Japanese politics. Although politicians have left the LDP in the past, defectors have barely numbered more than a handful until this June, when two groups, together numbering over 50, split away and voted in favour of a no-confidence motion against Miyazawa for his failure to push through political reform legislation.

The opposition parties have in the past failed to capitalise on the LDP's self-inflicted misfortunes. The largest, the Social Democratic Party of Japan (SDPJ), has been hampered by an ideological rigidness (particularly over defence-related issues) which has cast doubts on its effectiveness as a potential ruling party. Three smaller parties, the Japan Communist Party (fast losing its appeal in the post-communist era), the Komeito (neo-Buddhist but erratic) and the Democratic Socialist Party (hawkish on defence but indistinguishable from the LDP on many issues), have only limited support. Although the opposition did make significant inroads in the 1989 Upper House elections, they were unable to follow this through and they lost ground again in the February 1990 Lower House elections and the July 1992 Upper House elections. The public seemed to be swayed by the maxim of "better the devil you know" and to prefer the voracious but effective LDP to an inexperienced opposition-based coalition, with all its attendant uncertainties.

The July 1993 Lower House election was, however, different because for the first time a significant section of the LDP – the breakaway faction of former finance minister Hata Tsutomu reborn as the Japan Renewal Party – joined with SDPJ and the other parties to campaign on an anti-LDP programme. The election campaign was dominated by the rhetoric of political reform, with all parties pledging themselves to carry out such reform by restructuring the multi-member constituency system and by rooting out corrupt practices. Public opinion polls show that this issue did concern the voters most, even though their deep disillusionment with politicians means that they remain sceptical about how far and how quickly the system can actually be changed. The economy, despite being in its worst state for two decades, was, by contrast, a relatively secondary issue.

The results were not a total disaster for the LDP, for although it lost its majority, it remained by far the largest party with 223 seats, above expectations. As shown in Table 1, the new centre-right parties did well, with the Japan Renewal Party gaining 55 seats and the Japan New Party (JNP), formed by

Table 1: State of the Political Parties

	Lower House		**Upper House**
	1990 election	**1993 election**	**After July 1993 realignment**
LDP	**275**	**223**	**99**
SDPJ*	**136**	**70**	**73**
Renewal Party*	**—**	**55**	**8**
Komeito*	**45**	**51**	**24**
JNP*	**—**	**35**	**4**
JCP	**16**	**15**	**11**
DSP*	**14**	**15**	**11**
Shinto Sakigake*	**—**	**13**	**—**
Shaminren*	**4**	**4**	**—**
Rengo*	**—**	**—**	**10**
Ni-in Club	**—**	**—**	**5**
Independent	**21**	**30**	**7**

[* parties joining the new coalition government]

a reformist but previously LDP-backed prefectural governor, Hosokawa Morihiro, gaining 35 seats. The real loser was the SDPJ, which was widely seen as being opportunistic in agreeing to support Hata and his policies, despite past antipathies; its number of seats was halved to only 70.

The LDP's immediate reaction was to try to persuade one or two of the new opposition parties to come into coalition with it, but it failed to convince the JNP that it could really turn over a new leaf. The JNP, therefore, joined with the other opposition parties apart from the JCP to form an eight-party coalition government. Hosokawa's price for joining this coalition was the premiership, and so, in early August, he was installed as Japan's first non-LDP prime minister in 38 years. However, the coalition which has emerged is an inherently unstable one, with the parties really only united in one respect: their dislike of the LDP. Differences do exist over economic policy, but these can probably be massaged. More serious are the marked differences over defence, nuclear power, and foreign policy. In addition, Hata resents having the premiership snatched from him by Hosokawa and the left-wing of the SDPJ is uncomfortable at being allied with past political enemies from the old LDP. The new coalition's primary purpose will be to pass some form of political reform legislation and then call a new election within the next six to nine months. The inevitable focus on inter- and intra-party manoeuvering leading up to that election does not augur well for Japanese decisiveness in international affairs.

Domestic affairs

The net result of the pre-July 1993 political system was that LDP – and, indeed, opposition party – politicians have been preoccupied with managing their factional, constituency and business links. Factional in-fighting and manoeuvering for lucrative posts have been a constant. That is not going to change overnight; if anything, in the short-term, the July 1993 election results will intensify this tendency.

Japanese politicians' interest in domestic affairs has always surpassed their concern for foreign policy. However the growing complexity of international economic policies, particularly when they interact with heavily-politicised domestic sectors such as agriculture, construction and telecommunications, (where politicians are often closely linked with and beholden to "lobby groups") has helped to make more Japanese politicians at least aware of the international implications of their domestic actions.

The importance of the "triad" of the LDP, the bureaucracy and big business to the development of Japanese foreign and defence policies has been commonly asserted.[4] Certainly, by comparison with many Western countries the degree of policy consultation between these groups is high. However, these three component parts should not be seen as necessarily working together in perfect harmony, as standard bearers of the "Japan Inc" concept would argue. There have been, indeed, significant differences of opinion *within* each of these three components – for example, among different factions of the LDP or separate ministries – as well as *between* them, for instance between LDP politicians and bureaucrats. This inevitably brings tensions and, occasionally, inconsistencies into the policy-making process. In the foreign and defence policy field, these differences are more pronounced when policy is concerned with the present and former superpowers, China, the two Koreas, and UN peace-keeping operations than with relatively "low key" countries or issues such as the Association of South-east Asian Nations (ASEAN) or global environmental problems.

The Foreign Ministry has always considered itself the guiding hand of Japanese foreign policy, but it lacks a strong domestic power base by comparison with its fellow ministries and this weakens its bargaining power in inter-ministerial disputes over policy. Inevitably, with the growing reach of Japan's economic power and the increased complexity of modern international relations, the Foreign Ministry has found that not just its traditional rival on foreign economic policy, the Ministry of International Trade and Industry (MITI), but a growing range of ministries are involved in policy inputs. Although the prime minister's office can be called upon to sort out inter-ministerial impasses, few prime ministers are able to stamp their mark on foreign policy. In part, this is due to the constant turnover; the only prime minister to last more than two years in office in the last two decades, Nakasone Yasuhiro (1982–87), was also one who had definite ideas of his own about developing Japan's international role. Miyazawa, despite his English-speaking "internationalist" image, proved a disappointment. Hosokawa will find that the disparate nature of his coalition will make it difficult to lay out his new agenda in concrete terms.

Under the new, inexperienced coalition government, the influence of the bureaucrats should be heightened in the short-term, but they will themselves be distracted by the need to work out new inter-relationships between the component parties of the new coalition, big business and themselves. Already, the major employers' association, the *Keidanren*, has made it clear that it is going to review its future funding support for the LDP; big business will certainly diversify funding activities to more parties. However, as in the past, a number of key issues affecting the economy and relations with the United States and other partners will require political decisions. Initially at least, the new coalition government leaders are going to be less rather than more able to make these kinds of decisions. However, the progressive restructuring of the Japanese political system, particularly as the current shake-out inevitably promotes younger and more open politicians, should in the medium-term produce more capable and effective political leaders. The LDP has already seen the light in electing the youngish, reform-minded Kono Yohei to succeed Miyazawa as party president. There have been false dawns before, but this time generational change amongst the parties is certain. This cannot but make Japan less curtain-shy on the world stage.

ECONOMIC GIANT

While Japan's politicians appear parochial in nature, Japan's corporate sector increasingly wants – and achieves – global reach. The need to import natural resources and gain access to foreign export markets and technology has spurred Japan's integration into the international economy. Consequently, Japan's economic activities are an important underpinning to its foreign policy and are often vital in defining its relationships with its neighbours and partners.

Japan's postwar development has alternated between periods of great economic growth and periods of adjustment. In the process, Japan has overtaken its European rivals, steadily moved closer to the United States in size of economy, become a massive global trader and investor, and come to accept trade friction with its partners as the norm. But it has also become a mature economy. Although the economy registered GNP growth rates of around 5 per cent for four years in succession at the end of the 1980s, it has proved unable to return to the heady rates of earlier decades. Indeed, over the past 18 months the longest ever postwar economic boom (the "*Heisei*" boom) has turned into the worst recession in Japan since the 1973–74 oil shock.

The relatively high growth of the late 1980s masked two underlying trends in the Japanese economy, one negative, one more positive. The first was a rapid asset inflation, especially in land prices and the stock market, which created what the Japanese themselves call "the bubble economy". The banks began lending heavily against these assets and many Japanese companies were able to obtain vast quantities of new funds cheaply, but they often used these funds for *zaiteku* (financial engineering) through speculative investment. The end came in 1991, but, unlike its much earlier South Sea namesake, the Japanese "bubble" deflated rapidly rather than completely burst. The stock market fell steadily so that by June 1992 its level was more than 60 per cent below the late 1989 zenith. Then, from the end of 1991, land prices began to decline, though at a slower rate. The Japanese government worked desperately to ensure that the financial system did not collapse. GNP growth fell to 1.3 per cent in 1992 and it is unlikely to be much better in 1993. Domestic demand slumped, corporate earnings contracted, overseas investment fell to barely one-third of its peak level and, assisted by exchange rate changes and sluggish imports, the Japanese trade surplus in dollar terms rebounded to a new record high of US $ 126 bn in 1992. As the effect of the high yen takes time to work through, the figure for 1993 is set to be higher still. In early 1993 the stock market began to recover and Japanese government officials looked forward to the historically-usual six-month time lag between the bottoming out of the stock market and of the economy. The Miyazawa cabinet introduced two massive economic stimulation packages, in August 1992 and April 1993, but the political crisis has knocked back the time-scale for the second package's implementation, so the new coalition government will certainly have to consider a third stimulation package.

The second trend was a significant restructuring of industry. The Japanese have shown a propensity for turning economic shocks into blessings in disguise.[5] The 1973–74 oil shock converted Japanese industry to an all-out crusade for energy-efficient production methods. The 1985 Plaza Accord's master plan for cutting Japanese surpluses by manipulating exchange rates was only briefly successful: Japanese companies strengthened themselves by shifting some of their operations abroad and investing heavily at home in new plant and state-of-the-art equipment and in research and development (R&D).

Now, the current recession has hit the manufacturing sector hard. Although many of Japan's major manufacturing companies have declared poor results over the past year, and industrial output has declined for the past two years, their ability to survive rather than go under is clear. Labour-shedding, inventory pruning and cost-cutting have been the order of the day, making Japanese companies leaner and fitter to take advantage of the return in consumer confidence when it comes. Significantly, companies have cut back on capital expenditure rather than R&D expenditure. In addition, the lively debate amongst the Japanese business community, sparked off by calls for changes in work practices from the chairman of Sony, is likely, in the medium-term, to have the effect of promoting a more efficient use of time and human resources in the service industry. Japanese companies may be temporarily drawing in on themselves now, but the momentum to move outwards is not being lost. They will remain powerful global players, though not as all-conquering as they seemed in the late 1980s.

The new coalition government is unlikely to make any substantial alterations to the overall economic system, though a greater emphasis on the quality of life – trying to put some substance into the rhetoric of Miyazawa's earlier "lifestyle superpower" concept – will become apparent. Japan has prospered as a producer-oriented society; its next stage will be to accent the consumers. But, without removing the inefficiencies and barriers in certain sectors such as agriculture, finance and distribution, this reorientation will be slow and, to external trading partners, a frustrating process.

In June 1993, the Governor of the Bank of Japan said that he was optimistic about the longer-term future of the Japanese economy and dismissed the idea that Japan should learn to live with low growth as "a pathetic notion".[6] Japan will surely soon be back on its course of catching up the US economy, but less certain is the degree to which it will to translate this economic strength into political influence or even hegemony. That transformation depends not just on capability but will.

INTERNATIONAL PERCEPTIONS

In Japan, as elsewhere, policy-makers do not operate in a vacuum; there are close links between foreign policy, political values and imprecise but nonetheless undeniable concepts such as national identity and national purpose. Important to an understanding of the direction in which Japan might be going, therefore, are the perceptions and underlying elements of Japan's international outlook.

Self-confidence versus vulnerability

For the Japanese, sustained economic success has undoubtedly boosted national assertiveness and self-confidence. Although this has continued to be tempered by feelings of vulnerability – especially to external shocks – those concerns are certainly far fewer than one or two decades ago. At the time of the 1990 Gulf crisis, when the price of oil rose rapidly, the Japanese remained calm, convinced that as long as the oil continued to be available they could afford to pay for it. Even in the current economic downturn, the Japanese note that their growth rates are still higher than for most European countries, including of course Germany.

This heightened self-confidence does on occasion veer into arrogance, although this has been more explicit in best-selling literature than in foreign policy per se. The epitome of it was the 1989 book, *The Japan that can say no*, written by Ishihara Shintaro, a nationalistic LDP politician, and Morita Akio, chairman of Sony. But more common than this kind of swaggering cultural nationalism is a growing feeling that Japan should make its own decisions. This is apparent in heightened resistance to foreign pressure, *gaiatsu*. In the past, Japan has tended to accommodate pressure from its trading partners over export restraint and, more recently, on domestic regulatory or structural impediments. Although some officials and politicians keen to open up Japan have used this *gaiatsu* as a justification for pushing forward their own proposals, many Japanese now regret fostering the belief amongst external partners that Japan simply responds to the exercise of pressure.

Hierarchical worldview

The perception that Japan has arrived as "number one" has extremely strong connections with hierarchical principles in Japanese society. Inter-personal relations in Japan retain a strong hierarchical flavour, which is reflected in language and behaviour and which derives from the predominant pattern established under the Tokugawa era (1600–1868), though the origins can be traced back to much earlier Confucianist influences. However unconsciously, the Japanese tend to externalise these hierarchical principles into their image of the outside world. Being a "first-class" or a "second-rank" power has much more precise connotations for Japanese than for Westerners or even other Asians.[7]

The founding fathers of Meiji Japan admitted the general supremacy of Western civilisation and their poor ranking in the world order; by adopting the slogan of "rich nation, strong army" they strove to ascend this ranking ladder.[8] The first attempt to climb the ladder ended in defeat in war, but the postwar effort has been far more successful. Even so, in the 1960s and 1970s, the Japanese felt they were still ranking below the West. Not until the 1980s did the Japanese really feel that they were the equal of the West. The publicity photos from the annual G-7 Summits are replete with the symbolism involved. The photos from the early summits invariably showed the Japanese prime minister stuck on the edge of the group. By the second half of the 1980s Japanese prime ministers were edging nearer the middle and at the 1990 Houston Summit the then prime minister, Kaifu Toshiki, appeared centre stage, cracking a joke.

The corollary of this drive since the end of the 19th century to catch up with – and surpass – the West has been the enhancement of a feeling of superiority over other Asians and, further down the ladder, Latin Americans and Africans. Not only the lasting bitterness created by Japanese attempts to enforce this superiority on Asia in the first half of this century but also the psychological trauma the Japanese suffer in facing up to this past still affect Japan's relations with its Asian neighbours. Moreover, to take another extreme example from the best-seller lists, Hasegawa Keitaro's 1987 book, *Sayonara ajia*, in which he depicts Japan as a gleaming skyscraper towering above the rubbish dump of Asia, show that not all Japanese are able to escape from these assymmetrical perceptions even today.

Neither East nor West

Japan has had to grapple with the dichotomy of its positions in both Asia and the West ever since it was opened up to the West in the mid-19th century, but, while Japan is still of course geographically and culturally part of Asia, its postwar history has increasingly pushed it economically and politically into the "West".

Paradoxically, this dichotomy has fed into long-standing feelings of separateness and, indeed, isolation from the outside world, so that many Japanese feel neither fully part of Asia nor of the West. This has several implications for Japan's role in the world. Firstly, for the past four decades Japan's international relations have been dominated by the politics of managing one crucial relationship: that with the United States. For, unlike West Germany, which was gradually brought back into the evolving postwar regional order in Western Europe through membership of NATO and the EC, Japan found itself isolated in North-east Asia, surrounded by either communist or authoritarian neighbours and dependent ultimately on the United States alone. Secondly, the Japanese have not felt comfortable about their relationships with either the West or Asia and they have failed to establish the "mediating" or bridging role between the Eastern and Western cultures and systems that some Japanese intellectuals clearly desire.[9] Thirdly, the Japanese have tried to compensate through the recently-popularised rubric of "internationalisation", but the quantity rather than the quality of the interactions with the outside world has often seemed more important. Nonetheless, the globalisation of Japanese corporate activity is just one way in which longer-term exposure to different ideas and cultures is bringing about qualitative adjustments in Japanese thinking.

Separating politics from economics

For Japan, the fundamental "economistic" policy attitude since the early 1960s of giving priority to economic, rather than political, considerations[10] has deeply affected its interactions with the outside world. The policy of *seikei bunri* (the separation of politics from economics) was conceived in the 1950s as a device to get round political and ideological difficulties in trading with China, but gradually expanded to a general belief that it did not matter about the domestic policies or nature of any particular government nor, indeed, its behaviour on the international scene, as long as it was possible to do business with that country.

However, during the second half of the 1980s, Japan found it less easy to maintain such a profile. The transfer of dual-use technology to the Soviet Union by the Toshiba company, the emergence of Japan as South Africa's largest trading partner, the call for sanctions on China after the Tiananmen Square massacre, and avionics parts sales to Iran all demonstrated that the politics of commerce are now far more complex and subtle than in previous decades. The end of the Cold War has only heightened concerns about human rights and other "political" issues which increasingly intrude into Japanese commercial operations.

Threat perceptions

Even at the height of the Cold War, Japanese views on threats differed from those in the West. Of course, the Japanese were faced by growing Soviet forces in the Soviet Far East from the mid-1970s and by a communist government stubbornly refusing to make any concessions over the disputed "northern territories". But few ordinary Japanese could take seriously the idea that the Soviet Union would invade, not least while US forces and the US "nuclear umbrella" were in place. The Japanese, therefore, tended to see threats coming by economic means rather than military,[11] being indirect rather than direct, and arising from Third World disputes rather than superpower confrontation.

Ironically, while the end of the Cold War and the disintegration of the socialist bloc, at least in Eastern Europe and the Soviet Union, was generally heralded as enhancing economic issues and instruments at the expense of past military ones in international relations, Japanese officials were much slower than their Western partners in accepting the scaling down of the Soviet threat. Russian intransigence, like the Soviets' earlier, over the northern territories was crucial to this time-lag in perceptions.

However, now even the Japanese concede that the Russian navy is rusting away in Vladivostock and that the Russians are no longer a threat in North-east Asia. The Japanese do not feel militarily threatened by anyone, although they have some concern over North Korea's attempts to develop nuclear weapons and its recently-acquired capability to reach Japan with its missiles. Over the past year the Japanese have expressed some concern also over Chinese efforts to expand its blue-water navy, but, as will be discussed later, the most prevalent fear about China amongst Japanese is not a military threat per se, but the disruptive effects of disorder, instability, perhaps even Soviet-style disintegration in China which would result in thousands, even millions, of boat people heading for Japan.

Pacifism in one country

The feeling of a lack of a direct military threat overlay a much deeper concern amongst the Japanese as a whole to avoid entanglement in military affairs again. The distaste for the sufferings inflicted by embarking on a militaristic path in the 1930s and 1940s was epitomised in the postwar "Peace Constitution" and a broadly-felt aspiration that if they denounced war and avoided war-like situations then peace and stability for the Japanese would entail.

The psychological influences of anti-militarism – and anti-Americanism – which were so strong through to the 1960s have been declining but are nonetheless still there. Public opinion polls turned to a majority in favour of the existence of the SDF and the Japan-US security arrangements only in the mid-1970s. Out of a long series of wrangles in the Diet over defence issues emerged a set of limitations to Japanese military activity. Although they have frayed slightly at the edges over the past few years, their central tenets still retain a very broad degree of support. From the mid-1970s the government adhered to an informal guideline that defence expenditure should remain less than 1 per cent of GNP; this was breached in 1987, but defence expenditure has recently returned to below the psychological 1 per cent barrier. The SDF have now been accepted legally, but they can only act in self-defence and cannot participate in collective self-defence. Exports of weapons and their production facilities remain banned, with only a special but barely used exception being made for military technology transfers to the United States since 1983. Three non-nuclear principles (not to possess, produce or permit the introduction into Japan of nuclear weapons) have been established, although the entry of nuclear-weapon carrying US naval craft into Japanese ports remains a grey area of interpretation.[12] The July 1993 election set back for the SDPJ does not mean that the pacifist undercurrent is not still strong. This has been, and still is, therefore a strong inhibiting factor, which the Japanese government cannot ignore in policy-making.

GLOBAL PARTNER

For more than four decades, Japanese interactions with the outside world have been heavily coloured by the one crucial relationship with the United States. Nowhere are the linkages between politics and economics more potent than in this complex love-hate relationship. The US Ambassador to Japan throughout most of the 1980s, Mike Mansfield, used to refer to the US-Japanese relationship as the most important bilateral relationship in the world "bar none", whereas successive Japanese ministers and officials have called it, with more accuracy, the "cornerstone" or the "axis" of Japanese foreign policy.[13]

No alliance relationship is ever built on perfectly symmetrical and identical economic, political and security outlooks. The US- Japan relationship is no exception. Certainly the relationship is now far from being as assymmetrical as it was even a decade ago – one Japanese Foreign Ministry official even went as far as to argue that President George Bush's talks with Miyazawa in January 1992 showed for the first time that the two countries had become equal partners[14] – but it still has mismatches of capabilities and expectations.

Economic interdependence

Both pillars of the relationship – economic interdependence and security co-operation – have come under strain during the past few years. The rapid growth in Japanese trade surpluses not just with the world, but notably with the United States, during the 1980s led successive US administrations into complicated negotiations to open up the Japanese market and restrict Japanese export penetration. In the later 1980s, the bilateral trade deficit did come down, only to be replaced by a wave of large-scale and high-prestige Japanese investments in the United States – "buying up America" – and signs of the Japanese gaining the edge in several vital areas of high technology. The Japanese also ended up financing the US deficits (so that the Japanese unintentionally triggered off the October 1987 stock-market crash by selling off US Treasury bonds). An agonised debate about Japan broke out in the United States fuelled by a burst of "revisionist" literature, which actually represented a critique of the domestic American system but was expressed in terms hostile to Japan.

Many Japanese agreed that the state of the bilateral relationship was unhealthy, but most felt that it was the United States which was the patient most in need of curing. President Bush's brief collapse at a state banquet during his January 1992 visit to Japan was, therefore, cruelly symbolic. The litany of US complaints over rice, cars and trade in general provoked more condescension than concession from the Japanese. Worse was to come as the bilateral trade surplus, which rose in 1991 for the first time in five years, rose again in 1992 to reach US $ 49 bn. Although the Japanese investment flow into the United States has tailed off, the sluggish Japanese economy and the strong yen, which exaggerates the dollar value of exports, will ensure that the trade surplus only increases this year.

The security pillar

The relationship is as much about political and security co-operation, however, as it is about economic interdependence. The Japan-US Security Treaty, in its 1960 revised form, provides the basis for the US commitment to defend Japan and station its forces in Japan. The Treaty is lop-sided in the sense that it contains no provision for Japan to come to the aid of the United States in the event of an attack upon it. While the Americans have not requested that stipulation to be changed, they have made increasing demands over the past decade or so for Japan to do more in sharing the burden of defending itself and the East Asian region. These demands were spurred partly by the deterioration in East-West relations in the late 1970s–early 1980s and partly by the United States' own budgetary problems during the decade. Japan's response was to gradually strengthen its own self-defence capabilities, slowly increase the proportion it paid of the total costs of the US forces in Japan (the Japanese will be covering 70 per cent of these costs by 1995), and widen the political-security dialogue with the United States.[15]

Although popular support for both the SDF build-up and the maintenance of the Japan-US Security Treaty remained high during the 1980s, the end of the Cold War made the Japanese government more concerned about the relevence and the popularity of its approach. In fact, it has found itself caught between domestic pressures for a "peace dividend" through a reduced defence budget (the SDPJ has been in the van in urging this, but ironically found an ally in the Ministry of Finance which was looking for ways to trim the overall budget) and heightened US demands for burden-sharing. As will be discussed later, the Gulf War acted as a catalyst for the internal debate within Japan about its international role, but did little to help US–Japan relations. The United States was disappointed by the bungled Japanese legislative attempts to send SDF forces to the Gulf, while the Japanese felt that their considerable financial support for the Americans had not been appreciated.

The Bush administration laid its Japan policy on two foundations: the Structural Impediments Initiative (SII) talks to open up the Japanese economy and the "global partnership" concept to enhance political and security co-operation. Both showed some initial successes, but by 1992 as the trade surplus began to rise again the SII talks petered out and the rhetoric accompanying the "Tokyo Declaration", agreed during President Bush's January 1992 visit, was shown to be hollow. It was characteristic of the failure to develop real political and security co-operation that former US Secretary of State James Baker spent only three nights during his whole period in office in the capital of his global partner.

The coming of Clinton

Bill Clinton's success in the presidential elections was seen by the Japanese not just as a generational change, but as the start of a new US approach, although opinion was divided – and remains divided – as to how Clinton's rhetoric will work out in practice. Many Japanese expect him to be tougher on trade and market-opening issues and that differences in policy towards China and Russia could become more pronounced. Certainly, many of the new Clinton administration's economic policy-makers are known for strong views on Japanese trading practices and their proposals for "results-oriented" trade targets carry ominous warnings to the Japanese. But other Japanese interpret Clinton's call for a revised industrial policy to enhance US competitiveness as a belated recognition of US weakness: reinvigorating the US economy would, in the medium-term, stabilise bilateral economic relations and assist Japanese commercial activities. They also see Clinton's publicly-declared support for Japan becoming a permanent member of the UN Security Council, as well as the appointment of former vice-president Walter Mondale as the next US ambassador to Japan, as encouraging signs that the Clinton administration also wants to develop the high-level dialogue on broader themes.

It remains true, however, that the Clinton administration puts primary emphasis on the economic dimension of the relationship, so the short-term looks set to become more painful. Despite hectic negotiations to provide a "new framework" on economic relations for Clinton and Miyazawa to agree at the Tokyo Summit, both sides have different interpretations of the "objective criteria" for putting that framework into practice. Noting the success of a 1991 agreement on semi-conductors which has led to US companies achieving a 20 per cent share of the Japanese semi-conductor market, the Clinton administration wants a clutch of sectoral pacts with specific targets coupled with further negotiations to bring about broader structural changes. The Japanese, however, reject the idea of specific numerical targets (privately admitting that the semi-conductor pact was a mistake not to be repeated again) and are counter-proposing areas such as energy and environment in which co-operation could take place. Prime Minister Kaifu, on one of his early visits to see President Bush was bold enough to pledge Japan to become an "import superpower": domestic demand would help to boost imports from the United States. Miyazawa was less rash; on his visit in April 1993 he pointed out that the trade gap had been in existence for over a decade and there was "no reason why we should solve it overnight".[16] The political instability of the new coalition government is certain to handicap substantive discussions with the Americans. The net result is likely to be a reversion to the "old" framework of tough, contentious and prolonged haggling over economic issues during the coming months.

But what do the rising economic tensions tell us about the overall prognosis for the Japan-US relationship and Japan's own future international role? First, despite the popular appeal of books predicting a future war between Japan and the United States (these Domesday scenarios are usually better sellers in Japan than the US!), a trade war or, indeed, any other kind of war between the two is not a possibility in the immediate future. It is too simplistic to view the economic relationship purely in terms of adversarial Japanese trade and investment drives against the United States. The cross-patterns of trade, investment, and technology flows are becoming increasingly complicated, so that the two economies are now so intertwined and inter-locked that neither can afford to break away without suffering serious damage.[17] For example, the "big three" US car companies, often the most vocally critical of Japan, actually all have stakes in Japanese care companies; Honda, on the other hand, produces more cars out of its factories in the United States than out of its Japanese factories. Around 10 per cent of US imports from Japan are actually products from US companies set up in Japan.

Second, old attitudes are hindering a smooth rebalancing of the relationship. Both sides are still finding it difficult to adjust to the new status and power that each holds. The Americans remain uncomfortable with Japanese economic strength. They have been urging the Japanese to do more in the international arena, but they must then accept that an inevitable corollary is a greater automomy for Japan, which will make decisions sometimes at variance with US aims. On the other hand, the Japanese need slowly to wean themselves of the habit of always turning to the United States for advice or approval before responding to an international crisis or problem.

Finally, while the Japan-US relationship will clearly remain important to Japan for the foreseeable future, fundamental to Japan's attempts to provide a more rounded foreign policy will be the enhancement of relations with other partners, especially Europe and Asia. During the past decade, when Japan-

US relations have been poor, the Japanese have often turned to other countries or regions for temporary "compensation". Now, they need to broaden their activities away from the overpowering relationship with the United States on to a more committed basis.

REGIONAL LEADER

Japan faces a good deal of ambivalence when it looks to Asia. For some Asians, the legacy of bitterness and suspicion remaining from the wartime or longer colonial occupation is overlaid with apprehension that Japan is now trying to achieve by economic means what it failed to do by military means during the war, namely, dominate the region. Others respect the Japanese success in catching up – and even overtaking – the West economically; they have not only themselves benefited from Japanese aid, trade, and investment but have also looked for ways in which they might introduce certain elements of the Japanese socio-economic system to spur their own development. The Asians realise that they cannot live without Japan, but they do want to avoid becoming too dependent on it.

The Sino-Japanese "special relationship"

The Japanese have talked much about the "heart-to-heart" relationship with other Asians, but clearly, to the Japanese, the relationship with China is the most crucial for them in the Asian-Pacific region. Many Japanese feel alienated from the post-1949 Chinese experience and the failure, yet again, of the Chinese to get their act together in the way that the Japanese have, but they do still hark back to the old cultural linkages. To a surprising degree, despite the intermittent tensions in the association, both Chinese and Japanese politicians have a tendency to refer to the "special relationship" which they see between their two countries.[18] Special relationships, however, are rarely equally special to both partners.

It was politics that brought Japan and China together to establish diplomatic relations in 1972 – and Emperor Akihito's visit to China in October 1992, the first ever by a Japanese monarch, was ostensibly to commemorate that event – but it is economics that has held them together. And, despite the 1989 Tiananmen Square massacre, economics remains the key under-pinning to the relationship. Trade is booming and China, indeed, is well on the way to becoming Japan's second largest trading partner after the United States. Japan is now by far the largest provider of foreign aid to China and investment by Japanese companies is beginning to take off (in 1992 it was the country showing fastest growth in receiving Japanese Foreign Direct Investment (FDI) flows). However, although the trade balance has turned in China's favour in the last few years, tensions inevitably derive from the fact that it is a relationship in which China is highly dependent on Japan for economic inputs.

However, in the political dimensions of the relationship, it is Japan which is the more vulnerable to China. Much of this, of course, has to do with the emotional legacies of the past. Chinese leaders have often brought up wartime

Japanese actions not just as a means of pushing the Japanese off-balance but because of a deeply-held feeling that Japan has never fully faced up to its past. Emperor Akihito made only an anodyne reference to the past, so the Japanese are likely to be discomfited by this issue again in the future. Japan is also conscious that it needs the Chinese to act constructively in arms control and nuclear non-proliferation (most notably over North Korea) as well as to support Japan's medium-term objective of a permanent UN Security Council seat.

Despite some concern over the extension of China's military power projection capabilities and its revival of semi-dormant territorial claims, Japan does not feel militarily threatened by China. Rather Japan feels a very real political imperative to keep China stable – a weak and confused China would be worse than a strong China. Currently, Japanese concerns focus on regional growth differentiation within China and overheating of the economy which could lead to instabilities. This, to the Japanese, justifies their moves which have kept them one step ahead of the West in allowing China back into the international fold after 1989. The parallels with the way the Germans have acted towards the Soviet Union/Russia since 1990 are instructive. Just as the Germans did with the Russians, so the Japanese too wish to "pay" the Chinese – whether by means of aid or investment – to stay where they are.

Flying geese

Japanese economists like to refer to the phenomenon of the "flying geese" pattern of economic development in East Asia. Japan is depicted as being at the head, followed by the newly industrialised countries (NICs) and then the ASEAN countries, in a regular formation, with shifting comparative advantage as the countries advance in technological sophistication. However, one basic problem with this flying-geese pattern is that these geese are not of the same size or breed, nor are they flying at the same speed.[19] Thus the resource-rich ASEAN countries contrast with the resource-poor NICs and Japan; per capita income levels and export dependency ratios vary considerably. Growth rates, too, have differed widely.

By regional standards, Japan has matured into an affluent but less dynamic economy. Nevertheless, it continues to dominate – by virtue of its sheer size. As shown in Table 2, the combined GNP of the NICs and ASEAN is still less than one-third that of Japan. Even if China's GNP US $ 370 bn were added, the total would be less than half of Japan's GNP. This means that Japan is still a massive economic presence by comparison with its East Asian neighbours.

For all the major East Asian economies, Japan is either the largest or second-largest trading partner, investment source and development aid provider. Japan has consistently run a trade surplus with most East Asian countries as a whole, apart from one or two natural resource exporting countries. Japan's trade surplus with the four NICs has grown from US $ 20 bn in 1987 to US $ 46 bn in 1992, mainly because these burgeoning economies still rely heavily on imported Japanese components and intermediate technology to fuel their own export drives and their own efforts to penetrate the Japanese market (particularly a push on cheaper consumer electrical goods in 1986–88) have had only a temporary success. Since 1988, Japan's traditional deficit with the ASEAN countries has been shrinking as massive Japanese Foreign Direct Investment (FDI) in the region has stimulated demands for capital and intermediate goods; only Indonesia, because of its large oil exports, still maintains a sizeable trade surplus with Japan.

Table 2: Economic Indicators of the Asia-Pacific Region

	Population 1990 (mn)	GDP 1990 ($ bn)	GDP per Capita 1990	GDP growth rate (%) 1980–90	Export growth rate (%) 1980–90
Japan	124	2943	25,430	4.1	4.2
Singapore	3	35	11,160	6.4	8.6
Hong Kong	6	60	11,490	7.1	6.2
Taiwan	20	142	7,107	6.8	12.1
South Korea	43	236	5,400	9.7	12.8
Malaysia	18	42	2,320	5.2	10.3
Thailand	56	80	1,420	7.6	13.2
Phillippines	62	44	730	0.9	2.5
Indonesia	178	107	570	5.5	2.8
China	1134	365	370	9.5	11.0

[Sources: The World Bank, *World Development Report 1992*; Executive Yuan, *Statistical Yearbook of the ROC, 1991*]

The post-Plaza agreement restructuring of Japanese industry saw a large-scale movement of production offshore. Although the shares going to the United States and the EC grew strongly, East Asia also received considerable amounts of Japanese FDI. At its peak in 1989, over US $ 8 bn found its way to East Asia. Since then, although the global flows of Japanese FDI have declined drastically, East Asia's share has declined less markedly. In the 1992 financial year, Japan invested US $ 6 bn in East Asia and its share of total Japanese FDI rose to 18 per cent, its highest level for a decade. Two trends are discernable over the past few years: Japanese companies are shifting production away from the higher-cost NICs to the ASEAN countries (and, in the past year or so, to China), and, throughout the region, Japanese companies are establishing more sophisticated factories and exporting higher-value-added products.

Japan's Overseas Development Aid (ODA) has also traditionally been concentrated in the East Asian region. From the early 1980s, around 60 to 65 per cent of total Japanese ODA has gone to the region (around 30 per cent to ASEAN). Over the past decade China has been the largest recipient, followed by Indonesia; for these countries, Japan usually provides around 60 to 70 per cent of their annual aid inflows. Although the diversification of Japanese

ODA to other continents is slowly occurring, Japan is certain to remain East Asia's main aid provider. Although reluctant to admit it, since the early 1980s the Japanese government, under US pressure, has increasingly been taking account of the "strategic" element in the provision of aid – that is, the role that aid can play in promoting social and political stability.[20] Aid to Thailand, South Korea and Turkey in the early 1980s and the Philippines more recently (Japan played a key role in launching the Multilateral Assistance Initiative for the Philippines in 1989) reflect this approach. However, taking the region as a whole, commercial considerations have been more important to Japanese policy-makers: the close linkages between aid and investment, the tying of loans to Japanese company provisioning (though this is less overt than it used to be), and the reassurance of resource supply.

The East Asian economies, therefore, exhibit a high degree of dependence on Japan and the Japanese are well aware of this. Prime Minister Miyazawa once described South-east Asia as "a Japanese constituency".[21] Yet that does not imply a conscious Japanese purpose to create a yen bloc in the region. Trade, aid and investment flows have grown within the region without being overtly pushed by the Japanese government. Indeed, Japan has been extremely reluctant to take up the poisoned chalice of regional leadership.

Regional organisations

Unlike the European Community (EC), which has developed both a high degree of intra-regional trade and investment and also economic and political arrangements which entail subordinating sovereign rights, the Asian-Pacific region is still only at the embryonic stage of regional economic, let alone political, integration. Apart from the South Pacific Forum, which involves primarily the small Pacific islands, only ASEAN has developed to any degree as a sub-regional organisation. In north-east Asia, there has been no progress towards sub-regional organisational integration.

Until the late-1980s academics and business-men made the running on regional co-operative ideas, with governments giving only covert support. However, the most recent phase of regional integration began with an Australian initiative in 1989 for a governmental-level Asian Pacific Economic Co-operation (APEC). Japan has been particularly positive about APEC, once it had become clear that the United States, originally excluded from the Australian plan, would be a full participant.[22] Although the Japanese have some reservations about the Clinton administration's proposal to turn the November 1993 APEC conference into a summit-level meeting (the difficulties of getting the heads of government of the "three Chinas" round the same table are too complex), they have been active in putting forward ideas for moving the organisation forward, particularly in terms of jointly-planned co-operative manufacturing projects, such as in the automobile and electronics sectors.

By contrast, the Japanese have been far from positive about a 1990 Malaysian initiative. Malaysian Prime Minister Mahathir Mohammed proposed an East Asian Economic Grouping (EAEG), which deliberately excluded both the Australians and the Americans and was conceived as a regional counterweight to the emerging North American Free Trade Area (NAFTA) and the EC's 1992 programme; he also posited Japan as having a leading role in its operation. The Japanese had their doubts about the exclusion of the United States and themselves came under strong US pressure to try to forestall this grouping. With some other south-east Asian countries also having reservations, Mahathir has now watered down his proposal into an East Asian Economic Caucus (EAEC), which could meet on an ad hoc basis. This is less objectionable to the Japanese, but in practice it means that the Malaysian initiative is being talked into a slow death.[23]

APEC and EAEC have both been seen in terms of broader regional co-operation, with an inevitable slowness in institutionalisation and implementation. Japanese business-men are, in practice, showing much more interest in an evolving series of sub-regional "growth triangles". Some, such as the Malaysia-Singapore-Indonesia triangle are formal, while others such as the Hong Kong-Macau-South China one are much more informal. Ironically, the one visualised as evolving closest to Japan – the Russian-Chinese-North Korean Tumen River project[24] – is the one about which Japanese businessmen have the greatest reservations. In the EC, European industries and companies were frequently ahead of governments in structuring their operations so as to make the single market a reality. So, in the Asian-Pacific region, it is the corporate sectors, particularly the ubiquitous Japanese companies, who are leading the governments towards economic co-operation. This way, rather than direct governmental initiatives, is the preferred route for Japan.

The political security dialogue in the Asian-Pacific region is much less well-developed than economic discussions. International (or multilateral) security is not a prerequisite for national security, but it does contribute towards it. However, bilateral alliances rather than multilateral structures have been the pattern for the Asia pacific region. Ideas for a new politico-security architecture floated during 1990–91 by two relatively peripheral states, Australia and Canada, who were inspired by the intense European debate, failed to evoke a positive response from regional powers; Japan was no exception.

However, since 1992 the mood – both in Japan and the region – has begun to change. The Japanese themselves, while still cautious about an Asian version of the European CSCE, are beginning to promote embryonic ideas of a security "multiplex", which will add multilateral efforts to already existing bilateral arrangements.[25] When Japanese Foreign Minister Nakayama Taro, in July 1991, floated the idea of including security problems in the ASEAN post-ministerial conference (PMC) meetings with dialogue partners, it was greated with suspicion, but ASEAN gradually came round to the notion. The July 1993 ASEAN-PMC actually saw the launching of an ASEAN Regional Forum for discussing security issues in the region, which would involve Japan along with 17 other countries. The Clinton administration is certainly less negative to multilateral politico-security dialogues than was the Bush administration. The gradual development of these kinds of dialogues is a reassuring way for the Japanese to gradually expand their involvement. It also has the benefit of reassuring Asian neighbours about Japanese ambitions for a political and security role.

MILITARY MUSCLE

By both regional and global standards, Japan has become a major military power. Despite the constitutional and parliamentary constraints mentioned earlier, the Japanese SDF now has a total manpower of 246,000 men, with over 1200 tanks, 150 F-15 fighters, and 17 submarines and 64 destroyers/frigates. Obsolete weaponry is being steadily replaced (although well behind plan) and Japan has also agreed to purchase 4 AWACS surveillance aircraft from the United States. The total defence budget reached US $ 34 bn in the 1992 financial year, although personnel costs actually account for 43 per cent of this. If NATO accounting procedures were adopted, Japan would have the third-largest defence budget in the world. The Defence Agency argues that Japan should maintain "a minimum basic defensive power", but the constitutionality and effectiveness of such forces have remained controversial.

The end of the Cold War has changed the nature of the defence debate in many countries, but in the Japanese case the more important catalyst was actually the 1990–91 Gulf crisis. Ironically, Japanese participation in UNTAC operations in 1992–93 has proved more crucial for changing the nature of the debate amongst outside observers about Japan's defence role.

UN peace-keeping legislation

The Iraqi invasion of Kuwait took the Japanese government by surprise and throughout the crisis it was forced to walk a delicate line, caught between criticism abroad that it was prepared to spend money but not shed blood and criticisms at home that it was merely toeing the US line. The Japanese government did give substantial financial contributions (US $ 13 bn) to the multi-national forces, but its efforts to contribute personnel through a number of different methods were stymied by parliamentary opposition.[26] Emboldened by a gradual but perceptible shift in public opinion during the course of the crisis, the Kaifu government decided to send Maritime SDF mine-sweepers to the Gulf in April 1991, after the fighting had ceased. This deployment, the first overseas since the SDF's establishment in 1954, was only possible because the SDF missions did not include any combat-related activities in which the "threat or use of force", banned under the Japanese constitution, might arise.

In the autumn of 1991 the LDP made a second attempt to introduce legislation to allow Japanese participation in UN peace-keeping operations (PKO) (the first had foundered during the Gulf crisis). Lacking an overall majority in the Upper House, Miyazawa and the LDP had to rely on the support of the Komeito and the DSP; this was achieved by tortuously negotiated minor amendments.[27] The SDPJ plumped for an all-or-nothing confrontation with this tripartite alliance, using the time-honoured delaying tactic of the "ox walk" in the Upper House deliberations and boycotting sessions and proffering the resignation of its members in the Lower House.

These tactics backfired, for the SDPJ's rigid approach did nothing to dispel doubts about its abilities to become a governing party. Public opinion polls throughout 1991–92, although inconsistent, generally reflected slowly growing public support for the SDF's limited participation in UN operations.

The passing of the PKO law in June 1992 provoked widely differing views abroad: the United States and many Western countries welcomed it as a sign of Japanese efforts to contribute to the new international order, while some neighbouring Asian countries, particularly China and the two Koreas, expressed concern that this was the beginning of an inevitable resurgence of Japanese military might.

Yet the PKO law is closely woven with restrictions. The maximum number of SDF troops which can be sent in response to UN requests for deployment is 2000, they can carry light firearms but these can only be used for self-defence, they must withdraw immediately if a cease-fire breaks down, and they are only allowed to conduct medical, refugee aid, transportation, infrastructural repair, election-monitoring and policing operations. As the price of its parliamentary support, the Komeito ensured that the SDF was not allowed to participate in any operations that might involve military action and the DSP insisted on mandatory Diet authorisation for each despatch that might involve military activities. In addition, the law has to be reviewed after three years. These restrictions, therefore, preclude the SDF from participating in UN operations such as those in the former Yugoslavia or Somalia or from joining actions such as those undertaken by the multinational forces in the Gulf War.

The appointment of a Japanese national, Yasushi Akashi, as head of the UN Transitional Authority in Cambodia (UNTAC) increased the pressure on Japan to contribute to that operation and in October 1992, for the first time since the end of the Second World War, Japanese ground troops left on an overseas mission. Subsequently, 600 SDF personnel and 75 policemen have been active in engineering and election-monitoring projects in Cambodia. Despite the deaths of two Japanese in Cambodia – one a policeman, the other a civilian volunteer – Miyazawa remained steadfast in refusing to withdraw the Japanese forces, although a cabinet member did visit UNTAC in Cambodia to argue for the Japanese being kept away from the danger areas as security deteriorated in the run-up to the May elections. To the Japanese government, the very high turn- out in the Cambodian elections was a welcome relief and justification for its efforts. The Japanese government has seen the Cambodian operation as the focus of its PKO activity; it turned down requests by the UN Secretary-General to contribute to the UN Somalian operation, though it has now sent a small unit to Mozambique. Paradoxically, by the time of the Cambodian elections in May 1993, most Asian countries had come to accept the Japanese presence there and Singaporean and Malaysian leaders, indeed, urged that any premature Japanese withdrawal would be a dereliction of duty.

Although the Diet discussions of the PKO bills were couched in legal and technical terms, the debate was really about a more fundamental issue: whether the Japanese could be trusted, or, indeed, trusted themselves, to participate in overseas military operations without becoming a militaristic power again. Two elements are crucial to answering this question, Japan's attitude to its past wartime actions, and the manner in which Japan is adapting its defence programme and philosophy to the post-Cold War world.

Coping with the past

The Japanese take for granted that the present cannot be understood apart from the past, but in their relations with their Asian neighbours they prefer not to dwell too much on the past. Indeed, every hint or insinuation about their past makes the Japanese wince, and they would rather concentrate on building new relationships. The Japanese tend to dismiss Korean, Chinese or other Asian reference to the past as either a tactic to secure concessions or an irrational obsession, without realising the degree to which other Asians genuinely feel that the Japanese have not owned up to their past aggressive behaviour in the way that the Germans have done over Nazism and the Holocaust.

The Japanese, through imperial statements or prime ministerial speeches, have moved towards some degree of reconciliation with their neighbours. But, as the recent controversy over Korean "comfort women" forced into sexual service for the wartime Japanese army have shown,[28] they tend to take two steps forward and one step back. Compensation for the "comfort women" has now become a diplomatic issue not just between Japan and South Korea but also between Japan and several other countries. Japanese insistence that in the South Korean case all such claims for compensation were settled in the 1965 Japan-South Korea treaties may be technically correct under international law, but does little to settle the psychological traumas involved or improve the state of the relationship. Japan now seems to be prepared to go further than just legal niceties and really face up to, and apologise for, its past actions against Koreans and other Asians. If the new coalition government is more forthcoming than past LDP governments, the relationships may be less strained by these kinds of issues.

Rethinking defence

The rapid changes in the international security scene have presented the Japanese with a dilemma. Just as the 1991–95 Mid-Term Defence Programme began – which had been predicated on the continued qualitative expansion of Soviet military capabilities in the Far East – the Soviet Union disintegrated. The 1992 annual Defence White paper was forced to admit that not only the future role of the SDF but also the medium-term basis of the Japanese defence build-up programme had to be re-evaluated. Changing threat perceptions, an emerging arms race coupled with fears of a power "vacuum" in East Asia, tightening domestic budgetary restraints, increasing US demands for burden-sharing and a new coalition government form a complex equation with a number of possible solutions.

Some LDP politicians, such as Ishihara, openly advocate scrapping the Japan-US security treaty and pursuing sustained rearmament. However, successive LDP cabinets, as argued above, have shown no inclination to abandon the US-Japan treaty and the new coalition cabinet, despite the presence of the SDPJ, is unlikely to want to do so, although it will no doubt wish to continue – and speed up – the process of discussing ways to adapt it to the new realities. Ironically, both Japanese officials and regional observers now contend that the treaty is actually one way of constraining any Japanese tendency towards military adventurism.

Public opinion surveys show a slowly growing percentage (though still a minority) in favour of revising the constitution, especially Article 9, to allow greater freedom for Japanese military activities (those in favour rose from 22 per cent in 1986 to 33 per cent by 1991). During 1992–93 two LDP faction leaders came out in support of revising the constitution, though Miyazawa strongly opposed it. In practice, amendment of the constitution is effectively precluded in the near future by the requirement for a two-thirds majority in both Houses of the Diet followed by a majority vote in a national referendum, none of which are possible in the current political situation. More likely, however, are increasingly "grey area" interpretations of what is possible under the existing constitution, in line with those used to justify the despatch of minesweepers to the Gulf in 1991 and the PKO law in 1992. In mid-1992 a special LDP sub-committee, headed by a younger politician who has subsequently become Hata's right-hand man in the Japan Renewal Party, argued that, even under the existing constitution, the SDF could participate in UN collective security actions, but this view was not accepted by the then LDP mainstream.

Some observers argue that Japan could even forsake its non-nuclear principles, specifically if North Korea succeeded in manufacturing a nuclear bomb (followed conceivably by South Korea), and itself develop nuclear weapons. Japan undoubtedly does have the technical capability to develop nuclear weapons should it wish to be so.[29] But, the "nuclear allergy", deriving from the scars of the 1945 atomic bombing of Hiroshima and Nagasaki (which, incidentally, still tend to make many Japanese think of themselves as the "victims" rather than the "aggressors" in the war), remains strong. The Japanese government's persistent refusal to be pushed into normalising relations with North Korea until satisfactory international inspections of North Korean nuclear facilities have taken place is characteristic of this concern. If it were to try to go down the nuclear path, Japan would be out of step not just with the United States, which would certainly resist strongly such a Japanese move, but also with the United Nations which is now increasingly concerned about preventing nuclear non-proliferation.

Domestic economic and political problems could further constrain defence expenditure, so that Japan would be forced to work out a new division of labour with the United States, and, indeed, with other Western and regional powers, while staying within the framework of the US–Japan security treaty. This is the most likely scenario. The Finance Ministry, at a time of tax revenue short-falls due to the recession, is arguing hard for further cuts in defence expenditure. Only after strong lobbying from the Defence Agency, did it agree to 1.95 per cent growth in the 1993–94 defence budget, the lowest ever recorded; future years are likely to be even tougher. The Finance Ministry will find an ally in the new prime minister, Hosokawa, who, while not supporting the more extreme defence-cutting demands of the SDPJ, clearly does want to look for some kind of "peace dividend".

CONTRIBUTION TO INTERNATIONAL ORDER

Successive prime ministers and foreign ministers have stressed that Japan will never again become a military power; despite the passing of the PKO law, a direct military role is still to be avoided. This means that Japan's contributions to the international order will continue to be non-military.

Overseas development aid (ODA) has long been Japan's primary instrument for contributing to the international order. In 1992, for the second year in succession, Japan was the largest aid supplier to the world, with US $ 11 bn. With US and European aid budgets likely to be under greater pressure in the coming years and the Japanese pledging themselves at the Tokyo G-7 Summit to provide US $ 70–75 bn over the next five years, Japan is certain to remain top of the OECD aid league-table in total value (though near the bottom for aid as a percentage of GNP).

However, the reliance placed on Japanese financial contributions, both by Japan and a host of recipient nations (which at the time of the Gulf crisis even included advanced Western nations), is disconcerting to both sides and only helps to perpetuate the image of Japanese "chequebook diplomacy". The Japanese, indeed, are showing signs of resentment and frustration at being taken for granted as a "treasury" for financial "bailing-out" operations, whether for the Rio Earth Summit, Cambodian reconstruction or the Russian and East European new democracies. However, the increasingly complex linkages between commercial, technological and politico-strategic issues in the post-Cold War world are actually providing other opportunities and means for Japan to contribute.

Global macro-economic co-ordination

Japan is, of course, one of three major actors in the international economy. It therefore shares with the other two, the United States and the EC, an interest in co-ordinating macro-economic policies so as to achieve sustained economic growth and financial stability. The very nature of global financial markets ensures the growing interdependence between the three: changes in fiscal or, especially, monetary policy by one do have an impact on the others. The three will remain deeply involved in international economic bargaining in the 1990s, although the rate of progress on economic and monetary union within the EC will affect how the triangle is weighted. The three actors have different ideas of the rules of the international trade game; Japan needs to play a part in trying to promote more convergence between them.

Japan does also have an interest in reaching a successful conclusion to the faltering Uruguay Round of the GATT. Although Japanese officials and businessmen have concluded that a successful conclusion to the whole package would, on balance, benefit Japan – not least in helping to contain US unilateralism – its offers have been disappointing. Like its predecessor, the new coalition government will tend to put domestic political considerations first. In private, politicians agree that concessions on opening up the rice market (one of the major outstanding issues for the GATT agriculture talks) will have to be made, but in practice, while rural votes are likely to play such a crucial part in the next election, they will be reluctant to make concessions, particularly while it is easier to blame the Europeans and the Americans for holding up a GATT settlement.

United Nations

The Miyazawa government took advantage of the heightened international interest in making better use of the United Nations after the Gulf war to lay out its own bid. Having secured its seventh two-year term in the rotating seat on the UN Security Council, Japan is now lobbying for its name to be struck from the list of "enemy nations" mentioned in the UN Charter and for a permanent seat on the Security Council. According to the Japanese ambassador to the United Nations, Japan aims to achieve that status within five years.

While there is considerable international sympathy for the deletion of Japan – and several other countries – from the "enemy" category, Japan has been disappointed, but not surprised, by the lack of enthusiasm from France and Britain for its permanent seat proposal. Germany, which has similar ambitions, is naturally supportive, but for Japan the most encouraging sign has been President Clinton's support of the idea. Since it will clearly take time to build up sufficient support for reforming the Security Council structure, Japanese officials are keen, as an interim measure, to draw together representatives of both the UN Security Council and the G-7 member countries into an ad hoc nine-member forum to discuss economic, political and security issues.

As part of its learning process on security matters, Japan has also been edging closer to both NATO and the CSCE. Senior Japanese diplomats attended a NATO seminar in 1990 and in 1992 Japan was granted "guest" observer status at CSCE, in part due to a belated recognition on the part of the Europeans that if Japan was to provide financial aid to Eastern Europe, as it has been doing through the G-24 mechanism, then it should also be involved in political discussions as well. Such dialogues are likely to continue without ever becoming too detailed.

Russian reconstruction

Japan shares with the United States and the Europeans a need to prevent the former Soviet republics from continuing to spiral downwards into deeper economic and political chaos, which could place unbearable strains on the global financial and economic system. Associated with this disintegration are residual nuclear weapon dispersement and nuclear power plant safety problems.

However, the Japanese continue to give paramount importance to recovering the disputed "northern territories". Although the government has begun to think more flexibly about separating into two stages the desired return of the four islands, they have found dealing with Russian President Boris Yeltsin no easier than with Soviet President Mikhail Gorbachev.[30] Yeltsin has already twice postponed visits to Japan (in September 1992 and May 1993) and on his visit to talk with the G-7 countries at the Tokyo Summit studiously avoided the territorial issue. While Russian domestic political difficulties were the primary reason for these postponements, the obvious Japanese reluctance to provide economic aid – the "yen for land" deal at its crudest formulation – also acted as a chiller.

The Japanese remain unimpressed by Western – and Russian – suggestions that economic assistance is vital to ensure Yeltin's survival. While the Japanese did agree to join in the new package of aid endorsed by the Tokyo G-7 Summit, they are moving towards a three-track strategy. Firstly, they are beginning to disburse aid to the former Soviet Central Asian republics, with which they have no territorial dispute. Secondly, they are concentrating aid to Russia on nuclear-related facilities, for fear of nuclear waste contamination of the air and seas around Japan. Thirdly, they are discussing with Russian economists ways in which the Japanese post-Second World War reconstruction experience may be relevant for Russia's own efforts.

Arms control and non-proliferation

Japan has become increasingly concerned about the expanded global trade in arms (not least by Russia) and the dangers of nuclear proliferation, especially with North Korea so close at hand. Some Japanese officials argue that Japan, because of its own ban on arms exports, should be the "natural leader" in international efforts to curb the arms trade. This is, indeed, one area where the Japanese have been quietly pushing ahead: Japan is providing all the funding and the secretariat for a new international group regulating the export of goods which could be used in nuclear-weapon development, it co-sponsored with the EC the establishment of a UN arms registry system, and led the G-7 into thinking about new co-ordinating frameworks.

The Japanese government also introduced, in April 1991, new guidelines for its ODA programme, whereby it will curtail its aid to countries which are guilty of "continuous and excessive military spending", have poor human rights records or export arms or weapon technology. However, aid officials admit that they have no well-defined criteria for these categories. Decisions will tend to be made on a case-by-case basis. Aid to Guatemala was suspended in April 1993 because of a military coup, but was not in the case of Peru in April 1992 when the president (of Japanese heritage) suspended the constitution for six months. China, the world's fourth largest arms exporter to the Third World, is a particularly difficult case for the Japanese. Aid negotiators are therefore switching from infrastructure projects, such as railways and ports which could be used by China for military purposes, to aid for the environment and urban development.

Development and environment

The Japanese are showing that their own experiences can be beneficial to other countries, of both the North and the South, in dealing with associated questions of development and the environment. Japanese economists are also becoming more assertive in challenging the orthodoxies of the World Bank and the International Monetary Fund. They have submitted reports to the World Bank which demonstrate the advantages of a governmental role in economic development.[31] Although they have by no means won the argument within the World Bank, other Western countries, in their own aid programmes, are beginning to take more account of the Japanese experience in establishing benchmarks of good governance and economic viability in the developing countries.

Japan learnt the hard way from its own environmental problems in the 1960s and 1970s; in the process it has developed both environmental monitoring equipment as well as anti-pollution technologies. As with the case of acid rain drifting across to Japan from China, environmental problems do not respect borders. Financial and technological pooling with countries of both the North and the South provides another role for Japan.

THE WAY FORWARD

Japan faces a troubled transition. Externally, the relatively stable, if often unpleasant, Cold War structures, which actually worked well for Japan, have disappeared. The international economic order is in a state of flux, too, as economic growth and technological development redistribute economic power and rebalance the relationships between companies, governments and regional groupings. Internally, the political structure, which pitted the dominant conservative LDP against a socialist opposition and which, despite the gradual emergence of several smaller non-socialist opposition parties, effectively survived throughout the Cold War era, has broken down. The split in the LDP is the first step in the restructuring of Japanese politics through gradual mergers of the current myriad of small parties into something closer to a two-party system, but with neither major party being "socialist" in orientation. Economically, the current recession is proving longer and more stubborn than most Japanese expected. Continuing restructuring will be a crucial test of Japanese companies' ingenuity, though it will doubtless be one with which once again most will prove capable of coping.

In the short term, Hosokawa's unprecedented coalition government – and its constituent parts – is going to be concerned more with positioning itself for the next election than pacifying external trading partners or contributing actively to new initiatives in the international arena. There are significant policy and personality differences within the coalition which will ensure that Hosokawa will not have an easy time pushing through even his own pet ideas on political reform. But the reordering and consolidation of existing parties, which the next election will bring, will also help to confirm the generational and attitudinal change in Japanese politics. In the medium term, Japan will emerge with a properly pluralistic political system and leaders more attuned to international arenas. This does not mean that external partners will find these new leaders mere carbon-copies of western-style leaders, but at least they will be better equipped to articulate and carry out policies.

In the short term, Japan will remain reactive and uncertain in playing a global role. Even on the regional level, Japan will try hard to keep a low profile. But, in the medium term, the incremental steps forward over the past few years can turn into the basis for more positive contributions to political and security matters, which will do more to balance up Japan's inevitably widespread economic involvement in regional and global affairs. A Japanese intellectual once said that Japan had a first-rate economy and third-rate politicians. Despite its current sluggishness, the Japanese economy is still fundamentally strong and the country is certain to remain a global economic leader throughout the 1990s. The challenge for the new generation of leaders such as Hosokawa and Kono is whether they can upgrade Japan's political leadership. The key to a different Japan – one playing a more active political role in the world – lies in their hands, but opening the door will be no easy task.

NOTES

[1] *Japan Times*, 8 May 1993.

[2] Aurelia George, "Japanese Interest Group Behaviour: An Institutional Approach" in J. A. A. Stockwin *et al*, *Dynamic and Immobilist Politics in Japan* (London: Macmillan, 1989), p. 120. See also Arthur Stockwin's own contribution to that volume.

[3] Brian Reading, *Japan: The Coming Collapse* (London: Weidenfeld & Nicolson, 1992), pp. 262–74.

[4] See Reinhard Drifte, *Japan's Foreign Policy* (London: Routledge for RIIA, 1990); Robert Scalapino, editor, *The Foreign Policy of Japan* (Berkeley: University of California Press, 1977).

[5] Ronald Dore, *Flexible Rigidities* (London: Athlone, 1986), pp. 12–58.

[6] *South China Morning Post*, 22 June 1993.

[7] This mode of thinking is explored in several of Ronald Dore's writings, especially "The Internationalisation of Japan", *Pacific Affairs*, Winter 1979–89.

[8] Seizaburo Sato, "Japan's World Order", in Irwin Scheiner, *Modern Japan: An Interpretive Anthology* (New York: Macmillan, 1974), pp. 12–17.

[9] See the discussion in Shiro Saito, *Japan at the Summit* (London: Routledge, 1990), especially chapters 1 and 11.

[10] Masahide Shibusawa, *Japan and the Asian Pacific Region* (London: Croom Helm, 1984), pp. 22–25.

[11] Nobutoshi Akao, editor, *Japan's Economic Security* (London: Gower, 1983), pp. 6–7.

[12] J. M. W. Chapman, R. Drifte, and I. M. Gow, *Japan's Quest for Comprehensive Security* (London: Pinter, 1983); S. Javed Maswood, *Japanese Defence* (Singapore: ISEAS, 1990).

[13] On the background to US-Japanese relations see Roger Buckley, *US-Japan Alliance Diplomacy, 1945–1990* (Cambridge: Cambridge University Press, 1992); Takashi Inoguchi and Daniel Okimoto, editors, *The Political Economy of Japan: Vol. 2, the Changing International Context* (Stanford: Stanford University Press, 1988).

[14] *Japan Times Weekly*, 20 January 1992.

[15] Kiyoshi Araki, *Japan's Security Policy in the Regional and Global Context* (London: RIIA Discussion Paper, 1991), pp. 9–11.

[16] *South China Morning Post*, 14 April 1993.

[17] Drifte, *op cit*, pp. 88–90. See also the comment by Mike Mansfield in *International Herald Tribune*, 2 March 1992.

[18] Laura Newby, *Sino-Japanese Relations* (London: Routledge, 1988), pp. 88–90.

[19] Masahide Shibusawa, Zakaria Haji Ahmad and Brian Bridges, *Pacific Asia in the 1990s* (London:

Routledge, 1991), chapter one; Susumu Awanohara, "Japan and East Asia: Towards a New Division of Labour", *The Pacific Review*, Vol. 2, No. 3 (1989), pp. 198–208.

[20] Dennis Yasutomo, "Nihon Gaiko to ODA Seisaku", *Kokusai Mondai*, March 1989, pp. 37–54.

[21] *Mainichi Shimbun*, 17 January 1993.

[22] Peter Drysdale, *International Economic Pluralism* (Sydney; Allen & Unwin, 1988), pp. 204–222; James Cotton, "APEC: Australia hosts another Pacific acronym", *The Pacific Review*, Vol. 3 (2), 1990, pp. 171–173.

[23] *Far Eastern Economic Review*, 25 July 1991. Miyazawa's refusal, while on an ASEAN tour, to endorse EAEC incensed Mahathir. *Yomiuri Shimbun*, 18 January 1993.

[24] Takashi Sugimoto, *The Dawning of Development of the Tumen River Area* (Tokyo: International Institute for Global Peace, 1992), pp. 1–17.

[25] Gaimusho, *Gaiko seisho: Heisei san-nen-ban* (Tokyo: Ministry of Foreign Affairs, 1992), pp. 71–73. A private advisory panel on policy towards the region in December 1992 recommended to the prime minister the European CSCE as possible model for Asian regional security frameworks. *Nikkei Weekly*, 28 December 1992.

[26] S. Javed Maswood, "Japan and the Gulf Crisis: Still searching for a Role", *The Pacific Review*, Vol 5, (2), 1992, pp. 149–55; Araki, *op cit*, pp. 32–37.

[27] Naoki Saito, *The Passing of the PKO Co-operation Law* (Tokyo: International Institute of Global Peace, 1992), pp 1–22.

[28] See Brian Bridges, *Japan and Korea in the 1990s* (Aldershot: Edward Elgar, 1993), pp. 133–136.

[29] Reinhard Drifte, *Japan's Rise to International Responsibilities* (London: Athlone Press, 1990), p. 28. Ambassador Ryukichi Imai, a nuclear scientist before he became a diplomat, however, has argued that Japan lacked the engineers, scientists, and technology; "by the time we had the know-how and started to build the arsenal, such arsenal would already be more than ten years obsolete". *US–Japan Policy Interactions on Arms Control and Disarmament During the Reagan–Nakasone Era* (Tokyo: IIGP, 1991), p. 11.

[30] Wolf Mendl, "Japan and the Soviet Union: towards a deal?", *The World Today*, November 1991, pp. 196–200; Leszek Buszynski, "Russia and Japan: the unmaking of a territorial settlement", *The World Today*, March 1993, pp. 50–54.

[31] Takashi Inoguchi, "Japan in Search of a Normal Role", in *Asia's International Role in the Post-Cold War Era: Part I* (London: IISS, Adelphi Paper No. 275, 1993), pp. 64–65.

FURTHER READING

There is an extensive literature on Japan's politics, economics and foreign policy now available in English.

Balanced studies of the political economy include J. A. A. Stockwin *et al*, *Dynamic and Immobilist Politics in Japan* (London: Macmillan, 1988) and Gary Allinson and Yasunori Sone, *Political Dynamics in Contemporary Japan* (Ithaca: Cornell University Press, 1993). The classic "revisionist" text is Karel van Wolferen, *The Enigma of Japanese Power* (London: Macmillan, 1989).

On the Japanese economy, general surveys include Bill Emmott, *The Sun Also Sets* (London: Simon and Schuster, 1989) and Kyoko Sheridan, *Governing the Japanese Economy* (London: Polity, 1993).

Of the recent surveys of Japanese foreign policy, Reinhard Drifte's *Japan's Foreign Policy* (London: Routledge, 1989) and Kathleen Newland, editor, *The International Relations of Japan* (London: Macmillan, 1990) give the broadest coverage.

Journals which either exclusively or frequently cover contemporary Japanese topics include *Pacific Review*, *Japan Forum, Far Eastern Economic Review*, *Journal of Japanese Trade and Industry*, *Japan Echo* and the *Japan Review of International Affairs*. Of the English-language newspapers published in Japan *The Nikkei Weekly* and *The Japan Times* are the most useful.

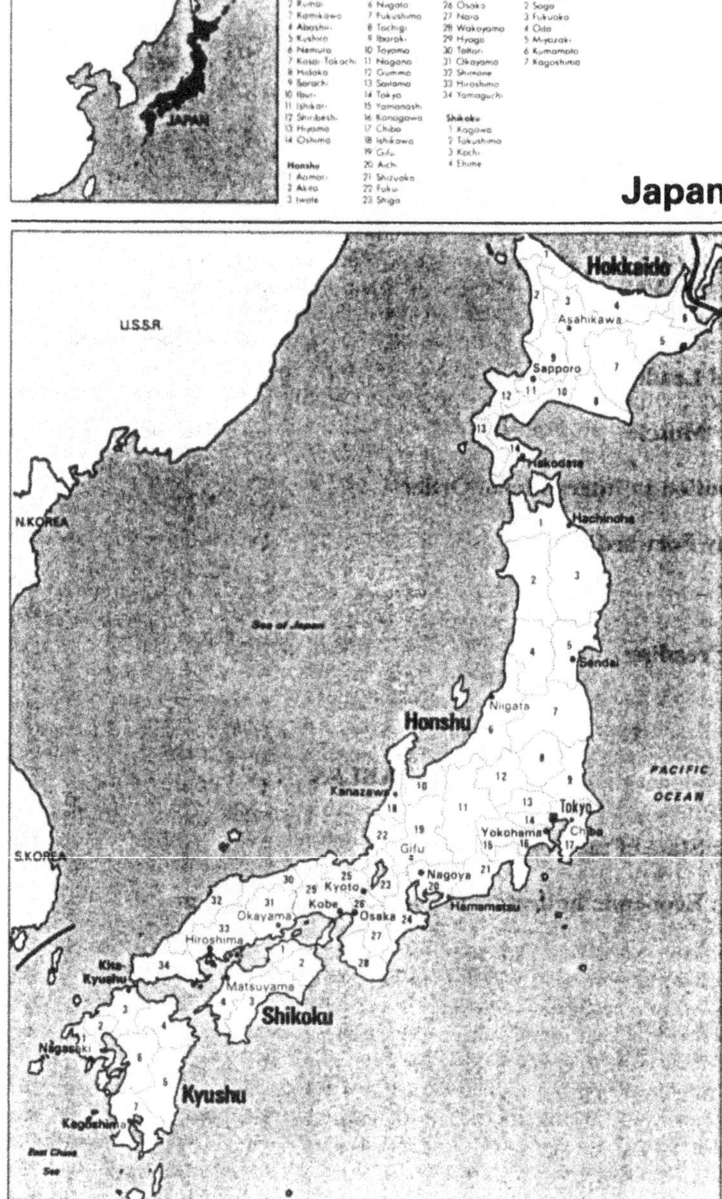

Map by courtesy of Control Risks Information Service

[9]

China's Coming "Revolution"

The dynamics of political change

David Goodman

Is a "revolution" in China imminent? The political future of the People's Republic of China [PRC] already seems uncertain and this could easily lead to dramatic change. Uncertainty results from both the personalist nature of China's politics and the reforms introduced since 1978. The possibilities for change derive not only from the reform process within China but also from events elsewhere, notably the collapse of communism in the Soviet Union and Eastern Europe, and the transformation of authoritarian regimes in East Asia.

A basic uncertainty in China's current politics is the transition to the post-Deng era. Deng Xiaoping may hold no formal position of power in the structures of the Chinese Communist Party [CCP] or the state, but he has remained the undisputed "paramount leader" since the start of the reform era in December 1978. Even in highly institutionalised political systems uncertainties about leadership may destabilise politics. In political systems such as that of the PRC, where politics seems determined by personalitites, the illness or ageing of the current leadership impose fairly obvious strains on political stability. At present there are concerns not only for Deng's health – with repeated rumours in the Japanese and Hong Kong press of his death – but for the health of others in the post-Mao leadership generation who together with Deng have been responsible for the reform era.

Concern about China's imminent generational change has been exacerbated by more substantial uncertainties about the form and content of politics which have been released by the process of reform itself. Although the CCP initiated reform measures at and after the Third Plenum of its 11th Central Committee precisely in order to provide more certainty to politics, in at least two ways reform has increased uncertainty. Since 1978 the CCP has actively encouraged wider political discussion on a range of issues that cannot but challenge its own position, even though that was certainly not its intention. For example, the role of the state in economics and society has been widely questioned, and become a major target of reform. The nature of "democracy" once regarded as a "bourgeois fallacy" is now also a legitimate subject for debate and seen as a worthy goal when correctly interpreted.

The once crystal-clear distinction between capitalism and socialism has become blurred, and not just at the level of ideology. The reforms it has initiated, particularly in economic policy, have created seemingly new social forces – most obviously, a whole range of new business people and entrepreneurs – that already seem to challenge the CCP's position. The CCP no longer has anything like a dominance of wealth, power and influence in society as it once did, let alone the monopoly associated with the era of the

Cultural Revolution and Mao's personality cult. In addition, reform China has been characterised by a high degree of economic regionalism, with an apparent decline in Beijing's ability to control the provinces.

The potential political consequences of economic regionalism have been a matter of no small concern to the leadership of the CCP. An important part of the CCP's claim to legitimacy has always been its ability to restore political unity after the early-20th century experience of warlordism. Events since mid-1989 in both China and the former communist party states of Eastern Europe have foregrounded the prospects of more cataclysmic change, including both the end of CCP rule and political disintegration. Time and again various leaders have either predicted that China might suffer a similar fate or argued that measures need to be taken to avoid such an outcome.

At the same time the rapid rate of growth of China's economy – approximately 9 per cent per annum in GNP through the 1980s and into the 1990s – that has now transformed China into one of the world's largest economies seems likely to have further consequences for social change and politics. Economic growth has been accompanied by a decline in the state sector's share of the economy. For example, by 1991 only about half the industrial output value of the PRC was being produced by the same sector. In contrast, most of the former communist party states of Europe have economies in which the state sector still massively predominates even in the post-communist era. Retail activities are virtually monopolised by the private sector which also accounts for just over a third of commercial activities.[1]

At first sight China's economy certainly seems to have developed some significant capitalist features. It may be somewhat far-fetched to expect China's capitalist development of the 1990s to give birth to democracy in precisely the same way that the emergence of capitalism in England and Western Europe is usually regarded as having led to democracy in the first half of the 19th century. However, it is reasonable to assume that rapid economic growth of the kind recently experienced in China is likely to produce pressures for political change. Elsewhere in East Asia during the last two years there would appear to be instructive and spectacular examples of this kind of interplay. South Korea and Taiwan have faced crises of systemic change after periods of economic growth based on authoritarian political systems.

China's development since the start of the reform era in December 1978 suggests then that dramatic change is not only likely for the 1990s, but already in great measure under way. The important questions for the future concern not so much the possibilities for significant change, but whether change comes violently or through some process of peaceful transformation; the nature of the forces driving the processes of fundamental change; and the shape of China's political system as its contemporary revolution unfolds.

China, in common with many newly and late industrialising societies, of which Japan is a clear example, has a propensity to cultivate a public belief in its own uniqueness at both official and popular levels. China, is certainly unique in many ways, as is every society. At the same time both the pressures it now faces and the newly emerging social forces it now contains have been experienced elsewhere, and those experiences may help explain the parameters of China's future development.

In particular, the three historical experiences already mentioned provide the essential perspectives that may be instructive to understanding the processes of social and political change in China, and their consequences. The experience of the USSR and Eastern Europe in the wake of the collapse of state socialism is the most obvious. Given 1989 and its aftermath rapid social change would seem to threaten both the continuation of communist party rule, and the ability of the CCP or the government to maintain the unity of the nation-state. With or without the formal dismissal of a ruling communist party, capitalist forms of development seem to have come to dominate both in Europe (East and West) and East Asia (communist and non-communist.) A second perspective that seems to have lessons for China's future is thus derived from the experience of modernisation in Western Europe and emphasises the emergence of capitalism and democracy. The third, which may both contradict and complement the earlier historical example of social change is the process of late development in East Asia which points to the relationship between economic growth and authoritarianism.

Discussion of political change in China usually concentrates almost exclusively on the personalities involved and factional interplay. Although speculative, such interpretations are extremely important, particularly in a political system that is highly personalist, as is the PRC. For example, Mao Zedong played a seminal role in the Cultural Revolution. Though some leaders of the CCP may like to argue otherwise, Deng Xiaoping played a critical and highly personal role in the start of the reform era and the evolution of reform policies. Deng may not have been the intellectual genius behind the ideas of economic reform, as Mao was with the Cultural Revolution, but without him governing coalitions would probably not have coalesced, and certainly not in the ways they have. On several occasions, most recently in May and June 1992 when his January 1992 "Journey South" reignited official enthusiasm for export and growth-oriented policies, he has intervened personally in the policy process to maintain the momentum of reform.

At the same time a focus on personalities and factions can only explain a limited amount about political and social change. China's reform era may have resulted from a change in national policy but its course and contents have not and could not be planned down to the fine detail in or by Beijing. Deng's "Journey South" in January 1992 largely provided political legitimacy and security for practice already well underway. In Hangzhou, for example, a large number of Chinese-foreign joint ventures had actually started in the year before Deng's "Journey South" was publicised, but their existence was not a matter of public discussion until such kinds of activities received Deng's imprimatur at the later date.

Fashions in explaining systemic political change can and do vary within a relatively short period of time not least because there can be no simple explanation. This study concentrates exclusively on the long-term social and economic causes of change rather than the short-term political catalysts. It starts by examining the key features of the reform era, and the ways in which political change has been related to the reform idea. It then considers each of the three readily available and apparently relevant paradigms of political change and examines the extent of and the ways in which they are applicable to China. It is of course relatively easy to identify the similarities between China's development since 1978 and each of the three models under consideration here. The parallels are what make them obvious perspectives for the attempt to interpret China's future in the first place. More difficult, because the exercise is necessarily somewhat open-ended, is the need to identify the differences between each model and China's experience.

CHINA IN REFORM

China's reform era is usually dated from the Third Plenum of the 11th Central Committee of the Chinese Communist Party which met formally in December 1978, and which had been preceded by a less formal Central Work Conference for about a month. Of course some features of the reform era, or necessary changes from the Mao-dominated era of China's politics, were already in place or underway. For example, although full diplomatic relations with the USA were not formally established until 1979, and were agreed at the time of the Central Work Conference of late 1978, nonetheless the way to substantive change in the PRC's foreign policy came when Nixon visited China and signed the Shanghai Communique in 1973. This rapproachement, more than the events of 1978, marks the start of the PRC's integration into the world economy.

At the same time, there was an element of conspiracy about the launch of the reform era that is often not fully understood. It is easy, by concentrating on the particularities of factional disputes during the last couple of years of Mao Zedong's life to interpret change only in terms of the interactions between the "Gang of Four" – Mao's wife and her three associates from Shanghai usually described as "radicals" – and their enemies. However, there was a more programmatic aspect to the opposition to the Gang of Four by the mid-1970s. That opposition had gathered round a group of veteran CCP leaders – many of whom had fought together before 1949 in the war against the Japanese in North China and later in the Civil War – and who had worked together in central party and government offices during the 1950s and early 1960s. Deng Xiaoping was an obvious leading figure in this group, as were Chen Yun, Peng Zhen and Bo Yibo. Though many had supported Mao Zedong and his initial ideas for fast development at the time of the Great Leap Forward, in the wake of that disaster they all came to revise their options and argue for less politically-determined and more economic growth-oriented policies. In the early 1960s they began to develop a new series of policy instruments, but were overtaken by the emergence of Mao Zedong's Great Proletarian Cultural Revolution of the late 1960s which also in almost every case cost them their positions of leadership. (Of the four mentioned, only Chen Yun remained in the leadership of the CCP at the height of the Cultural Revolution and even he was demoted.) By the time of Mao's death in September 1976 this group had coalesced into an alternative government, waiting in the wings, with a package of economic reforms they considered long overdue.

However, the image of conspiracy can be taken too far. Though the leadership had some idea of how it wanted to proceed, the strength of its unity lay in knowing what it had rejected rather than anything more positive. It was a reforming ministry, but in a very conservative way. Its *bête noir* was Mao's notion of "politics in command" as the organising principle for every aspect of policy in the PRC. Reform was explicitly founded on the principle that putting "politics in command" had severely undermined China's economic prospects, political stability and support for the CCP. The consequences of putting "economics in command" at the Third Plenum were necessarily more unknown and unknowable, not simply because the dictates of the market were eventually to take the CCP into new territory, but also because whilst the leadership had well-developed ideas on economic reform it was much less clear on the question of political reform.

The crisis facing the CCP leadership by the time of the Third Plenum was relatively straightforward. When it had come to power in 1949 it had been with the promise of economic modernisation and political stability, in contrast to the mass starvations, instability and lack of political unity that had characterised the first half of the century. Almost 30 years later the CCP's record on both was considerably tarnished. Though there had been economic growth and even at times increased prosperity, particularly during the early 1950s, for some 20 or more years the economy had virtually stagnated. For example, average wages had not increased from 1957 to 1977, and there had been occasions in between (as during the early 1960s) when economic crises led once again to famine and starvation.

Although political instability after 1949 was of a different kind to that which existed before, it was none the less real. From 1949 to the late 1970s there was a change in the basic developmental policies being implemented by the CCP on average every four or five years. Every time the general political direction changed so did the organisational forms of the state and the personnel who were responsible for the implementation of policy. In addition, both the Great Leap Forward of the late 1950s and the Cultural Revolution of the late 1960s were deliberately destabilising attempts by Mao to bring about China's transformation in line with his ideas. This lack of long-term stability undoubtedly helps to explain the relative lack of economic performance. At the same time from the 1960s on, elsewhere in East Asia countries with many less obvious advantages were transforming themselves into "tiger economies".

Economic reforms

As various leaders emphasised at the Third Plenum, the CCP had to start to deliver on its promises if it wanted to stay in power. It faced a crisis of confidence which threatened to undermine its position, and the policies that followed were designed to ensure economic growth and political stability, and to restore its legitimacy. The key economic reforms were to be more far-reaching than simply the introduction of market forces into a command economy. Following the obvious example of its East Asian neighbours China was to embark on an export-led growth strategy. In addition there was to be structural reform of the state economy: the rural collective economy was basically to be dismantled; local government was to disengage itself from enterprise management; and decentralisation was to be a guiding principle in both government and economic management.

Two early reforms that clearly signalled a break with the recent past were rural decollectivisation and the establishment of the Special Economic Zones. In the early 1960s and at a time of severe economic crisis those who were later to become the post-Mao reformers had first proposed the "household responsibility system" as a way of encouraging rural initiative in the wake of the failure of the Great Leap Forward and not least in order to meet the massive shortfall in food production. Though it was obviously popular it soon fell foul of Mao's collectivist vision for China. After Mao's death and even before the Third Plenum, which approved the re-introduction of individual household production, a number of local leaders had experimented with similar systems in order to increase rural productivity. Within two years the rural sector was decollectivised and the boom in the agricultural economy provided the basis for further economic reform.

The first Special Economic Zone [SEZ] was established shortly after the Third Plenum, in Shenzhen on the border with Hong Kong, to play a key role in the internationalisation of China"s economy. The SEZ was designed as an area of foreign investment with privileged and preferential economic regulation, particularly targeted at the fast-developing economies of Chinese East Asia: Hong Kong and Taiwan. Thus Shenzhen was followed in the early 1980s by SEZs in Zhuhai, also in southern Guangdong and oriented towards Hong Kong; and Shantou and Xiamen, the closest mainland areas to Taiwan. Later still an SEZ was established on Hainan Island when it became a province in 1988. The intention was not simply to attract general foreign investment but more specifically the new technologies that China lacked in return for raw materials and cheap labour. At the same time, the CCP leadership hoped to limit the impact of such internationalisation by confining wider foreign influence, as for example on value change, to the area of the SEZ. The SEZ marked a significant break with the recent past not simply because it was part of the internationalisation of China's economy, but also because the CCP's nationalist origins had led it from very early on to oppose the enclaves of foreign influence and extra-territoriality that existed in China before 1949.

Political reforms

Political reforms were designed both to support the drive for economic modernisation and together with the fruits of economic growth to restore the CCP's legitimacy. They resulted from the CCP's critique of its own past practices after the mid-1970s initiated at the Third Plenum and which culminated in the passing of a "Resolution on certain questions in the history of our party since the founding of the People's Republic of China" at the Sixth Plenum of the 11th Central Committee in June 1981. That process highlighted the lack of democracy, political uncertainty and instability, and the behaviour of cadres whose only motivation seemed to be the pursuit of personal power and privilege. Solutions were sought in an appeal to democracy; recognition and acceptance of partial interests, in both economics and politics; an emphasis on rules and regulations; and an attempt to ensure the abilities and virtue of the cadre force.

The problem for the CCP in initiating reform of any kind, but particularly political reform, is that it has almost no room for manoeuvre and runs the risk of creating a revolution of rising expectations, which it cannot meet. The CCP wants to reform the system it has created but still retain control: to give in to external demands but still to control the extent to which it meets those demands and their results. Nowhere is this problem clearer than in the CCP's appeal to democracy, not least because its meaning was ill-defined when reform started. At the time of the Third Plenum, even the CCP leadership, and including Deng Xiaoping, was prepared to talk of democracy as almost the unfettered will of the people. However, within a few months as debate became wide-ranging and possibly CCP-threatening, then the appeal to democracy became an appeal to "socialist democracy" with the intention to make the party-state system being renovated by the CCP work better.

The recognition of partial interests is perhaps the most interesting of reforms for a CCP which previously brooked no qualification to its monopoly of political power. It was seen at its most obvious in the new economic policies of the 1980s where while the prospect of overall economic growth was held out to the population as a whole, the individual was positively encouraged to take the initiative and responsibility in order to amass personal wealth. However, the political consequences of the CCP no longer claiming omnipotence or omniscience are equally as important since it now, albeit in a limited way, encourages the articulation of interests outside its control, as for example demands for better working conditions or higher social status.

In the 1980s the democratic and legal forms that had previously been deliberately subordinated to the CCP's political control were revitalised. The resultant political reforms did not provide an independent judiciary or a total separation of party and state, but they did provide a large measure of regularisation that had earlier been missing. Civil and criminal codes were passed, greater distinction between the executive and representative functions of government work were made and given organisational form. It became respectable again, and even desirable, to be a lawyer; and regular general elections – direct elections to county level people's governments – have been held since 1979.

The final set of political reforms have been directed at improving the performance of cadres. The critique of past practices targeted the excessive personal and institutional concentration of authority, the lifelong tenure of leadership and various abuses of privilege. The greater distinction between party and government activity has assisted in combating the over-concentration of political power but more significant has been a set of policies designed to ensure that the leading cadres of the 1980s and 1990s are younger, better educated and more specialised than their predecessors. These policies have been implemented with a great deal of success in a relatively short period of time. For example, the average age of provincial leaders and ministers has dropped considerably, and most are now college graduates, whereas even 10 years ago it was common to find few with any formal education beyond the most rudimentary. However, the real impact of such reforms is harder to gauge. As with the introduction of laws and regulations and other structural changes the test is in the manner of their operation, and a new political culture undoubtedly takes time to develop.

Political change was an integral part of the reform process – designed to ensure stability and sustained economic modernisation, as well as to restore the legitimacy of the CCP – but it does not automatically follow that the CCP has been able to manage that process exactly as it would like. The CCP has no blueprint for reform, and some of the developments of the 1980s were clearly unforeseen either in kind or degree. The most obvious example was the popular demonstrations in Beijing during April, May and June of 1989 when the CCP leadership was clearly unsure how to react. Less dramatic but potentially more serious for the future is the scale of economic regionalism that has emerged with reform and the growth of China's new rich.

THE COLLAPSE OF COMMUNISM IN EASTERN EUROPE: POPULAR PROTEST AND DISINTEGRATION

Two of the least intended, or at least relatively unforeseen consequences of economic reform, have been the increase in popular protest and the dramatic emergence of economic regionalism. The experience of Eastern Europe and the then Soviet Union in and after 1989 suggests that popular protest can overthrow ruling communist parties, and that when the communist party abdicates there is a further danger not only of political instability, but also of disintegration. Misleading as this picture may be, it is a fairly common series of assumptions that the examples of the USSR, Yugoslavia and Czechoslovakia provide little evidence to contradict.

The assumption of parallel development between the PRC and the former USSR has a fairly obvious basis. These were the two models of communist development, with substantial economies and populations, and heirs to imperial traditions. Indeed, in 1989 it even seemed to some for a while that events in China were leading a near-worldwide revolution against ruling communist parties. Not surprisingly, the events of 1989 and after in Eastern Europe have led many Western commentators to suggest that Russia's most recent past is China's future, and to predict not only the end of CCP rule and the PRC, but also the political disintegration of China into a number of smaller political systems.

Undoubtedly communist party rule created similar political and economic structures in the USSR and the PRC to some considerable extent. In the early 1950s and despite its recent past of guerrilla war, the CCP adopted wholesale many of the characteristic institutions of Stalinism along with aid and assistance from the USSR. Formatively, these included not only the common economy and its planned operation, but basically its unbalanced growth strategy which emphasised the development of heavy industry.

Differences between USSR and PRC

However, there always were significant differences between the structures of communism in the USSR and the PRC. During the 1980s these differences widened with radically different processes of reform, though both the CCP and the CPSU were concerned with reinforcing their legitimacy. Moreover, the reform process in the USSR demonstrated parallels and lessons to be learnt, and the CCP leadership itself is extremely conscious of the impact developments there may have on the PRC. Early in 1991, Deng Zhian (son of one of the more conservative-minded elders, Deng Liqun) penned a restricted circulation report on the possible impact of changes in the USSR. More concretely, in November 1991, central government was reported to have sent additional troops to Xinjiang because it was concerned about the demonstration effect of the declarations of independence by the Islamic former Soviet republics on the other side of the border.[2]

Communist party rule in the PRC has several notable features which it does not share with the former USSR. The most obvious is that it came about as the result of an indigenous communist movement, struggling for power through popular mobilisation for some 28 years, two civil wars, and war with a foreign invader. One result is that the CCP's nationalist and popular base of support has always been greater than that enjoyed in the USSR. This does not mean that the Chinese are not alienated from the CCP (some clearly are) but it does mean that disenchantment is a slower process and the party's support less ephemeral.

Economic improvements and industrial reform

Popular support for the CCP has also been strengthened by the performance of the Chinese economy, both immediately and over the longer term. Unlike the European experience of communism and despite its relative failure to deliver on economic modernisation before the late 1970s, the CCP has not presided over a long declining economic base but has brought considerable tangible improvements to the daily life of the general population. In fact there has been a general rise in the standard of living since before 1949. The successes are not as great as has sometimes been claimed but they are real enough, particularly in improved food consumption and housing, the provision of daily necessities and health care.

More spectacularly, during 1979–82 the CCP presided over a major re-orientation of industrial policy. This reform perhaps more than any other single factor explains why the events of 1989 represent different kinds of turning points for communism in China and Eastern Europe. A major limiting factor to reform in communist party states was always going to be the power, politically as well as economically, of the heavy industrial sector that lay at the heart of the Stalinist command economy. The effective start of the reform era in China was the successful attempt that immediately followed the Third Plenum to divert additional investment into the development of light and consumer industries. In the event the amount of additional investment was not phenomenally large – only about 3 per cent or 4 per cent of GNP on most current estimates – but it was enough to substantially alter the structure and growth pattern of the economy. Essentially through the exercise of political will, a small net transfer of resources broke the nexus of power that in other communist party states bound cadres, planners and state enterprises together in a situation of mutual despondency, all seeing the need for reform but unable to bring it about. Quite apart from the effect of this change on economic development, it has resulted in the emergence of a genuinely consumer-oriented retail market and hence social and political support not only for reform but also the CCP.

Social and political protest

Economic reform led to social problems and even political protest in the 1980s which have continued into the 1990s, but these have resulted from a rapid increase in the standard of living and rising expectations which have been largely unsatisfied. Basically such problems are the side-effects of economic growth and development rather than the economic stagnation and decline characteristic of the USSR, and are thus more likely to be directed at a specific government rather than the whole structure of the state itself. Even before the Beijing demonstrations of April to June 1989 such manifestations had become if not commonplace certainly not unknown on the streets of the capital.

In the mid-1980s Beijing bus drivers went on strike on a number of occasions for higher pay. A central cause was a hangover from the old command economy in which taxi and bus drivers would have been allocated such work on demobilisation from the People's Liberation Army. At the time there was basically no difference in pay or work conditions between the two. However, with reform taxi drivers were soon in a position to work more if not exclusively for themselves and certainly to earn more if they chose. Bus drivers had no such opportunities.

1988 and early 1989 saw extreme popular fears about inflation that led to runs on banks and fairly wild consumer shopping sprees, all of which contributed to the demonstrations of April to June 1989. Throughout the 1980s and into the 1990s a major problem for the CCP, and a major source of social tension, has been that urban and rural populations have basically opposed interests. Peasants have wanted price reform on all goods, especially agricultural products, and a free market for their produce. Workers in cities were more concerned about the inflationary effects of price reform on foodstuffs. In May 1993 this potential impact of reform remained the most important concern of most city dwellers in a number of opinion polls, well ahead of other concerns such as whether incomes were keeping pace with inflation or social unrest.[3]

By any standard but particularly by comparison with the former USSR and the communist party states of Eastern Europe the population of China is not highly educated, literate or urbanised. The Eastern European states had traditions of wide public participation in politics, and indeed of democracy even during the years of communist party rule. China's intellectual and political traditions are very different. Confucian philosophy stresses duties rather than rights; there is no notion of civil society; and the cultural tradition is fundamentally conservative looking back to a mythical golden age of harmony when there was limited political participation.

Economic regionalism

Economic regionalism certainly has been a major result of the reform process in China. The development of the southern provinces, Guangdong and Fujian, bordering Hong Kong and facing Taiwan respectively, has been quite spectacular through the 1980s and into the 1990s and has caught the international public imagination. It is an example which other regions – notably the East China provinces of Jiangsu, Zhejiang, and Shandong and Liaoning in the Northeast – are rapidly emulating, and indeed China's growth into the world's largest economy sometime early next century will be based on the development of such additional regional economic bases. However, a necessary corollary of this development is that all provinces, and not just the highest economic performers, now have more control over their own activities. One consequence has been that there are opportunities for provinces to engage in a certain amount of mercantilist behaviour and local protectionism, particularly at times of plan formulation when such actions can be used to extract promises from central government. This would seem to have been the case in the early 1990s when the Eighth Five Year Plan was being drafted and there were complaints aired in the official press about the emergence of provincial "feudal economies."[4]

No nationalities problem

Nonetheless, there is little reason to believe that the borders of provinces, or for that matter the new economic regions, in general represent the fault lines in China's political system. The PRC's regional politics are not and have not been the same as those of the former USSR. The disintegration of the USSR was essentially determined (paradoxically) by Stalin's constitution and its creation of constituent republics. Some, though not all, of these were previously existing political systems, but all were based on a dominant or sizeable nationality grouping. With notable exceptions, the PRC's division into provincial-level units is not based on the same nationality principle. The exceptions are the Autonomous Regions of Tibet, Xinjiang, Inner Mongolia, Guangxi and Ningxia.

A further key difference is the scale of the so-called minority nationalities' populations. Almost half of the USSR were not Russians, and in many of the Soviet republics non-Russians were in the majority. In the PRC only some 6 per cent of the total population are non-Han (non Chinese) peoples. Many, including most of the largest group (the Zhuang, of whom there are about 15m) are so well assimilated that their identification as a minority has itself become a source of discrimination at times. Outside Tibet, Turkestan (Xinjiang) and Inner Mongolia, non-Han peoples are frequently in the minority even in their dedicated areas of self-government.

Racial, ethnic, religious and political divisions – some of them with extremely long and violent histories – within the USSR were to a considerable extent institutionalised in its political structure, and certainly in its partition into constituent republics. Once central control weakened, unity almost necessarily began to be threatened. Where a previous political independence was still within living memory, as was the case with the Baltic States, the process of separation proved swift and undeniable.

Regardless of the CCP's ability to maintain a firm central control, the conditions for a USSR-style political disintegration to occur generally in the PRC do not exist. Though there are clear and important provincial differences in China, for the most part the dominant "state idea" remains that of China. There may, as in South China generally, and Guangdong in particular, be fierce local pride and an attitude of resisting interference from the capital, but these are necessary folk-myths and not a coherent desire for political separation.

On the other hand, it is entirely possible to see that movements for political separation in both Tibet and Xinjiang (and possibly, but less likely, Inner Mongolia) may well develop. The crucial difference is that there is, and has been for some time, a separate consciousness and political identity, which in both Tibet and Xinjiang has developed movements for independence in various ways. The demonstration effect of political distinegration in the USSR is not just an imaginary threat, as the repeated upheavals of the early 1990s in Zinjiang bear ample witness.

THE WESTERN EUROPEAN EXPERIENCE: CAPITALISM AND DEMOCRACY

Despite the huge historical and cultural distance between early 19th century England and late 20th century China there may well be similarities in the relationship between economic development and political change. Although the relationship is often oversimplified, the emergence of capitalism did create a new class of capitalists who exerted pressure for political reform and eventually democratisation. China's growth since the late 1970s has created large numbers of new rich. However, it is less clear that China's new rich are capitalists, or indeed if the concept of capitalism is even appropriate to describe the development of China's economy, and whether democracy is in fact a goal.

The impression is easily conveyed of a China that has gone or is going capitalist. The introduction of the market has dramatically altered both economic management and the business of government. Slowly but surely China appears to be developing institutions that are usually considered necessary parts of the infrastructure of capitalism, including credit and banking facilities, stock exchanges and commodity markets. Moreover, the impact of reform seems to have shifted economic wealth out of the state sector and into private hands. The 1980s and 1990s have seen the relative decline of the state sector's share of the economy, and dramatic increases in the collective, private and foreign-involved sectors.

Changes in the economy

State sector involvement in service, retail and commercial activities (except for financial services) is minimal and largely confined to the industrial economy. Even the state sector's share of industrial output has fallen. For example, in 1980 the state sector produced 76 per cent of the gross value of industrial output. By 1991 this had fallen to 53 per cent, and according to official estimates is likely to drop still further to 27 per cent by the year 2000. In contrast, the collective sector of the economy has grown from 24 per cent of the gross value of industrial output in 1980 to 36 per cent in 1991, and is targeted at 48 per cent for the end of the century. The private sector, which was virtually non-existent in 1980, in 1991 was responsible for 6 per cent of the gross value of industrial output and is expected to reach 13 per cent by the year 2000.[5]

Of course there are some senses in which China's economic development can and should be described in terms of capitalism. Perhaps the most important of these is that whatever the form and content of economic development in China it is clearly the process of modernisation which occurred in Western Europe and North America during the 19th century that provides its motivation. Not just technology but also ideas on management and economic organisation have been copied and adopted in a variety of ways. Sometimes the transfer of values can seem very bizarre. For example, one would-be industrialist in East China had money to invest and was looking for a product to develop. At the time he was reading a novel by Graham Greene in translation and came across one of the characters in that novel using a food-processor. Never having seen a food-processor he started investigating and eventually began to manufacture them himself.[6]

Certainly, the problems and difficulties experienced by governments, employers and the workforce are often very reminiscent of the experience of capitalist development elsewhere. Rapid urbanisation has accompanied economic growth and industrialisation with much rural land being switched from agricultural to industrial and other uses. Less than half the rural workforce is now officially estimated to be engaged in agricultural production, and there is said to have been the transformation of about 100m people off the land into a permanent migratory and transient workforce in the cities. Enterprises in the richer East China and in the south recruit their workforces from the young in the poorer parts of West and North China, pay them low wages and provide little if any health and welfare support. Equally, many of the new entrepreneurs do behave like earlier western caricatures of capitalists. Thus many say they do not provide their imported female workers with pension schemes, workers' or health insurance. The reasons given are that the women are young, have no thought of pensions, do not get ill, and in any case will leave when they become pregnant.

The new rich

China's new rich – the new social categories enriched by economic growth in the 1980s and 1990s – can be very rich indeed. One such is Chen Jinyi, an industrialist and property developer in the Shanghai-Hangzhou area, who has an asset wealth in excess of some 100m yuan Renminbi [RMB], and an annual income of 10m yuan RMB.[7] Chen emerged spectacularly into the public limelight with his "fire-sale" purchase of six bankrupt state sector factories in Shanghai in October 1992.[8] Chen, who was only born in 1960, started off by raising bees and making honey, managing to save about 10,000 yuan RMB in three years, and diversifying into textiles, and later soft drinks. He now heads a large corporation employing 2,000 people all of which has been developed to date from his personal assets but which is now considering going public on the Shanghai Exchange. It covers a number of subsidiary companies including a joint venture in textiles with a Taiwan investor and joint investments in property development with a number of local government authorities. By comparison the average annual income for the country remains under 2,000 yuan RMB, though the average urban worker's wage is about 250–300 yuan RMB a month or as much as 4,000 yuan RMB a year with bonus payments and other emoluments. An established industrialist or manager with a few hundred employees in an enterprise can expect to have an annual income of about 20,000 yuan RMB.

However, wealth alone is not a sufficient indicator of either capitalism or a capitalist class. The separation of state and society and particularly the independence of capitalists from the state are usually held to be key characteristics of capitalism, especially in its European and American manifestations, and important factors in the development of democracy. Whilst it seems reasonable to regard China's recent economic development as a form of capitalism, not least because of capitalism's motivating influence, it is clear that China's new capitalists and indeed the processes of capitalism are anything but separate from the state. On the contrary, and despite the evidence that the state sector's importance has declined, the state has played a central and continuing role in China's capitalist revolution.

Continued influence of the party-state system

Official descriptions of the structure of China's economy in terms of the state, collective, private and foreign-involved sectors can be misleading. The collective sector has remained part of the state economy. Although it has always been surrounded by an ideological justification that relates to its ownership either by a locality or by the workers in the enterprise, it is more accurate to regard the collective sector as that part of the state economy run by or associated with local government and not governed by the state plan. The state sector is that part of the state economy which is governed by the state plan.

Since the early 1980s the distinctions between the state, collective, private and foreign-involved sectors, which theoretically relate to systems of ownership, have become extremely attenuated. The collective sector in particular has become home to all kinds of activity. Under the imperative of reform, state sector enterprises have decentralised their activities and established subsidiary companies, but the latter are registered as collective enterprises. Private enterprises once they become larger, more technologically sophisticated, and economically successful almost invariably become collective enterprises, not least because the financial and tax environment is so superior. Even smaller less successful private companies want to register as collectives for similar reasons. Local government accepts approaches and suggestions for a degree of co-operation and collective registration because it, too, is becoming market-oriented.

The result of all these trends is a very heterogenous collective sector but one which nonetheless maintains strong links with both the state economy and the party-state system. Indeed, the continued influence of the party-state system permeates the economy and not only through the agency of local government. On all the available evidence a large proportion of the private economy "piggybacks" the state economy. The patterns of economic interaction, notably supplies and distribution, remain those established by the state economy. Entrepreneurs are often state employees who pay for the privilege of being allowed unpaid leave and to maintain their pension and other welfare entitlements not available outside the state sector. Moreover, as is only to be expected the CCP has made a determined and successful effort to recruit the new entrepreneurs, with only a short hiatus in that process during the second half of 1989 and into 1990.

Development of democracy

Under such circumstances it would be remarkable to find the new entrepreneurs articulating any demand for regime change of any kind, let alone a Western-style democracy, and there is no evidence to suggest that is the case. On the contrary, at this stage – as one might expect with a continually rising market – most of the energy of the new entrepreneurs is concentrated on making money. Moreover, the attraction of Western ideas, even of capitalism, must be kept in perspective. Throughout the 20th century those seeking change in China have articulated a common love-hate relationship with the West. The fruits of Western capitalism are attractive, but for the Chinese political nation the objective is a fundamentally Chinese modernisation, and for many the CCP still represents the best hope of achieving that nationalist goal.

Some Chinese intellectuals have flirted with Western ideas of democracy since the end of the 19th century, but it cannot be said that notions of democracy or even civil society have ever developed strong foundations. For the most part when democracy was spoken of in the PRC before 1989 the meaning was either that of "socialist democracy" – perfecting state socialism – or the "small democracies" – freedom of choice in work, home and marriage. Despite such symbolism as the "Goddess of Democracy" modelled on the Statute of Liberty which appeared in Tiananmen Square in May, the demonstrations of 1989 did little to develop a new discourse or build towards civil society. However, the 1989 movement could now develop its own mythology which may well play a role in China's political future. There is a foundation for the awareness of democracy that did not exist before and which may develop, particularly with increased exposure to the rest of the world.

LATE DEVELOPMENT IN EAST ASIA: GROWTH AND AUTHORITARIANISM

Although the Western European experience of capitalist development seems to hold few direct lessons for China's political future, the East Asian example may be more relevant. Confucianism – or some similar cultural phenomenon – is often said to be the key factor which explains the economic success of Japan, South Korea, Taiwan, Hong Kong and now China. While common cultural factors cannot be totally dismissed they must also be kept in perspective. If Confucianism really had been the key determinant then Vietnam and Korea, the most Confucianist of states at the end of the 19th century, would have modernised before Japan. On the other hand it is clear that feelings of affinity amongst the countries and economies of East Asia have been a major factor in development since the 1960s. Certainly the success of other economies in East Asia was a powerful influence on the CCP leadership's decision to reform in the 1970s.

East Asian economic development can be regarded as a form of late capitalist development in which – as with Germany and Japan in the 19th century – the state plays a leading role. Late developers have the obvious added advantages of being able to draw on the earlier examples and experiences of their predecessors. They do not need initially to develop their own technologies, particularly if their economies are sufficiently internationalised, for these can be imported. In addition, development strategies focus on production for the export market with appropriate measures of protectionism.

Economic growth is linked inextricably with an authoritarian political system which is able to direct and mobilise resources to the national goal of modernisation. As the economy develops and social complexity increases then the state has to adapt to internalise the new social forces it creates. However, the experience of South Korea, Taiwan and even Japan within the last 12 months suggests that such transformations of regime can occur peacefully, in contrast to the violent 19th century revolutions that marked the political economy of change in Western Europe. It is even arguable that in South Korea, Taiwan and Japan a change of regime has occurred without fundamentally threatening the state and still leaving its authoritarianism intact.

A nationalist goal

The usefulness of regarding China as an example of East Asian late capitalism is fairly clear, not least to the leadership of the CCP. Since the late 1980s the CCP has promoted an image of China precisely in that mould, with an emphasis on successful economic modernisation and authoritarianism as somehow more "Chinese" than the chaos and lack of social harmony that is bound to result from Western-imported democracy. Newspaper and journal articles, as well as films and television programmes have internalised the message to a high degree, and there can be little doubt that such instinctively reactive nationalism strikes strong popular resonances. The notion of an exclusive "Chineseness" has even spread to the attempt by the PRC State Education Commission, the equivalent of a ministry of education, to institute an international Chinese language standard, taught in "traditional Chinese ways".

From the perspective of East Asian late capitalism it seems possible that the PRC's political future might involve a slow and gradual transformation in a similar fashion to the development of politics in Taiwan and South Korea. Certainly this was a common view of China's political future among Western commentators before June 1989,[9] and there has been some evidence since of the kinds of processes that might be expected. For example, the decentralisation of both economic management and government has been matched to some extent by the evolution of the CCP's activities. CCP organisation is now extremely localised, though it is a moot point whether its real strength locally is as much political as social. One reason the new industrialists are keen to join is the function of the local CCP as a meeting point, much in the same way that Rotary and Lions Clubs operate elsewhere.

Decentralisation

However, China's experience is significantly different to its East Asian late capitalist neighbours in ways that may well influence the political consequences of social and economic change. Its size is a fairly obvious but frequently overlooked difference. China is massively larger than elsewhere and this has always created different problems for political control and economic direction. Even during the period of greatest Soviet influence China had a higher degree of decentralisation: policies were rarely set centrally with no room for local adaptation. Economic regionalism, entailing a high degree of local variation in national policy and even local regulation, is well developed in the south and east and will increase with economic growth. Federal solutions seem to be emerging in practice in the sense that central and provincial-level governments are informally reaching agreements about areas of responsibility. However, a legal federalism is not an acceptable political solution in the near future because of the associations with both feudalism and warlordism.

China's size and regionalism are also significant because of the role it consequently comes to play in East Asia. China is so big that only a relatively small growth, such as occurred during the 1980s, has created a huge magnet of attraction of investment in the region that adds an extra dimension to international relations in East Asia. Moreover, the economic regions that have developed within the PRC, are also becoming increasingly economically integrated with other specific parts of the East Asia region. Thus, Guangdong should perhaps for some time have been regarded as Greater Hong Kong;

Fujian's industrial development is almost three-quarters sourced from Taiwan; Japan and Taiwan investors are particularly active in Shanghai, Zhejiang and Jiangsu Provinces; and Korean involvement is significant in both Shandong and Northeast China. It has even been suggested that this aspect of China's economic development is a deliberate ploy by MITI to ensure that any possible future conflict between China and Japan is either minimised or resolved to Japan's advantage.[10]

The Overseas Chinese

The Overseas Chinese are the major vehicle for the PRC's economic integration with East Asia and the existence of that diaspora also marks a further significant difference from East Asian late capitalism. There are some 55m ethnic Chinese throughout the Asia Pacific region, with an additional unknown number of people of Chinese descent. The existence of Taiwan and Hong Kong has clearly influenced the way the PRC's economy has developed, and are likely to play a central role in the future of domestic as well as international politics. Of course, Hong Kong will become part of the PRC in 1997, but in the meantime the process of adaptation continues as much from the PRC side as from the Hong Kong side. In addition, meeting the challenge presented by both Hong Kong and Taiwan is something that concerns the CCP and generally has driven change in the PRC since the late 1980s. An obvious example is the way the popular music scene has been drastically liberalised through the introduction of Hong Kong "Canto-pop" and Taiwanese popular music. One of the great ironies of the PRC after June 1989 was that at a time when the CCP was protesting loudly and publicly about "harmful" Western cultural influences fomenting rebellion in China through the Voice of America and the BBC World Service, it was encouraging an influx from elsewhere in East Asia of popular music of kinds it would previously have not permitted. In fact 1989 marked a turning point in the PRC's policies towards East and Southeast Asia, which further increased the involvement in China of Overseas Chinese from those communities. In the aftermath of Western reaction to its suppression of the demonstrations in Tiananmen Square, the PRC quickly moved to resolve its outstanding diplomatic problems in the region enabling the not inconsiderable Chinese business communities of Thailand, Malaysia, Indonesia and Singapore to invest in trade with China.

Two traditions of modernisation

A further difference between China's recent economic development and East Asian late capitalism, particularly in Taiwan and South Korea, is that whereas the latter can look back on the period since the 1960s virtually as a single process of modernisation, the PRC since the late 1970s has experienced a period of growth based on economic restructuring. Economic modernisation had already started in the PRC in the early 1950s. There was not inconsiderable growth between 1952 and 1978, but the problem was that the economy had driven itself into a Stalinist dead-end. This economic difference is important because of its political consequences. By the mid-1950s the PRC had already created the structures of a modernising state, including bureaucracies and bureaucrats and an educational infrastructure. There are thus two generations of modernisers with different traditions to be found in China, rather than just one. The social categories created during the 1950s have one tradition, based on the structures of the state. The other rests with the new rich of the 1980s and the 1990s and the power of market forces. These two social forces may find it generally easier to co-operate than to be in conflict, but they may also moderate each other's influence.

AGENTS OF POLITICAL CHANGE

In 1991 it was not unusual to read predictions that the CCP had but a short time left as a ruling party in the PRC. In 1993 it is not unusual to read an extension of that argument that predicts that the PRC will break up into a dozen or more autonomous regions within five years.[11] Such forecasts are usually based on a number of arguments that outline many of the dynamics of change identified in the preceding sections. In particular they emphasise the problems of social and political mediation faced by the CCP; the economic power of China's new economic regions; the power and influence of the Overseas Chinese, who it is often claimed are largely anti-Communist; and an alienated peasantry. These are sensational stories and in the light of the events of 1989–91 in the communist world their many possibilities cannot be categorically denied. However, their sensationalism is more than a little suspect not least because of the failure to identify agents of change.

The most recent example may prove instructive. From a perspective of cultural determinism it is common to suggest that China's new economic regions build on the traditions of provincialism to threaten political unity. China's provinces are well-established economic, social and political units. They have their own languages (which are frequently not intelligible to other Chinese), cuisine and customs. They are large in their own right, with populations averaging 35 to 40m and economies equivalent to many countries elsewhere in the world. Indeed, perhaps it would be more accurate to compare China with Europe as a continent rather than to regard it as a single country.

Links between government and regions

Lack of political unity has been a major recurrent theme in China's history. However, the tradition of provincialism has not meant that the regions always instinctively opposed the centre. The establishment of separate regional government only occurred when the centre had collapsed, and under the condition that it was the duty of the regional authority to reunify the whole country. One reason that such a belief was articulated and translated into action was that there was no separate or distinctively local leadership, or rather that there was a community of interest and close inter-relationship between the local ruling class and the imperial government.

Leadership and organisation are key factors in political change. The local leaders of China's provinces and new economic regions remain as they have been since the establishment of the PRC not simply members of the CCP but its specifically-chosen appointees. It may be that for various reasons a higher proportion of natives serve as leaders in their home provinces, but they remain appointed from above with the process directed by the CCP. In terms of the localisation of interests, at least at provincial-level, the most that can be said is that they are the agents of the centre in the locality and the representative of the locality to the centre. If they vary from that prescription they are virtually assured of failure. The cadres of the party-state system apart, there appears to be no independent articulation of a provincial interest.

More generally, those who populate the party-state system remain the key, if not the only, organised agents of political change. Without exaggerating their abilities they both see the need to accommodate China's new social forces and to learn from the lessons of the collapse of communist rule in the former Soviet Union and Eastern Europe. The communist officials in Eastern Europe who placed themselves at the head of movements for radical change were third or fourth generation revolutionaries, facing major economic problems and surrounded by the apparent attractions of democracy. The current CCP leadership in contrast has the original revolutionaries and their successor generation at its head, faces different socio-economic circumstances and is surrounded by a political discourse in East and Southeast Asia that stresses the synergy between economic growth and authoritarianism.

The opposition in exile

Of course there is opposition within the PRC to the CCP and its policies, but accommodation with the party-state is an inherent part of political life not just for business people but even for those in opposition. The events of 1989 alienated intellectuals and drove many into exile where they remain. Those who were involved in the movement for reform at the time saw themselves as within the system rather than opposed to it root and branch, and that position remains an unreconciled matter of some debate amongst those now in exile. It is possible that the opposition in exile may develop new ideas and even the organisation to represent a significant threat to the CCP at some point in the future. However, at present they face enormous structural problems. They are divided, physically separate and disparate. They are fundamentally a movement of intellectuals, and whilst that leads to a certain influence it is also a check on their development as a mass movement. Moreover, they are outside China and thus somewhat tainted in terms of their need to appeal to reactive nationalism.

Prolonged economic crisis and decline has the potential to threaten the infrastructure that brings the party-state system and China's new rich together. However, at present though the latter may prefer on an individual basis to exclude the CCP from their enterprises they have no problem with working with it on a larger scale and there is certainly no motive for them actively to organise political change let alone revolution. For similar reasons, Overseas

Chinese business people who may well be anti-Communist in their domestic environments in East and Southeast Asia are attracted by profits in China.

A new economic – political relationship?

The less sensational story is that China will probably continue to develop, either with or without the CCP, as a fundamentally authoritarian and modernising political system. The result is likely to be a China that has common characteristics with other political and cultural systems – capitalist, communist and authoritarian – but a China that also has its own specific features. It may even cause the rest of the world to reconsider its understanding of the relationship between economics and politics, particularly as China, or more accurately parts of China, become increasingly more economically integrated with the neighbouring economies of East Asia. Since 1989 it has been common to assume the lack of alternatives in domestic socio-economic development either to state socialism coupled with economic stagnation or liberal democracy associated with free market capitalism. The capitalist transformation of China's state socialism offers the possibility that new social forms and forces may appear. Moreover the internationalisation of China's regional economies has the potential fundamentally to challenge the notion that strong states depend on a high degree of control over the national economy. At the same time modernisation has rarely, if ever, proved an even or planned process, and China – with its boom-bust cycles since the mid-1980s – has been no exception. It is clearly important not to confuse short-term consequences with their more long-term causes.

NOTES

[1] Chinese statistics are notoriously unreliable. Unless otherwise indicated all statistics are derived from the State Statistical Bureau's official publications, notably its annual *Zhongguo tongji nianjian* [*Statistical Yearbook of China*].

[2] *South China Morning Post* "Beijing sends more troops to Soviet border" 10 December 1991, p. 1; and "Warning over Xinjiang unrest" 11 December 1991, p. 11.

[3] See, for example: *South China Morning Post* "Poll of Mainland" 30 May 1993, p. 6.

[4] See, for example: Shen Liren & Tai Yuanchen "Woguo 'zhuhou jingji' de xingzheng ji chi bituan he genyuan" in *Jingji yanjiu* [*Economics Research* No. 3 1990, p. 12; and Wu Minyi "Guanyu difang zhengfu xingwei de rougan sikao" in *Jingji yanjiu* [*Economics Research*] No. 7 1990, p. 56.

[5] 1991 figures are from State Statistical Bureau *Zhongguo tongji nianjian 1992* p. 23; estimates for the year 2000 from *Wen Wei Po* 13 July 1992, p. 5.

[6] Detail here and elsewhere on economic enterprises in China is drawn from a longitudinal study of some 120 in Taiyuan, Hangzhou and Foshan currently underway at the Asia Research Centre, Murdoch University, Western Australia.

[7] One GBP equals 8.75 yuan RMB on the official exchange rate, and approximately 15 yuan RMB more openly.

[8] "Chen Jinyi – the new industrialist" in *Yancheng Wanbao* 31 October 1992.

[9] See, for example: H. Harding *China's Second Revolution* Allen & Unwin, Sydney, 1989, p. 300.

[10] Chalmers Johnson "Where does Mainland China fit in a World Organised into Pacific, North American, & European Regions" in *Issues and Studies* August 1991, p. 17.

[11] See, for example: Perception International 25 June 1993, in *PR Newswire* 6 July 1993.

FURTHER READING

Asia Research Centre, Murdoch University *Southern China in Transition: The New Regionalism and Australia*, AGPS, Canberra, 1992.

P. Berger and Hsiao Hsin-Huang (eds.), *In Search of an East Asian Development Model*, Transaction Books, New Brunswick, 1988.

C. Burton "China's Post-Mao Transition: The Role of the Party and Ideology in the New Period", *Pacific Affairs* Vol. 60 No. 3, 1987.

W. A. Byrd *The Market Mechanism and Economic Reforms in China*, M. E. Sharpe, New York, 1991.

W. A. Byrd and Lin Qingsong *China's Rural Industry: Structure Development and Reform*, Oxford University Press, 1990.

N. Campbell (ed.), *Advances in Chinese Industrial Studies* Vol. I, J. Child and M. Lockett (eds.), *Reform Policy and the Chinese Enterprise*, JAI Press, London, 1990.

N. Campbell, S. R. F. Plasschaert and D. H. Brown (eds.) *Advances in Chinese Industrial Studies* Vol. II, *The Changing Nature of Management in China*, JAI Press, London, 1991.

T. Cannon and A. Jenkins (eds.), *The Geography of Contemporary China: The Impact of Deng Xiapoing's Decade*, Routledge, London, 1990.

Chao Chien-min "Transition From Authoritarian Rule: Is Eastern Europe's Today Mainland China's Tomorrow?" *Issues and Studies* Vol. 26 No. 11, 1990.

Chiang Chen-ch'ang "The Social Aftermath of Mainland China's Economic Reform", *Issues and Studies* Vol. 25 No. 2, 1989.

M. Chossudovsky *Towards Capitalist Restoration? Chinese Socialism After Mao*, Macmillan, London, 1986.

F. Deyo (ed.), *The Political Economy of the New Asian Industrialisation*, Cornell University Press, Ithaca, 1987.

J. Domes "Four Ways Communism Could Die in China" in G. Hicks (ed.), *The Broken Mirror: China After Tiananmen*, Longman, London, 1990.

J. A. Dorn and Wang Xi (eds.), *Economic Reform in China: Problems and Prospects*, University of Chicago Press, 1991.

P. Drysdale *International Economic Pluralism: Economic Policy in East Asia and the Pacific*, Allen and Unwin, Sydney, 1988.

T. B. Gold, *State and Society in the Taiwan Miracle*, M. E. Sharpe, New York, 1986.

T. B. Gold, "Guerrilla Interviewing Among the *Getihu*" in P. Link, R. Madsen, and P. G. Pockowicz (eds.), *Unofficial China: Popular Culture and Thought in the People's Republic*, Westview Press, Boulder, Colorado, 1989.

D. S. G. Goodman (ed.), *China's Regional Development*, Routledge, London, 1989.

D. S. G. Goodman, *Deng Xiaoping*, Cardinal, London, 1990.

D. S. G. Goodman and G. Segal (eds.), *China in the Nineties: Crisis Management and Beyond*, Clarendon Press, Oxford, 1991.

C. L. Hamrin, *China and the Challenge of the Future: Changing Political Patterns*, Westview Press, Boulder, Colorado, 1990.

H. Harding, *China's Second Revolution: Reform After Mao*, The Brookings Institution, Washington, 1990.

G. Hicks (ed.), *The Broken Mirror: China After Tiananmen*, Longman, London, 1990.

D. M. Lampton (ed.), *Policy Implementation in Post-Mao China*, University of California Press, 1987.

N. R. Lardy, "Consumption and Living Standards in China 1978–83" in *China Quarterly* No. 100, 1984.

N. R. Lardy *Foreign Trade and Economic Reform in China*, Cambridge University press, 1991.

C. Lin "Open-ended Economic Reforms in China" in V. Nee and D. Stark (eds.), *Remaking Economic Institutions of Socialism* Stanford University Press, 1989.

B. L. McCormick, *Political Reform in Post-Mao China: Democracy and Bureaucracy in a Leninist State*, University of California Press, 1990.

B. L. McCormick, Su Shaozhi and Xiao Xiaoming, "The 1989 Democracy Movement: A Review of the Prospects for Civil Society in China" in *Pacific Affairs* Vol. 65, No. 2, 1992.

F. Michael, C. Linden, J. Prybyla, and J. Domes, *China and the Crisis of Marxism-Leninism*, Westview Press, Boulder, Colorado, 1990.

Leo J. Moser, *The Chinese Mosaic: The People's and Provinces of China*, Westview, Boulder, Colorado, 1985.

M. Moskowitz, "The Worldwide Triumph of Capitalism: Is It for Real?" in *New Management* Vol. 6, no 2, 1988.

M. Mushkat *The Economic Future of Hong Kong*, Hong Kong University Press, 1991.

A. J. Nathan *Chinese Democracy – An Introduction into the Nature and Meaning of "Democracy" in China Today, With a Report on the Remarkable but Short-Lived Democracy Movement*, Alfred A. Knopf, New York, 1991.

P. Nolan, *The Political Economy of Collective Farms*, Polity Press, Oxford, 1988.

G. O'Donnell, P. Schmitter and L. Whitehead, (eds.), *Transitions from Authoritarian Rule*, John Hopkins University Press, 1986.

J. Prybyla, *Market and Plan Under Socialism: The Bird in the Cage*, Hoover Institution Press, Stanford, 1987.

L. W. Pye, *The Dynamics of Chinese Politics* Oelgeschlager, Gunn and Hain, Cambridge, Mass., 1981.

S. G. Redding, *The Spirit of Chinese Capitalism*, Walter de Gruyter, New York, 1990.

T. W. Robinson, (ed.), *Democracy and Development in East Asia. Taiwan, South Korea, and the Philippines*, AEI Press, Washington, 1991.

G. Segal, (ed.), *Chinese Politics and Foreign Policy Reform*, Kegan Paul International, London, 1990.

O. Shenkar, (ed.), *Organization and Management in China 1979–1990*, M. E. Sharpe, New York, 1991.

D. J. Solinger, *From Lathes to Looms: China's Industrial Policy, 1979–1982*, Stanford University Press, 1991.

Su Shaozhi, *Democratization and Reform*, Spokesman, Nottingham, 1981.

L. R. Sullivan "Assault on the Reforms: Conservative Criticism of Political and Economic Liberalization in China, 1985–86" in *China Quarterly* No. 114, 1988.

Sung Yun-wing *The China-Hong Kong Connection: the key to China's open-door policy*, Cambridge University Press, 1991.

G. Tidrick and Chen Jiyuan, (eds.), *China's Industrial Reform*, Oxford University Press, 1987.

E. Vogel, *One Step Ahead in China: Guangdong under Reform*, Harvard University Press, 1989.

A. G. Walder, "Workers, Managers and the State: The Reform Era and the Political Crisis of 1989" in *China Quarterly* No. 127, 1991.

Wang Zhonghui, "Private Enterprise in China" in *Journal of Communist Studies* Vol. 6 No. 3 (September 1990).

Yang Dali, "China Adjusts to the World Economy: The Political Economy of China's Coastal Development Strategy" in *Pacific Affairs* Vol. 64 No. 1, 1991.

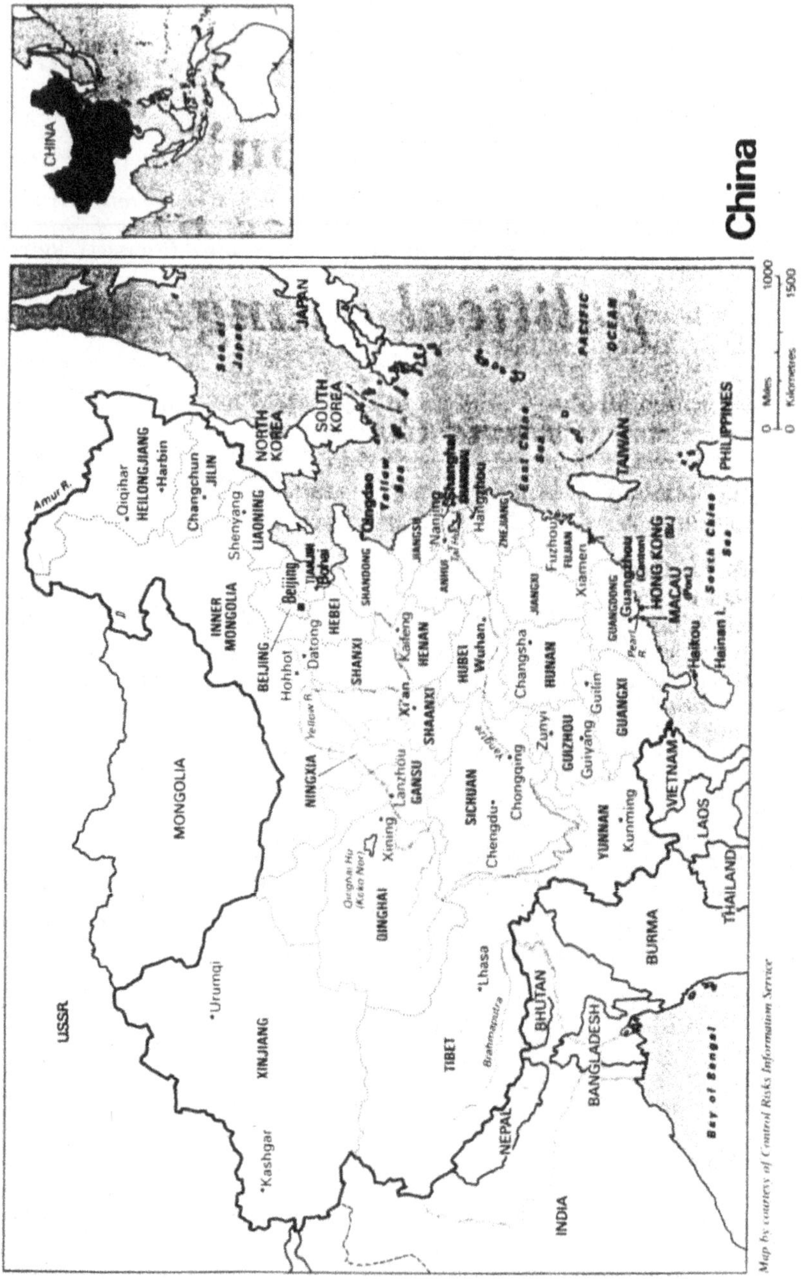

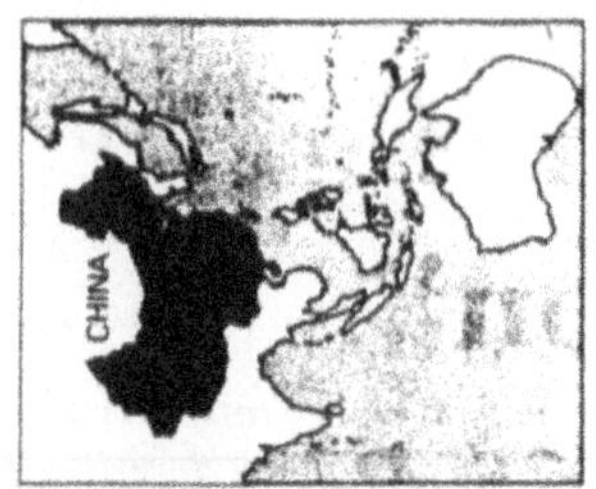

China

0 Miles 1000
0 Kilometres 1500

Map by courtesy of Control Risks Information Service

[10]

Nuclear Rivalry in South Asia

Strategic Imperatives and National Pride

Partha S. Ghosh

> ***The release of the atomic energy has not created a new problem. It has merely made more urgent the necessity of solving an existing one.***
>
> **—Albert Einstein:** ***Atlantic Monthly,*** **November, 1945.**

The phenomenon of the atom bomb is a unique one. During the past half-century that it has been available to the arsenal of mankind it has been used just twice and that too soon after the successful experiment in 1945. The impact of that use was so awesome in terms of human suffering that Albert Einstein, who was one of the scientists indirectly responsible for its making, lamented: 'If only I had known, I should have become a watchmaker.' Unfortunately, however, like any other category of human knowledge, this scientific expertise once acquired could not be unlearnt. In a lecture delivered soon after the end of the Second World War, J. Robert Oppenheimer, the leading architect of the Hiroshima bomb, cryptically remarked: 'The physicists have known sin and this is a knowledge which they cannot lose.' No wonder that five nations now have the bomb, that allegedly it is in the possession of another few states, and the technological know-how is available to all. The reason is not so much technological, therefore, that some nations have opted for it, some want to opt for it, and still more have already developed it secretly. The fact is that although it is still a weapon of war its relevance is more diplomatic—one of Nixon's arguments to enter into diplomatic relations with China was that a nation with 800m people and with nuclear weapons could not be ignored. In an actual war the decision whether or not to use it also lies entirely with the political leadership and not the military (recall for instance the Truman–MacArthur controversy during the Korean War) and this makes all the difference. The whole debate on nuclear proliferation is actually nothing but politics by other means.

In this study efforts have been made to posit the problem of a possible nuclear proliferaton in South Asia where two leading powers—India and Pakistan—have locked horns by accusing each other of nuclear ambitions. Since they have been in a constant state of conflictual relationship ever since their independence in 1947 the matter has assumed serious dimensions. Both the states are technologically and materially capable of producing the nuclear weapon, if they have not actually done so; both are resisting pressures from the dominant international community to sign the Non-Proliferation Treaty (NPT), though on different grounds; and both claim their sovereign rights to nuclear research for developmental purposes. But the issues that complicate matters lie in their divergent approaches to regional security and after the end of the Cold War the relative marginalisation of the region in the strategic map of the world. In some senses the region has become autonomous, but in others, it is now more vulnerable to external pressures. This is because no-one in the global system is willing to stomach the danger of a nuclear arms race from an area which is strategically less important but gaining in significance for international investment and trade in which the region itself has a stake. Herein lies the crux of the dilemma both for regional and international interests.

THE 'NUCLEAR BALANCE'

Although millions of words must have been written and spoken about the military nuclear programmes of India and Pakistan much is still shrouded in mystery. Most of what one hears emanates from Western sources which the regional political elites make selective use of to suit their respective national interests. Beyond this there are not many takers for these reports from the West. For example, although some of the American authors have dramatised the gravity of the situation by narrating the story of how India and Pakistan were on the brink of a nuclear showdown in 1986 and 1990,[1] these accounts have been dismissed in the subcontinent as sheer fiction. Most Indian analysts argue that India's own nuclear programme has not gone beyond developing the necessary technological capability to be ready to meet any provocation at the shortest possible notice and there are strong misgivings even in India about Pakistan's capability. According to P.R. Chari, the former Director of the New Delhi-based and the Defence Ministry-funded Institute of Defence Studies and Analyses (IDSA) and currently Professor of National Security Studies at the Centre for Policy Research, New Delhi, it is time that one should 'call Pakistan's bluff on its capabilities'. He says that 'a lot of our atomic energy scientists do feel that Pakistan really does not have the wherewithal to make nuclear bombs'.[2] Even K. Subrahmanyam, another former director of IDSA and one of India's leading defence analysts, who is otherwise convinced that Pakistan and not India has become a weapons state, concedes that too much attention need not be paid to Pakistan for its technological development. In any case it does not match with that of India. He says that the comparable situation actually exists between India and China.[3]

Yet if Western sources are to be believed, not only have India and Pakistan embarked upon defence-related nuclear programmes, they actually have developed nuclear weapons. According to Leonard Spector, a knowledgeable American observer, India has enough plutonium to produce as many as 75 nuclear bombs. Similarly, Pakistan has enough enriched uranium to produce at least 10 of them.[4] In late 1992, US Senator Larry Pressler quoting the CIA said at a press conference that Pakistan had developed seven bombs and was in a position to deliver them in a matter of hours. An NBC news of 1 December 1992 reported that in the Spring of 1990, in response to Indian army manoeuvres near the Pakistan border the latter had virtually prepared itself to drop one of its seven atomic devices from a specially engineered C-130 cargo plane, and that the then Pakistan Prime Minister Benazir Bhutto had subsequently alleged that her government was deposed by the President–Army clique because of her opposition to the plan.[5]

In a testimony before the Senate Governmental Affairs Committee on 24 February 1993, James Woolsey, the Director of the CIA, said: 'The arms race between India and Pakistan poses perhaps the most probable prospect for future use of weapons of mass destruction, including nuclear weapons.'[6]

The rationale

Granting at least that both India and Pakistan have agreed in principle to prepare themselves for any eventuality involving a nuclear threat some rationale for their action must be found. One analyst has identified seven reasons for this.[7] In the first place, India and Pakistan are in constant conflict which besides being ideological has also some serious territorial components. Kashmir is a disputed territory and in the Siachin glacier the two countries have been engaged in sporadic battles since 1984. In December 1987, poor communication and mutual mistrust almost led to war.

The second reason is that nationalism has always been a strong incentive for nuclearisation. India's emphasis on self reliance has assigned a significant role to the development of indigenous science and technology of which the dual use technology of nuclear energy is an offshoot. With regard to Pakistan it views itself as the technological leader of the Muslim world. Pride in technological sophistication and progress creates political–military confidence.

Third, both India and Pakistan enjoy strong domestic support for their nuclear programmes. One of the factors responsible for Zulfikar Ali Bhutto's popularity in Pakistan was his militant assertion that even if Pakistanis would have to 'eat grass' their nation must have the nuclear weapons to deal with India. The case is no different in India. However the opposition parties might criticise the ruling Congress Party for its commissions and omissions on every possible policy front, on the nuclear question they are firmly behind the government. On the eve of Prime Minister Narasimha Rao's visit to the United States in May 1994 they made a big furore in parliament cautioning Rao against being bullied by the Clinton administration into accepting the NPT. The Bharatiya Janata Party (BJP), the leader of the opposition parties, openly demands that India should go nuclear.[8]

The fourth reason stems from a penchant for prestige. India considers itself to be a great nation which should be entitled at least to freedom of choice insofar as the nuclear weapon is concerned. Pakistan expects that once it goes nuclear its prestige would grow tremendously in the 'Muslim Crescent' (Pakistan to Morocco) and Central Asia.

Fifth, the Gulf War, by demonstrating the efficacy of technology in modern warfare, has made both India and Pakistan aware that they should learn from Iraq's experience. The Third World countries have realised that they should not dare to challenge the United States without possessing deliverable weapons of mass destruction. A Pakistani commentator wrote that, 'the foremost lesson for developing countries [was] that had Iraq already developed a nuclear-weapons capability, the United States would not have been in a position to decimate Iraq's military might with impunity.'[9]

Sixth, with the dismemberment of the Soviet Union a new geostrategic centre of gravity has emerged encompassing the region extending through the Middle East and Central Asia. The region is full of potential for ethnic and nationalistic conflicts and nuclear proliferation. During the Cold War what looked like international stability by the West was seen as systemic instability by the Third World. The latter, therefore, has hardly any stake in perpetuating the present political order or in retaining the existing nuclear status quo.

The seventh factor stems from a growing realisation in many Third World regions that the end of the Cold War has resulted in the domination of the world by the developed world in the name of a 'new world order'. This 'new divide' in international politics has provided a greater urgency to assert Third Worldism which includes a declaration of one's sovereignty.

To these seven factors one may as well add the evolutionary variable. Both India and Pakistan have a long record of research in nuclear technology and at some stage are bound to look for more avenues of expansion. Since civilian and military research are intimately enmeshed these days any crossing of the floor from civilian technology to military technology is relatively simple. For example, with the high level of expertise in nuclear research it would be foolhardy to think that India would give up its strategic options despite whatever commitments it is forced to make to the world. The essence of Indian policy is something akin to what R. Chidambaram, Chairman of the Atomic Energy Commission of India, said recently in response to a question on whether India was making the atom bomb: 'That's a pointed question. And I would not like to comment on our nuclear weapons capability. Let me just say that we have built up an extraordinary range of know-how and expertise on all aspects of nuclear technology, especially in applications such as power, medicine and agriculture. There is nothing India cannot do.'[10]

INDIA'S 'PNE': THE WATERSHED

In South Asia the year 1974 was the watershed so far as the nuclear question is concerned. On 18 May that year India tested its first, and so far the only, nuclear device which the government called the Peaceful Nuclear Explosion (PNE). Whatever the political or diplomatic compulsion for Prime Minister Indira Gandhi to take this step it was received with great apprehension in the region. Pakistan was particularly disturbed and in August 1974 it put before the UN General Assembly a proposal for a Nuclear Weapon Free Zone in South Asia. India opposed the proposal and introduced its own resolution which urged the South Asian states to take their own initiatives towards a nuclear free zone. The UN General Assembly approved both the resolutions and asked the Secretary-General to convene a meeting of regional and neighbouring states so as to work out the establishment of a nuclear free zone in South Asia. But owing to differences in approach among the states, and particularly between India and Pakistan, the meeting could never be convened.[11]

Sri Lanka

For Sri Lanka the emergence of India as a 'nuclear power' from among the Indian Ocean littoral states had radically changed the strategic landscape in the Indian Ocean. Consequently, the context of declaring the Indian Ocean as a Zone of Peace also changed. Two subtle shifts occurred in the Sri Lankan position. On the one hand, its anti-West stance softened, and on the other, it started highlighting the South Asian context of its security while talking about the Indian Ocean region. In November 1976, the Sri Lankan representative at the UN, Shirley Amerasinghe, stated at the First Committee: 'We do not want any great power there. By the same token, we do not intend that we should drive out Satan by Beelzebub and allow some other powers within the group of littoral and hinterland states to take the place of the superpowers.'[12]

American reactions

Beyond the region, the nation most disturbed by the Indian test was the United States. The Indian PNE posed, first of all, a conceptual problem. Hitherto, in all cases of nuclear research and development in the five nuclear states the military programme had preceded the civilian nuclear programme. The PNE indeed had been an accepted concept in the United States and elsewhere and it was also executed but the presumption was that only the nuclear states had the privilege of indulging in the exercise. There were three visible reactions in the United States against India's PNE. First, overnight it became a dirty concept; second, all peaceful uses of nuclear energy were seen in the context of their economic viability, radioactive waste disposal, public health and environmental effects, reactor safety, nuclear terrorism, and, most importantly, proliferation risks; and third, strict restrictions were imposed on the sale of nuclear materials, equipment and technology to the Third World countries. President Gerald Ford secretly worked out a cartel of nuclear exporting countries which came to be known as the London Club. The meetings of the club commenced in 1975 but restrictions were made public in 1978.[13]

India's Tarapore reactor which supplied electricity to the country's most vital industrial and commercial zone, the Bombay region, was caught in these developments. The reactor depended on American fuel. The supply was technically subject to International Atomic Energy Agency (IAEA) inspections but it was not enforced as India was opposed to outside inspections. The basic assumption was that the use of the material and technology at Tarapore was purely developmental. But after the PNE, India was forced to adhere to IAEA safeguards (it is still under IAEA inspection). The strong US reactions against India's nuclear programme culminated in the enactment of the US Nuclear Non-Proliferation Act (NNPA) of 1978.

The NNPA was to hit India directly. After minutely analysing the act and also its antecedents, one scholar wrote:

> The legislation provided a statutory authority to the nuclear export restrictions that had already been clamped by the government on the basis of the London Club guidelines. In some important respects, the Act went even further: it made fullscope safeguards a condition for most nuclear exports and sought to unilaterally and

> retroactively rewrite the United States' contractual international obligations. The legislation effectively voided the US–Indian agreement for co-operation. The legislative history of the Act is replete with unsubstantiated allegations about India's abuse of US and Canadian nuclear assistance. . . . Analysts who continue to hurl such charges have conveniently turned a blind eye to some important facts: (i) there is no evidence that India violated its legal contracts with the United States and Canada; (ii) the agreements contained no explicit or implicit prohibition of a peaceful nuclear explosion; and (iii) the State Department's own conclusions do not support claims that US-sold heavy water was used in producing the plutonium of the PNE. India, before the PNE, had a surplus stock of heavy water, proved by its lease of nine metric tonnes of the material to Belgium, and—considering the rate at which heavy water degrades—it appears doubtful that any American-origin heavy water was still in use at CIRUS (Canada India US Reactor) in 1974. But such information has rarely been cited in US non-proliferation literature or congressional debates.[14]

Not only did the United States impose all kinds of restrictions on the export of nuclear fuel and technology, it took steps to alert its allies about the possible danger from India's nuclearisation. An internal note was sent by the US Mission to NATO on 5 June 1974, 21 days after the Indian PNE, assessing the politico-military impact of the test on international security. The note was eventually declassified with portions blacked out which obviously indicated the military-strategic importance that was attached to the PNE.[15]

The world is not unfamiliar with clandestine growth of nuclear weapons in critical Third World regions. But since most of these developments took place in the context of the Cold War, the leading Cold Warriors treated them with indulgence for it suited their interests. But so far as the Indian nuclear explosion was concerned it did not receive Soviet approval either, although India was considered to be virtually an ally of the Soviet Union. In the UN Security Council Indian action was unanimously denounced. Subsequently when the United States turned a Nelson's eye to the clandestine nuclearisation of Israel and South Africa the Soviets ceased publicly to criticise India but continued to give private counsel to the latter against its nuclear policy. According to Soviet scholar Sergei Lunyov although 'nobody has ever presented documentary evidence' against India's claim that its nuclear programme has nothing but peaceful purposes, 'even now there is some friction between the USSR and India over this issue and from time to time there are difficulties on the occasion of supplies of some Soviet materials and equipment that can be used in the Indian nuclear programme.'[16]

THE SECURITY IMPERATIVE

The South Asian security dilemma was previously attributed to the asymmetry between India and the rest of the region, most notably Pakistan. Ironically, of late, it is being viewed in terms of an emerging symmetry between these two powers for their alleged acquisition of nuclear weapons. Given the reality that in the past half-century they have fought three wars the last of which has led to the dismemberment of Pakistan, together with the current state of insurgency in Kashmir in which the Pakistani state has been actively engaged, though covertly, there are reasons for concern about the situation deteriorating into yet another war which might escalate into a nuclear show-down. Nuclear weapons seemingly play a positive role in maintaining peace by restraining governments which possess them from direct confrontation. Whether this will continue to be so in the case of India and Pakistan depends on their reasonableness and political good sense about which—in a way typical of Western attitudes to the Third World generally—the West is often condescendingly sceptical. The risk that the worst could happen may be relatively small but the fact remains that the nuclear question has compounded the South Asian 'insecurity syndrome' (Stephen Cohen's phrase coined 20 years ago) as never before.[17]

Since Pakistan views its security purely in South Asian regional terms its stance is that both India and Pakistan should renounce nuclear weapons through their simultaneous signing of the NPT. But as India's security concerns are both regional and extra-regional it cannot overlook the existence of a nuclear China next door in formulating its nuclear doctrine. The spectre of a possible future conflict with China continually haunts the political class of India. The wound inflicted on the Indian psyche by the Chinese aggression of 1962 may have healed but a nagging pain persists, the present Sino-Indian co-ordination of interests on select global issues notwithstanding. Indians simply cannot brush aside the fact that China has not only helped Pakistan to develop its nuclear programme, but it continues to supply its nuclear technology to other states in the region, namely Iran and Saudi Arabia.

The China factor

India's nuclear and missile policies are essentially dictated by the China factor. One might recall how the Chinese nuclear explosion of 1964 had unnerved the Indians. During his visit to London in December 1964 Prime Minister Lal Bahadur Shastri discussed with Harold Wilson, the British Prime Minister, the idea of seeking a nuclear guarantee from the superpowers to protect India against the threat of a Chinese nuclear attack. There was powerful pressure on the Indian government to launch a nuclear arms programme to meet the challenge posed by China. Shastri had to succumb to this pressure to some extent, and said, in 1965, that he did not rule out the development of nuclear weapons in the future. This was a sharp departure from the policy of Jawaharlal Nehru, who even in the teeth of violent criticism from his political opposition, particularly after the Indian military debacle in its war with China in 1962, had announced that India would never develop nuclear weapons under any circumstances. A public opinion survey carried out in 1968 by the Indian Institute of Public Opinion demonstrated that sizable support existed for developing an independent nuclear weapons capability.[18]

Against this background India refused to sign the NPT (1968) which was clearly discriminatory. The treaty extracted a perpetual guarantee from the non-nuclear states to remain non-nuclear but it did nothing to prevent the nuclear states from further proliferation. There were probably other more practical reasons too. Following the 1965 India–Pakistan war there was a cut-off of US arms aid. Although this loss was subsequently compensated for by a growing Indo-Soviet co-operation, the uncertainty over arms supply made the nuclear option look strategically attractive. Moreover, the military had generally been lukewarm in support of any nuclear option for it would have cut into their budget allocations. But following the US arms cut and more funds made available to conventional arms their opposition melted. Also, the launching of the first Chinese missile in 1966 had sharpened Indian anxiety.[19]

China's nuclear, missile and arms supply relationship with Pakistan has complicated the South Asian security system. During the 1962 war China annexed part of Kashmir which, together with another portion of Pakistan-occupied Kashmir ceded to China by Pakistan, enabled it to connect Xinjiang with Tibet and to build the strategic Karakoram highway to Islamabad. The deployment of Chinese nuclear weapons in Tibet and in Xinjiang province has increased India's vulnerability for many of its major industrial and military facilities are now within the striking range of Chinese missiles. In recent years, China has acquired the Multiple Independently-targeted Re-entry Vehicle (MIRV) and successfully launched a ballistic missile from a nuclear submarine. It has resumed nuclear testing which has broken an informal moratorium.[20]

In 1991, the United States imposed sanctions on both China and Pakistan because of transfer of missile-related technology. The sanction against China was subsequently waived as it agreed to abide by the Missile Technology Control Regime (MTCR). Despite these steps there are concerns that China might continue secretly to indulge in such deals in the future as recent reports of its assistance to Iran and Saudi Arabia tend to suggest. The Chinese strategy may well have been dictated by its perceived fear of India. It believes that by the close of this century India is likely to acquire the nuclear war fighting capability to augment its current conventional superiority along the border.[21]

The wider perspective

Against this background India considers it naive to view its nuclear policy within a purely South Asian regional framework. Its response to international pressure, therefore, has been one of looking at the issue from a wider perspective. Its strategy is moralistic—to insist that all nuclear nations dismantle their respective arsenals in a phased manner by 2010 which Prime Minister Rajiv Gandhi had proposed through a comprehensive Action Plan tabled at the UN Special Session on Disarmament in June 1988. By then the NPT anyway had become meaningless for even its sponsors' warheads had proliferated from 15,000 in 1968 to a staggering 55,000 by 1988.[22] One would have to be a simpleton not to realise that this proposal was just a bargaining strategy for the demand itself was unrealistic. None of the big powers has given any cognisance to this. The G-7 summit held in July 1994 has 'unequivocally' supported an indefinite extension of the NPT, as well as the continuing non-proliferation efforts in West and South Asia. The 1994 annual report of the US Department of Defense categorically noted: 'Nuclear weapons are an enduring reality and are not likely to disappear in the foreseeable future. Their numbers may decrease and the nature of the threat faced from them may change, but they simply cannot be eliminated from American defense policy and security strategy.' What the United States could do, according to the Pentagon, 'is respond to the demise of the old-style Soviet threat and the emergence of new threats to US security by appropriately altering force posture and outlining a new role for nuclear weapons in the national security strategy.'[23] But even so, the Indian position at least underscores the point that singling out South Asia for nuclear disarmament is neither good politics nor good security.

MISSILE PROLIFERATION

The problem of nuclear proliferation in South Asia is closely linked to the development and deployment of missiles in the region. India now has a fairly sophisticated missile programme which is largely in response to that of China. The successful tests of the *Agni* intermediate range missile, the *Akash* and *Trishul* surface-to-air missiles, and the *Nag* anti-tank missile, have shown that India's Integrated Guided Missile Development Programme has taken off. Besides, the short-range surface-to-surface *Prithvi* missile has been successfully tested. Consisting of two versions—one with a warhead of 1000 kg and a range of 150 km and the other with 500 kg and 250 km respectively—*Prithvi*, according to Defence Research and Development Organisation (DRDO) of the Government of India, is far more accurate than the Soviet Scud series or the US Lance. Over a 250 km range it would drift only about 0.1 per cent, which works out to a circular error probability (CEP) of 250 metres. Reportedly, the Indian Air Force has ordered 25 pieces of the 250 km type and the Indian Army 75 of the 150 km variety.[24]

India justifies its missile programme on the grounds that several neighbouring countries have deployed all kinds of missiles. Leave aside China which has an advanced missile programme and plans for a mobile Intercontinental Ballistic Missile (ICBM) during this decade, Pakistan's Chinese-supplied M-11 has a range of 300 to 800 km and Saudi Arabia's Chinese-supplied SS-2 has a range of 2000 to 2500 km. Besides, Pakistan has a secret programme of developing and deploying the short-range Haft-I and Haft-II missiles.[25]

According to A.P.J. Abdul Kalam, the head of India's Rs.10bn ($330m) defence research programme: 'Let us imagine a situation where we don't have strategic missiles and nations around us have either developed or purchased them.' Emphasising, therefore, self reliance in the field he says: 'Today our missile programme is playing a role in helping us stand on our legs. . . . Now no embargo can do anything to us. The MTCR has been rendered harmless. It can't even scratch us leave alone throttle our programme. All because we had anticipated the strictures and built critical technology ourselves.'[26]

India's *Prithvi* missile programme has caused consternation in Pakistan which argues that India has designs only on Pakistan. The Pakistani press was concerned at the development and appreciated Benazir Bhutto's government's political strategy of heightening its diplomatic activity at the UN to embarrass the Indian government further on the Kashmir question.[27] In an interview given to an Indian magazine the Pakistani ambassador to India, Riaz Khokhar, said: '*Prithvi* is a Pakistan-specific weapon. I don't think it is likely to be used against China. *Agni* is China-specific. *Agni* is directed at Iran, Saudi Arabia,

Kazakhistan. We are not afraid of *Agni*. But *Prithvi* is a purely Pakistan-specific weapon.'[28] The ulterior motive behind the statement probably was to sensitise the neighbouring Muslim states against Indian designs.

THE POST-COLD WAR SCENARIO

The end of the Cold War together with the disintegration of the Soviet Union has changed the international security scene drastically. There is no East–West conflict now but the overnight increase in the number of nuclear states from among the erstwhile Soviet republics has caught the imagination of international observers. It is against this background that all potential proliferators are being closely watched by the victors of the Cold War so as not to allow them to disturb their hard-earned triumph. An unprecedented pressure has, therefore, been mounted upon clandestine or potential nuclear states to make them subscribe to the NPT regime. Since South Asia is being viewed as one of the potential flash points of nuclearisation the pressure here is one of the most incessant and visible.

Neither India nor Pakistan, however, seems to be willing to give in to this pressure without resistance. Both are dodging it by taking recourse to their well known political strategies—for India, the discriminatory nature of the NPT and the China factor, while Pakistan lets India decide and then follows suit. But how long they are likely to be able to play their ball game is a moot point given the recent North Korean experience. Though this pressure appears to be coming only from the United States it is certain that behind the US is the entire developed world. On account of their donor status some of the developed nations have acquired clout in both India and Pakistan which the latter find difficult to brush aside. For example, Japan—which emerged as the biggest aid-giving country in the world in 1992 by surpassing the United States—has been considering for the last few years attaching a condition that all its aid-recipient states must sign the NPT and stop exporting weapons. If ever this is enforced, India and Pakistan together with China would be the first countries to be affected.

The tragic memories of Hiroshima and Nagasaki are still alive in the national psyche of the Japanese and so, despite their otherwise fragmented politics, on the question of nuclear proliferation they speak with one voice. Even earlier, after the 1974 Indian PNE, as the US Mission's internal paper to NATO noted, 'the Japanese Government, opposition parties and media have all reacted very negatively to the test and strongly condemned India.'[29] In August 1991, after protracted debate the Japanese *Diet* advised the government of Toshiki Kaifu to attach the clause that the recipient of Japanese aid must be a signatory to the NPT. The ruling LDP recommended a phased enforcement of the plan. In the first year the defaulting nations should be served with a warning, in the second year there should be a cut in the aid and eventually there should be a total withdrawal of aid. Mercifully for India and Pakistan this policy has not been adopted so far although during the Indian Foreign Minister Madhavsinh Solanki's visit to Japan in January 1992 Tokyo threw a broad hint that Japan might cut off its developmental aid to India unless it signed the NPT.[30]

AMERICAN CONCERN

The US concern at the horizontal proliferation of nuclear weapons dates back to the 1960s when it culminated in the signing of the NPT in 1968. In the latest phase this concern is particularly noticeable after the dismemberment of the Soviet Union. According to an estimate prepared by the US government, 1,000 to 2,000 scientists of the Soviet Union who had nuclear weapons design skills could be available to nuclear aspirants. On 15 January 1992, in a testimony before the Senate Governmental Affairs Committee, the CIA Chief Robert Gates said: 'Cuba, India, Syria, Egypt, and Algeria which collaborated extensively with Soviet science in the 1980s, are most likely to have the contacts and resident scientists to assist emigrating Soviets.'[31] Americans generally are haunted by a scenario of unrestrained nuclear proliferation. Writing in *Foreign Affairs*, a syndicated columnist stated:

> The danger from the Weapon State is posed today by Iraq, tomorrow perhaps by North Korea or Libya. In the next century, however, the proliferation of strategic weapons will not be restricted to Weapon States. Windfall wealth allows oil states to import high-technology weapons in the absence of a mature industrial base. However, it is not hard to imagine more mature states—say Argentina, Pakistan, Iran, South Africa—reaching the same level of weapons developments by means of ordinary industrialization. . . . The post-Cold War era is thus perhaps better called the era of weapons of mass destruction.[32]

Anti-proliferation strategies

Freed from the logic of nuclear deterrence which led the United States, as well as the Soviet Union, to amass vast nuclear stockpiles, Washington has now given top priority to developing anti-proliferation strategies that would deter potential proliferators, enforce international barriers to proliferation, and attempt to roll back instances of proliferation that have occurred, amongst other regions, in South Asia. The India–Pakistan nuclear dynamic most directly impinges on American's Middle East interests which are considered vital on account of their access to Persian Gulf oil, and with the Arab–Israeli military balance.

The objective of the United States is first to cap, then over time to reduce, and eventually try to eliminate the weapons of mass destruction and their delivery systems. Following its unilateral decision in July 1992 not to produce fissile material, it has urged both India and Pakistan to consider taking similar steps on a unilateral or bilateral basis. It has made known its strong opposition to any effort at the forthcoming 1995 NPT Review Conference to modify the treaty which has been adhered to by 155 countries. Reportedly, American and other Western intelligence agencies are in the process of preparing plans for co-operation with their counterparts in the former 'Iron Curtain' countries to combat nuclear proliferation.[33]

Together with nuclear non-proliferation, the United States strategy is also to prevent the proliferation of missiles on a global scale. President Clinton has inherited from the Bush administration the Enhanced Proliferation Control Initiative which targets missile proliferation on a global scale. According to the CIA director James Woolsey, Washington faces at least 25 countries, some of

Pakistan

SOVIET UNION
CHINA
NORTHERN TERRS
Gilgit
JAMMU
NW FRONTIER
PROVINCE
& KASHMIR
Peshawar
Islamabad
Rawalpindi
AFGHANISTAN
FEDERAL
CAPITAL
TERR.
TRIBAL
AREAS
Gujranwala
Lahore
Faisalabad
PUNJAB
Multan
Quetta
Bahawalpur
BALUCHISTAN
IRAN
Larkana
Sukkur
Dadu
Nawabshah
SIND
INDIA
Hyderabad
Karachi
Badin
ARABIAN SEA

0 Miles 250
0 Kilometres 400

Maps by courtesy of Control Risks Information Service

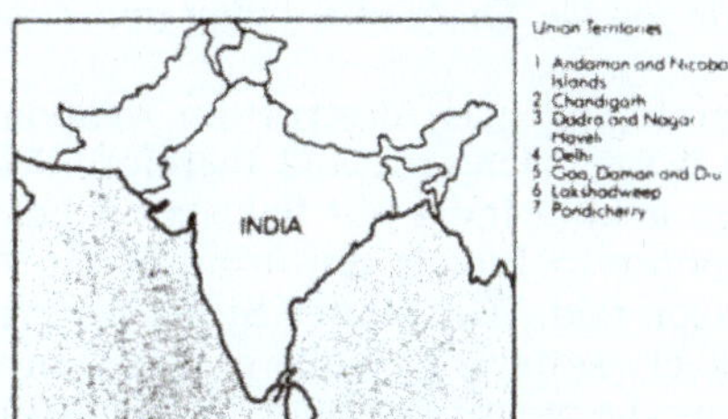

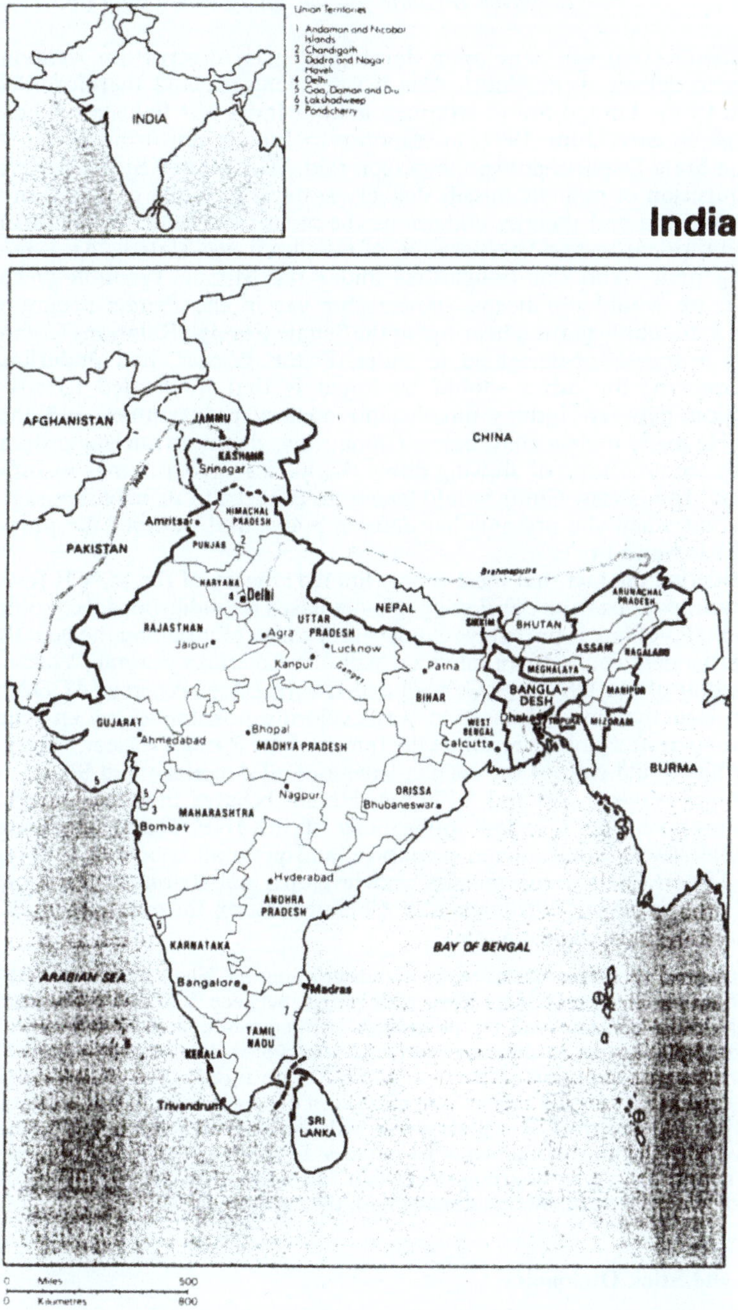

Union Territories

1 Andaman and Nicobar Islands
2 Chandigarh
3 Dadra and Nagar Haveli
4 Delhi
5 Goa, Daman and Diu
6 Lakshadweep
7 Pondicherry

India

AFGHANISTAN
JAMMU
KASHMIR
Srinagar
CHINA
Amritsar
HIMACHAL PRADESH
PAKISTAN
PUNJAB
HARYANA
Delhi
NEPAL
ARUNACHAL PRADESH
SIKKIM
BHUTAN
RAJASTHAN
Jaipur
Agra
UTTAR PRADESH
Lucknow
Kanpur
Ganges
Patna
ASSAM
NAGALAND
MEGHALAYA
BANGLA-DESH
MANIPUR
BIHAR
GUJARAT
Ahmedabad
Bhopal
MADHYA PRADESH
WEST BENGAL
Calcutta
Dhaka
TRIPURA
MIZORAM
BURMA
Nagpur
ORISSA
Bhubaneswar
MAHARASHTRA
Bombay
Hyderabad
ANDHRA PRADESH
BAY OF BENGAL
KARNATAKA
ARABIAN SEA
Bangalore
Madras
TAMIL NADU
KERALA
Trivandrum
SRI LANKA

0 Miles 500
0 Kilometres 800

them hostile, that are bent upon developing mass destruction weapons and missiles to deliver them. South Asia is one such area and therefore it causes concern to the United States although neither India nor Pakistan is hostile to America. In early June 1994, in response to India's test-firing of the *Prithvi* missile a State Department spokesperson said: 'The United States believes that the acquisition of ballistic missile delivery systems by India or Pakistan would be destabilising and thereby undermine the security of both.' Emphasising the US commitment to non-proliferation of missiles it was stated: 'As a matter of standing policy and our obligations under the Missile Technology Control Regime, we would not license exports for use in the *Prithvi* programme.'[34] Earlier, at his confirmation hearings at the Senate Foreign Relations Committee, the US Ambassador-designate to India, Frank Wisner, had underlined the same concern. But what should be noted is that he tended to stress the connection between India's missile and nuclear programmes and those of China. He made it clear that 'unless China slows down its nuclear programme, I do not see any hope of slowing down the nuclear programmes in India and Pakistan.' In his view China would 'cause no concern to its neighbours if she is transparent when she presents her defense budge and outlines the purpose of the defense build-up.'[35]

Considering the fact that there is only limited efficacy of the MTCR for it does not prevent nations from developing missiles based on indigenous technology, the United States of late is probably toying with the idea of attaining the goal through the disarmament route. In an interview with the American journal *Defense News*, the Director of the US Arms Control and Disarmament Agency (ACDA), John Holum, said that his organisation was exploring possibilities of an American initiative to draft a global version of the Intermediate Range Nuclear Forces (INF) Treaty that would call for the dismantlement of all American and Soviet missiles with ranges between 500 and 5,500 km. Holum believes that the United States should propose that the basic obligations of the INF Treaty are universally applicable which 'would invite, encourage, and press all countries to forego the threat of intermediate range missiles' and develop a global non-proliferation norm against the spread of ballistic missiles. Commenting on the catch involved in the proposal an Indian analyst wrote:

> A universal INF Treaty is not really non-discriminatory. Such a treaty would indeed eliminate a whole class of missiles, with ranges between 500 and 5,500 km. But it leaves those countries with the possession of inter-continental missiles with ranges above 5,500 km free to threaten the rest of the world. It also leaves the advanced countries with the option of continuing to build advanced cruise missiles, that have emerged as a powerful weapons system, as seen during the Gulf War. A global INF Treaty also leaves the US to press ahead with the development of a new generation of missiles that can shoot down other missiles. In short, a global INF Treaty will be little more than a partial arrangement that leaves all strategic advantages with the US while enforcing missile disarmament on the emerging powers.[36]

Carrot and Stick Diplomacy

Knowing the extemely complex nature of the South Asian nuclear tangle the

US wants to achieve its non-proliferation objectives through an equally complex political strategy of cajolery and arm-twisting. Ever since the 1970s, after the Indian PNE, the US has employed the threat of economic sanctions to make a recalcitrant state behave itself (the latest example is the North Korean nuclear crisis). In the early 1980s, the US government took recourse to the same threat to prohibit the government of India from abrogating its obligations under the agreement for nuclear co-operation and lift safeguards from Tarapore, including its spent fuel, which the Indira Gandhi administration had declared it would do. The possible sanctions that were threatened to be imposed included denying access to loans from the US Export–Import Bank and major international financial organisations and pruning the contributions to the Aid India Consortium through a co-ordinated multilateral approach. But since this was also the time when the Indian government was in the process of introducing economic liberalisations thereby opening avenues for foreign investments in India both countries found that discretion was the better part of valour and accordingly a compromise was worked out to suit both.[37]

In the current phase the United States seems to be using the Special 301 clause of its 1974 Trade Act to pressurise India on the nuclear question. In 1992, India was identified for the second consecutive year as a country not adhering to the norms of free trade and therefore to be subjected to punitive measures. Washington threatened to slash $60m worth of Indian pharmaceutical, chemical and other related products from its duty-free preference scheme. The pressure tactic worked as was evident from the fact that India did address the piracy of copyrighted materials and opened its market to US motion pictures.[38] Understandably, these aspects of relations also have their connections with the US–Indian nuclear diplomacy.

During his presidential campaign, Bill Clinton had promised 'to clamp down on countries and companies that sell proscribed technologies, punish violators, and work urgently with all countries for tough, enforceable nonproliferation agreements.' But during the same campaign he had also castigated President George Bush for his over concern for security and global matters at the cost of the US economy. It is essential for the United States to reconcile both these policies in its dealings with India. The latter is fast emerging as an important market for American trade and investment and in this situation to talk too much on the sensitive nuclear question may not be politically wise.

India of course has a much larger stake in US trade and investment.[39] The United States is India's largest trading partner—the two way trade passed $7bn in 1993 with over $4.5bn in India's account. It is also by far the biggest investor in India. During the past three years it has committed $2bn and is expected to remain as the largest investor for years to come. During Prime Minister Narasimha Rao's visit to the US in May this year the India Interest Group, a loose coalition of 30 top, diverse US businesses with a collective economic clout of $300bn—more than India's foreign debt and the GDP put together—helped pave the way for practically every delegation meeting, from the White House to key departments, Senators, Congressmen and chief executives.[40] It is important to note that prior to Rao's departure for the US there was considerable apprehension in political and media circles that Clinton might indulge in some arm twisting on the nuclear and missile issue. But nothing of that sort happened and the economic contents of the dialogue far outweighed other considerations. And within days of Rao's return the *Prithvi* missile was successfully test-fired and inducted into the army.

At the unofficial level there are proposals to give India a permanent seat in the UN Security Council in exchange for its signing the NPT. Questioning the validity of India's nuclear ambivalence, the noted South Asia expert Stephen Cohen argues that the Indian leadership would do well to prepare itself for a dynamic role in an emerging multi-polar world of five or six major powers. This preparation need not depend upon nuclear capability, for neither Japan nor Germany is actually contemplating acquiring that status yet, although they are already being recognised as global influentials. Considering Western resistance to India's going overtly nuclear Cohen wonders if India could diplomatically bargain for a permanent seat in the UN Security Council in exchange for its formal endorsement of the NPT.[41] Actually, it is a diplomatic trial for both countries. As Chellaney has rightly put it: 'The United States faces a painful policy dilemma: it cannot pursue an effective non-proliferation strategy without receiving co-operation from a country like India that itself has been a major target of Western technology-control regimes. On the other hand, India's own long-term security interests demand that it contributes to non-proliferation by seeking to deter the spread of weapons of mass destruction to countries in the Middle East and the Indian Ocean region.'[42]

With regard to Pakistan, the diplomacy of both Henry Kissinger and Zbigniew Brzezinkski and, in general, of the Politico-Military Bureau in the State Department favoured a trade off between conventional weapons and nuclear acquisition. In January 1981, Alexander Haig, the former Secretary of State, had spoken of the need 'to whet Pakistan's nuclear appetite' when Ronald Reagan became the president.[43] Cohen writes: 'I have no doubt in my mind that had the United States pursued a tougher policy toward Pakistan, then the latter would, by 1991, have been a nuclear military power. My own view (in 1981) was that linking the military assistance package to Pakistani nuclear restraint would defer but not terminate Pakistan's nuclear ambitions.'[44]

Ever since the days of President Jimmy Carter when Congress had passed the Symington and Glenn amendments to the Foreign Assistance Act of 1978, which prohibited aid and arms sales to countries suspected of having a nuclear weapons programme, US aid to Pakistan has been suspended several times. In contrast, the Indian programme has been deemed as 'dormant'. In 1981, in response to the Afghan crisis, there was a six-year waiver to the Symington and Glenn amendments to provide a $3.2bn aid package to Pakistan to enable it to bolster its conventional arsenal and thereby to discourage it from going nuclear.[45]

Of late, there has once again been an effort to dangle the carrot of conventional weapons to buy Pakistan's decision to 'cap' its nuclear arms programme. The Clinton administration has been pleading with Congress to grant a one-time waiver to the Pressler amendment to supply Pakistan with 38 F-16 aircraft. In May 1994, speaking on the occasion of his confirmation hearings before the Senate Foreign Relations Committee, the ambassador-designate to India, Frank Wisner, argued that the planes were meant as an incentive to cap Pakistan's nuclear programme and such incentives would also be offered to India for a similar action.[46] It is not clear whether Pakistan subscribes to this linkage or not. Both the President of Pakistan, Farooq Leghari, and the Foreign Minister, Aseef Ahmed Ali, have categorically stated that the supply of F-16s 'cannot be linked' to the question of 'a verifiable cap' over its military nuclear programme.[47]

But whatever Pakistan might say, that there is a secret threat of the stick is quite manifest from the recent controversy over the mode of inspection of the Pakistani nuclear installations. Islamabad appears to be veering round the point that it would probably not mind a 'non-intrusive' inspection which means non-physical verification of its atomic sites. Whether such a plan would be acceptable to the US Congress is, however, a moot point given the latter's insistence upon on-the-spot verifications.[48]

These carrot and stick policies are not confined to South Asia alone. Other countries are also lured to American aid and trade to bolster the NPT regime. The Clinton administration has promised to buy $12bn worth of uranium from the dismantled Russian warheads to fuel nuclear power reactors around the globe. Russia for its part has agreed to provide Ukraine with nuclear power generators in exchange for the latter's nuclear warheads and also an assistance of about half a billion dollars.[49] Given the attraction of the American economic carrot which Russia so desperately needs it is likely that it would continue with its policy of asking India to sign the NPT. Prior to Rao's visit to Moscow in the last week of June 1994, Vladimir Podoprigora, Chairman of the International Affairs Committee of the Federation Council, the Russian Parliament's Upper House, said that Russia as a nuclear power should, together with the United States, provide security guarantees to India, Pakistan and other South Asian states in exchange for India's readiness to sign the NPT.[50] He expected that the matter would figure in the Rao–Yeltsin talks. In the joint communiqué, however, no specific mention of the NPT was made except that both the countries agreed to 'make every effort to facilitate the early conclusion of multilaterally negotiated comprehensive treaties on the universal ban on nuclear tests and cessation of the production of fissile materials for weapons purposes.'[51] Seemingly, the Russians would prefer to continue with their private efforts rather than indulging in open diplomacy.

There is, however, an inherent fallacy in this carrot and stick diplomacy. If to cap Pakistan's, or for that matter any country's, nuclear ambitions it becomes imperative to pamper Pakistan through other means then why should other nations not expect similar pampering by threatening to go nuclear? The North Korean nuclear strategy is a case in point. It has been argued that by threatening to quit the NPT the North Koreans expect to extract concessions from the United States in terms of diplomatic relations, multilateral assistance, nuclear reactors for power generation, and so on.[52]

INDO-PAKISTAN CONFIDENCE BUILDING MEASURES

Owing partly to the US diplomatic pressure and partly to the region's own political compulsions India and Pakistan have taken a series of confidence building measures (CBMs) to palliate the danger of a war in the subcontinent. Between 1980 and 1992 both the Heads of Government or State have met as many as 22 times. Besides, foreign ministers, secretaries and senior officials regularly interact to discuss bilateral questions. The two GHQs maintain a hotline and use it whenever tensions mount on the border. In February 1992, it was this sort of communication only which prevented the situation from escalating when a Pakistan-based group of Kashmiri nationalists tried forcibly to cross the Line of Control.[53]

The most significant CBM, as far as the nuclear question is concerned, has been the 1988 agreement between India and Pakistan not to attack each other's nuclear installations. At the moment there are a number of activities sponsored by several of the Western countries, most notably the United States, through their track-two diplomatic efforts, to bring South Asian academics, journalists, government officials, activists and others to discuss their problems with the objective of preparing the environment for more and more confidence building measures.[54] South Asian academics themselves have suggested several ways of dealing with the problem bilaterally.[55]

The Kashmir Connection

There is an opinion held strongly by many that at the core of the Indo-Pakistan animosity is the unresolved problem of Kashmir which needs to be addressed before any effort can be made to work for nuclear non-proliferation in South Asia. Cohen argues that 'the road to accession to the NPT runs through Kashmir.'[56] Echoing these sentiments, the President of Pakistan, Leghari, said recently that a linkage between a final settlement of the Kashmir dispute and the issue of nuclear disarmament in South Asia could not be set aside.[57]

But the solution of the Kashmir problem is not easy. A whole lot of sentiments, emotions and nation-building dynamics are enmeshed in the issue making it virtually a zero sum game—one's gain is another's loss—which no state can politically afford. The only enduring solution seems to be the acceptance of the existing line of control as the international boundary. If the United States can use its good offices to make both the states agree to this solution it would go a long way to ensure South Asian security. Until then, to talk about nuclear non-proliferation in South Asia is to miss the essential point.

SOME PERSPECTIVES

Efficacy of the NPT: The NPT is the product of the Cold War when despite the confrontation of the two superpowers there was a tacit understanding between them to freeze the situation. Neither wanted Germany and Japan to emerge as nuclear powers and this was intended to be achieved through the expedient of the NPT. In that sense the treaty has been a success. But as far as its verification system is concerned there are glaring deficiencies which are probably built into the system itself. Iraq's Osirak nuclear facilities were bombed by Israel in 1982 to pre-empt the former's alleged nuclear ambitions. Since Iraq was a signatory to the NPT it made a mockery of the NPT regime.

It has been argued that so far there has been no foolproof system to denuclearise a nation that has crossed the nuclear weapon threshold and has the capability to produce the fissile material. This has been proved by the South African experience. The republic joined the NPT in 1990 and voluntarily gave up its nuclear weapons programme. But the IAEA which inspected the nuclear sites in South Africa was not able to find out whether the country had actually made the bomb in the past until South Africa itself confessed. Specialists have their misgivings about the accountability of all fissile materials produced by the country.[58] The problem is that despite an abundance of data, correct assessments are often not possible. Iraq's nuclear capability was not fully assessed until actual UN inspections took place. According to one expert early wrong US estimates were due not to 'data collection, but rather data fusion, caused by over-computerisation and jurisdictional concerns in the intelligence community.'[59] The recent controversy over the NPT-member North Korea's alleged nuclear ambitions provide yet another example of the sloppy nature of the NPT regime.

Taking a cue from the South African experience where, it has been argued, the reason that all the fissile materials cannot be accounted for is that their partial supply source is China, the same could hold good in the case of Pakistan's nuclear programme which has also been assisted by China. As such, no foolproof verification of the fact that Pakistan has been divested of its fissile materials is possible, at least to the satisfaction of India.[60] According to P.K. Iyengar, the former chairman of India's Atomic Energy Commission and one who played a key role in the Indian PNE, there is always the possibility of some fissionable materials which cannot be accounted for even in the safeguard regimes. He says that 'India uses fissionable plutonium in 100 kg units as reactor fuel while a bomb requires only quantities in kilogram in single digits. . . . Under the circumstances, can capping alone ensure non-availability of fissionable material for other purposes?'[61]

National Pride: The issue of the South Asian nuclear question cannot be grasped unless it is put against the background of India's image of itself as a nation and the way it conceives of its placement in the comity of nations. Though a poor state in terms of per capita GNP, in macro terms it is one of the world's largest economic and military powers.[62] It has been the constant grouse of many of India's strategic experts that India's reluctance to project its military culture has been the reason behind its being slighted by the guardians of the world system. One of them, Subrahmanyam, wrote a few years ago in the context of India's vacillation in going for the nuclear option:

> On the nuclear issue especially, the rest of the world cannot have a high opinion about the Indian will to power. In the wake of the Chinese nuclear test, the Indian leadership tried to secure nuclear security guarantees from Britain and was politely rebuffed. At the time of the negotiations for the finalisation of the Non-Proliferation Treaty India sought and failed to get security guarantees from the US, USSR, Britain and France. At the mildest disapproval of our nuclear test from the major powers India climbed down. Let us compare this with the behaviour of other powers in the world. The British, angered by the US McMahon Act which barred access to nuclear weapon design data after Britain fully co-operated with the US on the Manhattan

> project, went ahead and built their own arsenal at a time when Britain had food rationing and had just begun reconstruction of its war-torn economy. The French defied the US and overcame all the obstacles put in their way and developed their arsenal at a time when they had finished fighting one losing anti-colonial war in Indochina and were embarking on the next losing war in Algeria. The Chinese told Khrushchev, in the words of Marshal Chen Yi, that they would rather go without pants but would have the bomb. Bhutto vowed that the (sic) Pakistan would eat grass if necessary but would get the bomb. The Pakistanis resisted all the pressures of the US when the latter totally suspended all assistance to Pakistan in 1979 under the Symington amendment and reconciled itself to Pakistan developing a nuclear bomb. If in these circumstances the rest of the world, including Pakistan, were to have reservations about the Indian will to power, can they be blamed? [63]

'The harsh lesson of history,' Subrahmanyam further argues, 'is that if a nation does not have adequate power to hold itself together in the harsh international environment it is likely to be broken up. This age of coercive diplomacy continuously generates such pressures on composite nations.'[64]

While there is enough grain of truth in what Subrahmanyam says the fact remains that probably the tradition and culture of India (read Hindu) is such that most things are described in the negative. It is therefore non-violence, non-alignment, non-non-vegetarianism (literal translation of the Sanskrit word *niramish* meaning vegetarian food), and so on. It is this genius of India that has probably never been understood by the West. Mahatma Gandhi's political strategy of non-violence confused the British imperialists as much as Pandit Nehru's international diplomacy of non-alignment subsequently confused the all-knowing Americans.[65] In the same vein, India's nuclear diplomacy probably becomes unfathomable to the West. India is neither in favour of 'proliferation' nor 'non-proliferation' as the West understands these concepts. It tends to counter the Western diatribe of non-proliferation by emphasising its concept of non-non-proliferation—it will develop and perfect the technology to make the bomb, it is committed to the peaceful use only of nuclear energy, it will resist all pressure to sign the NPT. Each of these positions would sound exclusive and unharmonisable with the remaining two but India has proved that they can be integrated and projected as one single policy. Apparently Pakistan follows the same policy but by compromising on its NPT argument—if India signs it would also do so—it has blunted its ideological edge.

Given the diplomatic exchanges between the United States and India during the last few years it seems that the US might eventually relent and both states would find some way out of this proliferation controversy even without India subscribing to the NPT. The point must not be missed that after the end of the Cold War the emphasis for both the governments has substantially shifted to economic matters and there is some appreciation of each other's needs and expectations in this sphere.

CONCLUSION: NATIONALISM AND INTERNATIONALISM

The region of South Asia in nuclear terms is a potential flash point. Here three rival nations—China, India and Pakistan—sharing disputed borders and torn by historical animosities, are countenancing one another with nuclear weapons, or, at least, weapons-grade fissile materials, and delivery systems. What is also important, these states, who together account for about 40 per cent of the world's population, converge close to the borders of nuclear Kazakhstan, a one-time Soviet republic.

What the nature and composition of international response to the South Asian nuclear tangle might be is not yet manifest. But what is increasingly becoming clear is that more and more states would be roped in to address the question. Already in the place of five-power conference consisting of the United States, Russia, China, India and Pakistan a 5+2+2 conference consisting of the five acknowledged nuclear states plus India and Pakistan plus Germany and Japan has been mooted. It would not be surprising if more states are brought into the picture in due course. Given the recent North Korean experience it is certain that it would be the United States which would call the shots. In any case, by the time the NPT goes for review in April 1995 there will be some new developments.

Whatever might be the outcome of this conference and even if India and Pakistan are made to 'cap' their military-related nuclear programmes there is no guarantee that the South Asian 'insecurity syndrome' would be replaced by a security structure to which both countries would subscribe in mutual co-operation. One of the major obstacles to regional security is the Kashmir imbroglio which neither of the states seem seriously set to address. Their mindsets are so ridiculously fossilised that no change in them seems to be remotely possible. India harps on the tune that the starting point has to be the Simla agreement (1972) which had considered Kashmir as an issue to be resolved bilaterally and peacefully. But whenever Pakistan asks for a dialogue India unceremoniously rejects it on the ground that Kashmir is an integral part of India and, therefore, not negotiable. Pakistan for its part treats the Simla agreement as a dead document yet shows no qualms in taking every possible opportunity to call for a dialogue with India on Kashmir. Moreover, although it knows quite well that the UN resolutions passed in 1948 have little meaning now as they have been overtaken by other events still it makes reference to them ad nauseam.

A denuclearised South Asia, provided it is internationally guaranteed and made foolproof through a perfect system of verification (a tall order owing to inherent problems attached to the system), probably would not harm India's interest if seen from a purely South Asian regional perspective. It would help India maintain its edge over Pakistan in respect of conventional armaments. But India's security concerns are never viewed in narrow regional terms. A continent-sized country, having lived under colonial rule for about two centuries and being a nation with traditional pride in its cultural greatness, India conceives its threats more from beyond the region than from within. Pakistan is deemed as a threat only because of its extra-regional connections. It is, therefore, China, because of its physical proximity and territorial ambitions, and all those powers claiming stakes in the Indian Ocean region which continue to be pertinent to India's security concerns. To view the South Asian nuclear question from a purely South Asian perspective would be unwise.

India expects to compensate for its acknowledged position of not possessing nuclear weapons by a technology demonstration strategy which it perceives to be a deterrent to potential nuclear threats. The MTCR prevents the advanced nations from supplying the relevant technology to others but it does not prevent the indigenous development of missiles which India is poised to achieve. That it will have a snowball effect in the region is understandable and unavoidable.

The complex reality of South Asian security is that no segmented approach can encompass it. The nuclear question is just one segment, though a critical one. Keeping in view the nationalistic and rationalistic premises of all concerned the only enduring solution to the threat of a nuclear war can be nothing short of a total destruction of the nuclear arsenal from the face of the earth. If that sounds unrealistic then a segmented view of nuclear proliferation does not sound realistic either. Some day there has to be a harmonious blending of the concepts of nationalism and internationalism to save the world from the scourge of the nuclear holocaust. The battle cannot be won easily but won it has to be. 'My nationalism is intense internationalism; I am sick of the strife between nations and religions,' said that indomitable 'naked *fakir*'—Gandhi.

NOTES

[1] The book in question is, William E. Burrows and Robert Windrem, *Critical Mass* (New York: Simon and Schuster, 1994). *India Today* (New Delhi), 15 February 1994, carried long pre-publication excerpts.

[2] *India Today*, 30 April 1994, p. 48. Notably, a decade ago, Dr. A.Q. Khan, Pakistan's top nuclear scientist, had made it known that his country was years ahead of India in its uranium enrichment capability and if the Pakistan government so decided the bomb could be assembled. See Eric E. Vas, 'Pakistan's Security Futures', in Stephen Philip Cohen, ed., *The Security of South Asia: American and Asian Perspectives* (New Delhi: Vistaar, 1987), p. 96.

[3] K. Subrahmanyam, 'Capping, Managing, or Eliminating Nuclear Weapons?', in Kanti Bajpai and Stephen P. Cohen, eds., *South Asia After the Cold War: International Perspectives* (Boulder: Westview Press, 1993), pp. 179–180.

[4] See India and Pakistan chapters of Leonard S. Spector, *Nuclear Ambitions* (Boulder: Westview Press, 1990).

[5] Reuters report of 3 December 1992 citing an NBC broadcast of 1 December 1992.

[6] Testimony of CIA Director James Woolsey, 24 February 1993. US Senate, Governmental Affairs Committee, Hearings (Washington D.C.: USGPO, 1993), p. 11

[7] Philip P. Ritcheson, 'Nuclearization in South Asia', *Strategic Review* (Washington, D.C.), Fall 1993, pp. 39–40. American strategic thinkers, Lewis A. Dunn and Herman Kahn, have listed as many as 14 reasons for a country to seek nuclear weapons. For details, see Bhabani Şen Gupta and Centre for Policy Research, *Nuclear Weapons?: Policy Options for India* (New Delhi: Sage, 1983), pp. 17–19, 41–46.

[8] See this author's forthcoming article on BJP's foreign policy outlook, in *BIISS Journal* (Dhaka). At the party's National Council Meeting held in Vadodora in June 1994 it was reiterated that: 'We must declare that India is a nuclear state.' The party was 'not against global disarmament' but 'India must first have nuclear weapons before it can destroy them,' it was said. *The Hindu* (New Delhi), 13 June 1994.

[9] Mushahid Hussain, 'The Role of Advanced Weaponry in Developing Countries,' W. Thomas Wander and Eric H. Arnett, eds., *The Proliferation of Advanced Weaponry: Technology, Motivations, and Responses* (Washington, D.C.: American Association for the Advancement of Science, 1992), p. 18. Quoted in Ritcheson, 'Nuclearization in South Asia', p. 40.

[10] See his interview in *India Today*, 30 April 1994, p. 46. For a detailed study of the nuclear power profiles of India and Pakistan, see K.D. Kapur, *Nuclear Non-Proliferation Diplomacy: Nuclear Power Programmes in the Third World* (New Delhi: Lancers, 1993).

[11] Gamini B. Keerawella, 'Peace and Security Perceptions of a Small State: Sri Lankan Responses to Superpower Naval Rivalry in the Indian Ocean—1970–77', in Shelton U. Kodikara, ed., *South Asian Strategic Issues: Sri Lankan Perspectives* (New Delhi: Sage, 1990), p. 192.

[12] Quoted in ibid., p. 139.

[13] Brahma Chellaney, *Nuclear Proliferation: The US–Indian Conflict* (New Delhi: Orient Longman, 1993), pp. 291–292.

[14] Ibid., pp. 294–295.

[15] Text of the note in ibid, pp. 406–408.

[16] Sergei S. Lunyov, 'India's Role in South Asia: A Soviet View,' in Vernon L.B. Mendis, *India's Role in South Asia* (Colombo: Bandaranaike Centre for International Studies, 1992), p. 99. The paper was presented at a Colombo seminar on 15 June 1991. This view was corroborated by the US Mission's note to NATO, 5 June 1974, referred to above. It said: 'The Soviets share our concern about proliferation. They lobbied hard, though unsuccessfully, to get India to sign the NPT. At this point, they are wary of damaging their loose ties with India and have refrained from any public comment.' Chellaney, *Nuclear Proliferation*, p 407.

[17] One scholar has argued that deterrence as a theory has extremely limited efficacy in the India–Pakistan context. He has also drawn a scenario of nuclear war between the two countries and its devastating effect. S. Rashid Naim, 'Asia's Day After: Nuclear War Between Indian and Pakistan?', in Cohen, *The Security of South Asia*, pp. 251–282. For more general arguments against the theory of deterrence, see G.D. Deshingkar, 'Deterrence: With Weapons or Without?', *Alternatives* (New Delhi/New York), 4(1), July 1978, pp. 135–144; Achin Vanaik, 'Myth of Nuclear Deterrence', *The Hindu*, 25 June 1994.

[18] For details see Partha S. Ghosh, 'A Third World Perspective on Nuclear Disarmament', in David Carlton and Carlo Schaerf, eds., *Reassessing Arms Control* (London: Macmillan, 1985), pp. 95–96.

[19] See Shrikant B. Paranjpe, 'Parliament and Foreign Policy: A Study of the Role played by the Indian Parliament in the Formulation of India's Nuclear Policy', Report of ICSSR-funded project, mimeo, January 1993, p. 109.

[20] On 10 June 1994, China conducted its 40th nuclear test. On an average it has conducted one test every 39 weeks. The last test was on 5 October 1993, about 36 weeks earlier. The United States so far has conducted more than 1000 tests and the Russians about 700. For an analysis of the international implications of the Chinese nuclear tests, see D. Bannerjee, 'Meaning of China's 40th Nuclear Test', *Times of India* (New Delhi), 17 June 1994; and C. Raja Mohan, 'Chinese N-Test: A Signal to US', *The Hindu*, 13 June 1994.

[21] Ritcheson, 'Nuclearization in South Asia', pp. 40–41.

[22] Jasjit Singh, 'India and South Asia: The Strategic and Security Issues', in Bertram Bastiampillai, ed., *India and Her South Asian Neighbours* (Colombo: Bandaranaike Centre for International Studies, 1992), pp. 30–31.

[23] Quoted in C. Raja Mohan, 'Are Nuclear Arms Forever?', *The Hindu*, 20 July 1994.

[24] *The Hindu*, 19 June 1994.

[25] According to Middle Eastern intelligence sources Iran was to receive in the first quarter of 1994 North Korean *No-Dong* surface to surface missiles with partial Libyan funding. The missile is designed to carry a 700 kg warhead with a range of up to 1000 km. *Flight International*, 8–14 December 1993. Cited in *Journal of Indian Ocean Studies* (New Delhi), 1(2), March 1994, p. 76.

[26] See his interview in *India Today*, 15 April 1994, pp. 70–71.

[27] P.S. Suryanarayana 'Pak Response to Prithvi,' *The Hindu*, 1 July 1994.

[28] *India Today*, 15 July 1994, p. 155.

[29] Chellaney, *Nuclear Proliferation*, p. 407.

[30] Rajaram Panda, 'India and Japan in the Post-Cold War Era', *Reitaku Journal of Interdisciplinary Studies* (Kashiwa, Chiba), 1(1), March 1993, pp. 106–109.

[31] *New York Times*, 16 January 1992, p. A9:6. See also Batuk Ghatani's dispatch from London in *The Hindu*, 6 January 1992; Robert Pfaltzgraff, Jr., 'The Emerging Global Security Environment', *The Annals* (Philadelphia), 517, September 1991, pp. 23–24. By March 1992 some applications for jobs from Russian scientists had been received by the Department of Science and Technology (DST) of the Government of India. *Times of India*, 9 March 1992.

[32] Charles Krauthammer, 'The Unipolar Movement', *Foreign Affairs* (New York), 70, 1991, p. 31.

[33] *Sunday Telegraph* (London), 29 May 1994. Cited in *International Security Digest* (London), 1(6), May 1994.

[34] *Times of India*, 8 June 1994.

[35] Ibid., 26 May 1994.

[36] C. Raja Mohan, 'Making the World Safe for American Missiles', *The Hindu*, 7 July 1994.

[37] Chellaney, *Nuclear Proliferation*, p. 296. Later, France also compromised on the question of safeguards at Tarapore so as not to jeopardise its lucrative Mirage 2000 deal.

[38] Ibid., pp. 307–308.

[39] I have discussed this point elsewhere. See Partha S. Ghosh, 'Challenges and Opportunities: Indian Foreign Policy in the 1990s', in Bajpai and Cohen, *South Asia After the Cold War*, pp. 105–138.

[40] For details, see Sudeep Chakravarti, 'Indo-US Business Relations: Readying for a Boost', *India Today*, 15 July 1994, pp. 138–151.

[41] Stephen P. Cohen, 'A Way Out of the South Asia Arms Race', *Washington Post*, 28 September 1992; and 'India's Regional Impact', *Seminar* (New Delhi), 401, January 1993, pp. 69–74.

[42] Chellaney, *Nuclear Proliferation*, pp. 299–300.

[43] R.R. Subramaniam, 'US Policy and South Asia: The Decision-Making Dimension', in Cohen, *The Security of South Asia*, p. 149.

[44] Stephen Philip Cohen, 'The Reagan Administration and India', in Harold A. Gould and Sumit Ganguly, eds., *The Hope and the Reality: US–Indian Relations from Roosevelt to Reagan* (Boulder: Westview, 1992), p. 148.

[45] Arthur G. Rubinoff, 'Congressional Attitudes Toward India', in ibid., pp. 167–171.

[46] *Times of India*, 18 May 1994.

[47] *The Hindu*, 19 May and 6 June 1994.

[48] Ibid., 9 June 1994.

[49] Gursharan S. Dhanjal, 'A Detoured Nuclear Diplomacy', *Mainstream* (New Delhi), 26 February 1994, p. 21.

[50] See Vladimir Radyuhin's dispatch from Moscow, in *The Hindu*, 27 June 1994.

[51] Text of the Moscow Declaration, in ibid., 1 July 1994.

[52] Giri Deshingkar, 'North Korea and the US: Rogue States in Conflict', *Tinies of India*, 21 June 1994.

[53] Hasan-Askari Rizvi, 'Regional Nuclear Proliferation: Problems and Prospects', in Bajpai and Cohen, *South Asia After the Cold War*, pp. 212–213.

[54] For details of such activities, see Sundeep Waslekar, 'Track-Two Diplomacy in South Asia', Occasional Paper of the Program in Arms Control, Disarmament, and International Security, University of Illinois at Urbana—Champaign, March 1994.

[55] Two sets of such suggestions are given in Chellaney, *Nuclear Proliferation*, pp. 306–307; and Subrahmanyam, 'Capping, Managing, or Eliminating Nuclear Weapons', p. 189.

[56] Stephen P. Cohen, 'A Fresh US Policy for South Asia and India's Part in Influencing It', *India Abroad* (Chicago), 2 April 1993, p. 2.

[57] *The Hindu*, 6 June 1994.

[58] Subrahmanyam, 'Capping, Managing, or Eliminating Nuclear Weapons', pp. 184–185.

[59] Peter D. Zimmerman, 'Proliferation of Missiles and Nuclear Weapons', in Center for Strategic and International Studies, 'Agenda '93: CSIS Policy Action Papers'. (Washington, D.C., November 1992), p. 14.

[60] Subrahmanyam, 'Capping, Managing, or Eliminating Nuclear Weapons', p. 185.

[61] *Times of India*, 18 May 1994.

[62] According to the World Bank's latest development report India's per capita GNP by the purchasing power parities (PPP) calculation was a bare $1,210 in 1992 in 'current international dollars' which was less than Sri Lanka, Pakistan and even the so-called 'basket-case' Bangladesh. According to the same report, however, the Indian economy was the fifth largest in the world after the United States, China, Japan and Germany. *The Hindu*, 21 June 1994. A UNICEF report released in June 1994 revealed that there were 5000 malnutrition deaths daily in India. *Times of India*, 22 June 1994. According to the UNDP's human development report of 1994 India maintained its position as the world's top arms importer during the five years from 1988 to 1992. In 1992, it spent $1.2bn. India and Pakistan together accounted for about 30 per cent of arms imports by the developing countries, and over 18 per cent of all global arms sales. Ibid., 24 June 1994.

[63] K. Subrahmanyam, 'Role of National Power', in K. Subrahmanyam, ed., *India and the Nuclear Challenge* (New Delhi: Lancer International, 1986), p. 260.

[64] Ibid., p. 268.

[65] For a conceptual analysis of the cultural variable in diplomacy including that between the United States and India, see Raymond Cohen, *Negotiating Across Cultures: Communication Obstacles in International Diplomacy* (Washington, D.C.: US Institute of Peace Press, 1991). See also Partha S. Ghosh, 'United States and India: The Reality and the Hope', Occasional Paper of the Program in Arms Control, Disarmament and International Security (ACDIS), University of Illinois at Urbana—Champaign, March 1994.

[11]

Prospects for Peace and Stability in Northeast Asia: The Korean Conflict

Barry K. Gills

Following the partition of the Korean peninsula in 1945 and the emergence of two rival administrations in 1948, the 'Korean Question' was put before the international community, ie the matter of conflicting claims to domestic and international legitimacy, and the desire for national reunification. The Korean conflict was perceived abroad as primarily a geopolitical issue. The Korean War (1950–53) left a legacy of armed truce (the world's longest running armistice) and the most militarised border in the world, euphemistically known as the 'demilitarised' zone (DMZ). The Republic of Korea (South Korea, ROK) and the Democratic People's Republic of Korea (North Korea, DPRK) were both a product of the Cold War, but their antagonism has outlived it and continues to produce controversy. Long term regional security in Northeast Asia depends on a resolution of the Korean conflict.

During the Cold War, the division of Korea was tacitly accepted as a necessary element of stability. With its end, however, the continued division of the Korean peninsula, and the stubborn persistence of the Korean conflict, produced new threats to regional security. Paradoxically, the traditional 'Korean Question' was resolved through dual membership in the United Nations from autumn 1991. The international community, therefore, now recognises two states and accepts the legitimacy of both regimes. Nevertheless, the ideological and military confrontation between the two Korean governments has continued, and all parties maintain a commitment to the peaceful reunification of Korea sometime in the future.

Despite the formal equality of the two Koreas however, the reality of the respective status of each is quite different. North Korea is in crisis. The origins of the most recent phase of the Korean conflict lie in its relative weakness, both economically and diplomatically. The separate development of North and South Korea over a period of nearly five decades has produced sharply different outcomes. The economic failures of North Korea and its political isolation generated a new and serious crisis in the 1990s, affecting not only North Korea itself, but the region as a whole.

The most acute manifestation of this was the nuclear crisis of 1992–4, which brought a recalcitrant North Korea into direct confrontation with the UN and the United States. North Korea risked having UN economic sanctions imposed on an already crippled economy and faced the possibility of eventual US or UN military action. However, North Korea's behaviour should be understood as an expression of its general desperation. Essentially, North Korea played the 'nuclear card' as a bargaining chip, in order to extract aid and diplomatic recognition from the West. The death of the 'Great Leader' Kim Il Sung in

July 1994, at the very height of these extremely delicate nuclear negotiations, had the world momentarily holding its breath.

The succession of his son and heir Kim Jong Il, confirmed after several months of mysterious silence, marked the beginning of a new era. With the successful conclusion of the nuclear talks in autumn 1994, new prospects for peace and stability in Northeast Asia have appeared. North Korea is poised to accept the inevitability of opening up to the world economy, entailing domestic reform in the future. This opportunity should facilitate the trend toward increasing economic interdependence in the region, and the easing of ideological, political, and military tensions.

ORIGINS OF THE KOREAN CONFLICT

Much ink has been spilt over the causes of the division of Korea and the origins of the subsequent fratricidal war.[1] It is not possible adequately to review all the contending explanations here. Therefore, let us restrict ourselves to some central elements. In the broadest historical sense, the Korean conflict is a product of modernisation and development in East Asia, and particularly of the role of imperial Japan in this process. The colonisation of Korea profoundly changed its economic, social, political, and ideological makeup and set the stage for revolutionary upheavals in the wake of Japan's departure.[2] The ambition of the Soviet Union to expand its influence at the expense of Japan in 1945 ran head on into the American policy of containing Soviet expansionism. War-time co-operation was quickly translated into post-war competition.[3] The future mould of the Korean conflict was set in the first year of occupation by the Russians in the North and the Americans in the South.[4]

The partition of Korea in 1945, the inevitable consequence of military occupation via two separate zones of administration, had the effect of frustrating Korean nationalism and the fervently held desire for a unified independent state. Both superpowers underestimated Korean nationalism, although an examination of Korea's early colonial history would have instructed them in its tenacity.[5] This error proved to be a strategic one, since ideological and political polarisation on the peninsula led directly to the Korean War in 1950, when both sides in their turn made a violent bid for reunification.

In North Korea's view, it was a civil war, initiated for the necessary liberation of South Korea, a position shared by the Soviet Union.[6] In the view of the UN, however, North Korea was the aggressor for having invaded South Korea.[7] Likewise, the UN designated China as an aggressor, after Chinese forces entered the war and expelled UN troops from North Korea.[8] The question of 'war guilt' was thereafter crucial to the course of the Korean Question, bound up inseparably with the issue of legitimacy, including that of the role of the UN and of US forces in Korea.

Though the Korean War certainly had both genuine domestic causes as well as external ones, its internationalisation changed the nature of the Korean conflict thereafter. Despite the loss of several million lives, neither side won the Korean war and both accepted the inevitability of an armistice, finally agreed in 1953 after two years of tortuous negotiations.[9] The failure of the Geneva conference in 1954 to achieve any political solution to the Korean reunification issue led directly to the acceptance of national division as the new status quo.[10]

Nevertheless, the post-war settlement, which remained stable until the end of the Cold War, was fraught with a legacy of continued hostility between the two Koreas and their allies. This hostility was translated into further ideological polarisation between the two regimes, high expenditures on military preparation, economic competition to achieve industrialisation, and extensive diplomatic competition for foreign recognition and support.

THE COMPETITION FOR INTERNATIONAL LEGITIMACY

Throughout the Cold War era—a period of some 45 years—the two Koreas competed intensely for international legitimacy. Both regimes were actually quite successful in terms of developing an industrialised economy, a strong state, and in promoting an active diplomacy throughout the world. This process culminated in dual membership of the United Nations in the 1990s. Paradoxically, however, the apparent resolution of the Korean Question and the problem of legitimacy revealed the underlying weakness of North Korea at the end of the Cold War. The explanation for this paradoxical outcome lies in an analysis of the political economy of Korean diplomacy in the context of a changing international system.[11]

The annual debate on the Korean Question in the United Nations General Assembly (UNGA) was a barometer of the general state of competition for international legitimacy between the rival Korean regimes. The United Nations Commission for the Unification and Rehabilitation of Korea (UNCURK) submitted an annual report on the Korean Question, thus eliciting a debate between contending interpretations of the Korean conflict.[12] From 1947 to 1961 the composition of the United Nations General Assembly (UNGA) was such that an overwhelming majority was in favour of the US–South Korea interpretation of the Korean Question: ie that South Korea was the only legitimate government of Korea recognised as such by the UN; that only South Korea be allowed to participate in UN debates on the Korean Question; that the UNC/US military presence in South Korea was necessary to keep the peace; and that the role of the UN, and especially of UNCURK, was necessary and beneficial to the maintenance of peace and security in the region.[13]

This comfortable pro-Western majority in the UNGA began to show signs of weakening by 1961, when a large number of newly independent African states joined.[14] The asymmetry in the UNGA's Korea debates was thereafter steadily reduced, as a new coalition of socialist and non-aligned countries pressed for passage of pro-DPRK resolutions. South Korea was therefore placed somewhat on the defensive in the UNGA throughout the late 1960s and early 1970s, a period during which South Korean combat involvement in the Vietnam War cost it the support of many non-aligned governments. As a result of this increasing diplomatic competition, and in parallel with its ambitious industrialisation plans and export orientation, South Korea gradually retreated from strict anti-communist criteria in its foreign affairs in favour of a more pragmatic 'economic diplomacy'.

Table 1: UNGA Voting Patterns on the Korean Question 1965–75

1965	61 yes, 13 no, 34 abstentions (pro-ROK resolution: free elections and extension of UNCURK's role) 28 yes, 39 no, 22 abs. (invite DPRK to debate)
1966	67 yes, 19 no, 32 abs. (pro-ROK resolution) 34 yes, 53 no (invite DPRK to debate)
1967	68 yes, 23 no, 26 abs. (pro-ROK resolution) 40 yes, 55 no (invite DPRK to debate) 50 yes, 37 no, 24 abs. (invite both Koreas without preconditions) 24 yes, 60 no, 29 abs. (pro-DPRK: dissolve UNCURK)
1968	72 yes, 23 no, 26 abs. (pro-ROK resolution) 40 yes, 55 no, 28 abs. (invite both Koreas unconditionally) 67 yes, 28 no, 28 abs. (invite DPRK on precondition of its recognition of UN competence) 25 yes, 67 no, 29 abs. (pro-DPRK: dissolve UNCURK) 24 yes, 70 no, 28 abs. (pro-DPRK: cancel UN debate)
1969	70 yes, 26 no, 21 abs. 9 not voting (pro-ROK) 40 yes, 55 no, 27 abs. (invite DPRK unconditionally) 29 yes, 61 no, 32 abs. (pro-DPRK: UNC and US withdrawal from South Korea) 30 yes, 65 no, 27 abs. (pro-DPRK: Dissolve UNCURK)
1970	67 yes, 28 no, 22 abs., 10 absent (pro-ROK) 40 yes, 54 no, 25 abs. (invite DPRK unconditionally) 32 yes, 60 no, 30 abs. (pro-DPRK: withdraw all foreign troops) 32 yes, 64 no, 26 abs. (pro-DPRK: dissolve UNCURK)
1971	68 yes, 28 no, 22 abs. 12 absent (to postpone the Korea Debate to 26th UNGA session)
1972	70 yes, 35 no, 21 abs. (to postpone Korea Debate)
1973	Unanimous Decision, First Committee (to allow the DPRK to participate in renewed debate on Korean Question) Unanimous Decision, UNGA (to dissolve UNCURK)
1974	61 yes, 43 against, 31 abs., 3 absent (pro-ROK) 48 yes, 48 no, 38 abs., 4 not voting (pro-DPRK: withdraw all foreign troops; dissolve UNC)
1975	59 yes, 43 no, 42 abs. (pro-DPRK: withdraw all foreign forces; dissolve UNC)

The pattern of the annual voting on the Korean Question in the UNGA between 1965 and 1975, illustrated in Table 1, reveals both the strength of South Korea's position throughout the period, and the mounting challenge to the West's interpretation of the Korean Question. This challenge is reflected in the steadily rising vote for pro-DPRK resolutions and by the parallel proclivity to abstain on pro-South Korean resolutions, especially by non-aligned countries.

It would be a mistake, however, to conclude that the DPRK 'won' this diplomatic competition. In reality, the international community gradually moved away from the ideological and strategic criteria of the Cold War and toward a new consensus that emphasised the equal international standing of the two Koreas and their right to self-determination without foreign interference.

Nevertheless, North Korean reunification proposals did indeed receive a consistent increase in support throughout this period, culminating in a series of decisions that changed the post-war settlement of the Korean Question. First, the DPRK was given permission to participate in the UN debates on the Korean Question. Secondly, the UNGA unanimously voted to affirm the principle of self-determination for the Korean people, ie to recognise that the UN role should be phased out and the matter of international status and reunification should be resolved by the two Koreas themselves. Thirdly, the UNGA voted unanimously to dissolve the UNCURK, long depicted by North Korea as biased in favour of the West's interpretation of the Korean Question. Fourthly, in 1975 the UNGA passed a resolution which in effect called for the end of the UN and UN Commission's (UNC) role in Korea and the removal of all foreign troops.

This change in the international community's view of the Korean Question can be measured in the pattern of the UNGA voting. For example, the number of votes against the annual pro-ROK resolution in the UNGA (affirming the legitimacy of South Korea and the need for UNC/US forces to keep the peace), increased from a mere nine votes in 1959, to 11 in 1961–63, 13 in 1965, 19 in 1966, 23 in 1967–8, 26 in 1969, 28 in 1970–71, 35 in 1972, 43 in 1974, and peaking at 51 in 1975. Likewise, the number of abstentions on pro-ROK resolutions gradually increased, from 17 in 1959, 27 in 1961, 34 in 1965, thereafter hovering in the 20s throughout the next decade, but again peaking at 31 abstentions in 1974.

The decisions of the UNGA to postpone the debate on the Korean Question in 1971 and 1972 were taken at the initiative of South Korea and the United States. Many supporters of North Korea's position voted against these resolutions or abstained. The idea behind the suspension of debate was ostensibly to avoid 'unnecessary acrimony', which could spoil the new atmosphere for fruitful North-South dialogue between the two Korean regimes.[15] It also provided the ROK and the US with a respite during which new proposals were floated, most significantly the idea of 'cross-recognition' and dual membership in the UN.[16] The essence of this idea was that the principal supporters of each Korea would recognise the 'other Korea' as well, thus admitting that both were legitimate. This would have the effect of legally recognising the actual status quo, and thus reducing tension.

Effect of superpowers' detente

The new atmosphere surrounding the Korean conflict was a product of changed international circumstances, including detente between the superpowers, Nixon and Kissinger's breakthrough with China, the winding down of the Vietnam War, and the new importance of the Third World in global politics. The two

Koreas seized this opportunity to launch their first direct diplomatic contracts since the Geneva conference in 1954. In 1971 secret high-level discussions took place, leading to formal talks in 1972. These contacts led to the historic agreement on new principles of peaceful reunification contained in the Joint Communique of 4 July 1972.

The great powers accepted and facilitated this new atmosphere of reconciliation in Korea. Kissinger and Zhou Enlai reached an agreement on the principle of self-determination for Korea, making possible the unanimous decision of the UNGA in 1973 to allow the DPRK to participate in the UN debate for the first time. This also cleared the path for the decision by the UNGA to dissolve UNCURK. The entire international community seemed to be signalling a clear desire for the two Koreas themselves to produce a peaceful solution to the Korean conflict.

The final full UNGA debate on the Korean Question in 1975 produced an unprecedented situation whereby two irreconcilable resolutions on the Korean Question were approved by the UNGA. One called for the dissolution of the UNC and withdrawal of foreign forces, the other called for retention of the UNC's role. Though perhaps a symbolic victory for North Korea, the situation was left ambiguous as to which resolution had real authority and should be implemented. The United States thereafter emphasised its bilateral security arrangements with South Korea and demonstrated its defence commitment to the ROK through staging ever larger annual military exercises, known as 'Team Spirit'. North Korea continued to call for implementation of the pro-DPRK resolution. It was particularly active within the Non-aligned Movement in this respect.

The changing voting patterns in the UN during this period are better understood when one examines the underlying competition between the two Koreas for diplomatic partners. Again, whereas South Korea started out in a very superior position and generally maintained its strength, North Korea achieved a steady and impressive improvement in its diplomatic standing throughout the period. Table 2 illustrates the basic pattern of competition for diplomatic recognition between 1961 and 1975.

Table 2: Full Diplomatic Partners

Year	DPRK	ROK
1961	15	27
1963	18	67
1967	25	76
1969	32	80
1972	45	85
1974	60	90
1975	87	92

Table 2 reveals a leap in the total number of partners for the ROK from 1961 to 1963. The gain of 30 new full diplomatic partners in 1962 was due to a sudden realisation by the new military government of Park Chung Hee that

South Korea could no longer afford to be complacent; therefore the ROK simply capitalised on already existing recognition which had been allowed to lie dormant. North Korea's leap occurred between 1971 and 1975. Altogether, in the three year period immediately preceding the UNGA vote in 1975, over 40 countries established full diplomatic relations with North Korea. Of these, a majority were non-aligned countries. It is clear, therefore, that North Korea gained far more from the new 'non-partisan' attitudes of the international community than did South Korea during this period.

The competition for diplomatic recognition and support continued even after 1975, but in the absence of any annual UNGA debate on the Korean Question. The suspension of the debate was perhaps a natural consequence of the dissolution of UNCURK, the winding down of the UNC after 1975, the end of the Vietnam War, and the heightened security tension on the Korean peninsula after the 'axe murder' incident of August 1976.[17] The annual UN debate was suspended from 1976 by mutual agreement of the parties concerned, including North Korea.

After 1975 the DPRK managed for a short time to sustain rough parity with South Korea in the competition for diplomatic partners. In 1980, the DPRK had 100 partners to the ROK's 112. By late 1985, however, the gap was widening in South Korea's favour again. The figure in 1985 was 101 for the DPRK and 118 for the ROK, reflecting the diplomatic costs in North Korea of the Rangoon bombing incident in 1983, in which several members of the South Korean President's (Chun Doo Hwan) entourage died.[18] South Korea's level of international support improved again after the hosting of the Olympic Games in Seoul in 1988 and the fall of communist regimes in eastern Europe from 1989 onwards. The 'nordpolitik' pursued by South Korea was a natural extension of its gradual abandonment of ideological criteria in foreign affairs, and the natural complement to its ever more successful economic diplomacy.[19]

International recognition

Most importantly, there was a steady trend from the early 1970s onward for an increasing number of governments to recognise both Koreas. In 1980 the figure was 61, and by 1985 it was 67. With the end of the Cold War, this previous trend facilitated the entry of both Koreas into the UN as full members.

North Korea's entry into the UN did not occur 'willingly', however. On the contrary, its admission alongside its rival was a reflection of its weak position. Its principal allies, the Soviet Union and China, both saw advantages in cultivating close economic ties with South Korea. The USSR's shift began when Gorbachev delivered the Vladivostok speech in July 1986, in which he indicated new interest in economic development in the East, normalisation of relations, and reduction of tensions. The surprise summit between Gorbachev and South Korea's President Noh Tae Woo in San Francisco in June, 1990 led directly to agreement to establish full diplomatic relations in September. In the Moscow Declaration in December of the same year, the USSR endorsed South Korea's reunification policy and a nuclear free Korea. In the course of such dramatic improvements in relations, both the USSR and China accepted the

South's desire to join the UN and agreed not to veto its application. South Korea's desire to join the UN had been public knowledge since Noh Tae Woo's maiden speech at the UN in October 1988. China informed North Korea in the summer of 1991 that it would not veto South Korea's application for UN membership.

In these circumstances, North Korea abandoned its longstanding opposition to what it referred to as the 'two Koreas plot'. The option of allowing South Korea unilaterally to occupy a seat in the UN was of course unacceptable in Pyongyang.[20] Nevertheless, many Western states, including the US and Japan, did not open full diplomatic relations with the DPRK, despite its admission into the UN. In this sense, 'cross recognition' was not fulfilled, though virtually all communist and post-communist governments opened such relations with South Korea. Therefore, unlike the period of the mid-1970s, when changes in international attitudes to the Korean Question primarily benefited North Korea, this time the benefits were markedly to South Korea's credit.

NORTH KOREA IN CRISIS

The limitations of Juche

The origins of North Korea's post Cold War crisis extend back much earlier than the 1990s and are essentially political. North Korea's nationalistic 'socialism in one country' approach to economic development, enshrined in the principle of 'juche', or 'self-reliance', was accompanied by creation of a rigid political and ideological system. The Juche economic management system, stripped to bare essentials, is nothing other than ubiquitous party management of production, even at the lowest levels. Thus, bureaucratisation is its hallmark, despite its credo of anti-bureaucratisation. The Juche system, like Stalin's economic policies in the 1930s, produced remarkable short-term economic benefits, but was bedevilled with long term structural problems of growth.[21]

Within a few years of its establishing the Juche economic system in the late 1950s, some economists praised North Korea as an 'industrial miracle',[22] while the political system was transformed into a 'monolithic' regime under the monopoly of one faction, the 'Kapsan' group led by Kim Il Sung.[23] After the initial one-off gains of the system, largely due to extensive foreign technological and economic aid,[24] North Korea's economy has been beset by perpetual structural difficulties. From the moment the Juche system was fully in place, these structural difficulties became increasingly burdensome, obstructing the economy's prospects for intensive growth (based on technological innovation and productivity gains) as opposed to extensive growth (which relies on simply building more productive capacity based on the same old technologies).

Economic links with the capitalist world

It is a mistake, nevertheless, to think that Juche meant autarky or that the DPRK sought isolation from the world economy. From about 1969, in tandem with developments across the communist world, North Korea debated the desirability (or necessity) of opening economic links with the wider capitalist world economy.[25] North Korea decided to adopt a policy of establishing limited economic ties with Japan and Western Europe, given the continued embargo on US trade and investment. North Korea needed capital and especially technology from the capitalist countries in order to increase its lagging productivity. The previous 'dual line' policy, which emphasised military self-reliance, had cost the North Korean economy dearly during the seven year plan 1961–7, which had to be extended by three years to fulfil its targets.[26] The six year plan for 1971–6 emphasised the so-called 'three technical revolutions' in order to redress admitted imbalances between heavy and light industry, and between industry and agriculture.

North Korea's first experience in 'opening' to the West brought mixed results. At first, increased trade had a positive impact on the economy. The six year plan was completed 16 months early, in September 1975. Industrial growth during this period was reportedly 16.3 per cent per annum.[27] However, what began rather promisingly as a search for technology through trade rapidly led to serious financial difficulties. North Korea's new exports were mostly primary materials, such as minerals. The global recession in 1973–5 sent the price of North Korea's primary commodities tumbling and the terms of trade deteriorated to North Korea's disadvantage. By 1976 the DPRK was experiencing difficulty servicing its external debt, mostly held by Japanese and West European consortia

The even more severe recession of 1979–82 intensified the debt problem. North Korea defaulted and was unable to obtain further credit. Thus by the end of the 1970s the Juche system reached a crucial watershed. It needed fundamental reform in order to overcome its inherent structural bottlenecks. Instead, North Korea recoiled from involvement in the world economy and rejected reform, quite unlike its neighbour China, which did exactly the opposite.

North Korea's return to economic isolationism coincided with preparations for the succession from Kim Il Sung to his son, Kim Jong Il, beginning at the Sixth Congress of the ruling Korean Workers Party (KWP) in October 1980. A new economic plan for 1978–84 was implemented, calling for increased production and technical revolution. On closer inspection this plan merely called for extensive growth in the traditional industries: iron and steel, electricity, fertilisers, cement, mineral ores, and marine products. No political reforms nor any reforms to the economic management system were undertaken. Industrial growth during this period reportedly declined to an annual average of 12.2 per cent.[28]

Driven by necessity, in 1984 North Korea again tried to re-open to the world economy. A new law on foreign investment allowed joint ventures with foreign firms on favourable conditions. However, there were very few takers. Foreign tourism was also explored as a source of badly needed foreign exchange, but this too had very limited results. At the completion of the second seven year plan in 1984, there followed an admittedly difficult period of adjustment in 1985–6 without a formal economic plan. This was explained as being due to 'dispersion in the level and speed of economic growth', 'relative delays in the development of some economic fields' and 'the heavy burden of military spending'.[29]

The continued difficulties in technical proficiency led to mounting production failures. The ambitious 10 year targets set in 1980 were revised downward by Kim Il Sung himself in April 1987, in a new seven year plan for 1987–93. Yet this plan remained confined to the same extensive growth model as before. A sign of the decay was the new emphasis on heroic scale 'grand construction projects' and the mobilisation of the army to meet the economy's labour shortage problem. In the post-1989 period, Kim Jong Il was more visibly in charge of economic management. He promoted a drive toward 'flexible production systems', which however amounted to little more than primitive computerisation and robotisation. The stated goal was to upgrade the machine tool industry, central to the DPRK's economy, and enhance the application of science and technology to industry across the board.

The essential cause of the failure of attempts at opening was the desire of the regime to insulate the Juche system from external influences, so that ideological purity and party unity would not be undermined. However, without liberalisation such as that begun by other communist countries in Eastern Europe, by China (1978), Laos (1982) and Vietnam (1986), there was never much of a prospect that foreign capital would be attracted into North Korea. North Korea's rejection of liberalisation, decentralisation, and marketisation, not to mention democratisation, undermined its own position. This situation contributed directly to the DPRK's diplomatic difficulties and the spiralling economic crisis in the post Cold War period.

THE CURRENT ECONOMIC CRISIS

North Korea's current economic crisis developed in tandem with the momentous changes in the former Soviet Union and Eastern Europe. When the USSR established full diplomatic relations with South Korea in September 1990 it soon afterwards announced support for South Korea's reunification policy.[30] The reformist Gorbachev regime had no great love for the ultra conservative DPRK and saw advantages in Korean reunification, which would remove a source of military tension. Accordingly, the USSR cut aid to the DPRK, as did the Eastern European governments. China, by contrast, continued a modest aid programme. In desperation, North Korea turned to Japan and South Korea for a lifeline. Talks on normalisation of relations were initiated with Japan (via discussions in Beijing in November 1990) following a successful 'feeler' mission to Pyongyang by LDP 'godfather' Shin Kanemaru in September 1990. North Korea initially demanded $10bn in compensation for Japan's colonial period, even if only in the form of low interest loans.

Rapprochement with South Korea began with President Noh Tae Woo's Special Declaration on 7 July 1988, in which he expressed a renewed interest in dialogue with North Korea. Talks with South Korea were elevated to Prime Ministerial level in September 1990 and quickly came to focus on achieving a new 'basic accord' and a non-aggression agreement. In December 1990 the DPRK raised the issue of removing all nuclear weapons from South Korea. In the fifth round of talks in December 1991 South and North Korea signed an historic accord on political reconciliation, military non-aggression, and economic co-operation. In September 1992, in the eighth round of North-South talks, further agreements on co-operation were signed.

Nevertheless, in both cases, ie in relations with Japan and South Korea, progress toward economic co-operation was stunted almost immediately by the emergence of the nuclear issue. The US, Japan, and South Korea co-ordinated their diplomacy towards North Korea. Compliance on the nuclear question became the absolute prerequisite to any further progress in obtaining economic co-operation or establishing diplomatic relations. North Korea walked out of the normalisation talks with Japan at the end of 1992, after eight full rounds. Progress in the North-South Dialogue was stunted by North Korea's regression to the airing of old political grievances and criticism of South Korea's National Security Law. In 1993 progress ground to a halt and the talks were suspended.

Economic spiral of contraction

The trends described above, including the reductions in Soviet and Eastern European aid, contributed to an intensification of North Korea's long-standing structural crisis. As the figures below indicate, the North Korean economy descended a spiral of contraction. In such a highly integrated, centrally planned national economy, the failure of one link in the production system had knock-on effects all down the chain. The shortage of raw materials, energy, and transport became ever more serious. As a consequence, the production system became more and more dysfunctional.

In 1990 the North Korean economy suffered perhaps its worst year since the Korean War. GDP and external trade both declined by nearly 4 per cent and per capita GNP by 5.25 per cent. The trade deficit grew to some $600m, reflecting a sharp decline in trade with China, diminished receipts from Japan, and a deep deficit with the USSR. From November 1990 the USSR demanded payment in hard currency at world market prices for all commercial oil shipments. Both China and the USSR decreased their 'friendship' oil transfers, ie those on special concessionary terms. External debt grew to $7.86bn. Some reports claimed that as much as half of productive capacity was already idle by early 1991, though a more realistic figure was probably in the range of 30 to 40 per cent. Domestic coal production, a mainstay of industrial production, was reportedly down due to mounting supply bottlenecks.[31] Official reports put a brave face on the crisis, claiming that production quotas were being fulfilled ahead of schedule.[32] The DPRK even imported rice from South Korea in July 1991 as North Korea's previous food self-sufficiency turned into a chronic deficit, following several years of poor harvests.[33] The country's primary and indispensable source of foreign exchange was narrowed down to the remittances coming from Korean residents in Japan, estimated at some US $1·bn a year.

The spiral of contraction continued in 1991, as both industrial and agricultural production declined. State revenues were stagnant, shortages of energy and raw materials continued, and bottlenecks in transport compounded the difficulties of sustaining normal production. Trade volume fell from US$5.42bn in reference year 1988, to US$2.72bn in 1991, a drop of 50 per cent.[34]

The contraction in GDP continued in 1992, and is estimated to have shrunk by between 5 and 7.6 per cent, the fourth consecutive year of decline. Income fell 7.6 per cent, declining for the third successive year. Manufacturing output fell by an estimated 17.8 per cent; mining output by 6.1 per cent, and agricultural output by 2.7 per cent. Factory capacity was reported to be operating at as low as 30 per cent.[35] Oil imports from Russia and China continued to decline, as did domestic coal production, though some oil was imported from Iran (in exchange for weaponry) and from Indonesia. (Nevertheless, China remained the main supplier of oil to North Korea.) Breakdowns in infrastructure became more serious, particularly in electricity, the sewage and water system, and transport.

In 1993, North Korea's GDP contraction is estimated by the Bank of Korea (Seoul) to have been 4.3 per cent, while per capita income fell again for the fourth consecutive year, to a figure of US$904 per annum. Trade volume stood at US$2.65bn, compared to South Korea's US$166bn. Industry was reportedly operating at a bare 20 to 30 per cent of capacity, which was mainly attributed to worsening energy shortages. In the first half of 1994, the general shrinkage in the North Korean economy was estimated at between 5 and 7 per cent.

The severity of the economic crisis was revealed in figures for the food ration, which in 1992 was reduced from 700 grams per person per day to a mere 550 grams. The grain ration was only 10 per cent constituted by rice, the traditional staple, and 90 per cent composed of corn or other grains. Meat was scarce. By mid 1993 there were unconfirmed reports of 'food riots' after a very diminished 1992 harvest. If these are true, the riots were the first visible signs of public disturbance or rebellion in several decades. The food crisis continued to worsen in 1993, with reports of food distribution drying up outside the capital Pyongyang.

The crisis was in general worsened by the tightening noose of trade relations for an economy starved of foreign exchange. In January 1992 China and North Korea signed a new trade agreement requiring all trade to be conducted on a cash settlement basis through the use of hard currency. China reportedly refused a DPRK request to write off its debts in March 1993,[36] an indication that these measures must have imposed hardship on the DPRK. North and South Korea established a Joint Committee on Economic Exchange and Co-operation in May 1992, but its economic promise was quickly poisoned by the nuclear crisis. In September 1992 South Korea normalised diplomatic relations with China, opening the door to a rapid and large scale increase in trade between the two countries. The US and South Korea believed that this would force North Korea into accepting more flexible policies and the inevitability of opening up economically, if only to prevent itself from being bypassed by South Korean investors heading into China. That this was a real concern in Pyongyang is confirmed by the fact that in July 1992. DPRK Deputy Premier Kim Dal Hyon, while on a visit to Seoul, appealed directly to South Korean companies to invest in North Korea rather than elsewhere, ostensibly out of 'national sentiment'. Some analysts predicted at the time of ROK-PRC normalisation that North Korea would react by retreating into isolationism and by playing the 'nuclear card', ie encouraging the impression that it had the capability to develop nuclear weapons.[37]

THE NUCLEAR CRISIS

The economic crisis of North Korea determined that it had only limited time during which it could play the nuclear card. The most persuasive interpretation of North Korea's behaviour on this issue between 1992 and 1994 is that it saw the nuclear ploy as the most effective means of wringing more concessions from the West. Essentially the nuclear 'threat' was deployed in order to 'raise the price' of North Korea's acquiescence, especially in terms of economic assistance.

Although the DPRK signed the Nuclear Non-Proliferation Treaty (NPT) in 1985, it delayed signing the International Atomic Energy Agency's (IAEA) Nuclear Safeguards Agreement. When the nuclear crisis began in early 1992, North Korea refused to allow inspection of its domestic nuclear programme. Furthermore, the crisis must be understood in the context of the US announcement in August 1991, of the removal of all theatre nuclear weapons from South Korea.[38] In December 1991, South Korean President Noh Tae Woo announced that there were no nuclear weapons in South Korea. In the same month, North and South Korea signed the 'Joint Declaration on Denuclearisation of the Korean Peninsula'. (This agreement appertains only to nuclear weapons, since both Koreas have a substantial nuclear energy programme.) The DPRK then agreed to sign the Nuclear Safeguards Agreement and did so in April 1992. North Korea later confirmed that it had no desire to develop nuclear weapons capacity.

The first phase of the nuclear crisis

In the first bilateral high level meetings with North Korea since the Geneva Conference in 1954, held in New York in January 1992, the US made the issue of nuclear safeguards the key to all progress in all other areas,[39] while also insisting on progress in the North-South talks and on human rights in North Korea. The emergence of the issue of nuclear inspections reflected a heightened international urgency for stricter enforcement of the NPT, following revelations during the Gulf War on the extent of Iraqi nuclear development and the availability of highly sensitive technology.

North Korea was already involved in parallel bilateral negotiations with the US, Japan, and South Korea, designed to open the door to economic co-operation and full diplomatic relations. Led by the US, these three powers reached a common position on the centrality of the nuclear issue. South Korea came to the conclusion that its own security could only be guaranteed if it was allowed the right of inspection of North Korea's nuclear facilities. Washington and Tokyo both backed Seoul's demand for such inspections, in addition to IAEA inspections, and made Pyongyang's acceptance of these a precondition for normalisation of relations.[40] When South Korean President Noh Tae Woo held his summit in China with Premier Li Peng and President Yang Shangkin in October 1992, Noh asked China to use its good offices with North Korea to persuade Pyongyang to accept nuclear inspections by South Korea. During this period, moreover, the US began strongly to suspect that the DPRK was simply buying time to develop clandestinely its own nuclear weapons capability,[41] a fear shared by South Korea and Japan.

Therefore in 1993 the issue of nuclear inspections overshadowed all others in the diplomacy of the region, and tensions greatly increased. The IAEA issued an unprecedented request for special inspections of North Korean nuclear facilities on 24 February 1993. Controversy particularly surrounded the nuclear facilities at Nyongbyon (Yongbyon), and a suspected special reprocessing plant nearby. North Korea came under suspicion of having diverted civilian nuclear materials for the separation of plutonium, allegedly having taken place in 1989. The IAEA has the right to make inspections of all 162 signatories to the NPT to monitor for any such illegal diversion of civilian nuclear materials to military use.

The DPRK's response to the IAEA precipitated a full blown international crisis. North Korea regressed to a posture of intransigence and belligerence, ostensibly in defence of the principle of national sovereignty, but this had the effect of confirming Western fears of its hidden intentions. The DPRK refused to allow IAEA inspections of the nuclear facilities at Nyongbyon, and on 12 March 1993, announced a threat to withdraw completely from the NPT. On 9 March 1993, the DPRK declared a state of 'semi-war' existed, thereby alarming its neighbours and the international community.

US response

The US responded to these provocative moves with a two track policy of preparing contingency plans for possible military strikes against DPRK nuclear facilities on the one hand, and initiating discussion with its allies on the possibility of imposing economic sanctions against North Korea on the other. A deadline for DPRK withdrawal from the NPT was set at 12 June 1993. The outbreak of the crisis coincided with the annual staging of the Team Spirit military exercises in South Korea, the largest of their kind in the world. In the previous year Team Spirit had actually been cancelled, reflecting the atmosphere of reduced tension surrounding the breakthrough on basic relations between North Korea and South Korea.

In the months, weeks, days, and finally hours and minutes before this final deadline (12 June 1993), frenetic diplomatic activity took place behind the scenes—to prepare the UN, and US allies for possible military action or economic sanctions, and to attempt diplomatically to bring North Korea 'back from the edge' and restore regional security. China played a key constructive role, at South Korea's direct request, by using its good offices to persuade the DPRK to make concessions. China likewise worked to persuade the US to resume direct talks with North Korea. The US responded positively to these overtures and did indeed resume direct high level talks with North Korea at the New York venue.

However, the US did so only after realising that it did not have a viable military option in North Korea and that China would very probably veto economic sanctions in the UN Security Council. In the case of Russia, Yeltsin's government was reassessing its security commitment to North Korea under their 1961 mutual security treaty, which required automatic response if North Korea were attacked. Russia was not particularly enthusiastic about the prospects for a confrontation in North Korea. Therefore, the US could not muster the kind of consensus that had been constructed in the Security Council in the case of the Kuwait emergency in 1990–91. The argument that economic sanctions would cripple North Korea, already in a severe economic crisis, and thus perhaps lead to an aggressive response by a desperate regime, proved to be persuasive. North Korea clearly regarded the prospect of economic sanctions with great alarm, and gave the impression that approval of such sanctions would be interpreted as an act of war against itself.

North Korea used the resumption of talks with the US in New York to press an ambitious agenda of its own. These demands included a guarantee against nuclear attack, suspending Team Spirit, allowing DPRK inspections of US and ROK military facilities in South Korea, removing the 'nuclear umbrella' from South Korea, and finally, recognising the DPRK's socialist system (the DPRK presented the confrontation with the West as an imperialist plot to destroy socialism).[42]

In the final hours of the showdown, on 11 June 1993, the US and the DPRK achieved their hoped for breakthrough. North Korea publicly retracted its threat to withdraw from the NPT.[43] In further high level talks with the US in Geneva on 19 July 1993, North Korea agreed to resume negotiations with the IAEA on nuclear inspections, and to resume its dialogue with South Korea, stalled since the onset of the nuclear crisis.

The second phase of the nuclear crisis

This was not the end of the nuclear crisis however, but only of its first phase. The crisis raised its ugly head once again from the begining of 1994, when IAEA inspectors were again denied access to the suspect Nyongbyon facilities. The earlier cycle of tension reasserted itself in a virtual replay of events. The US led a renewed effort to persuade allies and members of the Security Council of the need to prepare for sanctions, and possibly other action, including military. The first six months of 1994 were dominated by this agenda. The US strategy was to place gradual but irresistible pressure on the DPRK to comply with IAEA inspections. As in phase one, direct talks between the US and DPRK were suspended as tension increased. The US position was that high level talks would only resume after the DPRK fully complied with IAEA demands.

In May 1994 nuclear fuel rods were removed from the Nyongbyon reactor for reprocessing, without external monitoring, thus denying the IAEA the ability to measure the age of the rods and thus ascertain whether nuclear materials had been diverted at an earlier time. It takes up to one year for the fuel rods to cool sufficiently to be worked upon. North Korea's atomic energy department maintained that despite this refuelhng at Nyongbyon, they were preserving the technical possibility of future measurement of the fuel rods. The IAEA's Director-General, Hans Blix, however, heightened the sense of urgency by arguing that it was already too late to ascertain whether materials had been diverted. North Korea's offer to allow inspection of 40 selected rods at a later time was rejected by the IAEA, which insisted on the need to see at least 300 while they were being removed.

Events came to a head in early Summer 1994. On 7 June the DPRK announced at IAEA talks in Vienna that it would 'never' allow inspection of two nuclear waste sites identified as possible alternatives for the verification of the diversion of nuclear materials. In an atmosphere of bitter acrimony, North Korea withdrew from the IAEA on 13 June 1994 and threatened once again to leave the NPT, making open threats of war against South Korea and Japan if economic sanctions were imposed by the UN. At the same time however, the DPRK's Foreign Minister, Kim Young Nam, informed the Americans that North Korea would allow inspections on condition that the US resumed high level talks.

The precipitate event at this stage was a punitive decision by the board of the IAEA taken in Vienna on 10 June 1994 to suspend all technical aid to the DPRK, costing North Korea a total of about £166,000 a year.[44] North Korea responded angrily by announcing its intention to expel the two IAEA inspectors currently in North Korea. This incident greatly heightened tensions on the Korean peninsula. South Korea began a national review of emergency facilities, both sides' armies were placed on heightened alert, and the US stepped up intelligence surveillance of the DPRK. On 13 June the DPRK announced its withdrawal altogether from the IAEA, thus signalling its total rejection of any further international nuclear inspections. North Korea declared that imposition of sanctions would be interpreted as a 'declaration of war'. This led to crisis telephone calls between world leaders and a crash on the Seoul stock market, as fears of war intensified. The US, Japan and South Korea strongly condemned North Korea's action, while re-emphasising their determination to impose sanctions. The stage was set for a confrontation.

Once again, however, the attitudes of Russia and China were critical to any prospects of successfully imposing economic sanctions against North Korea. China openly opposed such sanctions, while Russia's position was more ambiguous. Foreign Minister Andrei Kozyrev said Russia would accept imposing sanctions in stages but only after all other means had been fully exhausted. China's support for the DPRK's security was strongly reiterated in early June 1994, when Choi Gwang, chief of the general staff of the North Korean army, was warmly greeted in Beijing by President Jiang Zemin, who reaffirmed China's 'unwavering' alliance. China had the ability to scupper sanctions both via a veto and through continuing to supply North Korea with essentials despite any sanctions. Even the restoration of China's Most Favoured Nation Status by President Clinton did not seem to bring China round to support sanctions against North Korea, but the US hoped China would simply abstain.

South Korea's policy, under President Kim Young Sam, was basically that sanctions were 'inevitable' and that any price was worth paying in order to stop North Korea from developing nuclear weapons. President Kim Young Sam travelled to both China and Russia to convince their leadership of the need to discipline North Korea. South Korean foreign minister Han Sung Joo engaged in hectic shuttle diplomacy in tandem with US efforts to organise a coalition. However, South Korean efforts to persuade China to support sanctions came to nothing, given China's firm conviction that sanctions would only aggravate the crisis. American plans for sanctions included the option of banning remittances from Korean residents in Japan, a ban on commercial flights, a ban on nuclear co-operation, an oil embargo, and possibly a complete trade and economic embargo. In the context of their severe economic crisis, the North Koreans reacted particularly badly to the idea of a ban on remittances from Japan. Even Japan was concerned that this might be too provocative, depite its public support for sanctions.

The Carter mission and resolution of the nuclear crisis

The Korean nuclear crisis in June to July 1994 was on a trajectory that threatened an outbreak of hostilities. Given North Korea's intransigence over inspections and the equally firm position of the US on sanctions, based on the strategic interest that no precedent should be allowed to threaten the NPT, an error or miscalculation by either side could have led to war. As Jimmy Carter prepared to go to Pyongyang in mid-June, President Clinton moved closer to bowing to Congressional and Pentagon pressures to despatch additional US combat forces to South Korea, in preparation for a military emergency. Into this swirling maelstrom and amid the gathering clouds of war, a single diplomatic initiative, almost *deus ex machina,* transformed the diplomatic atmosphere and led to a breakthrough that restored regional security, despite the momentous intervening event of the death of Kim Il Sung.

Jimmy Carter, whose role as international peacemaker had already taken him to such crisis areas as Ethiopia, Nicaragua, and Haiti, decided to go to North Korea in the capacity of a private citizen, but to broker an agreement among governments. Carter's audacity led to some tensions between himself and the Clinton administration, and earned Carter the animosity of hardliners in Washington. Nevertheless, Carter outflanked both President Clinton, the vociferous hardliner lobby in Congress and the Pentagon, and certain elements of the American press. Carter later admitted that he had taken the decision to intervene because he was convinced that the Clinton administration was yet again poised to make a serious error of judgment in foreign policy, and that war in Korea was becoming a very real possibility.

The preface to Carter's mission was the visit to Pyongyang by Selig Harrison, of the Carnegie Endowment for International Peace, in early June. In an interview with Kim Il Sung, Harrison was told that North Korea was in fact willing to suspend plutonium processing on condition that it received economic assistance and Western diplomatic recognition. Harrison relayed the message, just prior to Carter's arrival, that North Korea would suspend the plutonium programme (a tacit admission that it existed) in exchange for a firm Western commitment to assist in replacing North Korea's graphite-moderated nuclear technology with an alternative. Before his departure, Carter was briefed by the US ambassador to the IAEA, John Ritch. Notably, a few weeks prior to this, Kim Il Sung denied entry to the DPRK to President Clinton's own chosen emissaries, Senators Richard Lugar and Sam Nunn, who were to convey a somewhat tougher message.

However, it would be inaccurate to think that Carter alone was responsible for the subsequent breakthrough. Indeed, on the eve of his arrival the US and its principal allies were preparing to proceed with sanctions in the UN, but in a version that would impose them step by step, allowing North Korea several opportunities to make concessions, and being careful not to cut off its vital economic lifelines. Meanwhile, China was being strongly pressured to abstain rather than veto sanctions. During a visit by Japanese foreign minister Koji Kakizawa to Beijing in early June, Chinese foreign minister Qian Qichen assured the West that China was urging restraint on North Korea.

Just as Carter embarked for Korea, the US ambassador to the UN, Madeleine Albright, publicly circulated a draft resolution for sanctions against North Korea, including reduced diplomatic contacts with Pyongyang, a mandatory arms embargo, and an embargo on technological and scientific assistance and further economic aid. The DPRK would have 30 days after passage of the resolution to comply with IAEA demands, before sanctions would be imposed.

Carter's outflanking manoeuvre on 17 June 1994, was worked by bringing a live CNN crew into his interview with President Kim Il Sung. This ploy generated a new media space that allowed North Korea, and its adversaries, to break out of the end game scenario and seize the moment for a peaceful solution. However, it was based on an unauthorised guarantee by Carter that the Clinton administration would back away from sanctions if North Korea made good its promise, delivered personally by Kim Il Sung to Carter, to resolve all outstanding problems in the nuclear crisis and abandon its plutonium programme. Carter pressured Clinton further by calling for renewed direct US-DPRK talks in his television interviews.

President Clinton did not immediately endorse the 'Carter agreement' and the US maintained its UN sanctions diplomacy. Nevertheless, Clinton was inexorably drawn into the logic of Carter's diplomacy. President Clinton acknowledged that if North Korea's compliance with IAEA requirements and its abandonment of plutonium processing could be verified, the US would resume high level talks with the DPRK. On Capitol Hill, the US Senate voted to strengthen the preparedness of US forces in South Korea with additional shipments of equipment, despite the Carter visit's results. White House officials were initially angry that Carter had contradicted elements of US policy, while the State Department was first to acknowledge that Carter had at least re-established a track to bring North Korea back into negotiations.

After a brief hiatus, the disarray Carter had caused in Western diplomacy gave way to a new consensus in favour of renewed efforts to reach a negotiated solution. This was based on an acceptance of the efficacy of offering North Korea a bigger carrot, while not altogether forgetting the stick. After Carter officially briefed the White House of the results of his visit, on 19 June, the US put the wheels in motion to restart talks with North Korea. Japan announced its willingness to offer financial assistance for converting North Korea's nuclear programme, and most significantly perhaps, both Koreas agreed to an historic summit meeting between Kim Il Sung and Kim Young Sam, scheduled for

25 to 27 July in Pyongyang. The invitation was conveyed by Kim Il Sung to Carter, who relayed it to South Korea.

Nevertheless, the basic condition for improvement in relations, and dropping the drive for sanctions, remained that the DPRK would allow IAEA inspections, abide by the provisions of the NPT, and freeze its plutonium programme. Both Japan and South Korea remained committed to clarifying exactly what had happened at Nyongbyon in 1989, to settle once and for all whether North Korea had diverted civilian nuclear materials to military use Russia's position was that it would support step by step sanctions after a 30 day grace period. However, reflecting Russia's new ambition to play a larger role in international affairs, it proposed an international conference on the nuclear crisis including both Koreas, the IAEA, the UN, China, Russia, the US and Japan.

On 27 June North Korea confirmed that it had accepted resumption of talks with the US, scheduled to begin on 8 July in Geneva, towards a 'fundamental solution to the nuclear issue'. The US revealed it would offer to take the first step towards normalisation of relations and establish liaison offices with the DPRK if North Korea agreed to allow nuclear inspections to resume. In preparation for the 8 July talks, the US, Russia, and South Korea quickly developed a plan for converting North Korea's graphite-moderated nuclear technology to a system based on light water reactors, less capable of diverting nuclear materials to military uses. Russian light water reactors would be provided to North Korea, to be financed by US$1·47bn of the US$3bn South Korean aid package to Russia. South Korea preferred to provide its own reactors, and US opposition to this idea led to lingering tensions over the issue between Washington and Seoul. The US was offering diplomatic recognition and economic assistance in exchange for firm DPRK commitment to abide by the rules of the NPT.

The death of Kim Il Sung

On the same day that the US-DPRK talks resumed in Geneva, the Great Leader Kim Il Sung unexpectedly died. The talks, though acknowledged by North Korea to have got off to a good start, were suspended temporarily to mark a mourning period for Kim Il Sung after his funeral on 17 July, and to allow for the succession to Kim Jong Il to take place. Likewise, North Korea requested an indefinite postponement in the North-South summit with Kim Young Sam. Washington played down any sense of alarm over the death, though South Korea's military was placed on high alert. The G7 issued a communique urging continuation of the US-DPRK talks, an eventual US-DPRK summit, and clear action by North Korea to 'remove, once and for all, the suspicions surrounding its nuclear activities'. The West generally preferred to see a stable transition of power in North Korea rather than a sudden deterioration, rebellion and collapse, which could have unleashed unpredictable events on the peninsula and threatened regional security. Therefore all powers concerned sat patiently by and waited for confirmation of the succession to Kim Jong Il.

The succession of Kim Jong Il, by all accounts, seems to have gone quite smoothly, beginning with pledges of loyalty by the Deputy Prime Ministers, the 700 MPs, and by military officials. Curiously however, there was a long delay in official confirmation of his succession to the positions of President and leader of the ruling party. Nevertheless, it was assumed that Kim Jong Il was in control of North Korea. Talks with the US on the nuclear issue were resumed in Berlin in early September. To the relief of the West, Kim Jong Il's approach to the problem was based on moderation and good faith with the understandings reached with his father. The new element was a request by North Korea for even greater economic assistance, defended as compensation for the lost investment in its existing nuclear electricity system.

Talks continued in Geneva in late September and October, and a landmark agreement was signed on 21 October 1994, having the personal approval of Kim Jong Il. This agreement opened the way to a settlement of the nuclear crisis and gradual integration of North Korea into the regional economy through normalisation of relations with the US, Japan, and South Korea. The package was surprisingly generous to the DPRK, including: provision of two US$4bn light water reactors, the right to store the fuel rods extracted from Nyongbyon early in 1994 and delay inspection of the two waste sites (until vital parts of the new light water reactors are delivered, perhaps delaying IAEA inspections by five to six years), the opening of diplomatic relations with the US, and provision of future supplies of energy

In exchange, North Korea accepted that international inspections would take place in the future, agreed to 'freeze' its nuclear programme and later dismantle it (after the new system is fully in place—perhaps eight years away) accepted light water technology, including from South Korea, and thus granted future access to South Korean technicians (as opposed to Russian ones), and agreed to resume negotiations with South Korea towards further normalisation of relations. Notably, this last item was the final sticking point in the talks, resolved by phone calls between Washington and Pyongyang. North Korea's intransigence on the matter of improving North-South relations is mirrored in Seoul's longstanding ambivalence with regard to the bilateral US-DPRK settlement of the nuclear crisis.

A consortium will be formed between the US, Japan, and South Korea to provide North Korea with new light water reactor technology. The UN Security Council was asked to approve a five year exemption from special IAEA inspections, though the IAEA aired a certain degree of scepticism over these generous arrangements. North Korea will dismantle its existing reactor, cancel two currently still under construction (50,000 and 200,000 kW), and close its reprocessing facilities where plutonium is extracted from spent fuel rods.

Implementation of this agreement began almost immediately. On 1 November 1994 the DPRK announced that construction on the two reactors had been ordered to be stopped by the state Administration Council. In addition, the Nyongbyon reactor was also ordered to shut down. On 16 November, the DPRK and IAEA agreed on the despatch of IAEA officials to monitor the nuclear freeze. The halt in construction of the two reactors and the freeze on North Korea's nuclear programme was officially confirmed by the IAEA on 28 November 1994. The IAEA delegation toured both Nyongbyon and Thaechon nuclear facilities during talks in Pyongyang from 23 to 28 November. The DPRK has agreed, furthermore, that after sealing the radiochemical laboratory at Nyongbyon, and after safely storing but not reprocessing spent fuel rods, the DPRK will thereafter place the fuel under IAEA supervision. Negotiations between US and DPRK nuclear technicians were conducted in Pyongyang from 14 to 18 November, reaching agreement on technical operational matters concerning the safe storage of the 8000 spent fuel rods stored in a cooling pond at Nyongbyon.

The nuclear framework agreement between the US and DPRK received initial backing from South Korea. However, the final round of diplomacy to confirm international support for the agreement was conducted personally by President Clinton at the APEC (Asia Pacific Economic Co-operation) summit in Indonesia on 14 November 1994. Clinton put the North Korean issue at the top of his agenda in meetings with President Jiang Zemin of China, Prime Minister Tomiichi Murayama of Japan, Prime Minister Paul Keating of Australia, and President Kim Young Sam of South Korea. To the satisfaction of the US, China showed very strong support for the new approach. From China's point of view it was probably interpreted as a vindication of its earlier position.

Further operational and technical discussion concerning the replacement of North Korea's graphite-moderated reactors with light water reactors, and technical matters on safe disposal of spent fuel rods from the 5 MW Nyonbyon reactor, began in Beijing on 30 November, 1994, and continued in Berlin. Talks on the practical matters of opening liaison offices in Washington and Pyongyang began in Washington from 6 to 10 December 1994. These talks were concluded satisfactorily and liaison offices were scheduled to open in spring 1995. These discussions took place in the State Department in Washington, the first time a North Korean delegation has ever been in the US capital for negotiations.

Following Republican party victories in US elections in late 1994, there was speculation that the nuclear framework agreement might come under scrutiny by the new Republican dominated Senate. Frank Murkowski, a Senate Republican previously very critical of the US-DPRK nuclear framework agreement, visited Pyongyang on 12 December 1994, but came away making assurances that the agreement would not be scuttled. With these events, the nuclear crisis in Korea seems to be over. A new era may be beginning, based on gradual reintegration of North Korea into the regional and world economy, accompanied by normalisation of relations with the US, Japan, South Korea, and other Western powers.

CONCLUSIONS: THE OPENING OF NORTH KOREA AND PROSPECTS FOR PEACE AND STABILITY IN NORTHEAST ASIA

North and South Korea have come a long historical road from the partition in 1945, the Korean War from 1950–53, the Cold War, and the long period of competition for international standing that culminated in simultaneous entry into the

United Nations. The prospects of peaceful co-operation, enhanced with the end of the Cold War, were nevertheless temporarily blighted by the onset of the nuclear crisis. The problems of economic and political development that caused North Korea to fall into such an unfavourable position still remain. However, there now seems to be a real prospect that North Korea will begin a process of change that may lead to a new and more stable situation.

The successful conclusion to the US-DPRK nuclear framework agreement has opened the way to a constructive period of diplomacy. Alongside rapid planned improvements in relations with the US, other governments are also preparing to improve relations with North Korea. **Japan**, under Prime Minister Murayama Tomiichi's coalition government, announced on 22 November that it would make every effort to establish diplomatic relations with North Korea as soon as possible. A delegation was initially planned to visit Pyongyang by the end of 1994, to restart the normalisation talks (suspended since November, 1992). However, this was postponed to spring 1995, on the grounds that the ruling three-party coalition government in Japan needed time to develop a consensus position on the meaning of the landmark 'Three-Party Joint Declaration' signed in October 1990, in Pyongyang by representatives of the Korean Workers Party (KWP), the Social Democratic Party (SDPJ) and the Liberal Democratic Party (LDP), Murayama's own party has long been an advocate of normalisation with North Korea. The DPRK, however, immediately revived its claim to compensation for the colonial period of Japanese rule. Pyongyang declared that it will only resume normalisation talks with Japan after Tokyo reaffirms the validity of the Three-Party Joint Declaration, and particularly its recognition of North Korea's claim for compensation.[45] Nevertheless, there is now a fairly good prospect that Japanese trade, investment, and aid will be stimulated by normalisation, though 'compensation' will probably be minimal.

Russia has also responded positively to the new atmosphere, and has begun efforts to improve diplomatic relations with the DPRK, which had deteriorated sharply after the demise of the former USSR. Above all, Russia must now redefine its security relationship with North Korea. There is still some possibility that Russia may revive its earlier proposal for a multilateral conference on the Korean situation. If so, this should be geared towards a comprehensive review of security arrangements on the peninsula. This is the prerequisite to ambitious future economic projects of regional integration or co-operation, such as the UNDP's Tumen river basin project. The future development of the Siberian and maritime regimes of the Russian far east depend considerably on the success of such a new framework.

In the case of **China**, the government was of course highly pleased with the US turnaround and the abandonment of sanctions. China has been reinforcing its political and security relationship with North Korea, as witnessed by its decision in October 1994, to withdraw the delegation of the Chinese People's volunteers from the Military Armistice Commission (MAC) This move conformed to DPRK policy, wherein the DPRK abandoned MAC in April 1994, and established an alternative body known as the KPA Panmunjom Mission. In tandem, North Korea renewed its call for bilateral negotiations between itself and the US to replace the armistice agreement with a peace treaty.

This approach excludes the ROK from the negotiations, on the grounds that the ROK is not a signatory to the armistice. North Korea's insistence on this formula in the past was long a source of tension between itself and South Korea. Unfortunately, North Korea's reversion to it recently is not a good omen for the future of North-South relations, nor is its reversion to sharply worded propaganda attacks on the government of Kim Young Sam. Another instance of this recently is Pyongyang's sarcastic attitude to the official transfer, on 1 December 1994, of peacetime operational control of the US-ROK Combined Forces Command (CFC) from the former American Commander-in-Chief to the Chairman of the South Korean Joint Chiefs of Staff. North Korea ridiculed this transfer on the basis that in war-time or a crisis situation, operational control would revert to an American commander. North Korean propaganda continues to stress alleged 'provocations' by the CFC. In mid-December 1994, North Korea claimed it shot down a US helicopter intruding in its air space, killing a crewman and capturing another.

Otherwise, however, North-South relations show a good prospect of a quite rapid recovery. South Korea responded to the US-DPRK nuclear framework agreement by taking measures to revive contacts, especially economic co-operation. For example, South Korea immediately announced it would lift the ban on ROK firms' investing in North Korea and remove travel restrictions on Southern businessmen. This offers the prospect of renewed planning for investment and joint ventures suspended during the peak of the nuclear crisis. The South Korean government now prefers to depict Kim Jong Il as a man interested in economic reform with a loyal following of technocrats ready to steer North Korea towards opening up.

Reform in North Korea

This last issue is certainly the most fundamental. Much of the future course of the Korean conflict and its ultimate prospects for a peaceful resolution depend on the attitude of Kim Jong Il's government to economic reform and opening up. Therefore the central question is whether Kim Jong Il is in fact a 'moderate reformer.' He was long depicted in Southern propaganda as a kind of madman, perhaps responsible for various bombing attacks and the nuclear crisis itself. For many years predictions of a coup after Kim Jong Il's succession to power, especially by the North Korean military, were practically an industry in South Korea. Now, however, with his succession seemingly smooth and secure, South Korea has realised that it is in its own interests to project quite a different image of Kim Jong Il and indeed to hope for stability in North Korea.

There is indeed some evidence to support the argument that Kim Jong Il is a moderate or even a reformist. First, he supported the US-DPRK nuclear framework agreement and implemented its first stage immediately. However, more persuasive evidence can be ascertained much earlier than this. At the beginning of the 1990s some analysts were already convinced that a genuine policy adjustment was under way.[46] The Kim Jong Il succession is thought by many observers to represent the transition to a more pragmatic technocratic approach to economic policy, as opposed to the traditional views of the older generation of leaders drawn from the partisans who fought alongside Kim Il Sung. Selig Harrison, for instance, is among those who have recently been convinced that the new leadership is seriously committed to opening the economy to foreign investment and trade.[47]

By the end of the 1980s, North Korea's interest in economic opening up reappeared, particularly encouragement for joint ventures in export oriented manufacturing, especially in light industries. In October 1992 the DPRK made a clear move in this direction by approving new laws to make foreign investment more attractive and secure. A new code on foreign investment was approved which allows 100 per cent foreign ownership, for the first time in DPRK history.[48] North Korea voiced an interest in a mutual investment guarantee with South Korea, to attract more Southern investment. The DPRK constitution was reviewed with a view to a revision that would sanction the policy of opening up to the capitalist world economy.[49] In December, 1992, there was a significant Cabinet reshuffle in Pyongyang which reinforced the position of figures associated with the policies of diplomatic opening up to the West, South Korea, and Japan, the policy of limited economic opening up, establishing special economic zones, and expanding foreign and export trade. Furthermore, the DPRK joined the UN Economic and Social Commission for Asia and the Pacific and voiced an interest in joining the Asian Development Bank.

North Korea's trajectory towards opening up to foreign trade and investment seems clear. The government set an ambitious goal of attracting US$3bn in foreign investment capital between 1992 and 96. It announced a policy of encouraging the formation of joint ventures with DPRK firms in the envisaged 'free economic and trade zones' designated for the Tumen river and East coast regions.[50] Pyongyang participated in UNDP planning sessions with the PRC, Japan, Mongolia and the ROK to develop the Tumen basin into a logistical focal point for the regional economy, envisaging a development programme of US$30bn over a 20 year period.

The DPRK Ministry of External Economic Affairs launched a trade expansion drive targeted at Japan, Thailand, Malaysia, Indonesia, and the ROK and acknowledged that the same settlement of payments system would be used for capitalist and socialist trade partners alike, ie, hard currency. The first 'private' business group, Kumgangsan International, was established in September 1991 with an office in Tokyo, to promote export expansion with South Korea. Trade with South Korea rocketed upward from a minuscule US$1m in 1988 to US$190m in 1991. North Korea exported mainly raw materials such as steel, coal, zinc, gold, and fishery products and ran a surplus on this trade.[51] In May 1992 the Joint Committee on Economic Exchange and Co-operation was established with South Korea to facilitate a wide ranging expansion of economic relations. South Korean firms were eager to invest, mainly to take advantage of cheap raw materials and labour, but also for reasons of language and cultural affinity, and geographical proximity. In early 1992 the chairman of Daewoo signed a joint venture agreement in textiles, while Hyundae's chairman negotiated one in tourism. Japan, however, already had a head start on South Korean investment. Japan could emerge as a major source of future investment in North Korea, and thus a rival to South Korea. As early as 1991, JETRO recorded 41 Japanese joint ventures with the DPRK, mainly in textiles and fisheries, with a cumulative investment of 3.1bn yen.[52] The nuclear crisis temporarily put all such progress on hold.

The above evidence makes the case that North Korea is serious about changing policy direction. But is it serious about genuine internal reform? North Korea has firmly rejected the Gorbachev model of transition to the market economy as an anathema, while remaining quite resistant to the Chinese model as well. Pyongyang is more interested in a Cuban style transition which keeps most features of the traditional system intact, while making a necessary historic compromise with foreign and private capital in order to earn foreign exchange and acquire foreign technology to increase productivity.

The Catch 22 of North Korea's policy of limited reform and opening up is precisely that this approach may turn out to be insufficient to solve its fundamental economic problems. If the economic crisis worsens this may eventually threaten political instability and reforms may come 'too late' to save the regime. It is therefore equally clear that the security problems of Northeast Asia that arise from North Korea's difficulties are not yet resolved. Since the fall of the Berlin Wall in 1989 North Korean statements on reform have emphasised the superiority of Juche socialism and the lack of need for reform, except to strengthen the leading role of the party and ideological work in all fields.[53] What is most lacking is still any sign of fundamental domestic economic reform such as decentralisation of management or market determined allocation of resources. Even the special economic zones, as planned, would simply be secluded enclaves under special supervision, cut off from the main economy.

The progress of further economic reforms in North Korea is now crucial to the future regional security in Northeast Asia and to the prospects for ambitious new approaches towards regional economic co-operation and integration. A new security framework that takes into account the security needs of all the states in the region will be a necessary prerequisite to achieving a smooth and successful transition to a new regional order. The denuclearisation of the Korean peninsula will make a very substantial contribution to this new environment. Normalisation of relations between North Korea and its capitalist neighbours will likewise improve the prospects of a constructive transition.

However, the longstanding problem of the armistice, ie, its replacement by a permanent and binding peace treaty, remains to be resolved and is now an urgent requirement to ensure regional security.

NOTES

[1] The literature on the origins of the Korean war is particularly rich and interesting; among the most important studies are: Soo Sung Cho, *Korea in World Politics 1940–1950: An Evaluation of American Responsibility*, Berkeley, University of California Press, 1967; Bruce Cumings, *The Origins of the Korean War: Liberation and the Emergence of Separate Regimes 1945–47*, Princeton, Princeton University Press, 1981, and Vol. II, *The Roaring of the Cataract, 1947–1950;* Charles Dobbs, *The Unwanted Symbol: American Foreign Policy, The Cold War, and Korea, 1945–50*, Kent, Ohio, The Kent State University Press, 1981; Peter Lowe, *The Origins of the Korean War*, London, Longman, 1986; and James Irving Matray, *The Reluctant Crusade: American Foreign Policy in Korea 1941–1950*, Honolulu, University of Hawaii Press, 1985.

[2] For studies on colonialism in Korea, see: Andrew C. Nahm, *Korea Under Japanese Colonial Rule: Studies of the Policy and Techniques of Japanese Colonialism*, Center for Korean Studies, Western Michigan University, 1973; Dae-Yul Ku, *Korea Under Colonialism: The March First Movement and Anglo-Japanese Relations*, Seoul, Royal Asiatic Society, Korea Branch, 1985.

[3] For Studies of Occupation policy, see: Soo Sung Cho, op. cit.; Bruce Cumings, op. cit., and (ed.) *Child of Conflict: American-Korean Relations 1943–1953*, London, 1983; Charles Dobbs, op. cit.; Gregory Henderson, *Korea: The Politics of the Vortex*, Cambridge, Mass., Harvard University Press, 1968, J. A. Kim, *Divided Korea: The Politics of Development 1945–1972*, London, Harvard University Press, 1975; James Matray, op. cit.; E. Grant Meade, *American Military Government in Korea*, London, King's Crown Press, Columbia University, N.Y., 1951. Michael Sandusky, *America's Parallel*, Alexandria, Virginia, 1983.

[4] Both camps of scholars (ie conventional and so-called 'revisionist') tend to agree on this point. See: Bruce Cumings, *The Origins of the Korean War*, op. cit.; and Robert A. Scalapino and Chong-sik Lee, *Communism in Korea*, Berkeley, University of California Press, 1972.

[5] See: Chong-sik Lee, *The Politics of Korean Nationalism*, Berkeley, University of California Press, 1963.

[6] See: *Current Digest of the Soviet Press*. From June 1960 onward for several months the Soviet Press, particularly *Pravda* and *Izvestia* ran learned articles by Soviet international lawyers arguing the case that the Korean conflict was a civil war.

[7] The UN passed key resolutions on 25 June 1950, and 27 June 1950, calling first for the DPRK to cease hostilities and withdraw behind the 38th parallel, then calling upon UN members to render assistance to the ROK to repel the armed attack. On 7 July 1950, the Unified Command was established under UN auspices to 'repel the armed attack and to restore international peace and security.'

[8] On 1 February 1951, the UN voted to brand China an aggressor, but only after intense behind the scenes efforts to negotiate a ceasefire, spearheaded by the Asian-Arab Group, had failed.

[9] The armistice negotiations took two years and 17 days, 575 regular meetings and some 18,000 words to arrive at a modus vivendi for the Armistice Agreement on 27 July 1953.

[10] For documents on the Geneva Conference from the US delegation, see: *Foreign Relations of the United States*, 1952–54, Vol. XVI.

[11] See: Barry Gills, 'The Political Economy of Diplomacy' in T.Y. Kong and Dae Hwan Kim (eds), *Korea in Transition*, London, Macmillan, 1995.

[12] The DPRK and its allies criticised UNCURK for alleged bias in favour of the ROK's interpretation of the Korean Question. This was an element in the DPRK's rejection of the competence of the UN and its campaign for the dissolution of UNCURK.

[13] Prior to the 15th session of the UNGA (1960) the composition of the UN included 21 non-communist European states, 20 Latin American (non-communist) states, 22 Asian states, nine African states, and 10 communist countries. Given this composition, the US could muster a simple majority almost automatically. With the influx of many newly independent African members in 1961 this simple majority became more difficult.

[14] The effect of the new membership composition in the UNGA was felt immediately in the debate over the Stephenson Amendment in 1961, where the US made a compromise to accept DPRK participation in the UN debate on the Korean Question on the precondition that North Korea first recognise the competence of the UN.

[15] Though official US and ROK statements cited the desire to avoid spoiling the atmosphere for the new North-South dialogue in Korea through 'acrimonious debate', as the reason for postponement of discussion of the Korean Question in the UNGA, critics believed that this was a retreat brought about by the steadily increasing support in the UNGA for DPRK proposals.

[16] For a good discussion of the cross-recognition formula and diplomacy surrounding it, see: Ralph Clough, *Embattled Korea: The Rivalry for International Support*.

[17] The axe-murder incident in August 1976 involved a clash between a UNC team and DPRK personnel along the demilitarised zone (DMZ), with UNC fatalities incurred by the use of an axe. It occurred at the same time as a Non-aligned Summit meeting at which North Korea was campaigning for support against US 'aggression' in Korea.

[18] The Rangoon incident involved a bombing attack against Chun Doo Hwan and his entourage while making a state visit to Burma in which several members of the ROK cabinet were killed. The KAL incident involved the Soviet shoot-down of a civilian South Korean airliner over Soviet airspace. North Korean diplomacy suffered an enormous setback after the Rangoon incident. Some analysts attempted to make a connection between this event and the recent preparations for the succession to Kim Jong Il.

[19] Charles Armstrong, 'South Korea's "Northern Policy" ', *Pacific Review*, 3 (1) 1990. South Korea's retreat from the Hallstein doctrine began as early as 1969, when it tolerated a shift by Chad and the CAR to open diplomatic relations with North Korea while previously having relations only with South Korea. See: Barry Gills, 'The Political Economy of Diplomacy', op. cit.

[20] North Korea rejected cross-recognition from the outset and campaigned against dual membership in

the UN from the early 1970s onward, on the basis that this would 'perpetuate national division'. North Korea's alternative was a confederation and a single seat in the UN.

[21] Barry Gills, 'North Korea and the crisis of socialism: the historical ironies of national division', *Third World Quarterly*, Vol. 13, No. 1, 1992, pp. 107–130.

[22] Joan Robinson, 'Korean Miracle', *Monthly Review*, XVI (9), January, 1965, pp. 541–549.

[23] R.A. Scalapino and Chong-sik Lee, op. cit.

[24] Erik Van Ree, 'The Limits of Juche: North Korea's Dependence on Soviet Industrial Aid, 1953–76, *Journal of Communist Studies*, Vol. 5, No. 1, 1989, pp. 50–73.

[25] A.G. Frank, 'The socialist countries in the world economy: the East-South dimension', in B.H. Schultz and W.W. Hansen (eds) *The Socialist Bloc and the Third World, The Political Economy of East-South Relations*, London, Westview Press, 1989.

[26] See: Joseph Chung, *The North Korean Economy*.

[27] Teruo Komaki, 'North Korea Inches Toward Economic Liberalization', *Japan Review of International Affairs*, Summer, 1992, pp. 155–174.

[28] Teruo Komaki, op. cit.

[29] Taken from statements by DPRK officials reprinted in *The Peoples Korea*, Choson Shinbo Company, Tokyo, Japan.

[30] South Korea agreed to provide the USSR with a total aid package of US$3bn, partly as a 'sweetener' for the non-use of the Soviet veto when the ROK applied for full UN membership.

[31] *Far Eastern Econonmic Review*, 10 October 1991, p. 75.

[32] BBC Summary of World Broadcasts, FE/W0164 A/10, No. 72, Jan. 1991; FE/W0174 A/6, No. 39, April 1991; FE/W0178 A/8 No. 99, 8 May 1991; FE/W0180 A/12, No. 87–90, 22 May 1991.

[33] BBC Summary of World Broadcasts, FE/W0196 A/7, 11 Sept. 1991; *Far Eastern Economic Review*, 10 October 1991, p. 75.

[34] Andrew Mack, 'The nuclear crisis on the Korean peninsula', *Asian Survey*, Vol. XXXIII, No. 4, April 1993, pp. 339–359.

[35] *The Guardian*, 20 August 1993, citing *Bank of Korea*, Seoul, ROK.

[36] BBC Summary of World Broadcasts, FE/1629, 5 March 1993.

[37] *Far Eastern Economic Review*, 3 September 1992, p. 8.

[38] Andrew Mack, op. cit. North Korea's military power is currently estimated to consist of an army of approximately 1m personnel, with 3,500 tanks; an air force of 92,000 personnel with 732 combat aircraft; a navy of 40,000 personnel, with 26 submarines and three frigates. South Korea has an army of 520,000 men with 3,150 tanks; a navy of 60,000 personnel with four submarines, 29 frigates, and nine destroyers; and an air force of 53,000 personnel and 403 combat aircraft.

[39] In 1968 there were direct discussions between the US and DPRK to resolve the crisis over the DPRK's seizure of the USS Pueblo. Informal political talks between the US and DPRK began in Beijing from December 1988.

[40] *Far Eastern Economic Review*, 8 October 1992, p. 7.

[41] Andrew Mack, 1993 op. cit.

[42] *Far Eastern Economic Review*, 3 June 1993, pp. 12–13.

[43] The nuclear crisis in North Korea was seen by Washington as a test case of confidence in the NPT regime. A show of force in North Korea was therefore thought justifiable to 'make an example' of the DPRK and protect global security interests. The impending review conference on the NPT scheduled for New York in 1995 made the US and other powers very sensitive to the long term viability of the NPT regime.

[44] The vote in the IAEA was approved by 28 of the 35 members of the board, including the major nuclear powers: the US, Russia, UK and France. China abstained, as did India, the Lebanon, and Syria. Only Libya voted for the DPRK.

[45] *The People's Korea*, 3 Dec. 1994.

[46] John Merrill, 'North Korea in 1992: Steering Away from the Shoals', *Asian Survey*, Vol. XXXIII, No. 1, Jan. 193, pp. 45–53.

[47] Selig Harrison, Carnegie Endowment for International Peace, cited in *The Guardian*, 11 July 1994.

[48] *The People's Korea*, October 31, 1992.

[49] John Merrill, op. cit., pp. 44–45.

[50] BBC Summary of World Broadcasts, FE/1169 A3/3 No. 10, 5 September. 1991; FE/1144 A3/3 No. 7, 7 August, 1991.

[51] BBC Summary of World Broadcasts, FE/W0183 A/7, No. 55, 12 June 1991.

[52] BBC Summary of World Broadcasts, FE/W0180 A/12, No. 91, 22 May 1991.

[53] See: Barry Gills, 1992, op. cit.

Korea

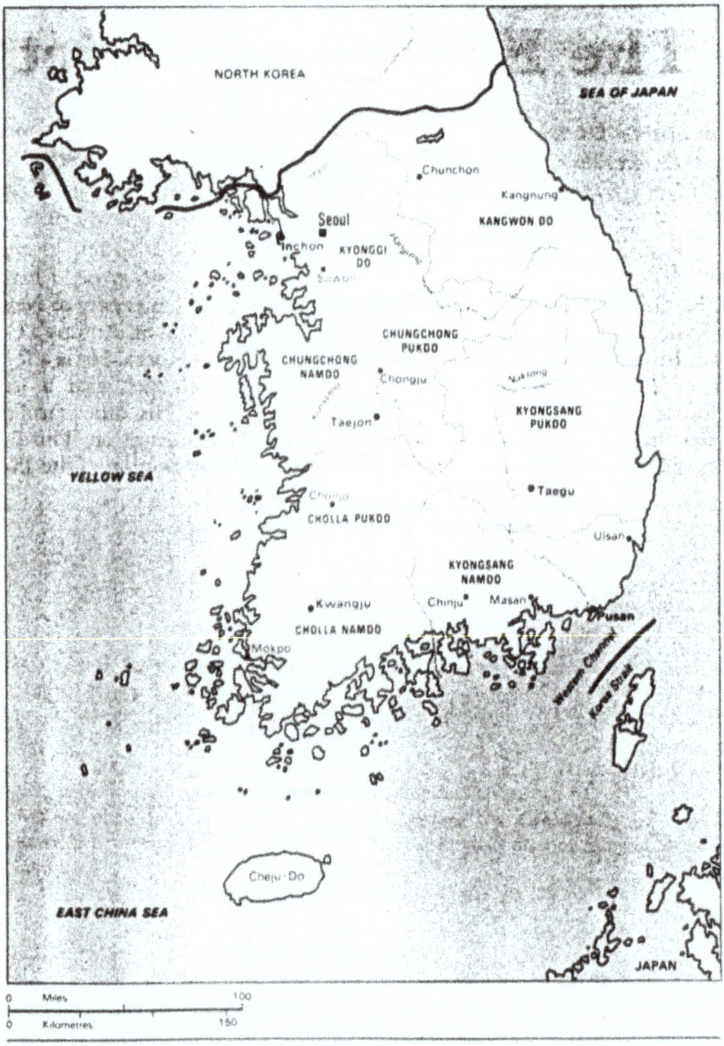

Map by courtesy of Control Risks Information Service

Name Index